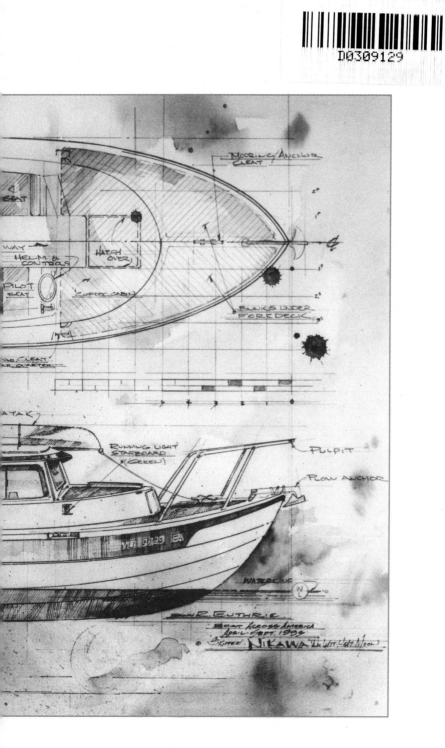

MOORING/ANCHOR CLEAT

SEAT

WAY —
HELM &
CONTROLS

PILOT
SEAT

HATCH
OVER)

CUDDY CABIN

1964

BUNKS UNDER
FOREDECK

CLEAT
QUARTER

5   4   3   2   1   0

A YAK

RUNNING LIGHT
STARBOARD
(GREEN)

PULPIT

BOW ANCHOR

VU 9729 EA

WATERLINE

W
L

JOHN R. GUTHRIE
BOAT ACROSS AMERICA
APRIL-SEPT 1994
SKIPPER NIKAWA Wildest Half Moon

RIVER-HORSE

BOOKS BY
WILLIAM LEAST HEAT-MOON

BLUE HIGHWAYS

PRAIRYERTH

RIVER-HORSE

WILLIAM LEAST HEAT-MOON

RIVER-HORSE

The Logbook of a Boat Across America

SECKER & WARBURG

LONDON

Published by Secker & Warburg 2000

2 4 6 8 10 9 7 5 3 1

First published in the United States of America in 1999 by
Houghton Mifflin Company
First published in Great Britain in 2000 by
Secker & Warburg
Random House, 20 Vauxhall Bridge Road,
London SW1V 2SA

Random House Australia (Pty) Limited
20 Alfred Street, Milsons Point, Sydney,
New South Wales 2061, Australia

Random House New Zealand Limited
18 Poland Road, Glenfield,
Auckland 10, New Zealand

Random House South Africa (Pty) Limited
Endulini, 5A Jubilee Road, Parktown 2193, South Africa

Random House Group Limited Reg. No. 954009

A CIP catalogue record for this book
is available from the British Library

ISBN 0 436 20530 0

Text maps by Ray Sterner and Stephen M. Archer.
Title page lettering and endpaper map by Ed Richardson.
Endpaper drawing and painting on page 67 of *Nikawa* by Rod Guthrie.
Photo credits: Robert Lindholm, pages 1, 3, 81, 105, 399, 463, 503;
David Pulliam, pages 191, 247, 427, 447

Papers used by The Random House Group Limited are natural,
recyclable products made from wood grown in sustainable forests;
the manufacturing processes conform to the environmental
regulations of the country of origin.

Printed and bound in Great Britain
by Biddles Ltd, Guildford and King's Lynn

Contents

My Lotic Mates   ix
The Boat   xi

I. THE HUDSON RIVER

A Celestial Call to Board   3
Up Rivers Without Sources   8
There Lurk the Skid Demon   14
A Drowned River   19
Where Mohicans Would Not Sleep   24
Snowmelt and a Nameless Creek   30

II. THE ERIE CANAL

The Pull of a Continent   37
Released from the Necessity of Mundane Toil   43
Like Jonah, We Enter the Leviathan   50
Knoticals and Hangman's Rope   56
We Sleep with a Bad-Tempered Woman Tossed by Fever   61

III. THE LAKES

Hoisting the Blue Peter   69
How the Sun Rose in the West to Set Me Straight   76

IV. THE ALLEGHENY RIVER

An Ammonia Cocktail and a Sharp Onion-Knife   83
A Flight of Eagles, an Iron Bed, and So Forth   91
Unlimited Sprawl Area   96
Zing, Boom, Tararel!   101

V. THE OHIO RIVER

Proving the White Man a Liar   107
The Day Begins with a Goonieburger   114
Enamel Speaks   123
Along the Track of the Glaciers   127
From Humdrummery on down toward Tedium   132
A History of the Ohio in Three Words   137
A River Coughed Up from Hell   146
A Necessity of Topography and Heart   149
Nekked and Without No Posies   156
Eyeless Fish with Eight Tails   161
The Great Omphalos in Little Egypt   166

VI. THE MISSISSIPPI RIVER

A Night Without Light on a River Without Exits   173
The Ghost of the Mississippi   178
Of Swampsuckers and Samaritans   181
To the Tune of "Garry Owen" We Get Ready   186

VII. THE LOWER MISSOURI RIVER

We Start up the Great Missouri   193
I Attach My Life to the Roots of a Cottonwood   200
A Language with No Word for Flood   203
Looking the River in the Eye   209
Clustered Coincidences and Peach Pie   214
Gone with the Windings   220
Pilotis's Cosmic View Gets Bad News   226

The Dream Lines of Thomas Jefferson 231
A Water Snake across the Bow 237
Sacred Hoops and a Wheel of Cheddar 242

VIII. THE UPPER MISSOURI RIVER

We Find the Fourth Missouri 249
The Phantom Ship of the Missouri Reeds 257
How to Steal Indian Land 263
A Conscientious Woman 270
Flux, Fixes, and Flumdiddle 275
Sitting Bull and the Broom of Heaven 284
How to Be a Hell of a Riverman 289
Yondering up the Broomsticks 298
Chances of Aught to Naught 303
We Walk under the Great River 308
Why Odysseus Didn't Discover America 314
Pilotis Concocts an Indian Name for God 321
Trickles, Dribbles, and Gurglets 325
My Life Becomes a Preposition 331
Little Gods and Small Catechisms 343
Eating Lightning 346
Imprecating the Wind 352
Into the Quincunx 356
Planning for Anything Less than Everything 369
Over the Ebullition 374
Ex Aqua Lux et Vis 377
Weaknesses in Mountains and Men 384
A Nightmare Alley 388
No Huzzahs in the Heart 393

IX. THE MOUNTAIN STREAMS

We Meet Mister Eleven 401
Eating the Force that Drives Your Life 409
An Ark from God or a Miracle of Shoshones 413
A Shameless Festal Board 418

X. THE SALMON RIVER

Bungholes and Bodacious Bounces   429

XI. THE SNAKE RIVER

My Hermaphroditic Quest   449

Kissing a Triding Keepsake   454

Messing About in Boats   458

XII. THE COLUMBIA RIVER

The Far Side of the River Cocytus   465

Place of the Dead   473

Theater of the Graveyard   479

A Badger Called Plan A   482

Robot of the River   489

A Taproom Fit for Raggedy Ann   493

Salt to Salt, Tide to Tide   498

An Afterword of Appreciation   505

If You Want to Help   507

My Lotic Mates

Without a copilot, there would have been no voyage,
and so this book is for Pilotis who was these seven:
Motier Duquince Davis, Robert McClure Lindholm,
Linda Jane Barton, Jack David LaZebnik,
Peter King Lourie, Robert Scott Buchanan,
Steven Edward Ratiner.

The Boat

If you want the specifications: she was made of fiberglass laminate over an end-grain balsa core two inches thick, with a flat hull aft a V-shaped bow; just under twenty-two feet long and about eight in beam, approximately seventeen hundred pounds empty, with an eight-inch minimum draft and about thirty inches when motored and loaded; called a C-Dory and built near Seattle in January 1995. The boat readily fit onto a small trailer.

She had only essentials: a compass, a depth finder, paired tachometers, and gauges for each of the two fifty-eight-gallon tanks that fueled the twin forty-five-horsepower, four-stroke Honda engines (efficient and environmentally advanced). The single window-wiper worked by hand-crank. Our radio was an Apelco marine-band pocket model. To save weight and increase range, we did not fill the freshwater reservoir, and to avoid head duty and have another reason to stop in river towns when we came across them, we left behind the chemical toilet.

Forward in the cuddy was a cramped V-berth, and in the pilothouse (headroom, six feet two inches) we could make a second, if narrow, bunk by lowering the small navigation table. Aft the pilothouse was an open cockpit or welldeck covered with a blowsy canopy, a nice place for sitting, sipping, and watching when we moored.

The hull, with molded lapstrakes to throw off spray, derived from the classic American dory perfected in the eighteenth century to carry fishermen into the rough coastal waters of the northeast Atlantic. Our C-Dory was not fast, but she was stable, sturdy, maneuverable, responsive, and yare. The fusion of her fiberglass upper and lower parts in effect made the boat a single unit. (Atop the pilothouse we carried a nine-foot, one-person Keowee kayak for places even the flat-hulled dory couldn't enter. For the shallowest rivers, we had a square-stern, seventeen-foot aluminum Grumman canoe and a tiny four-horse-power Evinrude motor which, when off the water, traveled with the trailer.

If you imagine a Maine lobster boat crossed with a turn-of-the-century harbor tug, you have our C-Dory, *Nikawa*, a name I coined from the Osage words *ni*, river, and *kawa*, horse, and pronounced Nee-KAH-wah. Indeed, she was a tough but sweet little river horse.

On the forward bulkhead, near the helm, I attached a wooden plaque, a proverb from the Quakers: PROCEED AS THE WAY OPENS. Aft, above the door to the welldeck and motors, I put up another, this one from Joseph Conrad's *Heart of Darkness*, the advice Marlow receives before ascending the Congo River: AVOID IRRITATION. I have spent my life trying to practice such simplicities, and when I fail, paying the costs; in April of 1995, we, my copilot and I, set out to test those admonitions in a venture of some moment and considerable chance.

1

THE HUDSON RIVER

NIKAWA IN NEW YORK HARBOR

ICONOGRAM I

The bulk of the water in New York Harbor is oily, dirty, and germy. Men on the mud suckers, the big harbor dredges, like to say that you could bottle it and sell it for poison. The bottom of the harbor is dirtier than the water. In most places, it is covered with a blanket of sludge that is composed of silt, sewage, industrial wastes, and clotted oil. The sludge is thickest in the slips along the Hudson, in the flats on the Jersey side of the Upper Bay, and in backwaters such as Newtown Creek, Wallabout Bay, and the Gowanus Canal. In such areas, where it isn't exposed to the full sweep of the tides, it accumulates rapidly. In Wallabout Bay, a nook in the East River that is part of the Brooklyn Navy Yard, it accumulates at the rate of a foot and a half a year. The sludge rots in warm weather and from it gas-filled bubbles as big as basketballs continually surge to the surface. Dredgemen call them "sludge bubbles." Occasionally, a bubble upsurges so furiously that it brings a mass of sludge along with it. In midsummer, here and there in the harbor, the rising and breaking of sludge bubbles makes the water seethe and spit. People sometimes stand on the coal and lumber quays that line the Gowanus Canal and stare at the black, bubbly water.

Joseph Mitchell
The Bottom of the Harbor, 1951

A Celestial Call to Board

OR ABOUT HALF A LEAGUE after we came out of the little harbor on Newark Bay at Elizabeth, New Jersey — with its strewn alleys and broken buildings, its pervading aura of collapse, where the mayor himself had met us at the dock and stood before a podium his staff fetched up for him to set his speech on, words to launch us on that Earth Day across the continent as he reminded us of history here, of George Washington on nearly the same date being rowed across to New York City on the last leg of his inaugural journey — and for the half league down the Kill Van Kull (there Henry Hudson lost a sailor to an arrow through the neck), we had to lay in behind a rusting Norwegian freighter heading out to sea with so little cargo that her massive props were no more than half in the water and slapping up a thunderous wake and thrashing such a roil it sent our little teakettle of a boat rolling fore and aft. I quickly throttled back, and the following sea picked up our stern and threatened to ride over the low transom into the welldeck. We had no bilge pump to empty it, and the cabin door stood hooked open to the bright blue April morning and the sea air of New York Bay.

My copilot roared, "Don't cut the motors so fast when we're riding a swell! You'll swamp us!" Only ten minutes out, we were nearly on our way to the bottom, sixty feet below. I turned toward the stern to see the bay rear above the transom just before the water raised *Nikawa* high enough to let the next wave ride under and shove her fast toward the chopping props of the freighter. Then her bow slipped down the other side of the swell, we pulled away from the big screws, and I idled to let the deep-water tramp move ahead until I got an open lane on her port

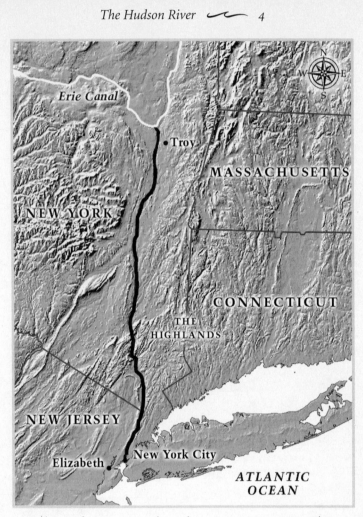

The Hudson, New York Harbor to Troy, 143 river miles

side. We pushed past, cut through the wake of the Staten Island Ferry, and headed on toward the Atlantic.

"And that's how it begins," said my friend, a blue-water sailor, one whom I shall call Pilotis (rhymes with "my lotus"). It wasn't, of course, *the* beginning, for who can say where a voyage starts — not the actual passage but the dream of a journey and its urge to find a way? For this trip I can speak of a possible inception: I am a reader of maps, not usually nautical charts but road maps. I read them as others do holy writ, the same text again and again in quest of discoveries, and the books I've written each began with my gaze wandering over maps of American terrain. At home I have an old highway atlas, worn and rebound, the pages so soft from a thousand thumbings they whisper as I turn them. Every road I've ever driven I've marked in yellow, the pages densely highlighted, and I can now say I've visited every county in the contiguous states except for a handful in the Deep South, and those I'll get to soon. Put your finger at random anyplace in this United States atlas, and I've either been there or within twenty-five miles of it, but for the deserts of Nevada where the gap can be about twice that. I didn't set out to do this; it just happened over forty years of trying to memorize the face of America. When someone speaks of Pawtucket or Cross Creek or Marfa, I want an image from my travels to appear; when I read a dateline in a news story about Jackson Hole, I want the torn Teton horizon and a remembered scent of pinyon pine in me. "Have you seen the historic tavern at Scenery Hill?" the Pennsylvanian may say, and I want to ask, How goes the ghost, and are the yeast rolls still good? No words have directed my life more than those from venerable Thomas Fuller, that worthy historian of olde England: "Know most of thy native country before thou goest over the threshold thereof."

Twenty years ago I had been down enough miles of American road that I could visualize the impending end of new territory to light out for — as my fellow Missourian, river traveler Huck Finn, has it — and that's when I noticed the web of faint azure lines, a varicose scribing of my atlas. They were rivers. I began tracing a finger over those twistings in search of a way to cross America in a boat. At first I was simply curious whether one could accomplish such a voyage without coming out of the water repeatedly and for many miles, but later I grew interested in the notion of what America would look like from the rivers, and I wanted to see those secret parts hidden from road travelers. Surely a journey like that would open new country and broader notions, but I could find no transcontinental route of rivers that did not require miles and miles of portages and heavy use of border waters — the Gulf of Mexico or the Great Lakes. For my voyage, I wanted only an internal route across the nation.

I'll skip details of how, during those two decades, I discovered inch by inch a theoretical route a small vessel might, at the proper time of the year, pursue westward from the Atlantic an interior course of some five thousand miles, equivalent to a fifth of the way around the world, ideally with no more than seventy-five miles of portage, to reach the Pacific in a single season. Travelers have boated across America before but never to my knowledge under those requirements. One night sixteen months earlier, in a thrill of final discovery, I found what I believed to be the last piece of this river puzzle, and at that moment I understood that I had to make the voyage at whatever cost. If a grail appears, the soul must follow.

In my excitement I phoned my great friend to join me, teach me the bowline and sheepshank, remind me of the rules of the road, to be my copilot, my pelorus of the heart to steer me clear of desolation, that fell enemy of the lone traveler. Pilotis said, "When my father was dying a few months ago, in his last days when he was out of his head, he lay murmuring — I had to lean close to hear him — he said again and again, 'Can you make the trip? Can you make the trip? Better be ready.' It was his celestial call to board. Now you ask me the same question, and I don't know."

My friend mulled things for some days and then phoned. "I can make the trip. I'll be ready. Find us a boat that can do it." And that's how we came to be, on the twentieth of April, sliding past the Norwegian freighter on our way to the Atlantic Ocean. Pilotis — my Pylades, my Pythia, my Pytheas — writes well, values memorable language, quotes it as I can never do. After I had nearly sunk us within sight of our departure dock, in the ensuing embarrassed quiet played to good effect, Pilotis said as if lecturing, "Nautical charts carry a standard warning addressed to 'the prudent mariner.' Revere that adjective above all others."

I, whose boating life to that moment consisted of paddling about in a thirteen-foot canoe and standing below-deck watches and chipping paint on a nine-hundred-foot aircraft carrier, realized more than I wished to admit why I wanted Pilotis along, but I only pointed out the worn stone walls of Fort Wadsworth on the north end of Staten Island near the Narrows. Frédéric Bartholdi, sculptor of the Statue of Liberty, considered that passage the Gate of America, an opening through which four centuries of ships have sailed for the Canaries, Calcutta, the southern capes, Cathay, but few for the Pacific via inland waters. Then we crossed under the lofty, six-lane span of the Verrazano-Narrows Bridge, the great Silver Gate looking improbably thin and fragile hanging above us, and pushed east beyond Coney Island and Gravesend Bay, on into the ocean. We paused at that western edge of the Atlantic so it might set in us a proper watery turn of mind and reset us from lubbers to sailors. Then, in the spindrift, Pilotis leaned over the side to fill a small bottle with brine from the great eastern sea, cork it up and stow it safely in the cabin until, we hoped, I could unstopper it and pour it into the Pacific just beyond the treacherous bar at the mouth of the Columbia River a continent away.

Then I brought *Nikawa* about, and we headed for New York City and the East River. I said in near disbelief, After twenty years of thinking about this possibility, it's happening! And Pilotis said, "Can you make the trip? Can you make the trip?"

Up Rivers Without Sources

THE DEPTH FINDER lined out a profile of the bay bottom, a place I began to imagine festered and festooned with antique arks and sloops — Dutch, English, Yankee — mired to the cold ooze ten fathoms below, the Hudson currents washing to the sea, working the wreckage and dunnage in the black and perpetual silence, where somehow the whelks learn to drone the sound of the distant surf and imbue it into their shells. Down in the weatherless deep there had to be jetsam from Henry Hudson's *Half Moon*, drowned ferrymen, bluejackets whose "Yo heave ho!" was forever gone, and concrete-booted malefactors trying to tread over the cinders blown from Fulton's steamboat, and sprawled across the bottom spars and anchors, capstans, soggy oakum, tar buckets, and sundered bare-breasted figureheads staring in wide-eyed disbelief at their ill luck.

Then my old nightmare: I am submerged in some unknown waters where I watch the drowned drag their weary grief across the mud, their long and faded locks rising from their skulls like kelp wafting in the slow current, barefoot sailors stirring the silt come down from the distant mountains, the agony of their end still on their faces, and a skeletal tar rises from the tangled rigging, turns, and motions me toward him, and I must approach closer and closer until I am almost against his moss-hung jawbone, and out from his eye sockets swims an eel, its toothy maw hanging with human viscera. I awake in strangled terror.

Pilotis said, "You're watching the sounder again. Leave the moss-bunkers and tomcod to themselves and try the day up here." I pulled the bow northward and aimed it toward Buttermilk Channel alongside

Governors Island, a place the Dutch of New Amsterdam knew as a 170-acre islet but that New Yorkers of 1900 saw as a wave-eaten place of seventy acres. We passed it, now built back to its earlier size with stone and soil from subway excavations and river dredgings.

The massive risings of Manhattan, monstrously fine in the sun and cutting deeply into the blue air, sat atop the skinny island that each year gets further Swiss-cheesed with diggings. Surely the tunnels and cavities under the pavement and foundations, if dragged up and stood on end, would nearly equal the bulk of what rests above them. From a mile down the bay, Manhattan looked fragile, more glass and glitter than stone and durability, the most staggering cityscape on earth, yet still only a grand temporariness before the Empire State Building one day collapses into the F train tunnel. The view gave me a small ascendance, a kind of superiority that water passage can bring: perhaps it was the sound of the eternal river against the hull or our moving freely past the bound and entangled city. I mentioned it to Pilotis who, after the usual consideration, motioned toward the Battery off our port side and gave a paraphrase of Melville (I quote it now exactly): "He spoke of landsmen 'pent up in lathe and plaster, tied to counters, nailed to benches, clinched to desks, how they must get just as nigh the water as they possibly can without falling in. And there they stand.' For us, we've traded safety to hear the Lorelei sing."

Bounded by water, Manhattan has a river at the end of nearly every through street; it's a place you can never be much more than a mere mile from the Hudson, Harlem, or East rivers, yet those citizens are islanders only because of a topography that rarely seems to inform their notions of where or who they are. If Manhattanites, other than the poor, want a river, they go to Maine, even New Jersey.

We went up past South Street Seaport, once a forest of masts and spars and home to packet ships owned by Captain Preserved Fish, then on we moved toward the high webbing of Roebling's great bridge. Somewhere below, the A train clattered through the dark and grimed tube buried in the sludge to haul the human freightage into Brooklyn, the "broken land" of the Dutch. Beneath us life was actually occurring — words passed, bagels noshed, books read, sleep rattled — under our keel, under the river and fetid muck and cold rock, and no one down there imagining us gliding above. We passed the cul-de-sac of Wallabout Bay where, although the water was cleaner than a generation ago, a few suicides and murdered folk still washed up in that wet potter's field, the cadavers chewed by eels.

The East River, local mariners allege, is one of but two in the world with a pair of mouths but no source. The truth is that it isn't really a river at all, no matter what it looks like; it's a strait only fourteen miles long, a narrow arm of the Atlantic that tidal currents sluice through to twist and torture the passage of small boats. But we were coming up it at its slackening, the flat hull of *Nikawa* sliding along as if the river were a farm pond, and then we went under the Brooklyn Bridge. Eighteen million people surrounding us, and we had the water almost to ourselves. I pulled the bow about, passed beneath to see the span again, and then turned us north once more. "What was that about?" Pilotis said, and I answered I'd waited a lifetime to see the bridge from underneath, an event I wasn't likely to repeat. "I hope we're not going to do the whole voyage twice," my mate said. "By that route, the Pacific is sixteen thousand miles away."

From the East River, the heaps of buildings of Manhattan seemed to leave little room for humanity, and the city looked strangely still, almost quiescent. Except for the trickling of yellow cabs along the perimeter, the place appeared empty. It didn't manifest power or vibrance but merely bulk, all of it enhanced by a certain worn charm the river lends: its six bridges and its satisfying narrowness, especially at midtown where Roosevelt Island splits the channel to create an intimacy never achievable over on the Hudson. From the city came no stink of combustion engines and almost no sound carried against the soft easterly off the ocean as if early Sunday morning lay over the place. But it was Thursday and the streets, entombed in long spring shadows, seemed to suck in morning light and Atlantic air, and the whole island inhaled that sweetness crossing the water.

Because I'd long heard of its legendary potential for torment, we detoured a mile northeast just to pass through and experience the pinched bending of Hell Gate, where tidal eddies and standing waves and — once — rocks sent hundreds of ships to grief after the *Tyger* first came through from Long Island Sound in 1612. For us, the passage was an early test to build our assurance in *Nikawa* and our own capacity to handle even more difficult water ahead. Trying to ride the flood tide up the Hudson, we happened to reach Hell Gate at its tidal pausing, a near hydrological calm that leaves it comparatively quelled. Even so, the pilothouse of a small trawler ahead of us began to roll, and we stopped to watch it before we moved into the swirlings and heard the turmoil speak through our hull in low thumpings and sharp bangings. *Nikawa* yawed flatly but didn't roll, and she shimmied forward through Hell Gate, and then we came about to take it the opposite direction before moving on past Astoria where once schoonermen lived under widow's walks. Pilotis put aside the chart and said, "Our first Astoria is fifteen miles upriver from the Atlantic and our last is fifteen miles east of the Pacific, and what's in between is our life for the next four months."

We took the Wards Island channel into the Harlem River, the other one with two mouths and no source. Like the East River, it too is a strait, although partly manmade, but even shorter and narrower with twice as many bridges as nautical miles. (A geographer might insist that Manhattan has no rivers at all; what it does have is an estuary and a pair of straits.)

It may have been Pilotis's comment about the two Astorias so far apart: suddenly I never felt luckier in my life. For the past sixteen months I had searched out and studied charts and maps of a potential transcontinental course. One evening, after poring over them with a magnifying glass and dividers to make a coast-to-coast voyage on paper with Pilotis at my shoulder, I finally went to bed exhausted. The whole night I dreamed of the twisted route with its leagues of unknown threats only to awake at dawn to the conviction we couldn't possibly complete such a trip, surely not in a single season, definitely not without long portages. That afternoon, Pilotis, ever-cautious Pilotis, revealed a similar dream and reaching a similar conclusion and a parallel belief that the voyage looked like a six-month venture over two years. How, I cannot explain, but that twin nightmare canceled mine, and I figured what we'd encountered in the dark was not foreshadowing but merely fear. I realized, while I *might* lack the nerve to undertake the trip, I was *certain* I didn't have the courage to tell friends I was backing out: with an audience below, once you're up on the high diving board you must at least jump.

So there we were, the four of us, river, *Nikawa*, Pilotis, and I, my friend wearing a strange smile and looking back toward the skirmishing waters of the East River; that smile of a small conquest was about to become known as the Hell Gate Grin. To a workman sipping from his Thermos under the Third Avenue Bridge I called through the window, We're bound for Oregon! His surprise was but a moment, then he yelled back with delight, "You're headed the right direction!"

Beyond the decay of Harlem and the South Bronx, Yankee Stadium and the football field of Columbia University, the riverside began to seem less fallen, not lovely but pleasant as if all had not yet been abandoned or destroyed, and the water appeared clean enough that, were Pilotis to go overboard mishandling a line, there'd be no cry to be put out of a poisoned agony. The shores there looked benign perhaps because the cold water, like a moat, lay between us and littered alleys and dilapidating warehouses. A friend, a woman forced into boating by her former husband, told me the evening before I hauled *Nikawa* east from my home in Missouri, "Follow two rules: Stay between the banks, and try not to ditch."

Ahead lay the wide Hudson. I cut the engines and we bobbed in the Harlem to wait for the railroad bridge, so low that waves sometimes lap at the tracks, to open. It was river engineers cutting through here years ago that turned Spuyten Duyvil Creek into a canal and the Harlem into a little strait.

The bridge soon pivoted to let us pass, and we entered the Hudson and turned north again, happy to have a river with a navigable portion that is naturally regular, an almost symmetrical shaft except for its run through the outreaches of the Appalachian Mountains called the Highlands. For two hundred miles upstream where it makes its grand turn out of the Adirondacks, the lower Hudson never shows an oxbow or even a truly twisted bend, in part because it is actually a fjord, the only one in the contiguous states, with a tidal reach of 140 miles north, as far as we would take it. At Yonkers, we moved below the statue of Henry Hudson high atop his column from which he looks *down*river and not *up*, the direction he was interested in, the one he hoped would take him to the far western sea. Pilotis said, "In a way, we're attempting what he failed in." And, after a moment, "I hope we make it beyond where he did." Yes, I said, we didn't come this far just to reach Albany.

To the west, across from Yonkers, rose the sheer basalt walls of the New Jersey Palisades, once the home of the movie business: from those cliffs hung Pearl White, her perils as Pauline playing in picture-show houses for a third of a century. One of the surprises of the Hudson, partly because the river sits deeply in its narrow valley, is the way New York City quickly disappears to leave a boat traveler suddenly in a world almost sylvan with more leafage and rocks and river than anything from human hands. It was hard to believe we had so easily passed through the length of a city with six thousand miles of streets by sailing right through its watery heart.

To starboard, separated from the river only by railway tracks, stood Washington Irving's home, Sunnyside. We could nearly have thrown out a line to tie up to the great wisteria he planted in the 1840s. It was he who wrote, "I thank God I was born on the banks of the Hudson! I think it an invaluable advantage to be born and brought up in the neighborhood of some grand and noble object in nature: a river, a lake, or a mountain. We make a friendship with it; we in a manner ally ourselves with it for life." As we approached Tarrytown, the western sky began to smear over, and we turned in to dock at the eastern foot of the huge Tappan Zee Bridge. Pilotis, whose daughter and a friend had come down to greet us, went forward to snub in our bow. The dock was high and strung with a web of crossed mooring lines of other boats. In an instant, a tangle of stretched cordage went taut and wrapped and lifted Pilotis off the deck into near strangulation. I jerked back on the throttles to keep the boat beneath the struggling feet, the lines slackened, my mate wriggled free and dropped back to *Nikawa*. In bemused calmness, pointing to Pilotis, the daughter said to her friend, "*That's* the experienced one who's supposed to know how to do things." Pilotis said, quoting our old mantra from Anthony Trollope's *Small House at Allington,* "'Umph!' ejaculated the squire."

With *Nikawa* secured, I whispered, The prudent mariner will not become entangled in docking lines. Pilotis said only, "We're thirty miles upriver." That's all it was, but the morning in New Jersey already seemed another existence away, as did the whole continent lying before us. Our feet securely on land, I put my arm on Mate's shoulder and said, We're well begun, my sailor. And we went up the hill to have a nice glass of stout.

There Lurk the Skid Demon

THE MORNING came on damp and befogged, and the big bridge across the wide Tappan Zee seemed anchored on the west to nothing but clouds, its trusses and girders mere cobwebs. Pilotis and I rose from our cramped bunks and walked the long dock to a shower room only to find as we dripped across the floor a few minutes later we had no towels. Said Pilotis, "We've taken too far your dictum that we'll carry not what we can use but only what we can't do without." As we dried on our shirttails, I heard muttering: "If you were a woman, you'd never forget towels."

I fired up the motors, hummed them to synchronicity, and in the lifting fog we pulled onto the quiet river just above where it goes from three quarters of a mile wide to two and a half across. The Tappan Zee, an Algonquian-Dutch name meaning "cold stream sea," is the first of two grand irregularities in the navigable Hudson, and its fourteen-mile length leads into the other, the Highlands. Our pilothouse windows fogged over, so we were glad to have the wide berth, although only someone from a small country like Holland would ever call this a sea. We ran against the ebb tide, but the broad water diffused the current, and we could hardly discern its movement to the ocean. Having no major tributaries below the Mohawk River, the Hudson is a remarkably constant thing, and to me who learned to boat on the vagaries of the Missouri, the Hudson is pleasantly predictable. On my home river in high water, a floating stick can travel two hundred miles downstream between one sunrise and the next, but here a piece of drift will ride two ebb tides a dozen miles down and catch two flood tides that will carry it back up eight, so that its 140-mile voyage from

Troy to the Battery can take — if it stays out of eddies and backwaters — three weeks.

Pilotis, thinking of our showers, said, "Sixteen months of preparation let us forget something as necessary as towels, so what else are we without? Maybe the next discovery can't be solved with shirttails." I said that adventure was a putting into motion one's ignorance. "I'll remember that when I go down for the third time." I said I'd looked long but had been unable to find a book of directions for crossing America by boat; for where we were going, there was no rutter. Digging into a bag of gear, Pilotis pulled out a sheet of paper and said, "That reminds me. We do have directions, a bon voyage gift from old Ed." Edwin Miller was our nonagenarian friend.

"It's a found poem," Pilotis said of the directions. "Ed picked it up in Japan in 1935. It's nothing more than a notice explaining rules of the road to foreign motorists. He hasn't changed a word except to title it and set it in stanzas." Pilotis read aloud:

Beware the Festive Dog

At the rise of the hand
of policeman, stop rapidly.
Do not pass him by
or otherwise disrespect him.

When a passenger of the foot
hove in sight, tootle the horn trumpet
to him melodiously at first.
If he still obstacles your passage,
tootle him with vigour
and express by word of the mouth
the warning "Hi, Hi!"

Beware the wandering horse
that he shall not take fright
as you pass him.
Do not explode
the exhaust box at him.
Go soothingly by
or stop by the road-side
till he pass away.

Give big space
to the festive dog

that makes sport
in the road-way.
Avoid entanglement of dog
with your wheel-spokes.

Go soothingly on the grease-mud,
as there lurk the skid demon.
Press the brake of the foot
as you roll round the corners
to save the collapse
and tie-up.

We moved north past Sing Sing sitting close to the water and affording prisoners a similar riverscape as one gets from the mansioned estates of the Goulds, Vanderbilts, Rockefellers, Roosevelts, and others not far upstream. Pilotis, believing that half the multimillionaires in the country should be serving time, found the shared view only just.

Across the water lay the broad, flattened convex shore aptly called Point No Point; resident author James Kirke Paulding in 1828 likened it "to the speech of a member of Congress, which always seems coming to the point but never arrives at it." Opposite was a topographic reverse, Croton Point thrusting its rooster beak well into the Zee. Then the river narrowed again at Stony Point where General "Mad Anthony" Wayne directed a peculiar encounter in 1779. George Washington asked him whether he would attempt an attack on the British garrison there, to which Wayne famously replied, "I'll storm Hell, sir, if you'll lay the plans." Washington allegedly said, "Better try Stony Point first, General." Preparing for the night attack, the soldiers, so the story goes, killed every dog within three miles to prevent a bark that would alarm the enemy, and they even unloaded their muskets to ensure a silent approach as they slogged across a marsh and climbed the heights to level a most spirited bayonet charge. Too late, the Redcoats began pouring down a steady fire of musketry and bad language. In twenty minutes the garrison surrendered, and the Yankees had one of their few decisive victories in the Revolutionary War–encumbered theater of the Hudson Valley.

Above Stony Point, the river passes through the Highlands, a kind of older wing of the Appalachians, where granite hills rise to only about fifteen hundred feet, but their bulk and situation right along both banks make them appear loftier. The Hudson makes three major turns there, each one distinguished by water, rock, and history. As we passed under the first, which the chart tautologically calls Dunderberg Mountain, the sky went back into the glooms again as lore holds it typically does. Dutch settlers believed their "Thunder Mountain," shoving the powerful Hudson a mile eastward, was the source of strange and nasty storms that struck ships sailing the Highlands and that this stretch lay under the mischief of other beings who haunted the forested dark cloves and the angled river, venting their spleen and indulging wicked humours by besetting boats with flaws and headwinds, countercurrents, rocky impediments, and unexpected mud flats. In truth, as we rounded below Dunderberg, the wind rose to smack our pilothouse and the current raced between the constricted shores and whopped the hull as if knocking for entry in a reach named the Devil's Horse Race. In that land — Washington Irving called it "the fairy region of the Hudson" — a prudent mariner will beware the Skid Demon, especially one of the heart.

Then we came under the looming of Bear Mountain. At its base, just above the Hudson, is a kidney-shaped lake once known as Sinnipink, and later after the bodies of British mercenaries turned the water incarnadine, it became Bloody Pond, a name changed to Highland Lake when a company in the nineteenth century cut ice from it to sell in New York City. Now it has returned to its history, although a bit cleansed: Hessian Lake.

At Bear Mountain Bridge high hills drop directly to the Hudson, and I slowed to an idle to see the location of one of the two great chains Americans stretched across the water in 1776 in an effort to keep British ships from using the river to cut the northern colonies in half. The two-foot-long links each weighed 140 pounds and lay on a huge boom of floating logs, but when the forts guarding the river fell to the enemy, the English broke open the chains, later shipping some links to Gibraltar, others eventually ending as exhibits in Hudson Valley museums. The combination of a lovely landform against a thickly historied river, all so close to the most powerful city in the world, is singular and, as such, has furthered the New Yorker's famed hubris into fatuous flights like this one from Henry Collins Brown in his inanely titled 1937 work, *The Lordly Hudson,* perhaps the biggest American river tome ever:

> This book is written primarily for those whom a beneficent Providence has permitted to dwell on [the Hudson] banks or in its lovely villages.

To less favored mortals, these pages are not expected to possess the same absorbing fascination. Yet a monograph of what is unquestionably the most beautiful river in the world is something the Hudson River man feels mankind should not be without. It is not his fault that everyone cannot live along the river. This volume is, therefore, designed also, as far as may be, to mitigate, to palliate existence away from the Hudson, if that is possible.

Four miles upstream we pulled into the willowed cove at the foot of Guinan's store in Garrison, the village that passed for nineteenth-century Yonkers in the movie *Hello, Dolly!* The temperature was dropping and the mist becoming rain.

A Drowned River

THE WOODEN FLOOR of Guinan's grocery and tavern creaked and leaked the antique scent of oiled wood and foodstuffs, and on the few shelves the few dusty tins and loaves suggested a kind of Old World paucity as if the owner were still in his native Ireland: rough-cut marmalade, custard powder, lemon curd, soda bread.

We went into the side room, its two walls of windows hung with river mist, West Point across the water disappearing in the grayness. Set into the small hearth was a footworn brass shamrock, and from the cold ashes a scent of burned wood; we had hoped for a fire. My friend the Photographer, who helped me haul *Nikawa* east and would soon take the trailer on to western New York for the first short portage, arrived at Guinan's in our tow wagon, a sport utility vehicle, with Jane Bannerman. She had come to Garrison on the train from New York City to tell us about the strange castle on Pollepel Island, a destination I was insisting on. Although our guest, she carried a generous picnic basket with finger sandwiches of ham and romaine lettuce, deviled eggs, a bottle of wine, and, tucked carefully to one side, sketchbooks from her European travels for us to see. A slender, attractive woman in her early seventies, she nodded when Pilotis spoke of our setting out from Elizabeth, New Jersey, her girlhood home. For years, her father had pleaded fruitlessly with city officials to install a traffic light at a particularly dangerous intersection. When she was twenty-five, Jane stepped into the street there and was struck by a car and suffered a head injury that caused partial deafness. Pilotis asked why she smiled telling of the event. "I was wearing black oxfords I disliked intensely, and one of them must have landed in a tree because I never saw it again. That was the end of wearing those shoes." Pilotis was scribbling notes, and I read, "In exchange for hearing in her right ear, Jane got rid of ugly shoes."

I asked her to tell us about that mysterious place we were about to strike out for, and she said, "My son passed the island on the train one evening, and he overheard a passenger tell another, 'A crazy man built that castle.' I guess it must look that way to others."

Her late husband, the builder's grandson, was Charles Bannerman, a New York City lawyer with little interest in the place, although he and Jane once took brief vacations there. She said, "I never found it easy to sleep in the residence. It was spooky and things happened at night. Cement cannonballs in the entablatures would come loose and fall. And electricity was never sufficient so we had to turn off one light before turning on the next. The house was dim here and dark there. It wasn't a place for me." She thought a moment and said, "I remember each room had an appropriate motto from the Bible carved in stone. In the kitchen, I think, was, 'She eateth not the bread of idleness,' and in the big room overlooking the Hudson, 'Come, behold the works of Jehovah.'" She sat quietly, then said, "I've forgotten so much."

When we went to the river again, Pilotis said, "She was just what you wanted — a lady to deepen the mystery." We passed below the high stone breastwork of West Point standing darkly in the weather, then made the sharp turn around the rock wedge that is the actual *west point* to enter a zigzag Hudson sailors call World's End, I think because, as you proceed, the sharp bend looks like a giant cul-de-sac. The bottom there is two hundred feet down, the deepest in the Hudson, and eddies and twisting currents and winds constricted by the ridges can create rough passage. Pilotis pressed against the window to watch closely. In the interest of promoting calm, I said, Everyone knows that a West Point freshman is a plebe, but what do you call the other three classes? My friend, keeping eyes on the water, said, "Sophomores, et cetera." No, I said, They're yearlings, cows, and firsties. "It's good to travel with someone so full of bar-bet knowledge." And I: Ask me what major league pitcher won the most games in a season. "Later! I'm navigating here."

The Highlands section of the river is distinct, mostly because the tallest hills rest against the deepest, swiftest, narrowest, and rockiest section of the lower Hudson, qualities that set it apart from what is upstream and down where the river widens into something more like a mountain lake. Over the 140 miles between Albany and the tip of Manhattan, the water drops only about five feet, and that means a negligible current if one ignores the tides. Except in the rugged Highlands passage, the Hudson shows itself for what it is today, a drowned river, with mud frequently two to three times the depth of the water. But in a time reckoned in millions of years past, it was then a fierce torrent that cut a deep trough through the hard rock there and onward for some hundred miles into the Atlantic. To see its present cleaving through the Highlands, those roots of higher mountains now washed into the sea, is to visualize the power the ancient river exerted.

The sounder picked up a large school of fish, perhaps migrating shad, as we approached Constitution Island, these days more of a peninsula because of a marsh that human works have brought about on its east side, a wetland now crucial to fish from the Atlantic that come up here to spawn. These days the Hudson usually looks invitingly clean, and the long efforts to reduce or eliminate filth are evident almost everywhere. But the pollutants that remain, while often less obvious than earlier algae blooms from untreated sewage or pools turned red by dumped paint, are more insidious because of their invisibility. A battery manufacturer once routinely discharged nickel-cadmium into a brook feeding Constitution Marsh, and even today the heavy metal comprises thirty percent of some sediments.

Not long ago, most Hudson Valley residents — except the poor — heeded state warnings and refused to eat anything from the river. Now, a generation after Congress passed the Clean Water Act, many fish, particularly anadromous species spending most of their life in the Atlantic, are appearing again on tables. Yet, at the very time we were climbing the Hudson, the 104th Congress, driven by right-wing extremists, was trying to undo the Clean Water Act, a strange and heinous effort given the effectiveness the law has had in improving American waters. Still, Pilotis and I found lingering a direct correlation between people's willingness to eat fish from the Hudson and the distance they lived from it: the farther they were, the greater their fear. But both on and away from the river, everyone we met spoke with anger about the deadly polychlorinated biphenyls that General Electric — under a state permit — for thirty years dumped into the Hudson a couple of hundred miles north of us.

Beyond the numerous biological arguments (such as self-preservation) for clean water and abundant life in the river is the poetry in the names of Hudson fishes. How impoverished the river would be without stonerollers, horny-head chubs, comely shiners, margined madtoms, northern hogsuckers, hogchokers, short-head redhorses, four-beard rocklings, mummichogs, naked gobies, striped searobins, slimy sculpins, and — more rarely — oyster toadfish, gags, lookdowns, four-eye butterfly fish, northern stargazers, freckled blennies, fat sleepers, and whole classes of bowfins, anchovies, needlefish, pipefish, silversides, jacks, wrasses, puffers, and flounders (left-eyed or right-eyed).

We beat along past Cold Spring, a pleasant village with a hospitable waterfront not far from a small source where General Washington quenched a thirst at a spring rising today hard by railroad tracks; despite some decorative stones, few modern travelers would think of drinking from it.

From the gloom, the massive, almost barren rock that is Storm King rose steeply from the west shore. Entering the Highlands, we were about to cross the Appalachians on tidal water. Close this gap and shut off the historic commerce that came through it, and New York City would be a Boston or Philadelphia. Storm King is significant in American law as the location of a rather recent and successful battle in court over threatened despoliation by a power company, a decision that established the right of citizens to bring suit on behalf of the environment.

I think no American river *per mile* is deeper in history, art, and perhaps literature than the Hudson, and some of its varied richness shows in the lore of the toponyms thereabouts. The river itself has been, to name a few, Cahohatatea, Shattemuck, Muhheakunnuk, Mahicanittuck, Mohegan, Grande Rivière, Angoleme, Río San Antonio, Río de Gomez, Río de Montaigne, Norumbega, Manhattan, Mauritius, River of the Prince, Nassau, Groote, Noordt, River of the Mountains, and (even today) the North. Along its banks no name is richer than Storm King, which Henry Hudson knew as Klinkersberg but Dutch settlers called Butter Hill, a description the local nineteenth-century "dude poet" N. P. Willis found not at all befitting its dominance of the lower river. He, according to one journalist, "bestowed in cold blood" the name Storm King. That label has stuck because it is more accurate than the others, given the way the mount twists wind and weather to alter them into afflictions as a heartless monarch does laws.

Even in the dark sky, the big rock seemed to cast a shadow over our course. I thought this reach a terrible place to die, and that turned me again to the depth finder: under us lay the Catskill Aqueduct, large enough to carry a locomotive and deep enough, were the Empire State Building placed on the tunnel floor, to leave only the top hundred feet of the skyscraper rising above the river surface. Inside the aqueduct each day, transverse to the flow of the Hudson, five hundred million gallons of cold mountain water rush down to New York City. Could tourists see that immense thing under the river, they might visit to gawk there as they do at Hoover Dam.

Beyond Storm King the Hudson opens again, its breadth more than a mile, and we moved along with little heed of the chart. Atop a wedge of driftwood, cormorants sat quietly hunched between sudden shrugs to throw off the damp day, shakes of beaks, and a settling again into inky stillness. "Okay," said my navigator, relaxing, "Who's the pitcher? Mathewson or Young?" Neither. "Koufax? Ryan? McLain?" No, I said, Charles "Old Hoss" Radbourn.

Abruptly distracted, Pilotis pointed upstream. "What in the hell is that?" Off our starboard quarter, emerging from the mist to menace the river, was the crazy man's castle. Prudent Pilotis, for the third time, said, "Are you sure about this little foray?" And then, citing *Jane Eyre*, "Curiosity is a dangerous petition, Jane."

Where Mohicans
Would Not Sleep

FOUR MILES UPRIVER from West Point and about three hundred yards off the east bank of the Hudson lies Pollepel Island, a hump of dark granite and gneiss sloping low on one side and rising about a hundred feet on the west, just enough to open to a good view of the river as it enters the Highlands. Across the water from Butter Hill, Pollepel was once Cheese Island, but those benignly bucolic names never fit the history, topography, or, above all, the weather. The Mohicans would not spend the night on the islet, and apparently, until Frank Bannerman bought it in 1900, the only ones to live there were a fisherman and his erratic wife who thought herself queen of England and waged long battles with storm goblins that rent the air with sudden squalls and meteorological occurrences more than passing peculiar. Since the seventeenth century, river travelers have attributed the capricious weather in the bends of the Highlands to elfin malfeasance.

Lore says old Dutch captains paused to douse their green crewmen in Pollepel water to immunize them against the bedevilment of hobs from Storm King and the dim, wet cloves around it. Another legend holds that the master of the *Flying Dutchman,* condemned to sail the seas forever, finally and gratefully saw his ship go down just south of the island on a hidden mud flat that today still grips the spars and ribs of the cursed ship to snag shad nets. And on the northwest shore lies an odd slant of rocks that wails like an injured woman when a certain northerly blows over it.

During the Revolutionary War Pollepel anchored a cheval-de-frise to halt movement upriver of British ships, but, while those sharpened, iron-capped timbers must have looked formidable, the enemy somehow passed through without let. The inconstants of Pollepel are so great that even warfare cannot properly proceed from it.

Pilotis and I had heard that Pollepel is sinking. Certainly it's one of the last islands in the lower Hudson, many others having disappeared not from subsidence but from being silted into peninsulas by human actions. We received warnings about goblins and deer ticks, so we took what precautions we could against the insects but didn't know how to proof ourselves against imps, and we believed the deep gloom was mere chance. As modern travelers we admitted no faerie to our plans and set out with a friend who had just joined us for a day, a reporter from my first hometown newspaper; he, looking remarkably like Shakespeare, was an earnest man, happier with a pencil than a paddle. We eased *Nikawa* up the channel east of Pollepel and shut off the motors for a downstream drift that would take us safely over presumed obstructions for a clandestine landing on what was now state land. We mostly discounted rumors of steel spikes and mines, even though one of the buildings carried big letters: BANNERMAN'S IS-LAND ARSENAL. Under the grim sky, Pilotis went to the bow with the sounding pole to call out the depth, but the wind began to rise and I had to spin the propellers every so often to keep our course. I could imagine the rocks, invisible as bogies, of Bannerman's old breakwaters lying inches from our blades. Pilotis liked nothing about this expedition and kept the phrase "holing the hull" bouncing against the pilot-house, but I wrote that off as the cry of a deep-water sailor who feels safe only with six fathoms under a keel. I repeated that we were in a flat-hulled boat specially chosen for river shallows. "Damn but you're insistent." I replied that in trying to cross the continent, our strongest ally was insistence, and Pilotis said, "How about intelligence?"

Bannerman's castle began to emerge from the dismals, veil after veil falling away, and slowly we could make out the turrets and crenelations, parapets, embrasures, and battlements, some built from nineteenth-century New York City paving blocks. The shadowy aura silenced us, and we drifted closer as though being pulled in. The Reporter put his pencil down and whispered to me, "Are you ignoring good advice?" and Pilotis raised four fingers to give me the depth, then it was three feet, and then came a godawful shattering whack, then another, as if we too had snagged on the *Flying Dutchman*. Pilotis, face full of alarm, whirled toward me and shouted, "You're on the bottom! You're on the goddamn bottom!"

I raised the stilled motors, and my prudent mariner yelled, "You just can't enter these places like Farragut charging into Mobile Bay! What's on your sign? 'Proceed as the way opens'?" I said the hitch in such advice was that much of the time we would *have to proceed* to learn whether the way was indeed open. When the motor stems came out of the water, we could see an anti-ventilation plate had snapped off. To fix it would be a major repair, and I knew we'd somehow have to continue over the next months without it.

I guessed we'd suffered the hit as we passed over one of Bannerman's breakwaters into what had formerly been a small harbor. The sounding pole indicated as much, so I started the engines, got up some headway, shut them off, raised them, and put us into a glide I hoped would let us reach deeper water. We'd have to use the canoe. A hundred yards south of the submerged breakwater, Pilotis went forward again and began working to set the anchor, but it took half a dozen tries before it stuck. We couldn't find the abundant Hudson mud and finally had to trust a less sure grip on rocks.

The Photographer was bringing the trailer up the river road from Garrison. I managed to reach him on the marine radio and make arrangements for our canoe to come out to the anchorage. We pulled on our rain suits, all the while explaining to the Reporter how to move the boat to safety should the weather change and the anchor slip. He said uneasily, "What if I can't remember all of this?" Pilotis mockingly answered, "Rely on your insistence." The Photographer, noticeably disturbed, told us a man had just committed suicide by walking into a tunnel as a Metro-North train rushed through. He added, "Ironically, quite close to the Breakneck Ridge stop." Pilotis said, "Nightfall's got more light than this day."

We boarded the canoe and struck out for a landing on the north of Pollepel, just above the old arsenal. Indeed, when we reached shore and started up the slope toward the fractured buildings at two P.M., the wind seemed to blow in not air but dusk. Pilotis carried a large corn-knife — allegedly only for brush — and kept one hand on it, allegedly only to prevent it from slipping from the belt. Forsythia blossoms, casting an unearthly yellow into the gray air like little jack-o'-lanterns, seemed to light our path more than the afternoon as we walked up under the tall shell of Bannerman's derelict dream. Years ago, his grandson Charles wrote, "Time, the elements, and maybe even the goblins of the Highlands, will take their toll of some of the turrets and towers, and perhaps eventually the castle itself." Seven years later, a night fire of unknown cause turned that eccentric structure — one of several along the storied Hudson — into a skeleton, and the immigrant Scot's most American longing for an instant ancestral dwelling became a romantic ruin, a fit end, some people thought, for a thing built on war profiteering.

We crossed the remains of the wharf in front of the arsenal where Bannerman used to store black powder, bombs, torpedoes, cannons, and more, all of it guarded by armed men, nasty dogs, and mounted Gatling guns. Now the seven-storey building was open to the sky, and trees and vines grew inside, right through heaps of cinders, broken glass, fallen brick, and steel girders serpentined by the fire. It had become like what it dispensed — a ruin of war.

After the First World War, the federal government tried to enforce the beating of sabers into plowshares by assuming greater supervision over secondhand arms merchants, and Bannerman's business following his death in 1918 became more of a big — very big — army-navy store with a fat illustrated catalog published well into the 1950s. It was full of uniforms and cannonry that outfitted Buffalo Bill's road show, movie regiments, courthouse lawns, and ten-year-old boys' imaginations: Civil War battle-rattle ($3.75), German bear-hunting sword ($14.00), Gatling gun barrels ($2.00), Spanish morion ($22.00), stone cannonball ($15.00), defused torpedo warhead ($20.00), as well as pith helmets, military ribbons and medals, buttons from the coats of Teddy Roosevelt's Rough Riders, and enticing descriptions: "Tree trunk from Civil War battlefield. Log is 42″ long, 12″ in diameter. Has 3 Minnie balls and one cannonball embedded. Packed for shipment." Everything sold only for spot cash.

Frank Bannerman, whom the *New York World-Telegram* described as a "one-time seller of death in wholesale lots," wrote in an early catalog: "St. John's vision of Satan bound and the one thousand years of peace is not yet in sight. We believe the millennium will come and have for years been preparing by collecting rare weapons now known as Bannerman's Military Museum, but which we hope some day will be known as The Museum of Lost Arts." And, in fact, some years later a portion of his immense collection did go to the Smithsonian. Bannerman's logic echoed that of Richard Gatling himself: "It occurred to me that if I could invent a machine — a gun — that would by its rapidity of fire enable one man to do as much battle duty as a hundred, it would to a great extent supersede the necessity of large armies and, consequently, exposure to battle and disease would be greatly diminished."

We walked up to the old residence, across the drawbridge, under the portcullis, and through the sally port. From the scorched and ruptured shell hung eroded stone armorial shields, cannonballs, and other architectural details no longer identifiable. Inside were floorless upper chambers, crumbling fireplaces clinging to the walls, stairs leading into space, and a litter of broken radiators, snapped pipes, exhausted dreams. As we wandered, we separated in the mist, and I found myself alone in a low, brick room like a dungeon. The ceiling dripped, darkness seemed to gnaw at the beam from my flashlight, and before and behind were cobwebbed corners and who-knows-what coiled under fallen plaster. I played the light over the chamber, across a rotting table and onto a thing that froze me: on top lay a wet face. I fell back, dropped my light, scrabbled about to grab the rolling beam, played it again toward the horrid visage and then onto a chair holding a sagging skeleton. As I backed up, I realized the face was a painted mask of the kind a Mexican might wear on the Day of the Dead, the image seared by one of the fat and moldy candles. The skeleton was a deflated piece of soft plastic. On the floor lay a stretched-out condom.

What in hell had gone on in here? I picked up the mask, one of several, tried it out. The temptation was too much. I went to the window and waited till I heard my friend, who believes not at all in goblins, crunching toward me. I lifted the mask to my face, stood low in the narrow window, and groaned. Pilotis looked up, recoiled violently, and jerked out the cornknife. I rasped out, Hello, Mate.

Too relieved to curse, Mate later recounted the incident with relish, since there's nothing a person of words likes more than an incident of survival.

We climbed to a second-storey room still possessed of its floor, or most of it, and sat down amid the rubble and rusting bedsteads to wait out a wind quickly turning vehement. It was one of the black squalls off Storm King we'd read about, and it beat the river relentlessly. Even from this high point on the island, we were unable to see through the pounded air, and we could only trust *Nikawa* was holding anchor or that the Reporter had moved her to safety, if there were such here. Said Pilotis, "Was this side expedition a good idea?"

I answered to the effect that there was little better for a traveler than reading about a distant place, absorbing its past, its legends, and then arriving to walk smack into them. For us, it wasn't just the old Scot's castle and his faux barony nor the strange island with its hobbed history; it was the whole aura of a weirdly weathered and demonic stretch of the Hudson Highlands. We'd taken chances to encounter something with an aspect beyond the probable, and we'd found it, perhaps by losing a boat.

Pilotis said, "You've always tended to equate caution with cowardice. I never knew a man so afraid of cowardice." I said that, at times, only risk could bring about such an intersection of books and life, tales and actuality, history and current moment, and it was for all that I'd come; surely we both knew that our time on the blasted island would long hold in our memories. But you're right, I said, if only we also could be sure of *Nikawa*. "Sudden, violent things never endure," Pilotis said.

The sky at last began to open and the wind drop, and we went down and pushed through the brush for a view of the river, and there, sweet and white in the quieting water, tidily at anchor, lay our little river horse, and soon we heard the canoe approaching to take us off odd Pollepel.

An hour later, *Nikawa* was sliding over a glassy Hudson and under the wondrously high and now abandoned 1888 railroad bridge at Poughkeepsie, the whilom home of brewer Matthew Vassar who proposed building a monument to Henry Hudson on Pollepel but, fortunately, failed to find support and founded a college for women instead. We moved past Hyde Park and the riverside mansions of Vanderbilts and Roosevelts. The cruise gave the Reporter a chance to recover from having been severely shaken in body and mind as he tended *Nikawa* through the squall. He said several times, "I thought she was going down. Capsizing on your second day out." We came, I said, to encounter the rivers. And he: "But not death." I mentioned I knew of a good glass of nerve-settling porter up on Rondout Creek, along what used to be the old Delaware and Hudson Canal, and Pilotis said, "Now there's something I'd like you to insist on."

Snowmelt and a
Nameless Creek

AT KINGSTON we were able to follow our plan of staying in
riverside towns when possible and found quarters up the hill
from Rondout Creek in a large old house with a yard full of
maple trees our host each spring tapped for sap to boil down to a fine
syrup that we dripped over breakfast pancakes just before we heard
the bad news. We were a day from the Erie Canal, the route to carry
us across New York to Buffalo. There are thirty-seven locks on the
canal, and at nine in the morning we learned repairs on the first one,
of all places, were not complete. Three days out, and already we were
going to lose a day.

"So what's twenty-four hours?" our host said. We wished he were
right, but the facts of a continental voyage in a single season change
the meaning of time. In order to find enough water in the western
rivers, especially the upper Missouri, we would have to catch the snowmelt off the Rocky Mountains, that brief but somewhat predictable
flushing in June which we hoped would enable us to float our canoe
rather than drag it across Montana. We wanted a voyage, not a hike.
Timing the snowmelt is rather tricky if one starts from, say, Iowa or
Nebraska, but to try it from the Atlantic Ocean is quite something else,
and the greatest problem in the East is the Erie Canal. In winter the
locks shut down, parts of its course are dry, and it doesn't open until
early May, too late to let us arrive with the June rise in the Far West.

Other water routes westward require miles and miles of overland
travel, and some necessitate skirting along much of the perimeter of

the nation; we were bent on traveling through the heart of the country with water under us in a measure never before achieved. To reverse directions and go from west to east presented knottier problems, the crucial one the Salmon River which is not passable upstream except by jet boat. We were, if you will, locked into our chosen route.

Using tables that show the usual peak of spring runoff on the upper Missouri and then figuring in a few days to accommodate a break-down, an injury, or an illness, I knew we needed to enter the Erie Canal, if possible, no later than April fifteenth, three weeks prior to the official opening. Months before starting out, I had gone to the Office of Canals to ask permission to pass through as soon as the Erie was completely watered. I brought in support from my friend Schuyler Meyer who had served on the Erie as captain of the old state tug *Urger* and hoped to join us. The authorities, recognizing the challenge of such a transcontinental endeavor, deliberated and finally agreed to let us set out on the twenty-fourth, but they warned of contractors not completing repairs on time.

I then reworked our itinerary, compressed it to the point of the nearly impossible, and removed virtually all capability of waiting out a force majeure, so we ended up with a schedule likely to try us nearly as much as the rivers would. Every day was now critical, and time became the unseen captain of our boat. I knew no way to circumvent it.

At Rondout, we could do little but deplore contractors and wonder whether a twenty-four-hour delay might turn into a week. Pilotis, not wishing to haunt me with my own advice, said nothing about proceed-ing as the way opens, but I couldn't stop myself from hearing the words of Manuel Lisa, the early Missouri River fur trader: "I go a great distance while some are considering whether they will start today or tomorrow." As I looked over our route, I thought how a jet plane could accomplish it in about four hours, a car in four days, a good bicyclist in four weeks; but we — *if* the staggering welter of things all fell into place hereafter — we would need almost four months before winter closed the mountain passes and froze the waters.

Helpless, Pilotis and I went off to the east side of the river to search for smoked shad whose Latin name means "most delicious." We heard their run from the Atlantic to spawn in the mid-Hudson flats was good that spring. Above Rhinecliff we found a little fish house, a family business for more than a century. The cutting room, redolent of fresh shad, stripers, and sturgeon, was next to a mechanic's garage filled with broken machinery and dusty mounted animals. A toothless old fellow dressed the shad and carried a tray of them to a small smoke-house where racks of fish, after a two-day soak in molasses and vine-gar brine, lay coloring in the clouds rising from the hickory coals. I said, Is it true poached shad testes are delectable? He said, "What?" and wrapped six fish for us to take upriver, and we went off to buy towels, returning to Rondout by suppertime.

Our enforced layover seemed to relax Pilotis and gave us time to work on our logbooks before we went to eat. After the meal, we propped back, and I talked about the creek — I never knew it to have a name — that ran near my boyhood home in Kansas City. One after-noon, when I was ten and messing about in it, I suddenly realized it wasn't a dead end: that flow around my ankles actually went some-where. Just like a road, it had a destination far beyond my sight. At home I dug into my father's maps and discovered that the creek, no wider than I was tall, meandered into a succession of ever-larger ones, all leading to the Missouri River and on to the Mississippi, the Gulf, the open Atlantic. I determined to put a note in a bottle and launch it nearly from my back porch on a voyage to Huck Finn's river, to New Orleans, perhaps the Mosquito Coast, or the mysterious Sargasso Sea, Casablanca, the very shores of the Sahara. I was woozy with a child's excitement as I realized that nameless creeklet was the first leg of a long voyage to Cathay, the Coral Sea, the Arctic. The waters of the world were one! Water linked the earth! The street in front of our house ran to the ends of two continents, but that creek led to the darkest jungles up the Congo, around the Cape of Good Hope, to the Ganges and bathing Hindus, even to the mountains of Tibet. I began planning voyages and reading about far places, books like *The Royal Road to Romance* by Richard Halliburton. Our creek was a threshold beyond which lay the realms of poesy.

Looking around the battered tavern where we'd just finished pitiful plates of potatoes and cabbage, lifting a chipped mug, Pilotis toasted, "To the realms of poesy, matey."

The next morning, we hoped the Erie Canal would be ready in another day, so we cast off from the small wharf on Rondout Creek, motored past the brick lighthouse, one of four remaining on the Hudson, and turned again upstream. The weather was fine and the water gave us only mild chop in a reach called the Flat. For the rest of the morning, the river showed us sand and mud shallows but little stone, and we clipped along, almost free of our greatest fear — under-water rocks that could abruptly end our voyage. As if an old tar, Pilotis sang pieces of song, some of them one chorus more than necessary, but I knew the river was at last full upon my friend.

By midday we reached Catskill and went up the tree-lined creek, a place not yet leafy, to hunt a beverage to go with our smoked shad. We found a winsome waitress named Rhoda whom Pilotis insisted on calling Rhonda, and, motioning toward me, said to her, "We have an unattached man here headed west in that boat tied up below. I'll leave the expedition if you'd like to join him." And she answered, "Last week I'da took you up on it." We went back to the river, got under way, and I said, You, Mate, are not yet expendable, even for the lovely likes of Rhonda, but one more chorus of "Blow the Man Down" may change that.

But Pilotis sang on, three runs of the Beach Boys' "Help me, Rhonda." We passed under the town of Hudson high on the east bank and on to Coxsackie to our portside. As the ridges began to recede from the river, kills flowed down to expend themselves in the Hudson, and then the water widened into the turning basins just below Albany, and industry lay here and there along both banks. Not long ago, that stretch of river was so severely polluted a public hearing on the Albany Pool, according to one report, caused men to grit their teeth and women to leave the room. Today, with improved sewage and industrial waste treatments and increased monitoring by ordinary citizens, con-ditions are better, but still that portion, like much of the Hudson, is an unfunded Superfund site.

The state government towers of Albany show well from the river, and they reminded me of traveler Clifton Johnson's comment near the turn of the century about the city: "One of its claims to distinction is the fact that it existed for over a century without a single lawyer."

Near there, Henry Hudson found a warm native reception — among several other violent ones — during his brief exploration of the river he called Manhattes. After sharing a meal of pigeon and plump dog with the Indians, he wrote (in one of the few passages extant from his missing journal): "The land is the finest for cultivation that I ever in my life set foot upon, and it also abounds in trees of every description. The natives are a very good people, for when they saw that I would not remain, they supposed that I was afraid of their bows, and taking the arrows, they broke them in pieces, and threw them into the fire."

Four miles upstream we stopped for the night at Troy, the first of several cities we'd see that have turned their backs to the river. At the town dock we refueled and met up with the man who was to lead us, under orders from the Canal Office, through certain construction areas. He had good news, if we could trust it: the first lock would be ready early tomorrow. I did a happy little jig. With that prospect before us, I invited all hands to Brown and Moran's brew pub, a few yards up the alley from the dock. In 143 miles, we had climbed only five feet above the Atlantic, yet the first river was all but behind us. Five thousand miles of water and weather lay ahead.

11

THE ERIE CANAL

LOCKPORT, NEW YORK

[Erie Canal packet boats] are about 70 feet long, and with the exception of the kitchen and bar, occupied as a cabin. The forward part, being the ladies cabin, is separated by a curtain, but at meal times this obstruction is removed, and the table is set the whole length of the boat. The table is supplied with everything that is necessary and of the best quality with many of the luxuries of life. On finding we had so many passengers I was at a loss to know how we should be accommodated with berths, as I saw no convenience for anything of the kind, but the Yankees, ever awake to contrivances, have managed to stow more in so small a space than I thought them capable of doing. The way they proceed is as follows — the settees that go the whole length of the boat on each side unfold and form a cot-bed. The space between this bed and the ceiling is so divided as to make room for two more. The upper berths are merely frames with sacking bottoms, one side of which had two projecting pins which fit into sockets in the side of the boat. The other side has two cords attached one to each corner. These are suspended from hooks in the ceiling. The bedding is then placed upon them, the space between the berths being barely sufficient for a man to crawl in, and presenting the appearance of so many shelves. Much apprehension is always entertained by the passengers when first seeing them, lest the cords should break. Such fears are, however, groundless. The berths are allotted [according] to the way-bill — the first on the list having his first choice, and in changing boats the old passengers have the preference. The first night I tried an upper berth, but the air was so foul that I found myself sick when I awoke. Afterwards I chose an under-berth and found no ill effects from the air. . . . The bridges on the canal are very low, particularly the old ones; indeed they are so low as to scarcely allow the baggage to clear, and in some cases actually rubbing against it. Every bridge makes us bend double if seated on anything, and in many cases you have to lie on your back. The man at the helm gives the word to the passengers. "Bridge!" "Very low bridge!" "The lowest on the canal!" as the case may be. Some serious accidents have happened for want of caution. A young English woman met with her death a short time since, she having fallen asleep with her head upon a box [and] had her head crushed to pieces. Such things however do not often occur, and in general it affords amusement to the passengers who soon imitate the cry and vary it with a command such as, "All Jackson men bow down." After such commands we find very few Aristocrats.

Thomas S. Woodcock
New York to Niagara, 1836

The Pull of a Continent

A S IF IT SLEPT, the river lay quiet when we arose at dawn to wash up and then fire the motors to stir the water so that it seemed to flow again, and above the curious lines of the art moderne Green Island Bridge we assembled our little convoy that the Canal Office required. On the west bank of the Hudson was an old and yet still operating powerhouse, built by Thomas Edison, where Captain Schuyler Meyer awaited in his forty-two-foot motor yacht called a trawler, and we fell in behind, followed by Cap's second vessel, the *Doctor Robert*. At the rear was a last-minute addition, a slovenly tour boat run by a grousing, jowly, slovenly man moving it west from its winter berth; he carried a reputation of trying to amuse tourists by using his loudspeakers to gibe lock tenders. Pilotis and I hoped to pull free soon of the sailing order, meeting up only when necessary.

The news was good: repair obstructions at the front of the Erie Canal were gone. We had lost only one day. The federal lock at Troy is the first — or last — on the Hudson, and it demarks the northern limit of tidal flow, the end of estuarial influence, as it does the farthest point Henry Hudson reached in 1609. There he determined the river was only that and not the imagined grand egress to the western sea. He turned the *Half Moon* around without knowing Samuel de Champlain just seven weeks earlier had descended by water from the north to within seventy-five miles of him.

We warily entered our first lock. Pilotis, on the bow, was a novice in canal procedures and edgy about casting a mooring line and missing a bollard to hold us fast in the swirling water that would fill the chamber. I was uneasy about wind spinning *Nikawa* as we slowed and lost

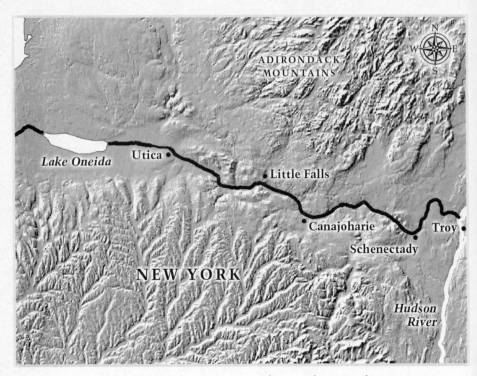

The Erie Canal east, Troy to Lake Oneida, 133 miles

steerage, so I came in fast, too fast. Pilotis's first toss landed in the water. The second bounced off the bollard. Then the wind grabbed our stern as the third throw looped over just in time to pull us securely to the slimy walls. I went to the welldeck to hold the stern line. The huge gates groaned closed behind, covering us in the dusk of a deep well, and water began rollicking beneath *Nikawa,* raising her slowly from the dimness again into sunlight. Fifteen minutes later, the forward gates opened to let us proceed a mile north of the three mouths of the Mohawk River where, at Waterford, we came upon a sign with one arrow pointing right to the Champlain Canal and another left to the Erie. For the first time I felt the westward pull of the continent in spite of the flow against us, perhaps because we were now running in the proper direction — toward the Pacific.

The Erie Canal, 170 years old that spring and in its first season ever without commercial barge traffic, is a marvel of nineteenth-century engineering, as travelers have remarked since 1825, but they do not commonly speak of its former 350 miles as a route of noteworthy beauty. Usually it's little more than "a nice journey through pretty country," and that's accurate, although the eastern end, above Cohoes Falls, where the Mohawk River drops over a great rocky shelf, is a splendid scape of land, water, and canal. Bypassing the cascade is a stair of five chambers, once the greatest series of high lift-locks in the world, stretching across only a little more than a mile, a hydrological escalator carrying the sweet name of the Waterford Flight, and indeed, our ascent was like a gentle rise in a hot-air balloon.

The first lock on the Erie, despite incomplete repairs, was ready enough to let us enter. Pilotis looped the pin on the second try, and the wind, passing across the chamber rather than into it, ignored *Nikawa,* and we soon started up between the eroded walls. Unlike its river sections, the canal for some miles beyond the Flight is an excavated cut, narrow and intimate, trees overhanging the water, the current slight, the bottom without treacherous surprises. As we climbed the locks in thirty-three-foot increments, the view back toward the Hudson Valley opened to the Taconic Range, and on the distant eastern horizon Massachusetts and Vermont appeared to lift into view. When we topped out and entered the channel leading to the Mohawk, we had risen 165 feet in less than two hours, and at last the Atlantic Ocean truly seemed *down.* If high water or farther repair work did not stop us, we thought we could reach Buffalo and Lake Erie in five days.

The earliest Erie Canal, the one called Clinton's Ditch, was, in its entirety, a slender, shallow, dug channel, but that old course in places is now a dozen miles away from the newer route. During subsequent reconstructions, engineers increasingly took advantage of lakes and rivers, especially the Mohawk, sometimes to the detriment of the natural waterways; Pilotis preferred the river sections, while I liked the canal cuts but, even more, the change from one to the other. When *Nikawa* passed under highway bridges, like Interstate 87 west of Schenectady, we motored along smugly free of striped concrete and truck mudflaps, and our sailor's life was easy. Then came Lock Seven.

The wind blew directly upriver into the chamber, and as I slowed so Pilotis could secure the bow, a gust took the stern and in an instant we got shoved sideways to the chamber walls, and the driver of the tour boat (permitted to travel the canal early only because of our passage) called over his loudspeakers, to the interest of all those watching — a locking-through generally draws spectators — "What the hell are you doing!" I spun the props to complete our shameful pivot quickly, and with a stellar toss Pilotis got the line to a crewman on Cap's trawler already tied to the wall, and we pulled in snug against her. To ease my chagrin, Pilotis said, "Sooner or later every rider gets thrown," and stopped me from going to the welldeck to address the tour boatman's supererogatory rhetorical flourish.

We proceeded on, into a long stretch of natural river, on past the Knolls Atomic Laboratory formerly manufacturing propulsion units for nuclear submarines, on beyond steep shale cliffs, then hooked northward where the Mohawk passes the arched stone remains of an aqueduct that once carried canal boats across the rocky river to easier passage on the opposite bank, on to Schenectady, the lightbulb city.

I told Pilotis of my visit there a year earlier when, at my late father's request, I looked in on his elderly colleague Miss So-and-so whose quiet elegance time had diminished but not erased, now living alone, rarely leaving her house, a place desperate for light and fresh air. She set out a pot of thin tea and limber Saltines and was pleased with the company, but whenever our conversation paused, out of apparent habit she would lift the receiver of her rotary-dial phone, although it hadn't rung, and hold it gingerly to her ear for several moments, then say softly, "Hello?" Waiting, then, "Anyone there?" Perhaps noticing my quizzical look after the fourth pickup, she said to me, "Just checking." I nodded, and she added, "It doesn't ring often, so maybe the bell doesn't always work." She mentioned Mr. Such-and-such whom my father had to give a pink slip years ago: "Yes," she said, "he joined the Silent Majority." I said, I had no idea he, of all people, had turned religious. She: "He didn't turn religious. He died." I see. "Yes, liquor finally took him." How old was he? "Ninety-seven." When I got up to leave, I mentioned my plans for crossing the country by water, and she asked would I go through Canada, and I said no, and she: "Yes, that's probably good. When I think of Canada, nothing comes to mind."

Cap had arranged to take aboard five students from old Eliphalet Nott's Union College to let them see the canal still living its history. It was Cap, two years earlier, who had invited me aboard the canal tug *Urger*, nearly a century old, to show me the Erie. On occasion, he gave me the helm of the ponderous thing. One afternoon, moving easily along, I fell into a lull and almost missed a channel buoy and had to turn the clumsy boat so swiftly I came close to dipping her gunwales. Thereafter the crew called me Captain Zigzag, a name to go alongside real canal captains Crash and Aground. Given those choices, I didn't complain about my moniker.

Schuyler Merritt Meyer's lineage was this: a father who represented as both assemblyman and senator a silk-stocking district in Manhattan in the early part of the century; an uncle, George Bird Grinnell, the famous ethnologist, who once showed Sitting Bull the city and learned the great warrior liked nothing so much as elevators; a childhood chum of Theodore Roosevelt's grandson Archie. Cap was tall, balder than he preferred, a man who laughed more than he fumed but did both well, a fellow of means and generosity, a philanthropist who lived much of each year aboard his trawler anchored near Manhattan. He helped found SCOW, the State Council on Waterways, a nonprofit association working to preserve the history, character, and especially the operation of the Erie Canal, a noble endeavor because the waterway, its commercial traffic unable to compete with trucks and now gone, needed new reasons for continuance. Hope for its survival lay in boaters traveling it, discovering its history, and those expectations were behind the Canal Office granting us early passage.

A few months earlier, when Cap learned of my intent to cross the country by boat, he was seventy-three, struggling to recover from serious surgery, and about to founder on his sharpened perception of mortality. Within hours of seeing charts of our proposed route, he began to revive, even more so when I mentioned I was four months away from leaving but still had no boat that I believed could make the voyage. He talked vigorously about finding me a suitable craft on the East Coast. A month later he'd discovered a fat, heavy, wooden cruiser built for offshore water; it was charmingly eccentric, of a character to match Schuyler's. He loved the boat, and I too admired it, as I did him, but I doubted its deep hull, cantankerous diesel engine, and the lease price. Even so, I thought long about it and came close to accepting. Then I declined. Annoyed, Cap bought the thing anyway, the very *Doctor Robert* then riding in our wake, and donated it to SCOW; to prove its riverworthiness, he decided to take it along much of our route, halfway across the United States to the head of navigation on the Missouri. I confess I didn't like his plan of following us but assumed that in the long river miles beyond the Erie Canal we would find independence. Helping Cap on his two boats were four men good and true. The tourist tub notwithstanding, Pilotis and I convinced ourselves the convoy was an inescapable accommodation to Meyer and the Canal Office, a necessity we could somehow try to enjoy for a few days.

Near Amsterdam the students disembarked, and we went through the next two locks so smoothly I saw Pilotis wearing the Hell Gate Grin. The trick for novice venturers is to learn quickly enough before inexperience does a journey in; I optimistically reckoned that each day of survival, each league of fast education, increased our chances of completing the voyage.

Pilotis and I wanted to tie up for the night at a pleasant park near an abandoned brewery — Bowler's — on the northwest side of Amsterdam, but Cap insisted we keep moving to where his plush trawler would have electricity and fresh water. To appease us, he let *Nikawa* leave the mandated sailing order and push ahead so we could gain a little solitude and time to look at the beautiful ruin of the 1841 aqueduct that crosses Schoharie Creek at Fort Hunter. Its fourteen arches, like something out of Roman Umbria, stood entire for a century until engineers, trying to prevent frequent jams of ice and driftwood, dynamited two of the pillars and so weakened the span that over the following years more arches collapsed, leaving fewer than half remaining from one of the finest structures on the old canal. Slide-rule men, never known for listening to people who have the longest experience with the country, would have done well to consider the Iroquoian meaning of Schoharie: "driftwood."

Five miles west, across from Fultonville, we pulled up in Fonda to a high concrete docking wall that made clambering ashore from our low decks difficult. The village was a tired place, and we ate a tired Chinese meal, and bought tired ice cream cones at a tired filling station, and walked tiredly back to our bunks. It was my turn to sleep in the cramped forward berth. The temperature dropped steadily, and what little warmth I could muster condensed on the uninsulated overhead so that droplets spattered down on me much of the night. It was twenty-six degrees by morning, and we were loath to leave our sleeping bags and step into cold and damp clothes, so we lay waiting for sunrise to thaw the air.

Released from the
Necessity of Mundane Toil

THE STARS had hardly thinned to vacancy when I heard a rumbling engine and Pilotis call out, "Cap's leaving!" It wasn't the worst way to meet dawn because we so hurried into our frigid duds I barely felt the discomfort. We didn't mind he'd chosen not to alert us before getting the motor yacht under way, but we did mind our thoughts of his heated cabin fragrant with fresh coffee and his hot plates of eggs and pancakes.

Pilotis stumbled about hauling in our frosted lines, and I fumbled the tardy *Nikawa* upriver and in behind Cap who, it seemed, was almost hoping to leave us behind and dash our chance to get through Lock Thirteen where we'd end up trapped till the season opened; perhaps he harbored irritation at my not having accepted the *Doctor Robert* now laboring in our prop wash.

The land through that portion of the Mohawk was little farms between small stands of timber, the sunrise bringing all of it into the colors of early spring. After the lock, we passed between the Noses, Big and Little, a break the Mohawk forced through the Adirondacks, an opening at least as important to the westering of America as the Cumberland Gap, for without it the Erie Canal would have been significantly more difficult to build. Even today, betwixt the proboscises run two railroads, two state highways, one interstate, the Erie, and the river.

We again proceeded ahead of the others to find the water quiet but for a lone canal-tender doing maintenance. Along one isolated bend we came upon, although we could hardly believe it, an animal once the most widely distributed in the Americas and today among the most elusive and mysterious: a crouched cougar lapping at the Erie before bounding in high arcs toward the north forests, its long tail whisking the icy brush. Pilotis: "That's something, if you're lucky, you see once and never again. Not in our time anyway."

Four miles west of the Noses is "the pot that washes itself," a translation of the Algonquian name Canajoharie; the "pot" is a surprisingly circular depression several feet across that gritty, swirling currents have cut into the rock bed of Canajoharie Creek; people drive out just to watch it work. The village is close enough to the canal to allow a small boat into the mouth of the stream below the old Beech-Nut chewing gum factory, and travelers can tie off and walk to Main Street and on down between a couple of blocks of stone and brick nineteenth-century storefronts all the way to the intersection with an old-style traffic signal at the center, the thing called "the dummy light." I once asked the mayor why that name: "Because it stands in the middle of the street." Said Pilotis, "Have you got a better Canajoharie story?" Not really, I said, except for that fellow here — the man who thumped his little boy's full belly to see whether he could eat more watermelon and who sold me a history of the Mohawk Valley and said, "My wife lives her days like forgiveness is the best revenge, and she's forgiven me day in and day out for ten years."

The forty miles of canal from Amsterdam to Little Falls was easy running through softly cambered terrain of wooded hills that become larger and more deeply timbered as they recede from the Mohawk Valley northward. Only ten miles away they rise to become the Adirondack Mountains, a tract big enough to clean the slow wind that rode over us on its way down along the great Appalachian corrugation. In several places the canal berms are low, and we found good views across the narrow valley. Here and there, Interstate 90, the New York Thruway, came within a few yards of the Erie, and drivers waved as if we were locomotive engineers, and we saluted, since their Thruway tolls underwrote the operation and maintenance of the State Canal System: we could boat across New York because they drove I-90.

In the morning sun, Pilotis at the helm, I sat back, feet propped up, and watched the canalmen putting out buoys for the new season, a farmer turning a fallow field, buds on the frosted bushery beginning to thaw; but the willows and sycamores, playing the vagaries of a northern spring more cautiously, had only bare branches as if winter had just gone, and that made me imagine we had a world of time to reach the snowmelt of the far Rockies.

Our conversation was doodling items of the sort people fall into when they are on water and content to believe they've earned an easy moment: as we passed Otsquago Creek I began rattling on how I liked American Indian toponyms and the manifold and usually fanciful translations attending them. I offered that Hudson was a better name for an automobile than a river and wished it were still the Mahicanittuck or the Mohegan; I said I wished the spelling of some upstate names looked more Indian: Skanektadee, Skoharee, Kanajoharee. After all, how much more native seems Tennessee than were it, say, Tenisi. And how about my state as Mazooree? "Not elegant." It's true, I agreed, one can carry even an Indian name too far. Take the Massachusetts lake due east of us, the one called, in its entirety, Chargoggagoggmanchaugagoggchaubunagungamaug, the longest American place name I knew, now changed to, if you will, a watery and weak Anglo one: Webster. I didn't actually speak the Algonquian name because my tongue couldn't make it through those forty-three letters. I tried to recite a piece of old verse (which I here give correctly):

> Ye say they have all passed away,
> that noble race and brave;
> that their light canoes have vanished
> from off the crystal wave;
> that mid the forest where they roamed
> there rings no hunter's shout;
> but their name is on your waters,
> and ye cannot wash it out.

We stopped at Fort Plain to wait for both Cap and the locktender, and we sat in the sunny welldeck and talked of whatever came to mind. I asked Pilotis what face of an American, other than a president or perhaps Ben Franklin, was the most reproduced visage. Pilotis cogitated. I hinted, Consider where we are. Pilotis ruminated. A New Yorker, I said. An answer: "Alexander Hamilton on the ten-dollar bill." I didn't think so and gave a punned clue: A man of the first water. Pilotis cerebrated. I said, The person carried a keg of Lake Erie water over this very route to pour it into New York Bay. Pilotis said disbelievingly, "DeWitt Clinton? Come on now." I asked, Do you remember the

little blue federal tax-stamps stuck to every pack of American cigarettes for almost ninety years? That face looking at the smoker was the
Father of the Erie Canal. How many packs of cigarettes had there been
in those years? Ten billion? A zillion? Sighing, Pilotis said, "This is what
happens to people released from the necessity of mundane toil."

We ascended Lock Fifteen and went on beyond St. Johnsville, the
old milltown where the citizens formerly made whiskey, cigars, player
pianos, and knitted underwear, a village I called Goodtimeville and
Pilotis St. Longjohnsville. A mile west, the canal leaves the Mohawk
and follows a four-mile cut, then rejoins the river three miles downstream from Little Falls and Lock Seventeen, at forty feet the biggest
elevation change on the Erie. Through the locks and up the slightest
slope of waters we had risen above the Atlantic the height of a thirty-
two-storey building; traveling at only eight miles an hour makes even
modest altitudes take on significance, much as they do with a hiker.

The lockmaster arrived early and happily let *Nikawa* through without the convoy, an accommodation to allow us to tie up at the tiny
wharf opposite the river from Little Falls. We walked the bridge just
above the remains of an 1822 aqueduct, at one time another distinctive
canal structure. Part of it still stood when I'd seen it a year earlier, but
too few people had cared to preserve it, never mind that it helped
make the village what it is, and the arches now lay a hopeless pile of
broken stone in the shallows. Little Falls sits along the narrow gorge of
the Mohawk, the Erie paralleling the river but forty feet higher. The
route here has shifted only a few yards from Clinton's day, and the
dark waterside cliffs have long been one of the often painted scenes on
the canal. Were Little Falls more alert to its history and setting, it could
be the gem of the Erie. On Ann Street we found a café where we
washed up and tucked into breakfast, then went back to *Nikawa* in
time to catch the convoy passing, and as we overtook it, received a
scowl from Cap.

A couple of miles west, the waterway leaves the Mohawk briefly,
rejoins it west of Herkimer for four miles, and then departs from the
river for good, although it's rarely more than a half mile away. Across
the Mohawk from Herkimer, the old nutcracker and BB-gun burg,
is Ilion, one of the canal towns named after ancient Mediterranean
cities — Troy, Utica, Rome, Syracuse. Like its predecessor, it has a long
association with war, weapons, and words through the Remington

Arms factory whence emerged not only guns (famous models and ones less so, like the Mule-Ear Carbine, the Zig-Zag Derringer, the rifle-cane) but also the creation of a practical typing machine. I said to Pilotis, The first typewritten manuscript accepted for publication came from a Missourian who wrote about a river, and he did it on a contraption made in Ilion. "That's got to mean Twain's *Life on the Mississippi.*"

The Erie now lay in long straight segments with only occasional warps from the engineer's transit line. As we left the big hills of the Adirondack rumpling, Pilotis and I fell into the drone of the motors, once more thinking how easily we were moving along and wondering how long it might last. At Lock Nineteen the tender kept us back until the convoy could come up, and even then we had to hold further for the chamber to fill, but we had a simple mooring to a concrete wall with good rings for our lines. We went aft to watch the water follow our course of the last days, and then Cap's boats arrived to tie up for the wait. The tourist tub lumbered alongside and began attempting a tricky and needless flanking maneuver, a showoff move, to ride in ahead of us. I was in the pilothouse to check fuel and looked up as the monstrous stern of the tub swung toward our forward quarter. *Nikawa* was about to be torn open and ground into the wall. I grabbed the radio and shouted for the helmsman to stop, but he just kept on flanking toward us, stupidly believing he had enough clearance. This was it — after only five days, our voyage was about to end.

Pilotis leaped to the rail, ran to the bow, and sat down to thrust out feet just as the heavy butt-end came up. With a shove made powerful by desperation, my mate moved us taut against our lines and by luck gained just enough inches to let the baneful tub clear our prow.

I stood in disbelief, shaking, still thinking the expedition ruined. On the water, the time between the easy life and disaster is but a moment. Blanch-faced Pilotis looked at me, and I said, You are one damn prudent mariner! Then I jumped off *Nikawa* and onto the wall, and in a voice of only a little less volume than the infamous loudspeakers of the tourist bucket, I dressed down the slovenly man and shouted something to the effect of wishing to see him never again on the same water with us. He only stared in feigned innocence.

I went back aboard and said to Pilotis, You saved this voyage by twelve inches and two feet. Thinking how months of preparation and thousands of dollars nearly went under, I got angry once more and started again for the wall, but Pilotis grabbed me. "Let it go. Let it go. He heard you — everybody heard you," and then, smiling the Hell Gate Grin, said, "By the way, exactly what is a 'moronic piss-brain'?" The gates opened, we locked through and left the convoy behind, and it felt good to show them our stern at Oriskany Flats. It was Thucydides, I think, who wrote two thousand years ago, "A collision at sea can ruin your entire day."

Between Utica and Rome, only fourteen miles, industries came down to canalside, although a screen of scrub trees camouflaged most of them, effectively creating an appearance of ruralness so that we slipped past downtown Utica before realizing sixty thousand people were moving just beyond the woody scrim of narrow bottomland. In river travel today, perhaps nothing is finer than arrival in the center of a town without having to undergo those purgatorial miles of vile sprawl, hideous billboards, and reiterated franchises where we become fugitives of the ganged chains in an endless surround of noplaceness, where the shabbiest of architectural detritus washes up against the center of a town. To come in by canal or river is to see a genuine demarcation between country and city and to fetch up in the historic heart of things the way travelers once did when towns had discernible limits, actual edges, and voyagers knew when they had entered or departed a place. To approach Boston or San Francisco by the bay or New Orleans or St. Paul by river is to arrive suddenly and merrily like Dorothy before Oz — out of the woods and into the light.

Years ago, engineers moved the canal from the center of Utica, Schenectady, Syracuse, and Rochester so that now the waterway skirts the hearts of towns, making it more a barrier than a boulevard, and the traveler no longer glides right through the nub of gaiety and commerce, no longer able to float along and look from a boat deck into shop windows, or see hustling clerks on a street errand, or pick up the scent from a lunch counter, or hear the newsboy's hark. What was once the Erie through these downtowns is today paved streets; only villages have kept the waterway close. Although the canal is unlikely ever to return to its earlier urban courses, city rivers everywhere across America still offer opportune avenues to enchant wayfarers.

Lock Twenty was full of drift and broken timber as though the woodchoppers' ball had been there the night before. Cap, perhaps thinking himself again at the helm of his Navy tug in World War Two, came on the radio: "I've made a command decision: we will *all* resume fleet order." It was my penalty for having earlier overtaken him too quickly — a wake from another boat drove him mad — and I grumbled until I noticed the clutter of logs in the water west of the lock; then we were content to have the trawler plow the way open.

We saw only the industrial edges of Rome from the canal, they too obscured by brushy trees as if nature were trying to hide human affronts. There the watershed changes, the flow no longer toward the Atlantic via the Hudson but now toward the St. Lawrence by way of Lake Ontario. The Indians knew that topographic detail well, for at that place, where the narrowing Mohawk turns north, they pulled out their canoes and carried them a couple of miles over a barely perceptible rise in the swampy country, to Wood Creek for a run down the twisting brook into Lake Oneida, the only major lake in New York to lie east and west, a fortuitous circumstance for early travelers and commerce. From the Hudson we'd been following a route as ancient as the Ice Age, a course later used by humankind for at least ten thousand years.

For us there was no portage-and-float down entangled twists of a boggy creek but rather a perfect alley of canal slicing through the lowland for fourteen miles of skunk cabbage and perched kingfishers, all the way to Sylvan Beach, the carnival village on the western edge of Oneida. The sun evaporated into an obscuring grayness hanging over the water, and our hope for a fuel-up before crossing the long lake tomorrow against a probable headwind also disappeared when we learned the waterside pumps weren't working. Pilotis found us a ride south a few miles to a room and hot shower which we followed up with a couple of drafts of a certain Irish stout of renown. While we guessed over the possibilities of lake wind and water, a scowling man came in from the rain, didn't bother to wipe off his spectacles, hat dripping into his double shot of rye intended to ease "a chill on the liver." His wife soon followed and asked why he was drinking whiskey. I didn't pick up his answer, but I did hear him break wind in something of a forced manner, and she said, "Don't you do that durn flatulitis at me, mister!"

Like Jonah,
We Enter a Leviathan

FIVE IN THE MORNING. Light wind, cold, no rain. We arrived to board *Nikawa* and, to our pleasure and consternation, found the convoy gone; should she run out of gasoline on Lake Oneida, we'd be on our own. The first lock west was thirty-three miles away, so, could we quickly find gas near there, the flotilla might still be within reach before we got locked out. Pushing for our independence, we received it at the worst time, and I wondered whether Cap had deliberately put our passage at risk. Pilotis said, "Is he competing against us to get to the middle Missouri first?" I don't know. Then, "Can *Nikawa* make it to the other side?" We've got no choice, I said, either we try a run now or get trapped until the navigation season formally opens.

On a map, the lake resembles a great sperm whale, complete with fins and flukes, swimming toward the Atlantic. Like Jonah, we entered at the front end, swallowed by a near darkness that couldn't entirely hide the fog, and *Nikawa* started down the sombrous gullet into the gut of the leviathan. We crept through the thick morning, passed the breakwater and onto open water and somehow immediately lost the buoys marking a route safe from shoals, so I set a compass course and tried to hold it against the chop and northwesterly that shoved and banged the boat and made us pay the price of a flat hull. I said nature seemed bent on using up our remaining fuel. Pilotis watched the obscurity ahead and I the compass and the depth finder fluctuating wildly in the rough water. Oneida hammered *Nikawa* hard, but to throttle back to ease the pounding would lessen fuel efficiency and reduce our chances of making the lock in time. Worse, the wind was certain to rise with the light — Cap's ostensible reason for leaving early.

Thirty minutes out, the sounder showed a much-reduced range of depths, and I had to slow to a creep. We began to half expect that sickening crack of propellers against rock, even though our chart indicated water just sufficient. Isolated in the murk, we couldn't be sure whether we were slightly north or south of Messenger Shoals, so trying to hook around them would be just as risky as holding our course, would use more gasoline, and slow us further. Feigning nonchalance, Pilotis tried not to let me see surreptitious glances at the fuel gauges, and I kept quiet about the last heap of snow melting in the Rockies, but I did say how the lake was supposed to be a cupcake of a run. One of the sweet and expectable aspects of life afloat is the perpetual present moment one lives in and a perception that time is nothing more than the current, an eternal flowing back to the sea. But trying to cross the American continent in a single navigational season disrupted that pretty illusion and put a live vinegarroon in my contemplative cap.

Pilotis, sweeping the fog with the binoculars, not an easy thing in a thrashing boat, shouted, "There's one!" and I eased in close to get the designation off the buoy, then replotted our course through the grayness and plowed forward, on and on, our ears suffering from the noise as much as our minds from the tension of going dead in the bad water. *Nikawa* edged past submerged pilings, then Shackleton Shoals, then a canal-dredge dumpground, then Frenchman Island, more piles, and finally we saw the western shoreline. As if we approached a great window, sunlight slipped under the drapery of fog, and we passed beneath Interstate 81 and went into the Oneida River to Brewerton. The crossing had taken not one hour but two, and there was no chance to catch the convoy before the lock. Said Pilotis, "We either find gas on the river now or we take a sixty-gallon hike for it." And I: If we get locked out, we'll have plenty of time to walk for gas, time as in weeks.

On the edge of the village Pilotis pointed to a boatyard and chandlery with a pump. As I hosed the gasoline in, the fellow asked where we were coming from, and Pilotis said, "A better question is where we're headed," and the man asked, "So where the hell are you going?" My friend answered, the man scoffed a laugh and said, "Send me a postcard if you make it."

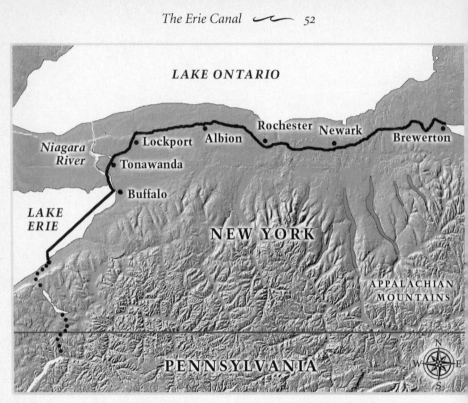

The Erie Canal west, Lake Oneida to Buffalo, 224 miles

We followed the river on through a two-mile canal cut and Lock Twenty-three. Because tenders sometimes work a couple of locks and must drive from one to the next, I expected that operator to follow the convoy and was prepared for bad news, but the gates stood open and waiting: Cap had told him to expect us. "The nature of this voyage," said my copilot, "is to encounter shit alternating with sugar so we keep getting sucked into continuing." And I said that was one more way a voyage was a metaphor.

We were beginning to enjoy locking through and the way it interrupted hours of mere steering, and Pilotis liked discovering whether the operator was one to give information and lore or only annoyance at our disrupting his oiling of machinery. Lock Twenty-three is in the middle of a woods and, like all the New York barge canal locks, kept in Bristol fashion: bollards painted, brass polished, shrubs trimmed. The valves and gates of every lock have a distinct voice, each giving a different performance: a basso profundo, a vibrato soprano, another not singing at all but only clattering and clanking as if drawing heavy chains across a dungeon floor, and everywhere the deep chamber walls amplify all of those harmonics and phonations into fine resonance. Twenty-three was our last descent on the Erie before we once again began the climb to Buffalo.

The Oneida River in its brief sixteen miles manages to flow to almost as many points as there are on a compass rose and follows the most ambagious part of the canal. The undeveloped wooded banks and marsh the river passes through made us feel an isolation not really there — downtown Syracuse lay just twelve miles south — but the trees enclosed us cozily after the windy and battering expanse of the lake. Where the Oneida joins the Seneca River stood a sign and an arrow pointing west: BUFFALO → 192 MILES. Such a marker, uncommon on American rivers, gave us a surge that life at eight miles an hour relishes. The Seneca took us in the opposite direction from our destination for a spell but then turned *Nikawa* again westward, where we found another sign, a realty one: TOWNHOUSES ON THE RIVER. Pilotis said, "Here they come." Yet for us it was only a chilly Wednesday in early spring on a forlorn waterway.

A whistling swan greeted us outside the lock at Baldwinsville, and this was the way we ascended: the big portals closing us into a near dark, thousands of pounds of flowing river pushing against the forward gates, leaking out a pattern in splatter and spray of a liquid angel, wings spread as if to fly out of the Stygian tank, cracks in the side walls funneling and dripping grace notes into the water, sounds in a deep cistern (nasal *deeblook-deeblook*, guttural *gahblunk-gahblunk*), a sense of foreboding and being trapped in a place not meant for humankind, a waft of fish, *Nikawa* bobbing atop the paused water, voices from unseen people above as if speaking from another realm, everywhere the fecund dampness of a boxed river waiting to sunder the concrete imposition, the valves below grating open and the upsurge churning and deepening and darkening itself, fathoming up, working to turn us like a twig, our almost imperceptible rising atop the boil that collects detained and inevitable flotsam and twists it in circling menace, chunks of log thunking the hull, the revolve of a bloated carp, eyeballs bleached and full upon us and its rot in our nostrils, an empty soda bottle pulled down to show us buoyance is but temporary, the nasty suck of a dozen whirlpools that would jerk us to the slimed bottom in retribution for this human outrage stopping the river, and the angel still unflown and drowning in the flood, and we are now in half-light, *Nikawa* straining against our holds, Pilotis calling something I cannot hear, and then our heads level with the pavement, the caution line of yellow paint (Don't fall in here, bub!), then we're above ground, and the machinery stilling to numb the water, the forward gates shudder against the river insistence, a vertical shaft of light splits them, widens like a theater curtain parting to reveal the mystery of the waterdance waiting ahead to draw us into the masque, the lockhouse horn sounding us free, and we breast off from the wall, the engines turning over, and we're again in the river, and the lockman calls something, but all we can make out is, "Oregon, you lucky bastards!"

Around a bend, we came upon the slow convoy, and, appealing to Cap's old Navy persona, I radioed for permission to overtake, and the formality pleased him into welcoming us back. We saluted, passed him slowly, then twisted on alone toward Cross Lake, a piece of natural water peculiar in its seeming to have a river pass athwart it. Rivers, of course, don't *cross* lakes. Usually, the best they do is to flow in with one name and flow out, enlarged, with another, but the Seneca appears to treat Cross Lake as a trolley does an intersection.

Then: there: the dire sound of the props striking something hard, a below-surface floater that rose to break the surface behind us and, in mockery, to disappear again, and with customary dread I stopped and raised the motors to look. All was well. We'd escaped again by pure luck. And so on we went. The river kept its meanders, the bigger ones dissected by canal cuts, but even still our compass swung fro and forth. In the afternoon, near the upper end of Lake Cayuga, *Nikawa* entered Montezuma Marsh, at another time a sanctum for highwaymen but today a national wildlife refuge that is one of the largest sheltering grounds for migrating birds in the Northeast. The leafless trees held cormorants raising their big, tenebrous wings in the manner of Draculas taking flight. Then followed several miles of shabby houses and fish camps, a large corn-processing factory in the middle of not much of anywhere, and then the marsh became heavy with willows, alders, maples, and winter-withered cattails. Near the heart of the swamp we came upon the grandest remains of the old canal, a romantic ruin waiting for its Wordsworth, a capital piece of nineteenth-century engineering: the eight remaining stone arches of the Richmond Aqueduct; fifteen feet above our deck, the packet boats once floated their passengers and kippage across, drawn by the aerial clop of mules.

Nikawa ran a long stretch of marshland and little else, nearly steering herself, gliding beneath the hover of an osprey, and to starboard a bullhead turned over violently in a quiet backwater, and the solitude put us in good fettle. Outside Clyde, we entered the lock and passed through expeditiously and gained enough time to tie up in town but saw no suitable place, so on we pushed to Lyons. We tied up to a fine little dock and went ashore to a laundry and waited for our wash in the Bridge Tavern, its interior somehow managing to draw enough light from the dim afternoon to gleam. We took seats at the end of the bar, not to drink but to eat and look out onto the canal as if we were making our way west in the tavern. We sat almost dozing until startled by a phone ringing like a death knell. When the annoyance ceased, Pilotis said, "Now I realize how *away* we are."

After retrieving our clean clothes, we returned to *Nikawa*, and still the convoy hadn't arrived, so we sat under the canopy, tilted back into a small libation; it was six o'clock, and I trusted we'd be spending the night at the dock. How good. Up motored the boats at last, we raised our glasses to them, and over the radio came Cap, furious about something that our toast and comfort only exacerbated. Another command decision: the flotilla would not stay here but would continue to the damnably high docking wall at Newark. Through the lock we wearily went, our sixth of the day, grumbling on west, and I waited for the time when Cap's demand for an electrical outlet would cease to shape our nights.

Knoticals and Hangman's Rope

OR SOME DISTANCE west of Newark, the view alternated between that of a goodly land and a faulty one. Twice an osprey clutching a fish passed overhead to lead us down the Erie; almost a rare species some years ago, the bird is a good omen because all things living along these waters evolved in the same riverine system, and to benefit one native creature is to benefit them all. But the route was banks bashed with litter and beat-up houses and slow pools sliming our hull with algae. To pass the degraded miles, we began listing the various seats fishermen brought to the canal: a concrete block, metal lawn chair, wooden folding chair, chopped log, cut telephone pole, upturned lard bucket, milk-carton case, soggy easy chair, soggier velveteen sofa, automobile wheel, auto rear seat, two stacked tires topped with a board, café booth (minus table), half an oil drum, theater chair, Windsor chair (missing a leg but propped with rocks); every one of them was empty. I called up Cervantes's words: "There's no taking trout with dry breeches," and Pilotis said, "True, but what about suckers and carp?" Wedged atop one stump was an old bicycle, mangled and bent, fished from the canal and encrusted with dried mud and dead mussels, a thing so skinny and misshapen it looked like a Giacometti sculpture.

That morning at breakfast with Cap and his men in the Newark Diner of traditional lines, a sailor's discussion broke out over, said a crewman, "a knotical topic": a knot is any lump in a rope, but precisely what is a hitch, loop, and bend? I, still trying to memorize the rabbit-hole-and-tree mnemonic story to help a novice tie a bowline, kept

quiet. Our waitress had eyes of different dispositions, the right drooping in sorrow, the left warm and sultry; one would close to suggest this
passion, the other to emphasize that. She too only listened, but as we
paid our checks she said to a couple of us, "Now you boys keep your
mast up and your keel down." On the street, a crewman said, "Was
that sexual?" and I asked which eye she had open.

For two miles around Port Gibson, the Erie artery forms a throm-
bus called the Wide Waters where a bed of the old canal joins the later
prism to create a turning basin. Westward, smack beside State Route
31, the embankment is low enough so that *Nikawa* cruised along as if
she were merely in another highway lane, and the faces of the surprised motorists nudged us out of taking our voyage for granted after
only one week. We guessed they must envy our freedom, but they
didn't see the tyrannies of wind and water. By running for seven days
from sunup to sundown, we'd not yet gone four hundred miles over
the easiest legs of the whole voyage. I thought of the nearly five
thousand miles still lying in wait, of snowmelt, of evaporating waters,
and I pushed the throttles forward only to remember the canal limit of
ten miles an hour and pulled them back. A strong walker could do half
that speed, and, without the many bends away from an intended
course, and free of meanders long and short, a hiker could reach the
Oregon coast three weeks before us. That, of course, was pernicious
thinking a good water traveler avoids.

Pilotis complained about there being no chart available for the
western half of the Erie; what we had was a photocopy of a third-of-a-
century-old, hand-drawn pilotbook we hoped was trustworthy. I said
I had wanted to assemble for our entire route a master atlas made
from U.S. Geological Survey 7.5′ maps, the best existing topographic
series for the whole country, but the cost was inordinate and making
them compactly portable nearly impossible. Besides, I rationalized,
poor maps, like muffed weather reports, make for adventure. Said my
friend, "And failure."

At Palmyra, a town so cut off from the canal we knew we were there
only from the chart, I stopped *Nikawa* to wait for the convoy and
poked around the pretty ruin of the stone aqueduct over Ganargua
Creek. The other boats arrived, and we got under way again, once
more leaving behind the plodding *Doctor Robert* and the infernal
tourist tub.

Zebra mussels covered the chamber walls of Lock Thirty, masses of them, and I warned Pilotis that canalmen took pains to avoid getting squirted in the face by the little striped things because they absorb and concentrate toxins. The exotic bivalves, about the size of a pistachio shell, filter more than a quart of water a day, and three quarters of a million of them can occupy a square the size of a small kitchen table; such efficient engines in their current numbers are able to filter Lake Erie in less than a month, even as they clog pipes and valves of water treatment and power plants. The mussels, ingesting organic detritus, have apparently clarified canal waters, a process that appeals to the eye but can disrupt ecological balances, as their proliferation does already endanger native clams and mussels. Within a decade after their arrival in America, around 1985, they spread from the western end of Lake Erie into the other Great Lakes and on into the Ohio and Mississippi from Duluth to New Orleans. Like kudzu on the ground, zebra mussels will cover almost any underwater surface and can sink docks, buoys, and long-neglected boats. Unlike native species, say bison or passenger pigeons or native clams, the extirpation of zebra mussels is now probably impossible. They, not us, are the exterminators.

At Wayneport — the first of the eight "port towns," a description carrying fossil history of the traffic once riding the Erie — we found the water down three feet and exposing lengths of wide mud banks mired with debris, but this wretchedness was good news since our concern — one of them anyway — was springtime flooding closing the canal. In contrast to our far western route, here the enemy was not drought but deluge. If the Genesee River, seventeen miles ahead, had not forced managers to close the big guard gates that protect the Erie against flood damage, we could likely set aside one more worriment. But, things always having to stay in balance, now we were hearing rumors of another construction blockage ahead. Pilotis: "We move in a perpetual foreboding that around the next bend the way will close." For a canal or river traveler, there is no such thing as a detour.

Fairport is an affluent suburb of Rochester, its prosperity evident in the excellent public dock next to the quaint lift bridge. We tied up again so Pilotis could phone the manufacturer of our depth finder to get unfathomable sentences in the instruction manual interpreted. I walked up Watson Street to buy sandwiches. As I waited, I listened to a somber man telling another this: "I was in the hardware store last week, and Langley came in, mad as all get-out. He threw a length of rope down on the counter and started in on Jenkins about the quality of it. He said it snapped on him. 'What were you using it for?' Jenkins says. And he says back, 'You know I been real down since Betty left. What do you *think* I was doing? I was hanging myself, if you have to know.' Of course, Betty leaves him about once a month. And Jenkins says, 'Hell, Langley, you never told me what you wanted it for. If I'd known, I could've sold you that heavy nylon stuff.'"

The day began to gloom up as we passed Bushnell's Basin and the old Richardson's Canal House, a restaurant and inn and one of the most beautiful restorations on the Erie; had we been free of the convoy, we'd have pulled in for the night. We startled a couple of mallards into the air, and a bicyclist passed us on a biking-hiking trail that will one day cross New York atop the towpath. Rochester sprawl has metastasized into Pittsford, another affluent historic canalside town, where we traversed a section of fine houses that Pilotis referred to as holding "the homefires of the urbanities." Then came rear ends of industries, parking lots, piles of rock and dirt — the usual sad unmitigations — but the wind rose and hit *Nikawa* and diverted us from further lamentation.

Lock Thirty-two held us for the convoy, then we entered the chamber first to avoid a shuffling for proper position. Perhaps we'd become cocky over our new locking expertise: I went in with enough headway to prevent the wind from working its wonted mischief, but our speed was too much for Pilotis to catch the mooring cable, and then the gusts had us, and in a trice they turned *Nikawa* sideways. As I cranked the wheel and struggled to realign, Cap started in over the radio at us, a flurry of impatience and a distraction I failed to brook when I heard for the third time, "*Nikawa!* What are your intentions?" Still well off the wall, I grabbed the transmitter and yelled, Cool it! You know very well the goddamn wind got us! A crackling, commodorial, and offended Cap said, "*Nikawa!* That is no way to talk over marine radio!" and he put his big trawler into gear and charged right in at us. Our bow got rocked toward the wall, close enough for Pilotis to snag the cable with the boat hook to pull us clear just in the nick. I respected Cap too much to say anything, but Pilotis hissed through the window, "Really, mate! You must stop harassing Admiral Hockle." The name was a knotical wisecrack to settle me down. When I settled, I said, Lend the admiral our AVOID IRRITATION plaque.

Except by means of aqueducts, it would seem as impossible for a canal to pass through a river as for a river to cross a lake, but not far south of downtown Rochester, the Erie traverses the Genesee at nearly right angles, as one avenue does another. If the guard gates were open, we should likely be free of high-water problems on the rest of the Erie, and one more potential trap would lie behind. We waited in keen anticipation. The gates came into view, both of them raised, the way open.

Near the intersection of canal and river are several small, graceful bridges designed by Frederick Law Olmsted, spans that give elegance to the old laboring Erie. Beyond to the north we could see the high buildings of Rochester. West of the far guard gate we started into the Long Level, a sixty-four-mile stretch without locks, the first portion of it cut through an immense stone ledge once an ancient seabed. The shale walls, rising to eighteen feet, closed off any prospect other than the cloven-rock channel itself to create a claustrophobic trough, but they also blocked the wind, so *Nikawa* could move over smooth water. What potholes do to a highway, mild wind does to a river.

On the high north bank we saw two boys fooling in the brush, the bushes moving in that certain way, that guilty rustling of lads up to no good. Small splashes pocked the channel, rocks perhaps, but before I could get us to the other side, we were under the devilment, and we watched something big roll to the edge and fall heavily toward us. Pilotis yelled a warning, but *Nikawa* was helpless at canal speed to maneuver out of the way in time. A terrific splunge of water rose over the bow, rocked the boat, drenched the windows. Pilotis said, "What the hell was that?" Surfacing violently, like an angry god thrusting his trident from the sea, was an automobile wheel. Pilotis: "There but for the grace of et cetera." Indeed. We averted what would have been a terminating disaster through no agency of our own, and I understood, more clearly than ever, that to reach the Pacific would take luck as much as preparation and prudence.

Near Spencerport we emerged from the miscreant Rock Cut only to catch the wind head-on, a bullying that beset us all the way into Brockport, and there we stopped. The convoy be damned, *we* were in for the night. Pilotis called for a room in a big Victorian house with knickknacks, whimwhams, gimcracks, and fribbles worrying every corner, shelf, and wall, but it was otherwise tranquil. At a canal-side grill, I found myself sitting transfixed on the water until I realized I was trying to sail a barstool west, and I turned my back on the venerable Erie.

We Sleep with a
Bad-Tempered Woman
Tossed by Fever

FIRST THERE WAS the soap salesman at breakfast, a man of ready and glad hand who asked but a single question, what were we doing in town, and when Pilotis answered, "Crossing the country in a little boat," the drummer nodded and began speaking about the difficulties of "marketing store-brand detergents vis-à-vis name brands." The meal done, he rose to hustle off to his accounts, and Pilotis said, "There goes a man whose curiosity never got the best of him."

Second: after we walked down to the boat, we learned the truth of the rumor: several miles west, at Albion, a bridge-construction barge was blocking the waterway, and the convoy would have to stay put until the Canal Office could persuade the highway department to let us through. We were enticingly near the terminus of the Erie, and I mumbled and mulled and decided we'd press on alone in hope luck would befall us and the slender *Nikawa* could squeeze through where the others could not. In that land of numerous low bridges, we would proceed to see whether the way might open.

The fifteen miles to Albion were easy and full of the delight of small lift-bridges clanging a bell at the traffic and rising promptly at our arrival. With each safely behind, we felt the accomplishment of mileage slowly earned, and I savored it for its inchmeal accumulation. That gray and mild morning, Pilotis cut a finger wrapping our anchor line, uttered an "Umph!" and I followed with, "Ejaculated the squire," a thing we did only when we were happy. We passed along the H villages of Holley, Hulberton, Hindsburg, then a stretch of old, hand-laid stone canal wall with recent breaks repaired by a load of coarse rock dump-trucked into the breach — another paradigm for our era. Twice we came upon mergansers that let us approach close before diving beneath our bow only to reappear in our wake, a game according to Pilotis, and I said, If only we could glide like that under the construction barge.

Then we saw it and knew *Nikawa* couldn't squeeze by, and I heard, "Stop thinking about snow in the Rockies." Amidst my mutterings, we coasted to a halt. Almost immediately, as if by the hand of a water spirit, the huge thing, like a garden gate, began to pivot, workmen with ropes over their shoulders pulling it aside, and we proceeded as the way narrowly, ever so narrowly, opened, and *Nikawa* slipped beneath the scaffolding, Pilotis singing "Low bridge, everybody down." Then I quoted the proud old Eriemen who boasted, "We bow our heads to nobody but God and the canal bridges."

Along the way were tidy farms, neat fields, and an apple orchard. By the Knowlesville lift-bridge we made fast to a wall at the old Tow Path Store, a false-front general merchandise of a type more common farther west. We filled fuel tanks, water jugs, and our little larder, and then went on, passed over Culvert Road, the only place automobiles go under the Erie, a detail once noted in *Ripley's Believe It or Not*. On to Medina for a walk and lunch. A man, perhaps a bit barmy, told the owner and cook for all to hear, "I never said I was Jesus. All I ever said was I'm related." Later, when I asked about him, a woman said, "He's not a lunatic — he's just a believer because his evangelical father used to punish him and his sister by pounding them with a Bible. It drove the girl into Hare Christmas."

We took to the Erie again and went on to Middleport where a couple of years earlier I swam in the canal with some tugboatmen, a thing most residents, remembering earlier days of foul water, still refused to do. Yet in truth the Erie Canal is probably cleaner today than ever, a result of wise federal and state environmental regulations — not to mention those rascal zebra mussels.

We reached Gasport, once the home of Belva Ann Lockwood who, in the days before women could vote, ran twice for the Presidency. It was in the village on the Fourth of July, 1839, that citizens raised toasts to the President, the Governor, Heroes of the Revolution, the Militia, Old Glory, American Democracy, the Plow, Literature, the Erie Canal, and — why I don't know — the Mississippi. Then came Orangeport, the only town in the United States, so I heard, to take its name from the color of a hotel. By early afternoon we saw the steeples of Lockport on its bluff. The old flight of five stone locks there has been well preserved right next to the somewhat newer and much larger ones that in just two steps took *Nikawa* fifty feet onto the top of the great Niagara Escarpment, the long shale ridge that is the cause of the falls. We were exuberant at reaching those last locks, for unimpeded water now lay between us and Lake Erie.

Waiting for the gates to release us, I violated our unspoken precept — few lines of endeavor are as encumbered with superstition as the sailor's — and unnecessarily talked of the next day: tomorrow Lake Erie and a short milk-run across water without speed limits, bridges, locks, construction barges, or the tortoise *Doctor Robert*.

We motored through Lockport and under what may be the widest short bridge or the shortest wide bridge in America — it looks more like a parking lot than a bridge — and into another rock cut, this one through the stone ledge that extends twenty miles west to Niagara Falls. On we went, down the canalized portion of Tonawanda Creek flowing an unnatural color of pale turquoise, past a long line of somewhat tired waterside retreats sporting miniature windmills, lighthouses, and plastic gulls, on through the twin Tonawandas and beneath five bridges, blowing our whistle in celebration under each, and then we entered the Niagara River, ten miles above the falls. The grand Erie, at 338 miles, the longest canal in America, lay at our backs.

The Niagara River is thirty-six miles long, a length hardly commensurate with its fame, but above the falls it's rather broad and would be more so were it not split by Grand Island. The current was swift, but no other boat traffic was bucking it, so we let our river horse run, and she fairly skimmed past the built-up shoreline under the overcast, and Pilotis cut loose with snatches of song. All was joy as we went beneath the Peace Bridge where the "headwaters" of the Niagara constrictedly flowing out of a full Lake Erie piled three feet up against the big piers, an unnerving display of power. *Nikawa* bounced up over a veritable rampart of lake water, but we figured it nothing more than fitting, since four fifths of the Great Lakes was rushing seaward underneath us; besides, our harbor was only three miles distant. The Black Rock Canal, offering protection from the open water at Buffalo, was closed for reasons we didn't know, an ignorance that was about to cause trouble.

The lake became progressively meaner, with ceaseless rises and falls (things I'd call neither waves nor swells) that began to thump us with a severity *Nikawa* had never encountered. Downtown Buffalo lay quietly a half mile off her port side. She labored up the crests, crashed into the troughs, and Pilotis couldn't stand without holding on; reading the chart to find a course to our harbor was nearly impossible, and the binoculars were of no more use than were we in a demolition derby. We had to shout over the tumult, and *Nikawa* was making almost no headway against current, waves, and wind. When I tried increasing the rpm's to counter, the violence turned intolerable. After fifteen minutes of torturing her over the assaults, the hull shivering with every drop, Pilotis yelled, "Can she take this?" I shrugged and struggled to hold the wheel on something like a course, but things only got worse. "It sounds like the hull is splintering!" It did indeed, but I shouted, It can't! "How do you know?" I don't, goddamnit! "I think we're in trouble!" That's when I knew my deep-water sailor was also scared, and that unnerved me even more.

Buffalo sat blithe and impassive to our plight, even though as the only boat under way anywhere near, we must have been quite visible. How could those citizens let us capsize in full view of safety? I called out that I was going to head for downtown whether or not there was a small-boat dock, and Pilotis shouted, "It's too goddamn shallow! You'll reef us!" Sounds good to me! Turning from a transfixion with the water ahead, my friend shook the chart at me: "For once be a prudent goddamn mariner!" So I fought my urge to park us up on Church Street, and to control my fear I tried to despise it.

After almost an hour we'd gone only a couple of miles, and in the falling light we couldn't find the entrance to our harbor at the mouth of the Buffalo River. I said nothing, but before dark would cover us, I'd determined either to reef the boat or hit the nearest shore. We handcranked the window-wiper to clear the spray, and Pilotis kept watch on our bilge-pumpless cockpit to see whether we were taking on water. We quit trying to speak in the noise and rode in grave silence as the wind-driven lake tormented us with only an illusion of forward progress.

Then in jubilation Pilotis shouted, "The breakwater!" I made the happiest left turn of my life, and we quartered the swells so that *Nikawa* rolled madly but no longer fell into the troughs. Behind the wall it was merely less rough as we found our way into Erie Basin, once the terminus of the canal, a long-gone exit that avoided such turmoil. Even with several turns in the channel, angles that usually baffle waves, our first chance to dock was impossibly rough, and we had to continue until we ran out of water and choices, and there we tied up our horse while she thrashed in her reins as if wanting to come ashore with us.

Standing on the solid wharf, we were sure it was moving, but it was only the wobble in our legs, and I laughed at my pigeonheartedness, and Pilotis laughed, and we threw our arms around each other like dancing bears, and little *Nikawa* banged her fenders, but there wasn't a drop of water in her pilothouse. We climbed a slope affording a good overlook of the boat and went into a restaurant with phony nautical decorations that seemed to jape us, and we spliced the main brace like sailors just pried from the maw of a deadly sea.

After supper we walked down to the dock to check our spring lines, found a bumper torn loose, and resecured things. We'd just heard there had been a three-day blow over Lake Erie, a body of water that yields its turbulence only slowly, but tomorrow there likely would be less wind. As we went to find a stable bed, Pilotis murmured, "I think we have a little rendezvous coming up." That night I slept with apprehension as if it were a bad-tempered woman tossed by fever.

III

THE LAKES

NEAR DUNKIRK, NEW YORK

ICONOGRAM III

The shallow basin and the position of Lake Erie make it the most tempestuous and choppy of the Great Lakes. The wide frontal storms roaring down over Lake Huron from upper Canada and Hudson's Bay strike Lake Erie with great force. The subtropical highs press in from the south. They engage in conflict over and around Lake Erie, and its shallow waters plunge and toss furiously. The winds can whip up tremendous seas on the surface almost without warning. The navigation charts are figured on a low-water datum 570.5 feet above sea level. The actual level fluctuates widely from half a foot below this datum in winter to four feet above it in certain summers. And the wind alone, sweeping up from southwest to northeast along the axis of the lake, may lower the level at Toledo by eight or more feet, while the depth of the harbors at the east end may rise by several feet. Likewise a strong east wind lowers the water at Buffalo and has, at times, actually laid bare the rock bottom of the lake near Fort Erie.

All through its maritime history Lake Erie has been unpredictable. Uncounted numbers of disasters, tragedies, and shipwrecks have overtaken men who have sailed over her blue surface. Time and again ships have put out from Buffalo under friendly skies only to be turned back or beaten to pieces by a raging sea before they reached Erie, Pennsylvania, or Long Point, Ontario. More voyagers have been seasick on Lake Erie than on Lake Superior. But with all her moods and whims, Lake Erie remains the most intimate and happy of all the Great Lakes.

Harlan Hatcher

Lake Erie, 1945

Hoisting the Blue Peter

THE LAST TIME I'd felt such apprehension as the one upon me
that Saturday morning happened the day I got out of a dismal
hotel bed to report for active duty in the Navy. Now I studied
Pilotis but couldn't determine whether I saw fearlessness or a façade of
insouciance, nor could I decide which response I wanted. Sometimes
the chicken-hearted love the lily-livered. I needed a good rousing
Sousa march, maybe my favorite, "High School Cadets," but a thumping version of "From Maine to Oregon" would have been more apt.
Although I'd been seasick only once during my naval tour, Pilotis and
I ate almost nothing before we made our way to *Nikawa*, where I
hoisted a blue peter of the soul to announce she would sail. The sun
was just appearing in a cloudless sky, the wind a moderate fifteen
knots, and our little boat lay quietly in her lines. So far, so good. Off we
went, down behind the long, high Buffalo mole, ready to take on the
second smallest of the Great Lakes which the old Jesuit explorers called
"seas of sweet water," but I think they had in mind only potability.
We kept to the smooth, protected channel as far as possible before
turning into the open lake. It was splendidly blue and not fraught with
whitecaps — all we needed was two hours of such sweet water. Barcelona, New York, our destination, lay fifty miles southwest, where the
Photographer, who had been off on his own assignment since Pollepel
Island, would meet us with the tow wagon and trailer in order to take
up our first inescapable portage. Life was good.

And so also were the first four minutes. Then *Nikawa* rose, rode
down, up again, higher, down farther, continually building until we
were soon into the violence of last evening. Goddamnit, I yelled, not

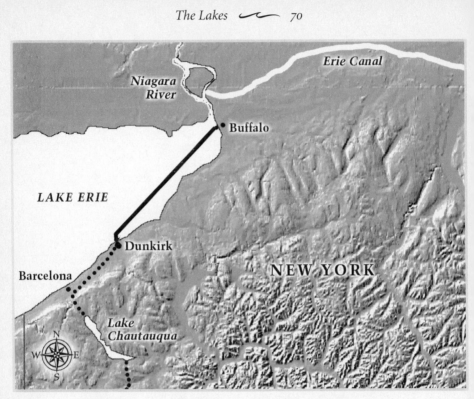

Buffalo to Lake Chautauqua south, 93 lake and portage miles

more of this! Pilotis, struggling to keep upright, said, "Do you want to turn back?" In the increasing racket we talked it over: these conditions might hold for several days or they could get worse, but were they likely to improve soon? After all, this was Lake Erie, with a comparative shallowness that leaves it prone to rapid and violent changes from wind, one of the reasons a recent book about the lake called the section we were about to enter "the graveyard of the Great Lakes." We banged along in ambivalence, hoping that beyond the next swell somehow would lie peaceful water. We did know one thing: we didn't want to turn about and put *Nikawa* broadside to the rollers. And, as always, we had to weigh the Rocky Mountain Snow Imperative.

And so, under innocuous skies, the lake beautiful in its menace, we bashed on, our motors laboring against wind and waves to push us forward, *Nikawa* rising up the swells so steeply we could see nothing ahead but the blue yonder and behind only the deep. After a while we were, in nerve if not mileage, beyond any point of no return.

If you've ever made the first slow climb up the initial ascent of a rollercoaster, when it's too late to disembark and before you is only heaven and fear, and if you remember that godawful pause before the cars drop into the screaming abyss, then you have a notion of what it was like that Saturday on that inland sea, except for one thing: we didn't *roll* down the watery hills because they were too steep and close together. Instead of broad backs they had sharp crests which held us a moment before the engines drove *Nikawa* off the edge into the trough to a crashing, splintering, shattering collapse. We weren't cruising on Erie so much as falling down it, and during any given hour we were airborne a not insignificant portion. At first the drops were three feet, then four, then six, and after an hour a ton of boat was falling seven feet every couple of minutes.

The navigation table almost immediately got jerked out of its locking mechanism and pitched to the deck, and charts, dividers, and pencils became missiles until Pilotis stumblingly caught and stowed them. My friend could only try to grip a small coaming above the entry to the cuddy, a poor purchase indeed that forced Pilotis into a simian squat to cushion the shock of the crashes. I had the wheel to grasp, but that did nothing to keep my skull from banging the overhead, and there was no end to hand-cranking spray off the forward window.

At every moment we watched for an indication that things were lessening, that the worst had passed, but in fact they went the other way. As we hit the bottom of troughs, the lake rose above the transom with only our forward movement keeping that crucial gap of air between us and the water, and I imagined some rogue wave breaking over into the welldeck (oh evil name) to snuff the motors. Without power, we'd be through in every sense of the word.

When I took my eyes from the compass, *Nikawa* instantly veered off our bearing, but with a choice of watching sky or nine-fathom water, I found the instruments almost a solace, and I was glad not to have a clinometer, but I did wish for a lethometer, a gauge I was inventing to show when conditions change from naughty to lethal. Where are the tocsins of life when one needs them?

On we crashed through the surge and plunge, making invisible headway, the indurate towers of Buffalo bobbing into view when we crested yet seeming to fall no farther behind. The south lake shore lay only five miles off, but over an athwart-the-swells course, so it might as well have been fifty miles. Still, I offered we edge closer to land in case of a capsize, but my deep-water sailor, so accustomed to a six-foot keel, would have none of it, and shouted out the hazards: shoals, sunken cribs, rocky shallows, dumping grounds, a wreck, sewer outlets. In one pause atop a crest Pilotis read the chart aloud: "Due to periodic high water in the Great Lakes, some features shown here as visible may be submerged, particularly near shore." In the early nineteenth century there was a proposal to build a canal from Buffalo to Portland, New York, along our very route, but the idea never went beyond a sketch.

It so happened that a direct course required us to hit the swells perpendicularly, the most violent way, and Pilotis argued for quartering them — that is, taking them at less than a ninety-degree angle to allow us effectively to broaden the backs of the rollers and come closer to sliding down along them; all well and good, but that tactic would nearly double our mileage. I held to the shorter bearing of head-on violence. Take it in the teeth and get it over with. As for power, to use too little would leave us standing still or being driven backward, and to clap on too much would almost assure the boat breaking up.

From time to time it came to me that this wasn't really happening; it had to be the insubstantial wandering of a sleeper who merely awakes in a sweat — nothing more; one good scream and surely I'd find myself in a Buffalo hotel room. But there was no waking. Never had I been frightened so long. Of the unwelcome emotions, I most hate fear.

After an hour of what I can only call terror, I realized my apprehension was the worst aspect of what was going on, and I sought some measure to kill or at least still it, to make death nothing more than a disappointment. In the bludgeoning — even the air in the pilothouse seemed to be tossing about — I came up with a solution: the wind was rising, the lake was not abating, and I unquestionably was going to die in a watery coffin of a C-Dory, so it was pointless to be afraid, for fear is useful only to those who yet have hope. River-Hearse. Scorn your cowardice, man! Proceed as the way opens! But was a way open just because it looked open? I've read that drowning, if you avoid the panic, is a fairly quick and painless way to exit. So, as best I could, I gave myself up for dead and tried to think of all those who might miss me. I can't say it worked entirely, although my descent into bathos did, to a degree, buck me back toward pluck, but I didn't suggest such a philosophy to my friend. Part of being skipper is to admit no impediments.

Pilotis called out that drinking from Lake Erie probably killed more people annually than sailing it. On we struggled, hoping the motors kept going, wishing the shoreline changed more quickly. A certain water tank seemed to be at the same bearing it was a half hour earlier — could the waves be giving us nothing but a beating and a fantasy of movement? My hands began to cramp around the wheel and my back ache from the slams, and Pilotis's legs tired from the continual half-squat, so we changed positions, and when I stood down I was immediately pitched to the deck. I couldn't believe the difficulty in staying upright, so I tried sitting, but that was impossible and dangerous. I took a grip on the coaming, only to have my hands repeatedly shaken off, and I too assumed the Erie crouch. We were being pitched around like a couple of beans in a bowl, but we were yet afloat, the most beautiful word I knew.

The console over the instruments tore loose, the screws ripped out, but the welldeck was wet only from spray, and the motors held steady, and I tried to conclude we'd lasted nearly four hours, so *Nikawa* wasn't likely to go down now. Built according to federal regulations, she was supposed to be virtually unsinkable, supposed to go under only to her gunwales before stabilizing. We could cling to her, but the temperature of the water in April would soon do us in. We had no real belief that our radio might bring rescue in time. With onboard space severely limited, I'd never planned to carry an inflatable life raft, a consideration that now led me to imagine how nice to see the *Doctor Robert* lumbering along behind; but Cap, clever seadog, was portaging his craft over this long leg to the Ohio. Why hadn't I listened to that old riverman Mark Twain: "Traveling by boat is the best way to travel, unless one can stay at home."

I grew weary with my incessant and fruitless expectation of progress, so I looked back at the wall of water — still pursuing, still waiting for us to falter and then have us — and as we scended a crest, Buffalo was yet heartsinkingly visible — but just barely. Using the tops of the swells as a crow's nest, I tried to match the skimpy shoreline details on the chart with what I saw, and at last decided we were off Irving, New York. If that were so, we'd gone about twenty-five miles, halfway. Then again, if that water tank were at Sturgeon Point, we'd done less than twelve, and our holding out was highly questionable. We carried a small GPS — Global Positioning System — that could pinpoint our location, but we'd not yet taken time to learn it, since we intended it for the Great Plains, not the Great Lakes.

As I tried to read the southern horizon, so dangerously and enticingly near, I looked at the houses bright in the sun, and I thought how in one of them a woman must be sitting down in her rock-solid kitchen to a hot muffin with marmalade, and next door someone's dad checked baseball scores from his anchored easy chair. I remembered making a drive the past September down the lake-shore road, a route rich with the sweet waft of ripe vineyards. Lake Erie was forcing me to admit I was a man of wheels, not hulls, who was in over his head. Wrong phrase. I remembered my Navy time and how, just before lights out, from the address system would float the hymn "Those in Peril on the Sea," with its opening words, "Eternal Father, strong to save, whose Arm hath bound the restless wave."

We crashed on, on, on, the noise beginning to wear us more than the slams and locking us in a separating silence. Climb, hang, crash, climb, hang, crash. Damn the torpedoes! No, that was Mobile Bay. Lake Erie was Oliver Perry on a cloudless afternoon like ours, stepping dirty and bleeding from a doomed ship to a fresh one, taking along his battle flag, "Don't Give Up the Ship!" Oliver Hazard Perry — there was a middle name no novelist would dare to match to such a history — he who was terrified of cows yet drove the British off Lake Erie and wrote to William Henry Harrison that immortal terseness: "Dear Genl: We have met the enemy, and they are ours." But we were no Perrys; our message would be: "Dear Mother: We have met the enemy, and we are theirs."

Pilotis called for a position. In five minutes I came up with a probable one: about thirty miles out of Buffalo. And then I noticed the swells seeming less awesome — was some Arm binding that restless wave? Yes, and it was that of Pilotis. Mate was quartering the swells. I yelled, We'll be out here till nightfall if you keep that up! But the binding continued. Soon after, I again took the helm, and we returned to frontal assault.

Pilotis shouted, "I think it's getting worse, blue sky or not!" Thunderous bashes, Pilotis thrown to the deck again, a wet spot on my head that could only be blood. "If that peninsula is Dunkirk, we've got eighteen more miles to Barcelona! In a rising sea!" Just then I became furious with the relentless spray across the pilot window, and I cursed and cranked the wiper violently. In the end, it's some lone detail that kills a venture, because every moment, every small occurrence, is a potential last straw in wait. Pilotis knew I wanted to keep water under us as no one before ever had on an internal American crossing, but my mate was right — things were worse. More cursing. The next crash knocked my hands from the wheel. We'd been at it six hours. My elbow was swelling from banging the bulkhead. All right, goddamnit, I yelled, Dunkirk it is! To live long enough is to come to a Dunkirk. Ask an Englishman. On our faces this time was no Hell Gate Grin. It was simply beat out of us.

I pulled the wheel to a new bearing, and we rode a runnel in behind the breakwater, into a placid cove, and in a normal voice Pilotis said, "Careful, shallows on both sides." Sweeter words I'd never heard. Our Battle of Lake Erie was done.

How the Sun Rose in
the West to Set Me Straight

T HE DUNKIRK DOCKS were rickety where they weren't collapsed, something like our constitutions, but the old wooden ways seemed to us like terra firma. For only the third or fourth time in my life, I found it almost incomprehensible that I was yet among the quick, but to stay there I'd surely used up too much of my predestined allotment of luck. Catching myself in such dreary determinism, I got hungry. My copilot found a phone and tried to call the Photographer to tell him we were a few miles shy of Barcelona, and there went another dollop of good fortune: Pilotis actually reached him, and the trailer was soon on the ramp and *Nikawa* out of the lake. I clambered underneath to check her hull and found nothing more than the whacks the Missouri River inflicted when I was first learning the ropes. We went up to Dimitri's restaurant where we could look onto the lovely blue water, and I heard a woman chirp, "I wish we had a boat. It'd be wonderful to be out there today."

I telephoned the builder of *Nikawa* to ask whether she could continue to take such beatings, and he said, "The C-Dory can take it. The question is whether a crew can." When I sat down to a hot bowl of Greek lemon soup and a stack of a sandwich, I wished I'd heard his words a day sooner: to have understood that the only weakness lay in me and not also in *Nikawa* would have cut fear by half and also laid out a challenge to lift a kitten-hearted sailor. We had no celebratory toasting because merely drawing breath was elation enough, and there was still Chautauqua Lake waiting in the warm afternoon. Seamen should hold off a week before trying to convey to a landsman what a hard voyage was like, but we didn't, and the Photographer, an excellent fellow but a worrier of the highest caliber, said, "Do you realize after ten days you're still in New York?" I said, Do you realize after another revelation like that you'll die in New York?

Off we hauled, down State Route 5, the Lake Erie road, and every so often we saw the water between gaps in the trees, again masquerading as a harmless piece of scenery. Riding behind us, dry and sassy, was our river horse, and I was then almost sure she had never really been on the lake, and I couldn't understand how something so small in the water could look so big out of it.

A moment of significance began when we reached rocky Chautauqua Creek where it empties into Erie at Barcelona Harbor: we turned south and took Portage Street, a route used for unnumbered generations, both red and white, to move between the far interior and the inland seas. On through pretty Westfield, the grape juice village, and southwest up a grade so moderate I had to point out it was a kind of continental divide, that our nearly imperceptible, thousand-foot climb had just taken us up and into the Mississippi River drainage basin, the same one holding Hell Roaring Creek, the farthest source of the Missouri River, just over the mountain from Yellowstone Park, fifteen hundred air miles west of us. The waters of Chautauqua Creek end up in the St. Lawrence, and those of Chautauqua Lake in the Gulf of Mexico; although their little tributaries at that point lie only inches apart, the distance between their Atlantic destinations is about two thousand miles. Now, for weeks to come, we would roll downstream all the way to the Mississippi, more than a thousand sinuous river miles distant. Elevation report: one quarter of a mile above the Atlantic.

Down the slope from the divide was Mayville at the north edge of Chautauqua Lake and, at the town limit, a sign: NEW YORK'S BEST TASTING WATER. Artesian springs won the village the title two years earlier, but Mayville had just lost it to Jamestown at the opposite end of Chautauqua. I liked a lake noted for the taste of its sources rather than for its violence.

We filled beverage jugs when we refueled *Nikawa,* then went to the head of the sweetly watered lake to launch, and told the Photographer where and when we hoped to arrive, and we were under way again. On a chart, long and skinny Chautauqua, once two lakes, looks like a pair of link sausages joined at Bemus Point where the water narrows from two miles wide to about nine hundred feet. Although cut by glaciers, the last working on it ten thousand years ago, and looking like and lying parallel to the Finger Lakes to the east, Chautauqua is not one of them. A place of modest beauty, its shores are completely humanified by an encasement of "cottages" and, at its southern end, the sprawl of Jamestown.

We held a course along the western shore and slipped under the long shadow of the bell tower on the point at Chautauqua Institution, an ecumenical endeavor that dispatched religious troupers into the American outback in the late nineteenth century to entertain and educate with tent shows called Chautauquas a people otherwise rather culturally desperate. The Iroquois name, perhaps then unknown to the Methodists, translates freely as "place where one loses the way." I stumbled into the meaning a couple of years earlier when I came to Chautauqua to give some talks, my version of a tent show, and on my first morning there I woke to find the sun rising in the west. Now, I knew that zealous Methodists can work wonders, but at last they had outdone themselves. I could see I was due for either conversion or correction. Figuring the latter easier, I went to a detailed wall map and happily found that the Methodists had not yet achieved celestial puissance. By arriving in the dark, I'd twisted my self-vaunted sense of direction and ended up believing I was on the opposite side of the lake.

Getting what we know to dawn on us is a fundamental human bugaboo, and my piece of lackwit is surely one of the most auspicious of this life, for it was the study of that wall map that kindled a crucial coalescence when I *saw* what I'd forgotten: the Allegheny, the great river of western Pennsylvania, looping up into New York to reach within seventeen miles of Chautauqua Lake. Then my interior dawning: the Iroquois and the French believed the true headwaters of the Ohio River were not the confluence at Pittsburgh but the source of the Allegheny in a remarkable pasture near Gold, Pennsylvania, where, within a circle of a few hundred yards, rise also the Genesee and, according to some, the West Branch of the Susquehanna. The "place where one loses the way," lying so fortuitously between the two great Eries — canal and lake — and the Allegheny-Ohio, was one of my missing links in an internal transwater route. At last I'd discovered a passage, if not to the Northwest, then at least to the Great Divide in

Montana. It was Chautauqua, true to both its Iroquois name and its Methodist intention, that finally led me into our voyage. Years ago my weary father, trying not to doze off one Sunday afternoon, said to me, "Keep an eye out and wake me before I fall asleep." I've spent much of my life attempting to do the same for myself.

Chautauqua was the easiest passage we'd yet undergone, nothing whatsoever to hinder us, and an hour after setting out, we were nearing destination and approaching the shore to watch for the boat ramp and our trailer. We were, after our Erie boat ride, traveling in a jestful casualness without a close watch on the sounder, chart, or an odd buoy off to starboard, and I ignored a rising wind. Following our damaging hit at Pollepel Island in the Hudson, I had written in my log in large block letters INATTENTION IS THE ENEMY. The north portion of Chautauqua is about thirty feet deep, but I knew the south end is much less, and still I took *Nikawa* right into an invisible rock dump, and off went the heart alarms as metal cracked loudly against stone. I raised the motors for inspection. We weren't getting away with that hit: the propellers were bent and jagged. Out-of-balance blades can ruin motors, but we had no alternative except to limp slowly along in search of the Photographer and his waving signal flag.

Two miles south at Burtis Bay we saw the banner and the trailer at the ready. Three men from a rod-and-gun club wandered up to watch us fight the crosswind. I got close enough to shout our landing plans, and the men warned the lake was low. *Rule of the River Road:* Good advice comes after the fact — bad before. I elected to avoid asking the Photographer to step into the cold water to hook the winch cable to the bow so it could line us up with the trailer, choosing instead to run onto the slips, a fairly easy task with a motorboat, but a ton of *Nikawa* catching gusts would require a bravura performance. Perhaps surviving Lake Erie made me imprudently audacious. I judged the wind, took a short run, and hit the trailer, backed off, recalculated, and hit it again. Over the blowing and engines, I thought I heard the fretful Photographer call out, "Umbrella!" On again I charged, and with terrible noises from behind, I drove our horse into the stable.

As we cinched her down and raised the motors for portage, I asked what he shouted that sounded like "umbrella," and he said, "Watch the umbrella." What umbrella? Pointing, "That umbrella." Madly twisted into a devil's nest around the sorry propellers were the ribs of an old bumbershoot. I said to the rod-and-gun boys, If you ever decide to take a boat across America, pay no attention to Lake Erie, but watch out for little old Chautauqua. And Pilotis said, "I've been thinking that if I ever write about this jaunt, I'll call it 'One Goddamned Scare a Day,' but now we've ruined the accuracy of that title."

I asked tiredly and rhetorically, Are we the hell out of this state yet? And one of the codgers said, "No you ain't, pal." We took up the eighteen-mile portage, hauled *Nikawa* along over wooded hills, and a half hour later crossed the Pennsylvania line after nearly six hundred New York miles which, were they straightened out, would land us in Cincinnati.

We pulled up in Youngsville, humble and plain as kraft paper but joyously out of the Empire State, and there we found a room, a bit ramshackle but large. While the crew washed up, I went to work on the propellers with hammer, pliers, and file; I'd chosen aluminum props because, unlike stainless steel, they can often be repaired on the spot. When I finished, they were again true enough for a try at the lower Allegheny River.

IV

THE ALLEGHENY RIVER

EAST BRADY, PENNSYLVANIA

ICONOGRAM IV

The Allegheny River, for the bulk of its length, has never been classed as "an excellent waterway of commerce." This is not surprising when you examine the very nature of the stream — for it is a river which is likely to be frozen solid from December until March, with ice piled in great packs and jams at perhaps thirty localities — piled mountain high with great ice blocks thrown into the most jagged contortions by reason of the grinding pressure brought to bear; then comes the annual "spring thaw" in which the Allegheny rids itself of the frozen constipation in one vast bowel movement which is a frightening spectacle to behold — urged by an enema of melting snow and drizzling rains which rile all the creeks to flood tide and cause a never-ending roar from each gully and ravine. The river stirs uneasily at first, winces, then with no warning whatever delivers itself of ice, drift, flotsam and jetsam, trees, logs, houses, barns, haystacks, cornshocks, barrels, dead pigs, bloated horses, boxes, barrels, packing crates, and other impedimenta which it has warehoused during the winter — all of the hodge-podge starts moving to the tune of thunderous cannonading of ice jams breaking, and one jam swoops down upon another, and with a continued crashing and rending the mighty discharge is on its way, now taking out bridges, piers, sometimes whole villages, with the natives of the bottom lands fleeing for the hills and terrified livestock jumping fences and racing away for Egypt or anywhere, so as to be shed of this cataclysm. "The Allegheny's bust loose!" This cry is passed from mouth to mouth, and hurries over telegraph wires, and shortly every owner of floating property the entire length of the Ohio River, some 1,000 miles long, is suddenly busy getting his houseboat, or raft, or steamboat, or fleet of barges out of the road of this demon destruction. For oftentimes the full force of this upheaval runs at brim tide for several days, and the broad Ohio proves a meager plumbing system to handle this cosmic diarrhetic discharge. Not until the Mississippi is reached does the destruction cease, and sometimes not even then — for case-hardened blocks of Allegheny ice have serenely sailed by New Orleans at intervals.

Frederick Way, Jr.
The Allegheny, 1942

An Ammonia Cocktail
and a Sharp Onion-Knife

THE MORNING came on sour with a sky working itself into a rain, the sort of weather a cynic would expect now that we had to leave *Nikawa* and take to our canoe for a couple of days. We got oilskins ready when we went to the Allegheny just above the mouth of Brokenstraw Creek, six miles downstream from the courthouse town of Warren. I had failed, weeks earlier, to execute a shakedown cruise in the canoe with its tiny motor, thereby violating the two most reliable, if homely, words of advice I've ever received, these from an Ozark cousin: Assume nothing. The bank down to the water was slick, but we soon had the canoe afloat, the motor mounted, and we assumed ourselves aboard. On the third pull of the starter rope, the new engine turned over, on the fourth it fired, and we waved to the Photographer who would haul *Nikawa* to the head of navigable Allegheny water.

The air was nippy but windless, and the river ran clear, visibility to about four feet, a good thing because the bottom was chock-a-block with rocks and boulders, although most of them were rounded and not likely to shear open an aluminum canoe, another fortunate circumstance since we immediately began cracking the propeller and motor stem over them, hard hits that kicked the engine nearly out of the water. Each time, I cut power fast and examined the plastic prop with trepidation, but we had nothing more than scrapes, and we quickly learned to float into the rock gardens and take up our paddles. At first, Pilotis would plunge one to measure the water from the bow

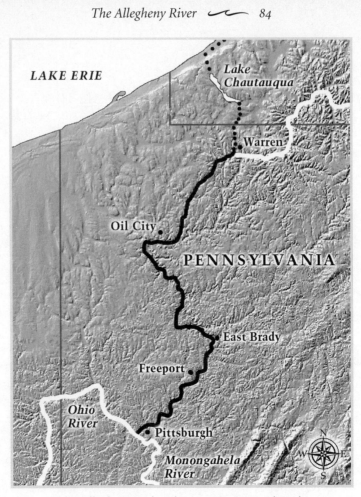

The Allegheny, Lake Chautauqua to Pittsburgh,
203 portage and river miles

but soon became proficient at *seeing* shallowness: like an old river leadsman, Matey cast out a glance instead of a weighted line and called the depth in feet, not fathoms, but later took simply to holding up fingers: when I saw only two digits I shut off the motor. Even so, the current and overcast made the dark bottom difficult to read, and we whacked the prop again and again, but it withstood the stones. I've always believed that two-cycle engines — lawnmowers, chainsaws, outboards — exist primarily to keep humankind from loving internal — infernal — combustion any more than we do. Those jerks on a starter rope are there to vex us into remembering we were never meant to use any tool requiring a spark plug. Yet each time, our baby motor started with a single pull, a dozen or more yanks every hour.

For some miles I gave myself a refresher course in reading currents, riffles, and changes in water color, and our descent slowly became easier as I began to understand the particularities of the Allegheny chutes and channels. Helped along by current and intermittent paddles and motor, we were doing about six miles an hour, a progress that relieved me of misinformation I'd heard about the northern end of the Allegheny. *Rule of the River Road:* A section within five miles of an informant's home is always passable, but ten miles farther, forget it. We had good canoeing, made better because I'd long wanted — an impossibility if one begins from an ocean — to start our voyage by letting a river itself take us downstream, pull us by its own native force into the country. Now, at last, we and the river were of one mind, both of us in quest of the Father of Waters. As I felt our lovely drift atop the Allegheny floating us in the right direction with few radical twists, carrying us on its back toward the Mississippi, I sat easily in the stern in full belief that we could reach the Ohio by water.

Given our fore-and-aft positions and the off-and-on noise of the motor, talking was difficult, so we watched the bankside theater and fell into musings, another river gift. Even though U.S. 62 follows the Allegheny closely on the east shore for many miles, the highway was rarely visible, and despite numerous and often shabby "fishing" cottages, we had a world to ourselves. Wooded hills cradled the narrow river, with interruptions only from the merge of small runs and by slender islands splitting the channel. All the way to Tidioute, sixteen miles, we passed under not a single bridge, and — never mind the dumpy houses alternating from bank to bank as the river terrace shifted east to west — we could almost believe ourselves slipping down through some eighteenth-century morning. The way was virtually free of debris and flotsam, a ditched washing machine the lone piece of junk, and the sky held steady, the pools slowly became slightly deeper — slightly was all we needed — and we had to paddle less and less.

Until now, we'd known few hours permitting idle reflection. For years I've been given to culinary dreaming whenever my travel slows or when I need occasional breaks from observing; that day I fell into remembrance of my perpetual hunt across America for genuine soda fountains once abundant but now as imperiled as a Topeka shiner. A friend had recently given me a small volume first published in 1863, *American Soda Book of Receipts and Suggestions,* that I pick up as the devout do a missal. Among the suggestions: "Don't use too much syrup; it makes a sickening drink," which I weigh against, "Remember that women like a little more syrup and three times as much foam and froth as men like." Among the receipts is this one:

Ammonia Cocktail

Aromatic Spirits of Ammonia . . . . 2 Dashes
Orange Syrup . . . . 1 Ounce
Bicarbonate of Soda . . . . ½ Teaspoon
Serve quickly!

I was trying to recall the admixture for that peculiar refresher called a phroso when we floated around a broad westerly bend and came upon tiny Tidioute (rhymes with "city boot"), the birthplace of Standard Oil, the ancestor of several of the largest corporations in America. Over the ridge lay the valley where the American oil industry began when "Colonel" Edwin Drake, a railroad conductor too debilitated to stand upright in the swaying aisles of a train, arrived in 1859 to explore black ooze leaking into Oil Creek, stuff then used mostly as a patent medicine. Claimed one advertisement:

KIER'S GENUINE PETROLEUM! Or ROCK OIL!

A natural remedy possessing wonderful curative powers
in diseases of the
Chest, Windpipe and Lungs;
Also for the Care of
Diarrhea, Cholera, Piles, Rheumatism, Gout,
Asthma, Bronchitis, Scrofula or King's Evil;
Burns and Scalds, Neuralgia, Tetter, Ringworm,
Obstinate Eruptions of the Skin,
Blotches and Pimples on the Face,
Biles, Deafness,
Chronic Sore Eyes, Erysipelas!

Five years later, a ne'er-do-well actor came into the valley to establish the Dramatic Oil Company, but he ruined his well by trying to increase its output, and a few months later John Wilkes Booth went off to ruin other things.

On the second terrace of Tidioute stood a clapboard hotel with a two-storey porch giving a historic view of the Allegheny. That Sunday it was closed, so we walked down to an ordinary place where I told Pilotis about my encounter in the hotel restaurant a year before when I'd come through by road to reconnoiter our route. In had walked an old fellow, pale as if he'd been partially erased, and ordered a sandwich. He looked so forlorn I spoke to him and bought him a mug of beer. He told me, "My wife was ten years younger than me, but she died last year." I commiserated, said I knew about losing wives, and he said cryptically, "A sharp onion-knife leaves a dry eye. No, I don't miss her so much. What I miss is my butt. I've got no butt anymore. It's like it fell off somewheres along the line. You get old and your butt disappears. Now, you take my balls, they're bigger than ever, hanging like a champion bull. It's Mother Nature's trick. It's all backwards. These days, what do I need them things for? What I need is my butt. That's what I do now — sit, just sit."

When we returned to the Allegheny, the glum sky remained such that every dry hour seemed like deliverance. The river carried us again into forested slopes for long and rather straight runs, and islands created chutes where we guessed out the deepest water, the through lanes. To the west, the hills began dropping, their far sides opening to agriculture and small oil fields we knew were there only from the map.

We passed a settlement called Trunkeyville, just down the road from Fagundus Corners. Pennsylvania, of course, has the most famous naughty town-name in America — Intercourse, a little south of Blue Ball — although for raciness I prefer Shy Beaver, Bareville, Desire, Tally Ho, or Mount Joy; and there are those renowned nonesuches Punxsutawney, Shickshinny, and Bird-in-Hand. But the toponyms I really like here are of another sort, partly because Pennsylvanians have sometimes acted as if there were a shortage of good and distinctive names. For their foremost university town the best they could come up with was State College, and for two other seats of higher learning they merely, and confusingly, appropriated nomenclature better left farther west — Indiana and California; they may have, however, gone too far into eccentricity, given it's an ivory tower, when they named one not too distant from our route Slippery Rock. Pennsylvanians have three Centervilles and eighteen other Center-somethings; there are four dozen towns with the key descriptive word of West, and three dozen beginning with New; and they must hold the national record for places suffixed with -burg and -ville, including one named, long before any-one had ever heard of a franchise burger, McVille. Citizens of one village just gave up and called it Hometown, and another community, in a fit of literalness, labeled theirs Factoryville, and yet another settle-ment apparently seeking the most perennially accurate name ever thought of, Airville. Perhaps erring too far on the side of plain humil-ity are Rock, Paint, and Transfer.

It's this flatness of imagination that makes me love other Pennsylva-nia town names. Take those that seem to come from some lost list of the Seven Cardinal Virtues of Commerce: Frugality, Prosperity, Econ-omy, Industry, Enterprise, Energy, Progress. Or those from residents who couldn't quite remember either the Boy or Girl Scout laws: Brave, Effort, Endeavor, Fairchance, Rough and Ready, Good Intent, Patience. Or those villages in need of the Junior Chamber of Commerce guys: Drab, Drifting, Distant, Drain Lick, Grimville, Leechburg, Scalp Level, Waddle, Cyclone, Panic, Fear Not, Little Hope. Couldn't they learn something from Lofty or Starlight or Acmetonia or Wampum? I ad-mire the logic of putting in opposite corners of the state, like boxers in a ring, Drinker and Dry Tavern, or keeping Virginville well away from Hooker. But the places here I like most are the loony ones, those that make you ask, "What in God's name were they thinking of?" Moosic, Blawnox, Nanty Glo, Orbisonia, Porkey, Mundorf, Equinunk, Coupon, Loyalsock, Paxtang, Wapwallopen, Turnip Hole, Shunk. And, of course, old Zelienople, once the "Chicken Dinner Capital of West-ern Pennsylvania."

That I had the quietude to look at the map and realize just over the west ridge lay Walkchalk and Whiskerville suggests our gentle descent of the Allegheny — a toponym, by the way, that led the New-York Historical Society in 1845 to advocate changing the name of the United States to the Republic of Allegania, mountains which "bind the coun-try together." A committee of eminent men cited Washington Irving:

> We want a national name. We want it poetically, and we want it politi-cally. With the poetical necessity of the case I shall not trouble myself. I leave it to our poets to tell how they manage to steer that collocation of words, "The United States of America," down the swelling tide of song, and to float the whole raft out upon the sea of heroic poesy. I am now speaking of the mere purposes of common life. How is a citizen of this

republic to designate himself? As an American? There are two Americas, each subdivided into various empires, rapidly rising in importance. As a citizen of the United States? It is a clumsy, lumbering title, yet still it is not distinctive.

The proposal brought other suggestions: Columbia, Fredonia, Vesperia, the Republic of Washington. South Carolina novelist William Gilmore Simms helped send the idea, no matter the logic of its arguments, to the dustbin of historical footnotes: "I conscientiously believe that if the nation was called *Squash,* [Americans] would not be conscious of any awkwardness."

Our Allegheny passage let us repair ourselves from the bruising of Lake Erie, and the river showed us mergansers, canvasbacks, teal, coots, an osprey, a bald eagle. Big fish, as silent and dark as shadows, moved slowly away from us, but I saw only their backs and couldn't identify them. Much of this natural plenty was the result of citizens working recently to clean the upper Allegheny, and we were in their debt.

On the east bank we passed a village once called Goshgoshing and later Saqualinguent, Indian names doomed on the tongues of Euro-Americans, so it became the simpler but still tricky Tionesta (rhymes with "my ol' Vesta"), but in the dropping temperature and darkening sky we kept to our course as the river began bending, although its happy trend was westward. The rain finally found a way through the thick overcast and prevented us from reading the river and seeing far enough ahead, so near Eagle Rock we went ashore where the Photographer could find us. We pulled the canoe up to an outbuilding and asked permission of a startled woman to leave it overnight, then we drove the tow wagon a few miles to Oil City, only to discover the 1924 Petroleum Street Bridge lying bank to bank on the river bottom; just days before, the highway department had blasted it off its piers to make way for a new one. In the dampness, our course abruptly dismantled like the bridge, we stood staring, disappointed, and dismayed. We walked the river edge to find a pull-out, but the steep banks gave no accommodation.

My prudent mariner, of all people, said, "Let's run it. We can get between those trusses." Cautious Pilotis, growing improvident, seemed suddenly infected with my passion to keep water under us for every possible mile. I reasoned what we must have, both now and later, was not two rash people but one ardent mind in compromise; nevertheless, I looked long for a route through the twisted girders. At last I said, If the bridge doesn't get us, the sheriff will — the area's buoyed off. With that somber decision, we hung up the day like an old wet coat. But we were satisfied to have found the sometimes rampaging Allegheny so friendly and to have floated it so easily so far.

A Flight of Eagles,
an Iron Bed, and So Forth

MAY DAY — not the distress signal, but the date. We retrieved the canoe from upriver and took it to the other side of the blown bridge being raised from the bottom a few feet at a time and torched into pieces of scrap to sell at four cents a pound. A farmer came along to buy a couple of half-ton cubes of collapsed steel to make into a garden bench, even though he didn't really want one and had no garden; he just loved the old bridge. He said, "I wanted to turn some of it into a barn and house, but I already have a house and two barns."

Pilotis was unusually willing to shoulder the canoe to the water, and I understood why when I heard an intoning from under the aluminum: "Who would fardels bear, to grunt and sweat under a weary life." Anyone happy to tote burdens just for a chance to recite Shakespeare is always welcome on such an undertaking as ours.

In the cool air, light wind, and broken sunlight, we were but five minutes onto the river when we hit the first rapids of note, and we bounced, took water over the bow, rode through to a deeper channel and on down past Franklin with its well-preserved Liberty Street, and then the river again took to the wooded hills. Gradually, pools became longer and more frequent, we paddled fewer riffles, the little motor pottering us between them, but the bottom of the Allegheny, now less lucid, still held many stone sleepers visible only as the canoe passed over their mossy backs. Large slabs of rock here and there slanted from the banks into the river, and we stirred ducks into long skittering withdrawals, their deep wingbeats dimpling the water.

River travel commonly makes this country appear as it ought to be: a sensible number of people blending their homes, barns, and businesses with a natural landscape free of those intrusive abuses junked up alongside our highways. Despite the continuous physical threat in moving water, going down a river can put travelers into a mellow harmony and make them believe all is not yet lost to the selfishness and private greed that so poison our chances for a lasting and healthy prosperity. To follow a river is to find one's way into the territory because a river follows the terrain absolutely — it cannot do otherwise. I'd come here in the belief that I could never really know America until I saw it from the bends and reaches of its flowing waters, from hidden spots open only to a small boat.

At Kennerdell we stopped under a bridge to stretch our legs. I told Pilotis about my preparations for our venture, about scanning my shelves and shelves of accounts of exploration and travel in America. One of the books I pulled down was *Journey to Pennsylvania* by Gottlieb Mittelberger, a German who came to the state in 1750 to deliver a church organ and remained four years. He was a man of common cloth but nonetheless with insight into the hard life of immigrants often exploited by agents and employers. He saw much in the new settlements to displease him. As I neared the last chapter and read his angst over the wilting of religiosity among new Pennsylvania Dutch, I was astonished to come across an anecdote about one of my grandfathers eight generations back, Conrad Reiff. Mittelberger wrote:

> I cannot pass over yet another example of the wicked life some people lead in this free country. Two very rich planters living in the township of Oley, both well known to me, one named Arnold Hufnagel, the other Conrad Reiff, were both archenemies of the clergy, scoffing at them and at the Divine Word. They often met to pour ridicule and insults upon the preachers and the assembled congregation, laughing at and denying Heaven and future bliss as well as damnation in Hell. In 1753 these two scoffers met again, according to their evil habit, and began to talk of Heaven and Hell.
>
> Arnold Hufnagel said to Conrad Reiff, "Brother, how much will you give me for my place in Heaven?"
>
> The other replied, "I'll give you just as much as you'll give me for my place in Hell."
>
> Hufnagel spoke again, "If you will give me so and so many sheep for my place in Heaven, you may have it."

Reiff replied, "I'll give them to you, if you will give me so and so many sheep for my place in Hell."

So the two scoffers struck their bargain, joking blasphemously about Heaven and Hell. When Hufnagel, who had been so ready to get rid of his place in Heaven, wanted to go down to his cellar the next day, he suddenly dropped dead. Reiff, for his part, was suddenly attacked in his field by a flight of golden eagles who sought to kill him. And this would have happened without fail had he not piteously cried for help, so that some neighbors came to his assistance. From that time on, he would not trust himself out of his house. He fell victim to a wasting disease and died in sin, unrepentant and unshriven. These two examples had a visible effect on other scoffers, similarly inclined. For God will not let Himself be scoffed at.

Pilotis said, "Another instance of 'Like grandfather, like grandson.'" Yes, I said, but Mittelberger's assertions about divine retribution are mendacious — Conrad lived in good health into his seventy-sixth year, but he *did* die unshriven — As for me, I can think of few better ways to go than to be taken by a flight of golden eagles.

We returned to the river and followed its bends, passing many houses and a steep, clearcut slope with eroding loggers' roads dumping mud into the Allegheny. As if to atone for those assaults, there followed a reprieve of rhododendrons richly green but not yet in blossom. At Emlenton, we tried to make a landing to get lunch but a severely rocky coast kept us off, so, crossing to the other side, we came upon long and overgrown wooden steps up the high earthen bank to I knew not where, but we packed up food, climbed, and found ourselves in the yard of a grizzled man working on two identical Fords, one with an adequate engine, the other an acceptable body; he'd paid fifty dollars for them both, and when he finished, he'd have a single tolerable car. We made thick turkey sandwiches, talked about weather, which led to talk about lightning, and that led to this from the mechanic: "My old uncle, back in the twenties, fell into a spell of bad times, and he finally decided to kill himself, but he wasn't never a man to bear pain too good, so he figgered on some easeful way to join the Lord. One night he was in bed duren a electric storm, and he saw a tail of smoke come out of a light socket, and then he knew what to do. Over the next week he took a metal bed, arn it was, out of the attic on up to a bare knob, over by Wood Hill, I think he said. He clumb up with it piece by piece and chained it into the ground. The next stormy night he went up to that bed and laid down on it. His plan was for lightnen to strike the arn bedposts and electrify him. He said it thundered and flashed and jolted for two hours. It was like that whole knob was shaken, but nothen struck the bed, so he come on back home and got into his real bed and had the best sleep he had in six months. The next day he got up and figgered the Lord had changed his mind and didn't want him, so he just went on about his business for another twelve years. Lived to be eighty-eight."

Pilotis gave over the bow seat in the canoe to the Photographer who had spotted us from the old Emlenton bridge, and we went on down the river, passed under the high span of Interstate 80 which effectively demarks the upper portion of the Allegheny only recently designated a Wild and Scenic River. While the first adjective hardly describes the country, the new status may help fend off developers who see dollars in every inch of riversides, just as it may also check the abuses of so-called "property rights"–spouting landowners who would do whatever they please, to hell with the neighbors. Today the upper Allegheny has a chance to avoid being turned into a long, skinny strip of suburbia, and the abandoned railroad grade along the east shore, now a trail, can bring in walkers and cyclists who will pass through leaving only tracks and money in the villages.

Foxburg faces the Allegheny with a line of pleasing old commercial buildings, and about a mile downstream we passed the mouth of the Clarion River, its name coming from someone, so I read, who heard "the clear sound of distant ripples," water speaking like a trumpet. On we descended, the sky obscuring, the riffles slowly disappearing in deepening water, the river growing broader, our run easy but for one violent underwater mystery that struck the canoe and motor shaft so hard we narrowly escaped capsizing. The Photographer said, "The Farm Bureau boys need to exterminate the whales in this river."

We came to the Narrows, a peninsula only a half mile across but eight miles around by water, and with last light we fetched up across from East Brady and went to lodgings overlooking the Allegheny in the large Clark House sitting there a century and a half and formerly serving river travelers when packet boats plied this far north. We poured out a round of Old Mister Smile, listened to our hosts tell about East Brady — they weren't sure why the East was tacked on since the only other Brady they knew was the former ironworks — and about the couple who "never married but wore out two engagement rings." Then we went out to walk the misty village and took a supper that, to say the best of it, we were grateful to find. On only three gallons of gas we had brought the canoe down 112 miles of the Allegheny to the head of navigable river, and tomorrow we'd return to *Nikawa*.

Unlimited Sprawl Area

ILOTIS AND I went off to a small boat shop to look for a repair kit to patch a deep gouge I'd put in the hull of *Nikawa* on Chautauqua Lake. To my surprise, the proprietor had one — only one — in a faded, dusty box long on the shelf, but he was afraid to sell it because he couldn't remember the price. Pilotis offered five dollars, the proprietor considered, calculated, deliberated — the Louisiana Purchase was concluded in less time — and eventually decided six was better. While I changed the engine oil, my copilot laid in a smooth repair, and we took *Nikawa* to the drizzled river, backed her in, and struck off downstream for Lock Nine, the uppermost on the Allegheny. Because the northern locks operate only seasonally and primarily for pleasure boats, and because we were arriving well ahead of the opening of the commercial navigation season, Pilotis weeks earlier had negotiated through the bureaucracy of the Army Corps of Engineers and finally convinced it to let us pass downriver on the second and third of May (another deadline I've not mentioned), a persuasion that opened miles of water for us. When we appeared at Lock Nine, the tender was ready, actually expecting us, and we accomplished the twenty-two-foot drop promptly. One more barrier behind.

Not far downstream we passed a large gravel-dredge staining the water for several miles, the clarity of the upper river gone, so that now it flowed in a green murk, a sign not just of silt but also excessive agricultural nitrates and phosphates. The Allegheny turned us northward around a small loop for a few miles, then took a fairly direct course toward the Ohio. Those reaches were bridgeless, and below Lock Eight the river uplands were smaller, the trees fewer and farther from the banks. Over a line of hills and fields to the west lay Butler, the home of Henry Marie Brackenridge, a law student and later an important chronicler of the Mississippi and Missouri rivers; in the early nineteenth century, he described how the largely Irish populace turned out for the first court held in the new settlement:

> A log-cabin just raised and covered but without window sash, or doors, or daubing, was prepared for the hall of justice. A carpenter's bench, with three chairs upon it, was the judgment seat. The bar of Pittsburgh attended, and the presiding judge [was] supported by two associate judges, who were common farmers. The hall was barely sufficient to contain the bench, bar, jurors, and constables. But few of the spectators could be accommodated on the lower floor, the only one yet laid; many, therefore, clambered up the walls, and placing their hands and feet in the open interstices between the logs, hung there, suspended like enormous Madagascar bats. Some had taken possession of the joists, and big John McJunkin (who until now had ruled at all public gatherings) had placed a foot on one joist, and a foot on another, directly over the heads of their honors, standing like the Colossus of Rhodes. The judge's sense of propriety was shocked at this exhibition. The sheriff, John McCandless, was called and ordered to clear the walls and joists. He went to work with his assistants, and soon pulled down by the legs those who were in no very great haste to obey. McJunkin was the last and began to growl as he prepared to descend. "What do you say, sir?" said the judge. "I say, I pay my taxes, and has as good a reete here as iny mon." "Sheriff, sheriff," said the judge, "bring him before the court." The judge pronounced sentence of imprisonment for two hours in the jail of the county and ordered the sheriff to take him into custody. The sheriff with much simplicity observed, "May it please the coorte, there is no jail at all to put him in. May it please the coorte, I'm just thinken that may be I can take him to Bowen's pig pen — the pigs are kilt for the coorte, and it's empty." "You have heard the opinion of the court," said the judge. "Proceed, sir. Do your duty."

We reached Kittanning, then building a lovely riverfront park overlooked by the courthouse up the hill, a town on its way to becoming a flower of the Allegheny. But at neighboring Ford City we followed a long, unbroken line of factories and warehouses of brick, some still in use, others shuttered, a reach of decrepit and derelict history. From there to its mouth at Pittsburgh, the Allegheny was worn-out industry, its course almost unrelieved of Rust Belt decay and decline except for a few interruptions of riverside trees. We moved atop a river carrying, since the days of white settlement, local products, all having their turn of demand and ready availability and subsequent depletion: timber, coal, oil, gas, glass, iron, steel, tin, aluminum.

The dammed and locked river, rebuilt for easy passage, gave us just that, and the shorelines were neither beautiful nor ugly but simply used and, in places, clogged with discarded factories, each marked with a brick smokestack long ago cooled, each revealing that typically American resistance to take old industrial land for new industry so long as fresh woods and farmlands are available for the squandering farther away. An Englishwoman, shocked in her travels across America to see the depressing number of abandoned commercial and industrial buildings, a rare thing in her space-conscious nation, once told me, "I realize now that USA stands for Unlimited Sprawl Area. Your wastefulness with buildings is deplorable, and most of you are blind to it."

Because the Allegheny locks lie close together and all of them were ready for us, we spent the day hooking up, descending, unhooking, and moving along more speedily than we had predicted. Every lock tender, unlike those on the Erie Canal, came out to take our line and loop it over a stanchion and return the free end to Pilotis. The details of this simple maneuver varied from lock to lock, with each man having a new set of directions, so we simply waited to be told how to do it his way, and that made the tenders think we didn't know an oar from a shovel, which may be why one bystander we talked with shook his head and asked, "You think you're actually going to make it across?" I answered we'd gotten this far from New York City in a couple of weeks, and he said, "Oh hell, my daughter drives that in five hours."

Immediately below Lock Five is the debouchure of the Kiskiminetas River; although only twenty miles long, it's the largest tributary of the Allegheny. It and its connecting rivers and canal from the nineteenth century could have been our way from the Atlantic to the Ohio had the network, including a portage railroad that hauled canal barges over a mountain, not been abandoned years ago. It was down the Kiskiminetas that water poured from the great and deadly Johnstown Flood in 1889, flushing bodies — and one tool chest with its contents unharmed — all the way to Pittsburgh. A few years ago, the river was declared "biologically dead," primarily because of acids draining from old mines, but there too, new regulations demanded by active citizens have somewhat improved it.

Opposite the mouth of the Kiskiminetas is Freeport, at the virtual juncture of four counties, sprawling its fringes into three of them, an unusual circumstance since its population is not even two thousand. A couple of miles below, in a misty and woody bottom, we tied up at the long dock of the River Forest Yacht Club. To judge from the number of the big things in winter storage on the first terrace, a more accurate name would be the River Forest Houseboat Club. The Photographer radioed and soon found us and showed the way through the trees to the road, past a rusting tow truck with doors labeled:

FRANK CRASH
AUTO WRECKING

Our rivering done for the day, but with the sun nearly in its happy and notorious relation to the yardarm, we went into Freeport to search out our favorite Irish stout to accompany a recounting of the miles and planning of the next day, one, we learned, that would be hampered by repair work at Lock Four, a snag leaving little room for miscalculation. In Freeport, about which even a kindly visual description would misrepresent were it to avoid the adjective "grim," we went up and down in search of some real ale, stepping into one place after another to find only television-commercial lagers. We might as well have been looking for a phroso. The Photographer said, "We need a GPS," to which Pilotis said, "We have one. Besides, we know where we are — approximately." Replied the Photographer, "No, we don't have a Guinness Positioning System."

We ended up nine miles northwest in glad serendipity, a frequent outcome of such real-ale searches, this one named Saxonburg with a Main Street from the nineteenth century, a fair village founded in 1832 by German immigrant John Roebling who developed there his patented process for "wire rope," the stuff he used thirty-seven years later when he designed the Brooklyn Bridge. Roebling's son Washington, the chief engineer for the span, wrote, somewhat in jest, that his father saw western Pennsylvania as "the future center of the universe with the future Saxonburg as the head center, which was then a primeval forest where wild pigeons would not even light." John encouraged his countrymen to immigrate and first named the village Germania but advised them not to bring tools, for in America "nobody could cut down a tree with a German ax."

In the big attic room of the Main Stay Bed and Breakfast, near

Roebling's home, we did our requisite logbook work, then went next door to the Saxonburg Hotel, a solid building put up the year of the engineer's arrival, and there we found our stout, not on tap but at least bottled. I tried to start a conversation about the massive aesthetic differences between Saxonburg and the dolorous manifestation of the town on the river, and I hypothesized that the dissimilarities were today likely the result of only one or two citizens insisting on communal attention to history and beauty. I said, You know — the power of the lone voice calling us to excellence. Pilotis: "Not now, Skipper. Now is beverage time. Happy Hour's a phrase first used among seamen, but I don't remember that they ever had one called Hypothetical Hour." To calm my restive crew, I immediately unzipped the pant legs of my trousers, turning them into hiking shorts. The hostess, watching with something between alarm and fascination, said, "Now that's one I haven't never seen done in here before."

Zing, Boom, Tararel!

WE AROSE AT DAWN and hurried along so we could pass through Lock Four ahead of the repairs that would shut it down till noon. At last there was deep blue sky in Pennsylvania, but directly above and precisely following the Allegheny Valley lay a slender, dingy muffler of fog, with the surmounting hills in full sun. *Nikawa,* not even visible until we were out on the long pier, was socked in tight on a day beautiful beyond the river, and we would not reach Four, only three miles away, soon enough to avoid the closing. In some concern, we drove to a breakfast café and set to work on logbooks, a way to avoid killing time, although we did give it a good choking.

The place was full of folks more or less the shape of biscuits and the pallor of white gravy, both of which they were putting down in quantities that convinced me a chemical analysis of their corpora would reveal them to be eighty percent identical to your standard Appalachian-country biscuit with gravy. Pilotis silenced my commentary and nodded toward the Photographer happily dipping into a platter of them. I don't mean to make mock of biscuits-and-gravy, a jolly food like mashed potatoes or Jell-O, but it is to a rural café what schnapps is to a Wisconsin tavern where one hears the outsider ask, "Are you really going to drink that swill?"

Perhaps the overflowing talk in the restaurant was the result of the plates of b-and-g; certainly we had no trouble raising conversations there. One fellow, who found the thick gravy disappointingly thin that morning, told me of his soldier days in World War Two when he was aboard a civilian train: "I was dead broke, and here we were on our way to Philly for three days leave before getting shipped out. I came up with a plan. I took off my cap and went down the aisle and asked people — civilians — for a contribution to build a memorial to Missus Williams, the Mother of the Unknown Soldier. It worked to the tune of thirty bucks and change."

When we returned to the river, the brume was nearly dispersed, so we headed toward Lock Four. Pilotis's earlier phone calls again made the difference: the construction crew moved a barge aside to let us edge through, and *Nikawa* was down and gone. The river continued heavy with industry, more vacant shambles too, but there were still many trees along the banks to soften the harshness. The Allegheny became a kind of watery quarry, its bottom being dredged — that is, sucked — for its glacial gifts of sand and gravel, but the color occluded further. Pilotis said, "Hard to believe this is the same river we were on three days ago, probably even some of the same water." Then, watching the muddied surface, "What else in nature begins its existence, its journey, clean and pure but finishes so soiled and sullied?" I said, You mean, besides humankind? Still staring at the Allegheny, Pilotis mused, "If the beginning of a river is its head, why is its end a mouth? Why not a foot or a toe? Or a rectum, especially since that's the way civilization treats it?"

With Lock Three soon behind us, we came into Pittsburgh and the last lock. *Nikawa* made another rapid descent, the tender signaling us on out with his steam whistle that set Pilotis to singing, and we began passing under the many bridges of William Pitt's town, he the Great Commoner who pleaded for cessation of hostilities with America but refused to recognize its independence. We passed Herr's Island, once an eyesore with an abandoned slaughterhouse but now on the way toward becoming landscaped and not inexpensive housing. Beyond the old ketchup factory, we went under the Sixth Street Bridge which isn't quite high enough to ensure a successful suicide, so the dedicatedly downhearted climb the big cables to the tops of the towers for the jump.

Mayor Thomas Murphy, who grew up not far away, once told me his mother always said when he left the house, "Be home before dark, and stay away from the river." Now he and rowing clubs and others were reawakening residents to its three rivers. The Allegheny was wide and empty, giving us an unobstructed view of the downtown catching shafts of light breaking through a dark sky blowing out of the west. It's excellent to see Pittsburgh from the bluffs — to realize its remarkable topographic setting where the Allegheny and the Monongahela join at that regular triangle to form the Ohio — but perhaps even better is the view from the water where the buildings rise in a way unmatched by any other river city in America (New York is a harbor city).

The Photographer had found a safe dockage for the night at the Pittsburgh River Rescue Station on the north side of the Allegheny, across from the Golden Triangle, the place those citizens of Vulcan began their town. With our man aboard and clicking his camera, the rescue crew motored up, gave welcome, then led us to a fuel stop and on to our mooring.

To celebrate a safe descent of the Allegheny, we went off that night to an old factory — at last a reused building — this one converted into a brewery of lagers which we ale lovers nevertheless duly appreciated, as we did a plate of pickled herring, but the accordion man in Tyrolean hat and lederhosen was another matter. My manliness would never admit that I try to flee when I see a belly organ coming near, but I will say that should I never hear one again I'll account myself well served. We endured an enfilade of schussbooming polkas and Teutonic schmierkäse. Then that one, "*In München steht ein Hofbräuhaus,*" with its infernal "*Eins, zwei, g'suffa!*"

The accordionist saw our navy blue sweatshirts, NIKAWA writ boldly across them, and he took an interest and decided to give a special concert inches from our ears. Half deafened, half insane, I was able briefly to quiet him by describing our attempt for the Pacific, but the musician was soon ready for "Beer Barrel Polka" when the Photographer saved another moment by asking him what he thought "Nikawa" meant. The music man stood puzzled *and* silent, then said, "*Jawohl!* It translates, 'White man must be crazy,'" and then out rolled those damn barrels of fun — zing, boom, tararel! And that's how, blues on the run, we got ready to descend the thousand miles of the river Ohio.

V

THE OHIO RIVER

NIKAWA AT PITTSBURGH, PENNSYLVANIA

ICONOGRAM V

Below Eureka the Ohio winds in a series of broad sweeping curves, with the sharp rubble banks of the upper valley giving way to swampy, spongy shores on both sides. As fishing is good here, the stretch is a frequent port of call for shanty-boaters. These boats, generally flat bottomed, but often built to resemble an ark, cruise the thousand miles between Pittsburgh and Cairo, Illinois, each year. The shanty-boater lives in the small cabin on his craft; the river and its banks provide his food; driftwood for heating and cooking is to be had for the taking, while a little backdoor begging at farmhouses usually provides him with castoff clothing. More energetic shanty-boaters work a few days each week ashore; they are invariably jacks-of-all-trades, their footloose life developing in them both an amazing versatility in handicrafts and an earnest desire to practice these crafts as seldom as possible.

Not all houseboat dwellers are shanty-boaters, this term being applied mainly to those whose wanderlust keeps them from settling in one spot for any great length of time. Cheerful, hospitable with what little he has, shiftless and slovenly, the typical shanty-boater leads a fairly carefree existence. His whims and moods are dictated by the vagaries of the river, which gives him sustenance and transportation. When left high and dry, he shores up his boat and waits for high water to put him afloat again — a few months of waiting mean nothing in his life of leisure. He is generally law-abiding, but his neighbors include a few elements who impart a bad reputation to all shanty-boaters by distilling and selling cheap whisky, and by hiding criminals until all trace of them is lost in the vague peregrinations and trackless wanderings of the boats. Yet his fellow boatmen include a number of Gospel preachers — elderly men, as a rule, who have grown weary of worldliness and dedicated themselves to the regeneration of the water gypsies. These preachers travel continuously, and their boats are welcome wherever shanty-boatmen congregate.

West Virginia: A Guide to the Mountain State,
American Guide Series, 1941

Proving the
White Man a Liar

HEN TORTURE is imminent, suicide beckons, although it's
rare a captive has the choice. In Pittsburgh, at the place
the Allegheny becomes the Ohio, was once a sandbar called
Smoky Island with a peculiar and dark history, and the darkest of its
incidents started ten miles down on the sister tributary, the Monongahela, nearly at the mouth of the Youghiogheny River. In 1755, General
Edward Braddock, a Briton of hauteur — a quality inimical to a frontier America requiring new ways and attitudes — came marching up
with almost two thousand soldiers, nearly three quarters of them
English, to try to capture the French Fort Duquesne at the Point on the
forks of the Ohio. This impressive contingent was the best his young
aide-de-camp, George Washington, had ever seen, but Braddock was
the wrong leader, and his contempt for the new land and its people
was a deadly flaw. When Washington warned him of possible ambush
and recommended firing from cover as the Indians did, Braddock
reportedly said, "What! A Virginia colonel teach a British general how
to fight?"

As the Redcoats and their supporting colonial soldiers marched
through a narrow ravine, they found themselves trapped in volleys of
invisible musket fire from the slopes. Braddock, insisting on standard
European rank-and-file order, saw his regulars forced into shooting
blindly toward the woods while the Americans tried to get to protected positions. Quickly, the much smaller contingent of French and
Indians, mostly the latter, put the British into a panicked scramble; the

general had five horses shot out from under him, the last just before he took a bullet in a lung. More than half his royal troops and all but one of his mounted officers fell. He himself was probably shot by Thomas Faucett, an American under his command. Faucett never denied the allegation, insisting, rather, he did it so the Redcoats and their brothers Jonathan could fight from behind trees and save their lives. Washington, the last mounted officer, though ill with fever and his coat perforated by four bullets, assumed command to direct the remaining troops back to safety where, three days later as the arrogant general lay dying — he who had smilingly told Benjamin Franklin, "These savages may, indeed, be a formidable enemy to your raw American militia, but upon the King's regular and disciplined troops, sir, it is impossible they should make any impression" — said weakly to Washington, "We shall better know how to deal with them another time." The Virginia colonel had Braddock buried in a road and then marched soldiers and drove wagons over the grave so the enemy wouldn't find it. The British who could not join Washington's retreat were less fortunate: Indians herded them naked back toward the Point and took them at nightfall to an Allegheny sandbar, tied them to stakes, piled embers on their feet, and thrust glowing iron rods into their nostrils and ears while children fired novice arrows into them.

A story has come down about one soldier who sought to save himself agony. He loudly boasted he knew of a plant that would render him invulnerable, so his captors untied him and dared him to prove it. Picking the nearest leaves he saw and rubbing their juice around his neck, he spoke some mumbo-jumbo, laid his head on a log, and challenged anyone to test his immortality. A warrior took up an ax, swung it hard, and cleaved the soldier's neck, thereby proving the white man a liar. Nine years later, Governor John Penn offered bounties on Indians: $150 for a male older than ten, $134 for scalp of same, $130 for a female or boy, $50 for the scalp of a woman.

Fort Duquesne is gone, and close to where that horror happened, the Pirates and Steelers play ball at the river edge. The morning we passed by, Three Rivers Stadium stood dismal in mist, but the big fountains across the river, the ones nearly atop the site of the fort, spewed up their glory to a city triumphant. Pilotis took the binoculars to scan the ridge above the Duquesne Incline and managed to spot the

Photographer and his signal flag waving goodbye before he pulled the trailer west to meet us — we trusted — in a few weeks and two thousand miles away in Sioux City, Iowa, below the first dam on the Missouri River.

From Pittsburgh almost to Louisville, six hundred miles downstream, bottomland highways lie close to both banks of the Ohio and make it, for its length, one of the most visible and accessible big rivers in the country. Only two generations after the slaughter of imperious Braddock's troops, another British fellow, Thomas Ashe, wrote in 1808:

> The Ohio . . . has been truly described as beyond competition the most beautiful river in the universe, whether it be considered for its meandering course through an immense region of forests; for its elegant banks, which afford innumerable delightful situations for cities, villages, and improved farms; or for those many other advantages which truly entitle it to the name originally given it by the French, of "*La belle rivière.*" This is the outline of a description given several years since, and it has generally been thought an exaggerated one. Now, the immense forests recede, cultivation smiles along its banks; numerous villages and towns decorate its shores; and it is not extravagant to suppose that the day is not far distant when its whole margin will form one continued series of villages and towns.

Like so many of the earliest river travelers — those in canoes, bateaux, flatboats, keelboats, and the first paddlewheelers — we were about to descend the Ohio as the water rose, although timing was no longer necessary since virtually the entire river seventy years ago was dammed into pools for the benefit of navigation, a process called canalization. Unlike those of, say, the Missouri, the Ohio barriers do not control floods; during high water a towboat and its barges pass right over the low crests of the dams, while at other times traffic must use the system of twenty locks. So off we went, singing the old refrain:

> Hi-O, away we go,
> Floating down the river
> On the O-hi-O.

The rising Monongahela sent rafts of woody drift into the Ohio, some that *Nikawa* could dodge or avoid by changing course, but others we simply had to plow through with nothing more than hope. Emsworth, the first lock, was full of floaters, many of them natural, the

The Ohio, Pittsburgh to Huntington, 309 river miles

remainder human crud ranging from tires on rims to tampon applicators — *la belle rivière* — so, to keep the props clear, I did my best to
coast to a tie-up on the wall. Although heavy barge traffic often forces
a small boat into long waits, we entered alone and quickly descended,
our teapot preposterously small in the massive chamber. That first
dam cleared the drift for some windless miles to give us a slick-water
run between low banks full of industry, power plants, and railyards,
but on the bluffs were fine old homes at Coraopolis and Haysville and
Sewickley. From the early days of coarse rivermen and aesthetically

dim industrialists, Sewickley has tried for greater elegance, shedding its earlier labels of Dogtown, Contention, and Devil's Race Track to take its current name, one that may look regally English but is in fact Indian, "sweet water." Later, wishing to have domiciles rather than industries, the town banned factories and even trolleys.

I have not said that the design of *Nikawa* made her look like an illustration from a children's reader, and her lines sometimes drew people who — more often than we cared for — used the word "cute." At Dashields Lock, the tender came out to see the boat. Before he lowered her, I asked where we could find a good lunch along the river. We pursued his suggestion past once steely Aliquippa, on past Ambridge that has surrounded its predecessor village, Economy — perhaps a not unexpected result, given the celibacy practiced by its German Rappite founders.

The village was the third and last home of communalists who settled there in 1824 after giving up on Harmony and New Harmony, and indeed they found they did better as Economists than Harmonists. Their celibacy derived from their certainty that the Christian Millennium was nigher than anyone could believe (their great church clock has only the hour hand, a reminder of their sense of time). Against the Second Coming they tried to be ready with bodies pure of recent sexual taint, not to mention — hidden in Father Rapp's cellar — a stash of half a million dollars intended to get them to the City Celestial. That epochal Last Generation not yet in sight, they managed to hold on eighty-one years before their abstinence left them shorn of believers. Yet they did leave a grand architectural inheritance of more than a hundred beautiful buildings along the banks of the Ohio and nearly twenty thousand fascinating and scrupulously designed worldly possessions. Where the half million went, I don't know.

Upon leaving Pittsburgh, the Ohio heads north as if to empty into Lake Erie less than a hundred miles away, something it did until the glaciers thousands of years ago pushed it back to assume a southwesterly course — another piece of fortuitous topography that very much contributed to linking the eastern half of America to the beyond. Without the Ohio and the Missouri, all people west of the Mississippi might today speak Spanish or vote for members of a parliament, and how different the Civil War would have been without the broad Ohio effectively separating much of the nation. At Monaca, a glass and steel manufacturing town like others nearby, the Ohio makes its great glacially wrought turn, and across the water lies the mouth of the Beaver River at the northernmost point of the Ohio. There we went a mile upstream to Bridgewater and found a good dock near the café the lockman had told us about. The place was once an ice cream stand, and before that a filling station, and filling was what we wanted: we ate tureens of spicy pinto-bean soup and tostadas, all of it fresh from the stove, and the dreary day seemed to withdraw. A young mother came in, child at her side; as customers made much of the girl, a man asked whether she was talking yet; said the woman: "She babbles one word, 'Mall,' and that means me *and* the shopping center."

Below the Beaver, the hills of the Ohio become higher and edge right to the water, a combination that has prevented significant industrial encroachment for some miles, and at last *la belle rivière* looked just that. At Montgomery Lock a drizzle came on and seemed to wash us back into the uglier aspect of railyards, then we passed a nuclear power plant across from Industry, the name perhaps accurate beyond its founders' dreams, and four miles farther we left Pennsylvania. Now on the south bank was the Northern Panhandle of West Virginia, and across the river lay East Liverpool, Ohio, a town I'd known before only from the road and thought it possessing a worn grime similar to that of its English counterpart. But from the river we saw old homes atop the high bank, slender steeples, and a graceful 1905 suspension bridge. It was for such changed views I had come. Wellsville, five miles below, with more historic houses along the bluff, was downright inviting, and there the Ohio began its 260-mile southwesterly drop before shifting to a more westward course at Huntington, West Virginia.

A repair crew held *Nikawa* off for a while at New Cumberland Lock. When we entered, Pilotis took delight in tying to our first floating mooring bitt, a pin or small bollard that moves with the rise and fall of the water to make securing a boat much easier; those plaintive squeaking, stridulating rollers added a new voice to the chamber music of mechanically profundo valves and soprano gears, that one strikingly like the song of humpback whales.

The afternoon finally began to dry but the clouds remained low, and, having done sixty miles, our longest run yet, we turned into a protected cove near a titanium processing plant. Pilotis began laughing, then said, "Get yourself ready," and pointed. Tied to a pier was the

Doctor Robert fresh from its overland transport to Pittsburgh. "Here you go again." No we don't, I said, not anymore — we're now a convoy of one. We warped in behind to refuel. Down in the engine well of the character boat stood a mechanic and Cap, both splattered with oil. "Never mind," Cap said. "Don't ask." But I did, and his lone crewman, Mr. V—, answered: "The diesel just quit above Montgomery Dam. We began drifting toward it. Dead in the water. Wasn't a thing we could do except get on the radio. A towboat managed to reach us in time and put a line on us. One hell of a scare."

I thought of how Cap once referred to *Nikawa* as Tupperware, and I looked at Pilotis, who said softly, "That was nearly our boat." I whispered that the *Doctor* would be a suitable vessel if only she could tow behind a dry dock; from then on, to us she was the *Dry Docktor*. That evening we borrowed a clunker of a station wagon from the marina and pursued a tip and drove a few miles south to one of the "mother towns of Ohio," Steubenville, laid out by Bezaleel Wells; the first steamboat built there was named after him, although its frequent breakdowns earned it the moniker *Beelzebub*. We met Cap and Mr. V— at the High Hat Café for a round of martinis followed by plates of chicken sautéed with banana peppers and mushrooms, a recipe the owner's mother had brought from Italy, all of it so good that Cap laughed and toasted and told jokes and for a while forgot about his *Beelzebub*.

The Day Begins
with a Goonieburger

THE SUN ROSE and with it our appetites for a hearty meal; by the time we drove the borrowed clunker to the 1000 Franklin Café in Toronto, Ohio, "hearty" had defined itself as hamburger, a craving only Americans can deeply understand. The choice was a Billyburger or a Goonieburger. "Either is appropriate for you," Pilotis commented needlessly. The waitress didn't know who or what Billy and Goonie were, but she said of the Goonie, "It comes with everthing includen tomaters." And the Billy? "It just comes with everthing." Pilotis ordered the Special, fried fish, and asked, "What kind is it?" Replied she, "Jumbo fish."

By the time we boarded *Nikawa*, noon was upon us. Our course was about as due south as a river can run, the Ohio curving just enough to give us the joy of anticipation, of waiting to see what lay around the bends, an important occurrence for water travelers who never have their route perceptibly climb or descend as does a highway to the sweet and sour of the unexpected; people who think driving across southern Florida or central Kansas is an encounter with ultimate levelness should try a stretch on a river.

The thousands of nineteenth-century traders and settlers who put out onto the Ohio to take them deep into the newly gained territory commonly carried a small book at first simply titled *The Navigator* (but with a ninety-six-word subtitle) which they purchased from the author's print shop in Pittsburgh. Zadok Cramer gave terse but trenchant "particular directions on how to navigate" the Ohio and the

Mississippi to readers employing boats they built themselves or bought cheaply, craft intended for a single downriver float: flatboats (arks, barges, broadhorns, Kentuckys), keelboats, skiffs, and who knows how many hybrids, all of them sharing one significant element: they had no propulsion but gravity — that is, the current. Cramer advised:

> The first thing to be attended to by emigrants or traders wanting to descend the river, is to procure a boat, to be ready so as to take advantage of the times of floods and to be careful that the boat be a good one: for many of the accidents that happen in navigating the Ohio and Mississippi, are owing to the unpardonable carelessness or penuriousness of the boat builder, who will frequently slight his work or make it of injured plank, in either case putting the lives and properties of a great many people at manifest hazard.

Because the Ohio is no longer a freely flowing river, we found our descent almost as simple as driving an auto, if you discount that at every moment our road moved under us in several directions at the same time, and one other thing: towboatmen who, with their gigantic loads, showed contempt for a small thing like *Nikawa,* a scorn not surpassed by interstate truckers for automobiles.

Steubenville has long been a town of suspension bridges, and the newest of them, the Veterans' Memorial, is a stunning piece, all of its myriad supporting cables depending from a single, central tower that looks like — take your choice — a tuning fork, a wishbone, or a clothespin rendered by Pop sculptor Claes Oldenburg. At Coketown, appropriately, we caught a scent of coal smoke, an odor once so prevalent on this river it could have been bottled as Eau de la Belle Rivière. And then came Wellsburg, with trimmed lawns to the water, a delightful old inn, and Pilotis wrote on the chart "nice place," although one eminent guide to West Virginia described it in 1941 as "an unromantic-looking industrial town for a long time more widely known for its 'gin weddings' and 'marrying parsons' than for its glass plants and large paper mills producing great quantities of paper bags."

The men of the Pike Island Lock took *Nikawa* in at their leisure. Again we had to furrow through a nasty field of woody drift and plastic flotsam. Once we started descending, the wheels of the floating bitts howled and screeched, and Pilotis said, "The Lock Mess Monster is dying." Then we were free, went past the Sisters Islands, taking one on our port, the other starboard. I've never seen an island I didn't want to explore, perhaps because, unlike us, they seem so entire unto themselves with their capacity to withstand the relentless river and their isolation that spawns mystery.

At Wheeling, West Virginia, we came upon another suspension bridge, in days gone the longest in the world, drift stacked against the piers neatly like cordwood; the Tenth Street span connects the city with Wheeling Island (the largest inhabited one in the Ohio and a rarity with its road links to shore). The historic structure of twin stone towers has the look of a small Brooklyn Bridge, although it's been around more than a third of a century longer, the smoke-grimed rocks revealing its age as if wrinkles. Built in 1856 and the oldest on the Ohio, it and its 1846 predecessor changed river law in two Supreme Court cases argued between Wheeling and Pittsburgh; the latter, fearing loss of its river trade, claimed the bridge interfered with navigation and won the first decision, but Wheeling prevailed on appeal, with the new law holding that the height of steamboat stacks must be governed by bridge clearances. When the span collapsed during a windstorm in 1854, the packet *Pennsylvania* continued to lower her chimneys in derision as she passed Wheeling, but the mockery lasted only until the present thousand-foot-long version went up. For us it was good to go beneath a bridge that has looked down on the stovepipe hat of Abraham Lincoln, the mustache of Mark Twain, the sooty funnels of a hundred thousand steamboats, the rifle muzzles of Union soldiers, and every other Ohio River traveler since before the Civil War.

Formerly a river town, Wheeling today turns its back to the Ohio, showing bum-ends of old brick office buildings and warehouses and a wretched four-storey auto garage that largely negates a new park along the bank. The name Wheeling probably derives from several early settlers, venturing down the Ohio in quest of land, whom Delaware Indians captured, decapitated, and set their heads as a warning on poles along the river, a site subsequently called *wih-link,* "place of the skull." Local residents, as you might guess, offer other etymologies.

On we went in the quiet, reflective afternoon. A river — with its attendant cascades, eddies, boils, and whirlpools — is the most expressive aspect of a natural landscape, for nothing else moves so far, so broadly, so unceasingly, so demonstrably, and nothing else is so susceptible to personification and so much at the heart of our notions about life and death. Across generations and around the globe, humans, we double-footed jugs of seventy percent water, have seen rivers as both our source and the way out of this world. The Osage Indians use the same word, *ni,* for water, river, sap, breath, life. To the ancient Egyptians and Greeks, the afterworld lay on the far side of a river, a bourn from which no traveler returns. But, the marine sailor might ask, what about seascapes? I've found the ocean, despite its continuous movement and manifest moods, too overwhelming to comprehend as anything other than an implacable immensity. The sea is the wind made visible, but a river is the land turned liquid. No engineer ever tried to bridge an ocean, dam a sea, or turn its currents another direction: oceans surpass our capacities too far. River travelers, even ones not poetically inclined, soon begin to conceive the water as friend or foe, to view it as possessed of a will, and at times even a primitive mind capable of acting companionably or inimically. In this country, bankside inhabitants often call themselves with pride "river rats," a self-inflicted insult expressing their humility before that force controlling their lots and their lives.

I've driven more than a million miles over American highways, but I don't recall loving, for itself, even one road. How can you love an unmoving, stone-cold strip of concrete, ever the same except for its aging, its attrition? But a river comes into existence moving, and it grows as it moves, and like a great mother carries within itself lives too varied and multitudinous for our myriad sciences even yet wholly to number and name. I say this now because we had just accomplished our thousandth wet mile, and during that passage I felt we were atop something animate and wondrously strong and strange which, were I but once to fail in my respect, would take me in a moment to its deadly bottom.

About then, Pilotis called my stare from the sounder.

Of the ancient monuments of America, few are as considerable, abundant, and fertile with mystery as the aboriginal mounds standing like sentinels all along the Ohio, Mississippi, Missouri, and their tributaries. These hundreds upon hundreds of earthen constructions — mostly simple tumuli, but also ones shaped into serpents, bears, birds, and platforms to hold temples — commonly lie hidden among shoreside trees. But why are they usually along rivers? I think the Osage expressed it: *ni,* river, breath, life.

The largest conical earthen mound in the New World is at Moundsville, West Virginia. Called Mammoth, or Grave Creek Mound, it is at least two thousand years old and once held the remains of Indians wearing copper bracelets, bone and shell beads, a gorget or two; but its most famous artifact was a sandstone tablet inscribed with a couple of dozen characters variously interpreted as "ancient Greek, Etruscan, Runic, ancient Gallic, Old Erse, Phoenician, Celtiberic, Old British, Appalachian." Translations of those twenty-four marks seem to express more the mind of an interpreter than the inscriber:

Thy orders are laws.
Thou shinest in thy impetuous elan,
and rapid is the chamois.

*

The Chief of Emigration
who reached these places
has fixed these statutes forever.

*

The grave of one who was assassinated here.
May God revenge him,
strike his murderer,
cutting off the hand of his existence.

*

I pray to Christ,
His most Holy Mother,
Son, Holy Ghost, Jesus Christ, God.

*

United States of Egypt.
Built by States of Eastern Union.

*

I knelt on the island,
Øn's yule site on Meadow Island,
now the island is a Hodd.

*

Your hope to be imbued with measure
of purity, manners, industry,
misery, folly, strength.

*

Bil Stumps Stone
OCT 14 1838.

And in 1948 another interpreter opined the characters were actually an image of the back end of an automobile, a prognostication carved by a

giant prophetess. The tablet, now lost, was likely inauthentic except as
an artifact planted during the first excavations of 1838 to lure tourists
to the gallery dug into the heart of the sixty-nine-foot mound, a dim
and damp exhibit hung with Indian skeletons and lighted by gutter-
ing candles, a spook show designed to thrill paying visitors. Atop the
tumulus the purveyors built an observatory, later replaced by a dance
platform, replaced by a saloon, replaced by a Union artillery position
in 1863; around the perimeter at one time was a horse track. When
these efforts failed to make enough money, citizens proposed leveling the mound to provide fill (the fate of a hundred other mounds
nearby), or building a post office at the summit, or turning it into the
Tomb of the Unknown West Virginia Soldier. In 1909 the state reluctantly and belatedly accepted this preeminent ancient monument and
for some years assigned the care of it to the penitentiary across the
street. It was convicts who restored it to something like its original
contours.

We passed several strip-pit coal mines and their high tailings, the
kind of mounds industrial people leave, massive cicatrices symbolizing
not mystery or an honored death but rather nothing more than extracted power and consequent exhaustion, corporate barbarity and
final uselessness, with an appendant poisoning of land and water. Yet a
few of the tailings recently had been "reclaimed," their new slopes
trying to come into kindly disposition with the landscape once again.

At the Mason-Dixon Line, the wind came on as if to cuff a couple of
Yankees, and where the direction of the hills and river let it get at us, it
bashed the water into a jogglety, noisy course that intervening quiet
stretches served not to give relief so much as to point up our banging discomfort. It was then Pilotis identified the worst of a wind-
hammered river, a small and crucial discovery: "It's not the jarring
that wears me down — it's the din, the racket. In this fiberglass we're
riding inside a big snare drum." On and on, the corrugated water beat
its tattoo into our bones. The next day I bought earplugs.

The enclosure of Hannibal Lock gave us a brief reprieve and added
a soothing music from its floating bitts, as melodious and plaintive as
American Indian flutes. And then we were back to an open twenty-
three miles down the throat of the wind, but we complained little
because the way was free of boils and rocks. About every hour we came
upon a big sycamore or cottonwood making a long and eventually
fatal lean over the river, and sometimes from a large limb dangled a

rope swing, a heavy, knotted cord for swimmers to drop from. Even in the cool air, the lines tempted us. On one sycamore that had completed its tilt and joined the Ohio to become a sawyer — a bottom-stuck tree breaking the surface to saw up and down in the current — stood a great blue heron in leggy elegance, aloof as if the suzerain of backwaters. Old steamboaters believed the birds embodied the souls of river pilots, for who knew the chutes, channels, and shoals better than a heron?

Steep, wooded bluffs lay close to the banks, creating a section of beauty that, at last, fully deserved the lost French name of the Ohio. Then came Paden Island, a mile-long cluster of trees, its upper ends swept back to a point, an overgrown sandbar generations ago when Obadiah Paden got it from Chief Munsie who dwelt there and one night dreamed the white man made gifts of his rifle and engraved powderhorn. Following an alleged native custom that holds a person appearing in another's sleep responsible for fulfilling the dream, Munsie, upon waking, went to Paden and told him of the vision; the white man, wishing to keep the peace, turned over the gun and horn but then went silent for several days. Some days later he found Munsie and related his own dream about the chief giving him the island. After that, they say, dreamers hereabouts kept their sleep to themselves.

The island marks the head of the Long Reach, at sixteen miles the farthest straight run on the river and also the beginning of a sixty-mile stretch of slender islands that survived canalization, although several of them lie so close to the banks they can hardly be distinguished as separate from the shore. To starboard was an Ohio settlement whose first residents, a number of them undoubtedly illiterate, years ago wanted an utterly simple name: Dog? Wet? Pot? Elf? They settled on Fly — insect or verb, I don't know. Across the river is Sistersville, a village of some late-nineteenth-century quaintness, once called Ziggleton, where Charles Wells and his wife had twenty-two children, the eighteenth and nineteenth the sisters of the present name. The Wellses called their next child Twenty and the following Plenty, but when the last arrived they lost their humor, and she was merely Betsey. Having tired of creating names, they just flat gave up procreating children.

Nine miles down the Long Reach, on the West Virginia shore, we passed Friendly, the name from the Quakers and not a description of local demeanor, despite some cheerful citizens treating it as a daily reminder. On the opposite bank lies what's left of New Matamoros, which the Ohio WPA *Guide* describes as "now a stilled community of old, severely simple business structures and shuttered houses," a possibly inevitable fate for a place named "killer of Moors" (even if the slayer, Saint James — Santiago — happened also to be an Apostle).

Because we were running smoothly and I wanted to try to gain a little on the Rocky Mountain Snow Imperative, Pilotis served up sandwiches while we moved, although I was tempted to stop at St. Marys, as agreeable a town as there is on the Ohio. In the 1830s Alexander Creel, an inconstant man, came down the river on a steamboat, allegedly in the company of the Virgin who appeared at the rail, pointed to shore, and advised (in language that, to my ear, sounds notably uncelestial, although I must confess never to have heard it spoken): "There you behold the site of what will some day be a happy and prosperous city." Creel bought the land in 1834, but perhaps for the same reasons as mine, or maybe having eaten one too many Goonieburgers, he came to doubt the divine flea-in-the-ear. He sold his holdings and moved a couple of miles downstream where he stayed for fifteen years until he learned a county seat was about to be selected, whereupon the Virgo Sapientissima again apparently proffered her presagement; he bought back the site, platted it, and named it after his realty adviser, a better decision, history suggests, than a link with any apostolic swordsmen.

Above Willow Island Lock, Pilotis, scanning downriver with the binoculars, said, "Here it is again," and soon we were behind a boat tiredly trudging the current, and I said over the radio, Prepare to launch torpedoes. There came no response from the *Dry Docktor*, and when we overtook her, no whistle of recognition, only a weary Cap bent over her wheel. Once in the lock together, Pilotis hailed Mr. V—, who simply lifted a weak thumbs-up. We were wayworn too, ever the more so when our exit got us entangled in floaters, and we had to raise the motors to unwind branches and monofilament fishing line. Ten miles farther at Marietta, we entered the muddy Muskingum River and tied up at a small fuel dock. Pilotis jumped off to find us a room in the old rivermen's hotel, the Lafayette, but slipped on the pier, went down hard, and while decumbent yelled, "Goddamnit to hell!" While the day had not been difficult, we felt our thousand miles as if we carried them on our backs, and all I could think to do was get off *Nikawa* and help my friend up.

While I pumped in the gasoline, I noticed a new softball floating in a thick mat of flotsam, so I pulled it out, then another bobbed to the surface, another, and one more. It was as if some unknown sport fish were laying them. When Pilotis returned, I began juggling. Now, I can't juggle even knotted handkerchiefs, let alone softballs, so the spheres were soon hitting me on the noddle, the knees, the foot, and I cried out, "'Umph!' ejaculated the squire." The ludicrousness drew a smile from Pilotis and also a fellow who couldn't believe my incompetent display; he was a coach of women's sports at Marietta College and said the softballs belonged to the team. I turned them over, and he took two tired sailors on a convivial tour of the river town. Slowly we got from beneath the burden of miles, and I wondered how the evening might have gone without such adventitious flotsam.

Enamel Speaks

S PRING WAS IN profusion that morning — its scent along the
avenues of dignified Marietta, its angle of light against the brick
shops, its promise in the gait of citizens on Front Street — but the
season didn't draw us immediately to the river. Instead, we walked the
town, the oldest (they say here) in Ohio, and we found a couple of
conversations, a breakfast, a grocery, a bookshop, all the time my
notepad filling:

— *Child to mother in coffee shop: "Do pearls make oysters hurt?"*
— *A young woman to her friend after stumbling on curb: "I'm not
sure-footed, but I'm not afraid to fall down."*
— *From Francis Galton's 1867* The Art of Travel: *"Neither sleepy nor
deaf men are fit to travel quite alone. It is remarkable how often the
qualities of wakefulness and watchfulness stand every party in good
stead."*

At last, with a small sack of books under my arm, we walked to the
water, boarded *Nikawa,* and followed the Muskingum into the Ohio,
on down past a long run of skinny islands, remnants of the many
before the dams drowned them. Mark Twain said, "A river without
islands is like a woman without hair. She may be good and pure, but
one doesn't fall in love with her very often." Under a beneficent sky we
did the dozen miles to Parkersburg, West Virginia, where years ago
residents had the sense to create on a river hill a picnic garden out of
the former hanging-ground and the linguistic courage to call it Nemesis Park; now, if they would only have the courage to stop certain
dimwits from turning their historic downtown into a parking lot, a
process that makes pointless the big floodwall separating the city

center from its rivers, the mass of concrete giving lower Parkersburg the feel of a penitentiary exercise yard.

A year earlier here, in the quaint Blennerhassett Hotel, I met Enamel, whose name I learned from the grocery store nametag pinned to her shirt. She was forty, of melodious voice, serious, and able to tie a knot in a cherry stem in her mouth using only her tongue, a bar skill she'd learned in her whiskey-sour days. When I asked how her name came about, she corrected me: "It isn't Enamel — it's Enna-*mell.* My grandmother, who couldn't read too good, saw the word on a fancy brooch in a jewelry store and thought it was classy, maybe like Tiffany. It's a good name because I can tell if people know me or not. One gal was claiming to be my friend but making up tales about me, but everyone knew she was lying because she called me Enamel like I came out of a paint can. But I took her boyfriend from her — then we broke up when he started writing the date on dusty furniture. Of course, *he* couldn't ever help clean. He wasn't any good anyway. All's he wanted is you-know-what. And a dust lady."

The Ohio turns directly west at Parkersburg, and two miles along lies the island where a wealthy and eccentric Irish immigrant, Harman Blennerhassett, settled in 1797 to conduct experiments in the natural sciences. After shooting down Alexander Hamilton, Aaron Burr arrived there in 1806 to seek underwriting for his design of setting up an empire somewhere southwest of the lower Mississippi. Convincing Blennerhassett he would be surrounded by a utopia of intellectuals, Burr got the Irishman to join the treasonous plan, and on a dark December night he started down the Ohio to join the conspirators, but President Jefferson learned of the schemery and dispatched militia who caught them near Natchez, Mississippi. The traitors were charged but never tried. Had the plot succeeded, the United States might have been smaller by a third.

Nikawa slipped between green shores, the day happening easily, and Pilotis hummed a strange barcarole just before we entered a section of the Ohio which appeared to lose its urgency to reach the sea; it twisted and bent and bowed, often traveling a curving eight miles to gain only two straight ones. That day we hoped to cover about a hundred river miles, but the crow-flight distance was only about half that. Still, the Ohio, partly from its current, although much hidden in the dam pools, and partly from its sinuousness, gave us proof of its infixed destination, its destiny to lose itself when at last it loses its way in the begetting sea. Its gravity-driven motive moved us powerfully, if blindly, in a way our engines could not, and it seemed we and nature became a single intention, and we were but a small message in a corked bottle thrown to the current, to wash up someday on a far shore. All of this yielded a concord, one strong enough to put Pilotis into a doze I presently interrupted by quoting Francis Galton on the qualities of wakefulness.

When we descended Belleville Lock, I heard my mate singing quietly on the bow, playing the mooring line back and forth, and then we went on through the afternoon with Pilotis sometimes at the wheel, sometimes me, sometimes conversation, sometimes not, but always a contentment in our clement travel; even the drift was benign, pieces of it actually getting out of our way and taking flight as we kept misreading slender, dark cormorants for floating sticks. Then Racine Lock, then around the big northern bend with little Pomeroy, Ohio, perched atop it like a feather in a cap, the late sun casting over it a flaxen light. Because the village opens to the river to show inviting front sides of buildings, we almost hung up the day there, but the pull of the Ohio was greater, and we rolled on a few miles more to Point Pleasant, West Virginia, a place surely named on an afternoon like ours, although in the earliest days of the settlement Henry Clay described it and its excellent setting as "a beautiful woman clad in rags." The first white man known to see the point between the Ohio and Kanawha rivers was Pierre-Joseph de Céloron. In 1749 he came from Lake Erie on the same route as ours to *la belle rivière* to claim it and its tributary country for Louis XV by burying along the Ohio four inscribed lead plates. Incredibly, two of them have turned up, the one at the Point coming to light exactly a century after the Frenchman left it.

I knew of a well-situated bed-and-breakfast there, one with a good river view and near Céloron's hiding spot, so we turned into the Kanawha (river folk pronounce it Kah-NAW) and searched for a tie-up, but we found nothing suitable or even safe, so we went back into the Ohio another four miles to Gallipolis and passed the riverside town square where the citizens remind themselves of the 1878 arrival of yellow fever in the village with a monument made from the broken rocker shaft of the steamboat that brought the disease. We entered silty Chickamauga Creek, bounced over a sunken log, and came upon a quiet little backwater harbor with a gasoline pump and an owner

who let us moor for the night. We had joked the *Dry Docktor* would be
there, and indeed she was, Cap and Mr. V— as mellow as we, a mood
we polished with supper together at a grill across from the river park
where teenagers swarmed Saturday night like a glom of mayflies during a hatch-out.

Along the Track
of the Glaciers

MY FIRST MATE said, "This is the kind of day airline pilots call 'severe clear.' It seems you could jump in and take a swim in that blue sky." We left Gallipolis and made our way around the big loop of river marking out the southernmost tip of Ohio, the first half running nearly cardinal compass points: south, west, south again, then a series of slightly less true courses up the other side of the great bend. The Ohio country between the stretches of river is largely national forest, and the West Virginia shore also is wooded all the way to the bottom of the loop, where industrial Huntington spreads out along the flats.

A fifth of the distance across the continent, we had traveled few leagues not shaped by the last Ice Age and its several glaciations. Moving generally transverse to the flow of ancient snowpacks, we were at that point — as elsewhere — virtually following a sea-to-sea route cut or deformed by great chisels of ice: if you trace over a map of America the southern limits of the last few glaciers, you have a reasonably accurate chart of our entire course. Our passage depended absolutely on water, ancient and modern, frozen and otherwise.

More than any other kind of travel, floating a river means following a natural corridor, for moving water must stay true to the cast of the land, and we liked knowing our way was so primeval and, what's more, that in every mile we were recapitulating human routes of the previous eight thousand or more years. No other form of travel can do that, for no trail, no road, is so old, so primordial, so unchanged in its path. The river, alone in nature, makes its own destination, and we enjoyed feeling that the high-banked Ohio, its course as untransformed as any long river east of the Rockies, was taking us there; not even the locks and dams much altered the perception. In our search for the essence of American water passage, this retrocognition was of the first order.

A strand of ring-billed gulls rose from the smooth surface and skimmed it, and we overtook a line of barges in hopes of getting through Byrd Lock before they arrived, but it wasn't necessary; for our first time, the tender sent us into the auxiliary lock, the one half the length of the twelve-hundred-foot main tank. Even so, *Nikawa* in the chamber was but a cockhorse, and some of the Sunday visitors smiled and waved to us, to give underdogs courage, yet the faces of others betrayed a wistfulness, as if their lives were little more than anchors.

We had a long, slick-water, bridgeless run down to Huntington and its nine-mile shore with Riverfront Park, a greensward that somewhat ameliorates the big ugly floodwall typical of towns on the "new" Ohio. When Huntington, the largest and newest West Virginia city, was about to spring up in 1869 next to the settlement of Guyandotte, a newspaper published a list of attributes the older village offered, and a future citizen of Huntington conceded those advantages but said it would "take a search warrant to find them in the annual crop of dog fennel, popcorn, and empty pint bottles." Soon after, an eastern visitor described Huntington as "a right big little town."

A few miles beyond lies Kenova at the mouth of the Big Sandy River that separates West Virginia from Kentucky. Then, for twenty-five miles, tows pounded the water, and barge terminals and repair facilities, cement plants, refineries, floating harbors stacked with big containers, aerial power cables, and heavy truss bridges lined the banks. It was the kind of place an automobile traveler gets depressingly snagged in, but *Nikawa* bounced over the chopwater and soon had us free again.

I've not said much about towboats and their massive train of barges (the earliest vessels actually towed, that is *pulled*, their loads, but today a more accurate name would be pushboats); I've been silent about how they bulldoze the river for miles, about how we had to keep out of their way, about our necessity to take an oncoming one, sometimes nearly a quarter mile long, on the inside of bends (where the shallows are), so that the violent prop wash and tons of barge swept away from

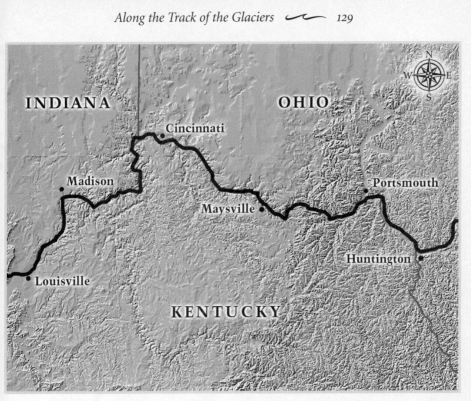

The Ohio, Huntington to Louisville, 295 river miles

our little jug. While I've found captains and pilots to be polite on shore, in a wheelhouse they usually ignored us when we radioed our intention to pass them port or starboard, and when we waved, our arms seemed invisible to them. What the hell, they're the big boys of the river, and they act it; but once out of their sailing line, given the millennia of seniority tiny boats have earned, we refused to accept the river as theirs only. We figured we were doing something they could not do, and we believed our transcontinental quest gave us equal right to passage.

It may have been the several large carp carcasses floating in Greenup Lock that led Pilotis to ask after we exited, "If all the millions of fish were pulled from this river, how much lower would it be?" We'd be dragging sand, I said. "Do you think as much as an inch?" I hoped it might be more because I liked the idea of the fishes helping keep us buoyant, and that in their absence we'd find the way harder, perhaps impossible without banging one gravel bar after another. Pilotis: "Carried across the country on the backs of fishes."

At Portsmouth, the Ohio yields most of its southerly course to run much more directly west for better than a hundred miles; that kind of topographical detail gave us a sense of accomplishment and a small boost to our will to continue — a determination challenged whenever we looked at a map of the United States and saw how much country yet lay before us. At times we talked about explorers, settlers, early travelers, wilderness, of how America perhaps more than any other nation built itself and many of its cherished myths around westering, a concept then and now most evident and the source of the greatest theme in our history: the journey. Westering is only logical from a country whose people all have ancestors from the eastern hemisphere, whose leaders considered Westward ho! a manifest destiny to be executed for the good of humanity — never mind those already dwelling there who sometimes got in the way. The American fate was to drive on to the sea where the sun sets, to take up the land, remake it according to our own images. We, so goes the gospel of our historiography, we descendants of the purported ancient Garden, were foreordained to create a new one. Whether that impulse was noble I leave to others, except to argue that our destiny would look considerably more estimable had our ancestors — and we — conceived the New Eden in terms less those, to keep the biblical context, of Mammon. Whenever I found myself faulting something along the river, I was usually, as I heard a professor once say, "deprecating mercantilistic esurience."

So, that afternoon, on we westered atop the remade Beautiful River to Portsmouth, a town with a first cause deriving from the Ohio itself, born of it, but now making itself into something else, a leopard wanting to become a lion. Portsmouth seemed bent on forgetting, denying, and hiding the river, turning itself into a place where the land voyager cruises up in the family sport utility vehicle, ties to a parking slot, and rafts the aisles of the megamall. I don't intend curmudgeonry toward Portsmouth, for I consider the flatboat as one of the ancestors of the window van. From river rats to mall rats. Nevertheless, a traveler on the Ohio doesn't see the town but rather a high, long, and forbidding concrete floodwall like a medieval rampart; lettering WELCOME across the fortress alleviates nothing, and the huge mural on the city side, while a tour de force, is painted history substituting for the reality of the river beyond.

Below the mouth of the Scioto River (with its tributary Peepee Creek), we came upon the *Docktor,* but there followed no response to our hailing. Five miles farther we found a cove with a good pier, gasoline, and food, and we ceased our run. Twenty minutes later, in limped Cap's boat. We took mooring lines from Mr. V— who looked disheveled and dispirited, and we asked how it had gone, but he only shook his head. When the boat was secure he finally spoke: "This thing has turned into a hell ship." I said to Pilotis, *Beelzebub.*

Later, after attitudes got redressed with a glass of rum, the sanctioned beverage of our fellow voyagers' vessel, we learned they had run afoul of a drifting towboat hawser that wrapped around their propeller and shaft like tentacles of a giant squid and left them dead in the water again. Cap, amazingly, had managed to summon a fleet diver from a towing company, but he was unable to cut through the tangle, and the *Doctor Robert* had to be lifted out of the river by a crane to remove the line. The story struck a chill in us because their ill-luck monkey could jump to our horse, but all I suggested was Cap might swap boats with a worn cruiser tied next to him, the one named *Why-U-Ask.*

From Humdrummery
on down toward Tedium

SLEEPING ABOARD *Nikawa* was a choice between a straitjacket and claustrophobia, the first coming from a mummy bag on a narrow bench where a turn in the night could mean ending up on the pilothouse deck, the other from the cuddy requiring a bent recumbence beneath an overhead resting virtually atop one's brow. Night to night, our only relief was to change places. Still, I liked sleeping aboard, lying snug if nothing else, and listening to the lap of water against the hull and sometimes being rocked easily into a slumber that came quickly but demanded patience in tolerating frequent wakings from cramped muscles or near rolls onto the deck.

When I was home I'd dreamed of the river, but on the river I dreamed of home. That Monday morning, well past sunup, my sleep had me trying to write an article on food, although I couldn't find the precise topic. Then, at last, a brilliant breakthrough: I came up with something! I got the title: "How to Make Theater Air in Used Olive Bottles." I awoke in exhilaration, sat up, hit my head, crawled out of the cuddy, washed, and found my copilot already in the café. I shared the dream, then listened to another from that night: Pilotis browsed in a grocery and avidly read labels on soup cans; on one low-calorie chowder, "Only two servings per teaspoon." I said, Have we been at this river stuff too long?

Filling our fuel tanks before we set out, the young pump girl, hearing of our voyage, said to me, "Oh, God, I want your life!" Had I an urge to savage youthful dreams of a nobler sort than of soup tins or used olive jars, I might have told her what it took each day to earn the good moments. While a river can offer the adventure and romance of slow-moving freight trains you can board almost anywhere to let them take you who-knows-where, it otherwise is demanding, restrictive, exhausting. For every hour of excitement, for each sublime riverscape, there can be three or four hours of humdrum repetition that makes merely staying alert a mental tussle.

Of the twelve hundred books on my home shelves containing accounts of exploration and travel in America, a number are about river journeys. That Monday, as we reached the quarter-way mark of our try at crossing the continent, I realized I would hereafter read them in a new light: those with never a dull moment were suspect, if not mendacious, for to travel a river that is not white water is to go slowly, often drudgingly. One of the reasons the voluminous journals of the Lewis and Clark Expedition have power lies in their honest portrayal of frequent tedium, often conveyed by the simple phrase "we proceeded on." Because moving water is — and I do not overstate this — death waiting, the pilot cannot just put the boat on cruise control, sit back with two fingers on the power-steering wheel, and daydream through a spell of monotony. The river is no blue highway because a river removes reverie. I think that's the reason, at the end of a day on the water, Pilotis and I were more tired than events usually seemed to warrant. Our most reliable and consistent antidote to humdrummery, in other words, was risk, and at every moment it called us, impelled us to heedfulness when nothing else did, even as it wearied us.

My usual remedy for tedium on a highway is to stop and walk a place, but on a river that's harder to do. The Rocky Mountain Snow Imperative aside, many villages called to us, but a landing and tie-up was frequently unwise or impossible, especially so early in the season, with uncertain weather and rising waters keeping docks from going in or being open. We loved the isolation available on a river in spring, something harder to come by in July, but we had to pay for it. In one place the problem could be as simple as an impassable bank of grease-mud lurking with skid demons, or an impenetrable scrub, or in another it might be security. Pilotis had a clear vision of naughty boys covertly undoing our mooring line to watch an unattended *Nikawa* drift downriver, over a dam, onto rocks, under a barge; indeed, a small boat is a difficult thing to secure by any means other than one's presence.

And so it was that day as we passed allurements. Vanceburg, Kentucky, shone in the sun, the brightly red roof of its courthouse against blue sky; and Maysville, as pretty a town as there is on the Ohio, appeared even more inviting, the golden dome of its courthouse gleaming like high justice, steeples like slender fingers beckoning the miserable and fallen, Federal-style orange tin roofs, white antebellum columns, green lawns bright with May, and all of it climbing the narrow river flats for a few hundred feet before the rise became too steep for anything but oaks and hickories at last in full leaf. Here on the rim of the South we had reached midspring through both time and space, and at last we wore short sleeves. Often, where we could not stop I tried to relate memories from my other travels in the place, or Pilotis swept a village with binoculars and concocted a tale of what might be there.

At Ripley, Ohio, the spot Eliza carries her baby to freedom over the river ice-floes in *Uncle Tom's Cabin,* we found that rare combination, a village showing historic and handsome waterfront buildings, a stairway up the slick bank free of floodwalls, and a dock with a little barge café and a sign we thought might be missing letters:

FRI D CH CK N TOD

Said Pilotis, "It could mean Friday Chuck and Todd, whoever they are, will be here, or if the food's German it could mean on Friday they serve chicken and death, but I hope it means Fried Chicken Today." And it did. Chicken Jim cooked up five thousand pounds of barbecued bird a season, but not just then as he tried halfheartedly to clean out the café, a place deeply piled and waiting for either spontaneous combustion or a lawsuit. I estimated the sprucing could take until the river froze over, especially if he continued to use paint and a paintbrush instead of a shovel and broom. A quiet, polite man, he asked where we were coming from, and I said New York City. Expecting Pittsburgh or Wheeling, he stopped in mid-drag on his cigarette and said, "What?" Pilotis nodded, and Jim asked, "Can you do that?" I said, This is the easy side of the Mississippi. "Yes," he said, "I hear the water's rising real good on out west there."

We climbed the terrace to town. Trucks hauled to market cured tobacco, and we walked Main Street in quest of worthy food, but the recommendations required wheels, so we settled for a bland sandwich, a sorry thing compared to what Pilotis might have assembled aboard

Nikawa. Worse, we couldn't find a good conversation; the best I did was overhear a wrinkled gentleman, long a member of the Borrowed Time Club, whose drooping patty melt did not match his erect posture, say to his lady, "Would you make a pudding tonight, plum blossom?" Like an army, I travel on my stomach, and I told Pilotis my only disappointment on our voyage was the frequent unmemorable food we'd had to accept, and Mate asked, "Did you ever consider carrying bikes?" and then answered, "Of course. Where would we put them?" I said, The river giveth and the river taketh away.

Filled but not satisfied, on down the Ohio we went, through its wooded shores, past Augusta, another appealing village with a century-gone aspect, then a line of house trailers disfiguring the north bank for some miles. Meldahl Lock we descended with ease, although Pilotis became intrigued with a floating boat cushion and tried to fish it from the water and would have missed the mooring bitt had I not said, Do you remember talking about tedium and risk this morning? The response, in sarcasm, "Aye, Captain."

Along the nearly thousand miles of the Ohio, perhaps nothing in our generation marks it out more than the regular appearance of big power plants and their high smokestacks leaking into the sky. Many barges haul coal to those places, and even in this day more than half of the deadly mercury released into the air of Ohio and other nearby states comes from yellow smoke like that rising innocuously above us near Meldahl, an effluent that ends up in the water and makes even occasional eating of local fish dangerous for children and pregnant women. Utility companies still are not required to control airborne mercury and a number of other pollutants, and corporate people making a living from the river have shown the same likelihood of changing their ways voluntarily as turnips to sprout feathers.

Then came Point Pleasant, Ohio, birthplace of Ulysses Grant, and we followed a long bend northwest to New Richmond with its historic river hotel, and on around the curve to the bluffs of east Cincinnati where we began searching out a night mooring. Always thinking of ourselves as boatmen (a genderless term) but never boaters, we continually tried to avoid marinas, preferring a more natural experience of finding an inlet or some odd cranny, even in tough tie-up areas at city centers. Much of the bank of Cincinnati is, as it has been since paddlewheel days, given to a sloping stone and concrete landing useless to a small boat, so we motored back and forth in the declining light on water beat up by towboats. At last, near the mouth of the Licking River in Newport, Kentucky, we found a square of quietness on the inside of a big restaurant barge, and I asked permission to stay overnight, taking a chance on security.

As we tightened mooring lines, Pilotis called out, "I can't believe it!" Swimming up to *Nikawa* and eyeing her intently was a beaver. There, under the shadows of skyscrapers and interstate bridges, was the economically preeminent beast of westering America, the creature that drew in most of the first white people, an animal once eradicated from this river through numerous causes, not the least of which was massively polluted water. She dived under the barge where, we learned, she had built a lodge.

We took quarters nearby, showered, and went out but could find none of that peculiar and highly local delectability called Cincinnati chili within foot distance, so we walked back to the River Café and watched the Queen City across the Ohio light up and turn it into a wet and wavery kaleidoscope. Underneath us was a beaver lodge, and I said, I need to be careful — these rivers are starting to make me optimistic.

A History of the Ohio
in Three Words:
Mastodons to Condoms

THE MORNING DOWNPOUR came on so heavy it turned the window glass into a curtain, nothing visible beyond, and the room was still dark an hour after dawn, so I went back to bed — there would be no rivering in that weather. At ten, when the rain eased but didn't cease, we sogged down to the barge café and ate club sandwiches and watched the oldest overnight steamboat on American waters, the *Delta Queen,* arrive and tie up at the Cincinnati landing. Through what was now just dreary air, we saw but couldn't hear the steaming notes of the calliope tootle and warble up to dance the mists, and a man watching next to me said, "She's the most beloved boat in America." He'd taken a six-day trip on her a year earlier, a voyage he chose after somebody told him a person living in daily view of the Ohio as he did should know the differences among a towboat, tugboat, and barge. "I used the words interchangeably, and I've probably seen that river six days out of seven for the past forty years. So I took the *Delta Queen* to learn what the river is really like, because you don't know anything from just crossing on a bridge a dozen times a week. Cincinnati is, or was anyway, a river city. In 1860 that commercial waterfront was six miles long. Today, I'll bet not one person in twenty knows the depth of the channel, the average speed of the current, or who's in charge of the dams. People in Denver go up Pikes Peak. People in Cincinnati try to stay off the Ohio."

We went down to *Nikawa* and found her still tidily tucked in, but the welldeck was just that, a well with two inches of water, so I bailed her, tightened the little canopy, and we struck off into the gloom and passed under Roebling's great suspension bridge of 1856, the noblest on the Ohio. Cincinnati has four nineteenth-century bridges, the most on the river, but the others, all truss spans, lack elegance and romance. From there to the mouth at Cairo, Illinois, the Ohio takes no more long turns northward, content to permit only seven small humps in its passage southwest. The narrow bottoms were full of industry — oil, asphalt, cement, chemicals, coal piles, railyards, transformer stations. It was the kind of place bombardiers draw a bead on in wartime, and the overcast day made things even grimmer, so we motored on in silence. Twenty miles out, *Nikawa* reached several benchmarks at once: the Indiana line, the Central time zone, and the halfway point of the Ohio. As if to dramatize it, the sun broke through and Pilotis said, "I know you've planned the voyage with due process, but sunlight at this very moment? Are we flaunting our powers?" Better that than to speak of our luck, I said.

Lawrenceburg, Indiana, almost two hundred years old like many of the other river towns and villages along there, has an appealing main street which a highway traveler misses because of the bypass and which the Ohio traveler also misses because of the big levee (the 1937 flood still topped it) built on what was once Gamblers' Row, a place of boisterous vice infamous from Pittsburgh to New Orleans. Today things have settled down to a casino boat and whiskey making, legal vices in the minds of certain brow-dripping evangelicals. A half century ago a reporter wrote an anonymous squib about this piece of the Ohio:

> The river banks are peopled with families who live in shacks or house-boats. They raise a small patch of tobacco for their own use, and subsist mainly on catfish and greens, accepting the periodical high waters with philosophic calm. They move up the hills into deserted barns until the water recedes, and then return to their shanties to resume their usual occupation of gazing dispassionately at the river.

The heavy rain and rising water had flushed from the leafy hills much drift and flotsam, mostly the two things of greatest buoyancy, pieces of trees and objects of plastic, but there were also several Emblems of the Ohio — floating automobile tires — as well as less dangerous mats of maple seeds we could churn through. Atop one drifting log sat a pair of migrating terns, wing to wing, doing nothing as is the wont there but gazing dispassionately at the river; even when we passed, they just watched like visitors getting to know the Ohio.

The air warmed, the wind rose, and we moved from glassy water to ripples, the changing conditions more apparent to the ear than the eye: the hull of *Nikawa*, with its sensitivity to the surface of water, conducted sounds like a crystal goblet and registered the river, slicks to slaps, each tinkle and trickle, gurgle and gulp, whack and whomp. *Nikawa* spoke the river, gave it tongue, and said how to proceed as the clattering chattered, nattered, jabbered out a course. Leagues back we'd learned to heed the hull — not that I always remembered — and on that day I moved us along according to my eye only, over the gleaming water toward a western horizon whispering, Hurry, sundown soon, and I obeyed it, even as the wind stiffened, the water rattled, and I began to grouse about conditions. Pilotis tapped the plaque above us and said, "Does Captain wish to proceed as the way opens or just bang us the fuck through?" I throttled down, put in earplugs, followed the sounder to deeper — that is, easier — water where things were better. An exotic scent of marigolds and eucalyptus wafted into the pilothouse, although either odor had to be impossible then. Because we saw no dock out yet, we didn't stop at Rising Sun, Indiana — across the river from Rabbit Hash, Kentucky — although it looked good in the afternoon light and we needed a bracer, maybe a phroso; perhaps somewhere in the village was a relict fountain and an ancient sodaman who knew the secrets of a Tenderfoot Punch (2 ounces rum, 1 tablespoon Nesselrode pudding, grape juice, dash of bitters, shaved ice). Traveling a prairie creates strange hungers, but a river brings on peculiar thirsts.

We went on down, down past the mouth of Big Bone Creek. A mile or two over the hills was a spring where beasts of another age — mastodons, Arctic elephants, three-toed sloths — came to lick salt from the margins and sometimes mired themselves in the bog. Late-eighteenth-century travelers reported heaps of bones embedded or lying about, and people made tent poles from mastodon ribs and footstools of vertebrae, and they carried off souvenir ten-pound molars, ivory tusks the length of two squatty men, femurs as long as one tall woman. Hearing of the incredible prehistoric boneyard in 1805, Thomas Jefferson sent out an expedition to gather a large and representative collection; in the next thirty-five years diggers removed skeletons of twenty elephants and a hundred mastodons to stock American and European museums until the salt lick was all but empty of fossils. By the start of the Civil War the spring was little more than a spa for young ladies "gone into decline," whatever that meant, and obese seniors seeking a cure for adiposity in the sulfurous water. As for the Jeffersonian collection, an unwitting servant ground it into fertilizer. Underneath *Nikawa* now was salt and a saline history from Big Bone Lick.

By the time we reached Patriot, Indiana, we were convinced this stretch of the Ohio was by far the most littered water we'd seen. Except for pockets here and there, from the Atlantic our route had been surprisingly free of floating trash, even the East River, but that section of *la belle rivière* seemed to be a drain where debris from the past five hundred miles came to go down. For about an hour we kept a list, almost everything on it plastic:

> miscellaneous pails up to five gallons (4)
> lard buckets (3)
> milk jug cases (2)
> laundry baskets (2)
> fabric softener bottles (8)
> Thermos bottles (3)
> ice chests (2)
> dock floats (3)
> mounted auto tires (4)
> rubber glove (1)
> prophylactics (2)
> doll heads (3)
> toy autos (2)
> Big Wheel tricycle (1)
> football helmet (1)
> balls, you name the sport (17)
> Playtex tampon applicators (gobs)
> motor oil quarts (galore)
> bleach jugs (more than galore)
> juice and sodapop bottles (a gazillion)
> disposable lighters (whatever happened to Zippos
>   guaranteed for life?)
> cigarette filter tips (now we're talking depressing)

We reasoned that few of these things had been tossed directly into the river, but rather most had washed into it from places some distance off the Ohio, probably the preponderance from the old Appalachian method of disposal I call OTHOOS — over the hill, out of sight. The rafts of cigarette filters came from people pitching butts out car windows onto highways and town streets where rain washed them down creeks. What Pilotis called "crotch rot," tampon applicators and condoms, came from those who would, were it possible, flush their broken Hoovers and Maytags down the toilet.

When we got into Markland Lock — the disharmonic noise of this one was excerpts from a John Cage score — I commented over the radio about the trash, and the tender said, "It's okay — Ohio Clean Sweep people will be out next weekend." The Sweep is a noble annual effort by volunteers to pick the shores clean, but as in all things, a new attitude is the only lasting solution: to educate people so they connect spiritually with rivers is to change what goes over the hill, onto the street, down the toilet. Pilotis proposed that all commodes be imprinted PLEASE CONSIDER THOSE ON THE OTHER END — US. I said, To a Zen Buddhist, flushing is a spiritual act.

Off to starboard lay Vevay (pronounced VEE-vee), an Indiana village founded by Swiss who once made wine from rootstock brought from the Cape of Good Hope but gave it up when they realized a bushel of potatoes — requiring only planting and harvesting — traded for as much as a demijohn of their claret-like red. Thinking of phrosos (forgotten), Vevay vino (gone), or water one could drink straight from the Ohio (unwise), I told Pilotis we ought to storm onto the courthouse lawn and do what J. D. Salinger said Lincoln should have done at Gettysburg: simply stand up and shake a fist at a self-destructive people.

Holding the Indiana WPA *Guide* and ready to read aloud, Pilotis said, "Here's a Vevay story to quell your dudgeon, another sad tale but of a different sort, one that sounds like the seed of a novel. There was a woman here, Mary Wright, an ironic name as you'll see, who owned a fine Clementi piano. She was, and I quote, 'the daughter of an aristocratic but impoverished English family that came to this country in 1817 and settled on a land grant near Vevay. Deserted by her English fiancé, she lived bewildered and heartbroken in this wild, rough country. An accomplished musician, she found outlet for her grief and loneliness in weekly concerts she gave for the pioneer folk of the community. On each occasion she descended the ladder from the second floor of her father's rough log cabin, attired in court dress and jewels, and with a gracious bow seated herself at the piano and played her entire repertoire. Then without a word she would retire to her second-storey room, and the guests would quietly depart. These concerts continued for forty years without the piano ever being tuned, or the introduction of a new composition. The dress grew faded and the jewels tarnished, but the same dignified procedure endured year after year. The only time Mary Wright ever left the house was to wander alone in the moonlight. She was found dead in her room in 1874, at the age of eighty-two.'"

And then happened a peculiarity, as if an omen for us to divine: a rough-winged swallow flittered toward *Nikawa* and alighted on the pulpit rail, looked at us, turned to peer down the river, rode a mile, then was gone, and Pilotis said, "One more thing you couldn't put in a good novel."

The mouth of the Kentucky is at Carrolton; for a river nearly three hundred miles long, it enters modestly, slipping quietly from narrow shores suggesting the perpendicular cuts it makes through the limestone country it drains.

Twelve miles farther we found a dock alongside an eatery and bar atop an old barge at Madison, Indiana, and we strolled up to town in the humid air, past the women's softball game, up to the long and historically remarkable Main Street lined with pre- and turn-of-the-century buildings, several peeled of later obtrusive façades and restored to integrity, buildings that made us want to stay. So we walked a block off Main and came across a big antebellum house, now a bed-and-breakfast, and Pilotis went inside to inquire, but there was no room. The proprietor called another place and found a vacancy some distance away and a long hoof up the bluff road.

Not wanting to start out, I fell into conversation with a carpenter working on the house. I spoke of the trash in the Ohio, and he said, "Don't tell me. I'm a bank walker. For twenty-five years I've walked both sides of the Ohio, forty miles of it, looking for Indian artifacts. That river is an interstate of floating things. I saw an outhouse in a tree once. The trash sorts itself out into levels. Fishing lures and bobbers here, bleach bottles higher, tampon inserters above that. You know, like birds of a feather. When a sewage treatment plant overflows, the riverbanks are full of things you'd hope to see somewhere else."

The carpenter, Patrick Kelly, a tall and angular Ichabod Crane of a fellow with a kindly and generous demeanor who tidily flicked his cigarette ashes into his shirt pocket, found his first arrowhead when he was eleven and had stopped along a corn field to pee: there, wondrously at his feet, the point lay. In the following thirty-one years he'd found hundreds more Indian artifacts — stone knives, drills, axes, scrapers, a few pipes — as well as recent coins ("They get recycled fast") and one gold watch, its interior rusted into a blob ("The case disappeared at the same time as the first Missus Kelly"). To help defray his young son's college education, he hoped eventually to sell the collection and the careful cards he kept on each find.

I asked whether he knew about the cabin site of Harlan Hubbard, the Kentucky artist who in 1944 salvaged yellow-pine timbers and planks from an old riverside building and assembled an ark he and his wife floated down to New Orleans, a voyage Hubbard described in his book *Shantyboat*. Later, after they left the bayous and returned to the middle Ohio, the couple built along the river a cabin out of rocks and trees, an experience he wrote about in *Payne Hollow*. Hubbard interested me because his undertakings and books are so intensely American: a river journey, turning a piece of woods into a house, finding a tenable existence between wilderness and civilization. I told Kelly about *Afloat on the Ohio*, Reuben Gold Thwaites's account of an 1894 voyage, one of the good American river narratives.

Our conversation went on long enough for him to offer us a lift up the bluff, a winding climb that seemed to go higher than the ridge itself, up to the Cliff House, an 1885 brick and portico mansion named by James Whitcomb Riley, the Hoosier poet, who slept there and gave a reading in the parlor. Now surrounded by ferns and big trees, the place had been hit by a tornado a couple of decades earlier, but the damage inspired renovation. Inside, in room after wallpapered room, were elaborations: marble fireplaces, beveled-glass fanlights, gilded mirrors, a grandfather clock, candelabra, oil lamps, two pianos, a foot organ, a breakfront carved with stringers of trout and a brace of doves, a wooden deer-head supporting a whatnot shelf, a dining table set with sterling silver napkin-rings depicting a menagerie of species. Our second-floor bedroom gave a long view down the Ohio beyond the roofs and spires of Madison. Near the window was an antique baby crib holding a doll, its face an unearthly pallor, its eyes evaporated; the thing looked like toy death. Our host said, "Somehow, some way, that doll's head comes off in the night." It'll be nice to have it in the room, I said, and she took me for a man without sarcasm.

When Kelly hauled us back down the bluff to Main Street, he told of the open construction ditch he'd noticed at the old river landing in Vevay. He said, "If I see a hole, I jump in to look around because I don't ever dig, and in that one I found this thing stuck in the side, six feet down." He handed me a small, much worn coin with a hole drilled through, apparently to accommodate a chain or thong. "What do you make of it?" I looked closely and, although some of the legend was gone, I could read CAROLUS IV and make out what seemed a Spanish coat of arms. I guessed it was Charles IV of Spain, king when Europeans started floating down the Ohio. "Take it," he said. "Write me if you learn any more." (It proved to be a fifty-centimos piece minted between 1788 and 1808 and quite possibly worn as a medal by an Indian.) "I can't make a step along those riverbanks without wondering what's under my feet. That's where the past lives, you know, underneath. In 1972 I found a broken piece, probably a knife, I mean an Indian stone knife, the kind people would call a spear point. Twenty years later — I couldn't believe it — I found the other half. When I matched the pieces together, the blade was almost five inches long. Broken pieces I call heartbreakers, but that one was a lifetime maker."

Before Kelly left, he directed us to an excellent meal I can't describe because the amiable café owner, whom I also can't describe, joined us for an hour or more and gave disquisitions on his life, philosophies, and plutological theories, saying things like, "I just married six days ago. A perfect woman. But it won't last." You know that already? "Of course. I'm a skirt chaser." That can endanger things, I said. "I go down to the river almost every day to clear my mind, get some tranquillity."

After the café man returned us to the ridgetop and we were upstairs, Pilotis said, "Add that to the list of ways we use our rivers: purification of skirt chasers. What are you going to do with that conversation?" Save it for my novel.

The bluff caught the high night wind and moved the curtains into wandering shadows that crossed the room back and forth, back and forth, and they whispered from the dim corners where they went to hide when the currents ceased; then the air stirred, and out they came again to slip over the old crib, ruffle the coverlet, caress the pallid, blind head, and I slept deeply until three. Suddenly I sat bolt upright in bed. Pilotis, alarmed, called out, "What?"

Listen, I whispered, there's something coming across the room. A scratching like toenails, tiny claws over the oak floor, stopping, starting, making for the crib. Dry dragging, scrabbling, something small, sinister.

"Cut it out," Pilotis hissed. I struggled to find the light. In the brightness, through the bathroom window, a breeze scattered dead leaves across the room. "Put that nefarious crib out in the hall." You put it out, I said. Neither of us did. After all, we were adults, scorners of phantasmagoria.

A River Coughed Up
from Hell

AFTER A BRIEF STORM passed over to leave blue sky and let us get on down to the river, we heard the weather might turn again, so we set off to keep from losing altogether the improved day. A rainbow, intensely colored but flattened as if stepped on, lay over Madison when we looked back, and Pilotis sang some ditty, commented that the Corps of Engineer charts for this lower half of the Ohio were far better than those for the upper portion, sang again. I sat happily at the wheel and for the hundredth time delighted in simply steering our course, and I spoke of how I was still almost incredulous the voyage was happening after I imagined it for so many years, and Pilotis said, "A journey long dreamed is the greatest one — even if you don't reach the destination." I answered that I wasn't ready even to contemplate not getting to the Pacific. "Maybe you should." I know this, I said, I disappoint myself most when I betray my dreams. "Failure isn't betrayal." In this instance it is.

We ran the gentle Ohio, and I offered that it was the longest river in America to have such regularity in the rise of its banks, shores so uniformly distant, its breadth at Pittsburgh only somewhat less than at the mouth. It was a watercourse European explorers could comprehend, unlike a Missouri, that quintessential big American river with a deception around every bend, a wile behind each towhead, a sleight under every bar, the one Mark Twain called "villainous." When Pilotis took the wheel from time to time, I often went to the welldeck and stood watching the Ohio fall behind, our motors pushing us toward Oregon, and those moments never failed to inspire me.

Pilotis carried small vials of ginseng made from the root of the wild panax, supposedly taken from the Changpai Mountains in Manchuria, mixed with royal jelly and water, a solution to impart vigor. That day, I felt the need of a roborant after my ghost-ridden night, and I swigged down two doses and, like Dr. Jekyll, waited for transformation, but all that changed was the day. A swarthy sky crept up from behind, crawled up our wake, an eastern darkness that increased at unnatural speed, and the wind began to pick up the river, throwing it, turning it back like a thin blanket, and shredding it and pitching the tatters against the bow, then over it and onto the windows. The noise of the hull against the water increased, and Pilotis asked, "Earplug time?" and I said, No — there's something different about this turbulence — we need to keep listening. "Mostly what I'm hearing is swearing."

We banged on through the worsening. Pilotis radioed an approaching tow to ask about the weather, but the boat refused to respond; when we overtook another, again came silence. From the weather band we got this: *Tornado watch / Possibility of large hail / Damaging thunderstorms / Dangerous lightning / Until eleven P.M.* The nouns were alarming and the adjectives worse.

I tried to keep in the lee of the hills as the storm began to run the river, and the chop turned to three-foot swells, and we crested and dropped, but neither of us mentioned Lake Erie. Pilotis said, "There's a fortune waiting for the guy who invents boat shock-absorbers." The foudroyant sky overtook us, and bolts began spiking the horizon, each one seeming to zap down closer, and again we could hardly hear each other. We both kept eyeing the steel bow-rail sticking up into the electrified weather. I yelled, Find us a creek! A cove! We've got to get the hell off this river!

But there was nothing, and we were slamming harder, and the clouds were tornado black. I shouted, Find something on that goddamn chart! Pilotis held it up to show me the most uncreeked shoreline I'd ever seen, so on we thrashed, and the Pacific seemed very far away, quite beyond the thrust of our feeble motors and our pummeled hull. The interval between thunderbolt and thunder became briefer, and the river turned to an evil yellowy black like something coughed up from Hell.

Try the radio again! I called out. An obliterated reception gave us answer. We came around a broad bend, and I asked, What's that off the port bow? "You're not going up that sonofabitch, are you? It's a mudhole!" But I turned and entered the mouth of a twisting creek, and the thundergusts cracked over us, but we were no longer the highest thing within two hundred yards, and the muddy water was quiet. We came to a strand of docks, and I pulled up to one where we put out secure spring lines to hold *Nikawa* tight against the wind should it sweep down into the hollow. On a slope above, a flag stood straight out from the pole as if wooden.

"Skipper, that cruise loosened my fillings," Pilotis said as two domestic geese swam up to hiss and snap at me, miniature versions of the weather. "Appease the darlings of the river gods." I offered the birds some bread which they gulped between snaps and hisses. We'd made only twenty-nine miles, but we didn't care: now we had time to write in our logbooks, eat a cold supper, sit back safely in harbor, and perhaps let the storm rock us to sleep. I went up the hill to arrange for the dock, and the lady said, "Oh, heavens. I couldn't charge you in weather like this." I said, Ma'am, you should charge us for saving our lives. She smiled. "And how much would you pay for that?"

A Necessity of
Topography and Heart

NOT LONG AFTER DAWN, when I went to the welldeck to dip up a basin of water for washing hands, Pilotis appeared and, as if addressing no one, said, "Why is a creek like a dog?" And then, stretching, answered, "Because you don't know where it's been." I knew where my hands had been — cleaning the boat — and I sudsed away shamelessly. Eating little, we shoved off early into the overcast but stormless morning, the river quiet, and soon we passed the old Louisville waterworks, its minaret one of the distinctive landmarks on the Ohio. Across at Jeffersonville, Indiana, a boat-building town for more than a century and a half, the *City of Evansville*, a floating casino, was about ready to slide down the ways.

Louisville is where it is because the Falls of the Ohio, once the only significant natural impediment within a thousand miles, are where they are. The broad ledge, while not high, was just enough to stop steamboats and necessitate that cargo be hauled overland to a vessel on the other side; around that simple portage of goods, the city grew. During high water, paddlewheelers could execute a thrilling ride through the falls to avoid the haulage, and one nineteenth-century writer reported the flooding river sweeping houses over, occupants crying out from windows and rooftops. McAlpine Dam sits upon much of the ledge now, but near the north side, the base of the Falls of the Ohio is still visible at low water, and from the limestone paleontologists have found a large fossil bed, an album of ancient sea creatures long gone before the Ohio made its first run over the rocks.

After being blown off the river the day before, we were hoping to have a good run that Thursday, but the McAlpine Lock operator was a man who neither moved us along nor explained over the radio why he made us tie to the approach wall for half an hour. Like many of the lockmen on the Ohio, he refused to give any information, and my attempt to interest him in our long voyage ended with his silence quieter than Rocky Mountain snowmelt. So there we sat, both locks empty of boats. Finally the gates opened, we entered, the gates closed, and — we waited some more. Eventually we began a slow descent, but four feet down the water stopped moving and we sat again. Then we started back up. Pilotis spoke my irrational concern: "Did you violate some ordinance? Are they going to call us over?" Had I left the radio on while we grumbled about McAlpine operators? Then the upstream gates reopened, and I was sure we were going to get some directive. It was as if I'd just glanced in a rearview mirror and seen flashing red and blue lights. Pilotis went aft with the binoculars to look upriver for a police boat, then called out in annoyance, "Oh, good god!"

I went back, took the glasses, and there slogging up was — what else? The *Docktor*. We were being held up for her. She came in and took a bitt behind us, and after another delay we started the descent once more, and we talked stern to bow. Cap said, "It's been raining to the west. That damn Missouri River of yours is starting to flood again. Trees, docks, all hell's coming down into the Mississippi." I said, For a minute there I thought you had bad news. "I don't think we'll try it," he said. "Current ten to fifteen miles an hour against us. And the drift. Waterfronts are under. Way too much risk." Hell, I said, there's only twenty-five hundred miles of it.

An hour and a half later we were at last free of the infernal McAlpine Lock and could skim down the pebbled river as if we were a water strider, and Pilotis said, "So that flooding, what do you think?" I shrugged. "I know this — you can't always go where you want when you want." But on this voyage, I answered, to go where we want, we have to go *when* we want. "So then, did you put up that 'Proceed as the way opens' just to mock yourself?" I said, The only way to test the waters is to get out on the waters, and, as you know, most of the time it's too late to turn back when you understand you should turn back. Two years ago the Missouri flooded for half a year. "And what's six months against your life?" Pilotis said. This voyage *is* my life — I can't

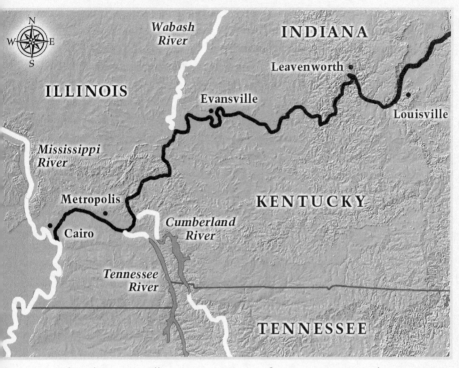

The Ohio, Louisville to Mississippi Confluence, 378 river miles

get along from here without getting to the other side of the country —
it's a necessity of topography and heart — you know what's been happening in my life — I've put everything into this voyage — my land-
ward life resumes at the Pacific Ocean. "Skipper, you sound like Meriwether Lewis." I said, Sometimes all you can do is commit to the flood
and believe yourself lucky.

The Ohio clicked under the hull, water of happy texture, and we
were finding the good run we'd wanted, but of course on the river all
things sooner or later come into balance, and our counterweight just
then was gasoline tanks nearing empty. Below the reach of Louisville industry, we passed some shoreside houses, new places, then we
were again between hills rising from a narrow bench that opened every
so often to tilled plots atop eight-foot-high earthen banks. We found
no fuel at West Point, Kentucky, and nothing at Brandenburg sixteen miles farther. From there the Ohio takes to meandering through

sparsely populated country where horseshoe bends and oxbows make it run an errant seven or eight miles to gain only twelve hundred feet westward. The river turned rough and drift beset us, so we had to slow down here, weave around floaters there, all of it killing fuel economy, and twice we had to stop to clean the props of branches, but the twisting green hills gave recompense in their rumpled sublimity.

About every twenty minutes, *Nikawa* encountered tows moving coal, their big wakes banging us. The fuel-gauge needles kept dropping, and Pilotis said, "If we go dead in the water, what's the drill when a tow comes on? What do we do to keep from getting sucked under those barges or minced in the propellers?" If one engine stops, we'll use the last gas in the other to run to shore. "And if the shore is impossible?" Look at it this way, I said, worrying about gas keeps our minds off floods.

Before the Ohio was engineered into dams and pools, it was, although not a particularly rocky river, full of sandbars, islands with blind and tricky chutes and channels, and the usual obstructions of snags. Published maps were little more than sketches, and many travelers, struggling with burdensome flatboats, relied on verbal charts like Samuel Cummings's *The Western Pilot;* typical instructions from the 1847 edition:

> Two miles below N. Albany, will be seen in low water, a bar on the left, which will drive you over to the right, above a white house, on the Indiana side, you must keep the right shore until you get near Yellow Wilson's, or a large brick house that formerly belonged to him, then incline to the left, and keep down until opposite the left-hand point, called Hughes's Bar. Then if you run the lower channel, make a long crossing for a clearing with a white house on the right side. If the upper channel is taken, run square in for a cluster of trees about 250 yards above the house, then keep nearest to the right-hand shore until you reach the point below on the right.

We wore on through the gray day, deeper into the meanders where the banks were too high to let us see potential salvation like a road or a farm. Said Pilotis, "We've got one small chance for gas at Leavenworth. After that, there's nothing for fifty miles." *Nikawa* doesn't have fifty miles in her, I replied. Pilotis put the chart down wearily. "Why is this never easy?" Because this is America, I said. I was thinking that we often fail to understand how wild this land is even today, sometimes mistaking the ruining of wilderness as a subduing of it.

Pilotis spotted a little dock under a steep bank on the Indiana side, turned the field glasses on it, studied it, and I said, Yes? "Can't tell yet." Now? "Not yet." You know what I want to hear. "It might be. Give me a few more yards. Could be." Don't disappoint me, Mate. "Looks good." I'm starting to get happy. "Oh, god. I think it's a barrel. Damnit! It's a goddamn red barrel!" Get out your hiking boots. "Hold on. I think behind the barrel there's a gas pump!"

And indeed there was a pump, a locked one with no one around anywhere. I said, We're here to stay till we get the key. "What if the storage tank's empty? Or the pump's broken?" We climbed the long stair up the clay bank to a trailer sitting in a space cleared in the woods. No one there either, so we wandered on to a road and followed it into the remains of old Leavenworth, a settlement severely set back by the great flood of 1937. Only a few closed-up, weathered buildings were still there, and in the cinereous weather we found not a soul. If you've seen one of those movies where a couple of survivors of some Armageddon come up above ground to discover only screen doors banging in the lonely wind, cobwebs long empty of life, and dust whispering about, then you know how Leavenworth was. We walked on, turning toward the river again, and near the edge we came to The Dock, not the kind we wanted, but a homely café. Inexplicably, it was open.

The cook stepped from the kitchen to see who the hell had wandered in. "Off the river?" she said. We sat at the counter in front of a large refrigerator with a hand-lettered sign punctuated with equal signs as if the phrases were equations:

NO = VULGAR = LANGUAGE
WATCH = YOUR = MOUTH

Pilotis warned a look at me although I hadn't said a word. We thought ourselves and the cook the only ones about, but then from a side room we heard a rough, threatening Appalachian voice: "Weasel's gonna eat up your liver," and a child began to whimper. The cook saw our expressions, and she said, "That's her mom = The kid ordered chicken livers = Weasel's her dog."

The gasoline man wouldn't be home till nightfall, so we settled in against the afternoon and ordered a plate of fried fiddlers (whole catfish), hush puppies, slaw, and potato salad. In Italy, country *food* is taken seriously, but in America, country *eating* is the serious thing, and we honored the custom, all the time in hopes someone would enter and get curious about two marooned sailors. At last the café owner, Peggy Apple, a tall woman in her sixties, walked up, asked the question we wanted — how we came to be there — and our telling of the river miles got her interest, then her sympathy, and she offered to drive up the highway for gasoline while we finished our fiddlers. Although she was able to return with only ten gallons, I figured it enough to get us the sixty miles to Cannelton.

We took *Nikawa* on around the meanders, past what had to be the fifth or sixth Knob Creek we'd seen in the last couple of days. The twists in the Ohio made for a weird compass: Kentucky lay south of us as it had since the state line, but then it went north, then east, then west, and south again, yet always it lay on our port side. Finally the river straightened to run a course absolutely due south, made a broad turn west, and again assumed a perfect 180-degree heading.

Once when I was near here, I met an old fellow of some charm, a teller of tales from the twenties; at the end of our first conversation, he gave me his card:

> VYISDER ZOMENIMOR
>
> ORZIZZAZZIS,
> ZANZERIS, ORZIZ.

I looked at it and said I thought his name was Hiram Hiller. He broke into laughter. "And *I* thought you could read."

Pilotis figured a good overnight stop would be Stephensport or Cloverport, Kentucky, but we found no suitable mooring, so we ran on, on over a stretch of broadly spaced swells with smooth backs that gave us a carnival ride again, but this one was a gentle carousel horse that took us up and down along the shores of Breckinridge County, Kentucky, where the citizens seemed bent on paving the riverbank with discarded kitchen and laundry room appliances mortared together with plastic flotsam.

We turned into Deer Creek, stopped to make sure we could pass beneath the small highway bridge — *Nikawa* did so by three inches — and there upstream we lay to. In spite of the hindrances, we'd come 132 river miles (only half of that mileage directly west), our longest run yet. We hitched a lift a few miles down to Cannelton, the old steamboat-coal town, and took quarters in the Castlebury Inn, once an 1867 commercial building. After washing up, we walked a mile to a good salad bar, talked about floods, and toasted to surviving another river day. While I was waiting for a pass at the hot peppers and green olives, a young man said to his wife, "That makes no sense, honey. Why are you doing that?" She smiled at him and said, "Because shut up, that's why! I'm a girl."

Nekked and
Without No Posies

THE YOUNG WOMAN, a seller of caskets, found southern Indiana good country. "Lots of old people here. It's almost ideal demographics." Pilotis asked whether she ever found her work depressing. "I get equibalance from my other line, homeopathic remedies." Her system sounded sure-fire to me: if the root extracts and natural tonics failed, one had the comfort of that coffin at hand. She said to me, "Cynicism is a poison, bad for the brain cells."

Our host drove us up the road to Deer Creek with a stop at Lafayette Spring where water gurgled deep within a long, dark cleft in an eroded sandstone outcrop before emerging to roll a few yards down into the Ohio. Lafayette himself washed ashore there when the steamboat he was aboard struck a snag and sank in 1825; in the river the aged nobleman left his baggage, carriage, and, supposedly, eight thousand dollars in gold. Near that spring Abraham Lincoln and his parents entered Indiana from Kentucky on the way to a new homesite in the woods, an event commemorated by a bronze plate bolted to the rock: LINCOLN — HUMBLE — HOMELY — LONELY — GIFTED — GREAT. That peculiar laud somehow reminded me of Lincoln's joke about the man tarred and feathered and ridden out of town on a rail, who replied when asked how he liked it, "If it wasn't for the honor of the thing, I'd rather walk."

The kind of day we'd longed for since setting out fifteen hundred miles ago finally began to happen, although I first thought things were shaping up in the more usual way of weather: challenge, alarm, weariness. The clouds had lifted, but now the sky was saffron from sulfurous coal smoke, the air botched with stink from a pulp mill, and the river yellow-brown like an Appalachian dustyard dog. When we radioed our request to descend the Cannelton Lock, the operator told me a newsman had heard of our approach and was trying to hunt us down. I told him to forget he'd seen *Nikawa*.

An upriver-bound tow, ready to enter the lock, called to ask us to pass him on a two-whistle — that is, to his port — so our diminutive wake would not push him against the bank. That our dory could move anything so massive was indication of the instability of the river road. Beyond the lock the water was as quiet as if in a bottle, and we ran past Tell City, another Swiss town, this one with a floodwall and an arrow-pierced apple painted large on it.

The bottomlands became wide enough to give industry sprawl space, and the entering streams bore names like Lead Creek, Muddy Gut, Big Slough; it was an area for a swift and unhindered run among hills dwindling to a mere rolling terrain as we neared the valley of the Mississippi. I propped back at the wheel, took off my shoes, and steered with my stockinged feet, a stunt to rouse Pilotis who seemed to be waiting for the next perturbation.

The Anderson River, a name my mate thought one of the least interesting in the country, entered at Troy, Indiana, about where seventeen-year-old Abe Lincoln built a small scow to take travelers out to midstream to board passing paddlewheelers. A Kentucky boatman hailed the boy into court for operating a ferry without a license, but Abe argued his scow didn't cross the river, so it wasn't actually a ferry and therefore needed no license; the judge agreed, a decision less important than the suit itself, which introduced Lincoln to the law. In that way, the Ohio helped make a President. Farther on downriver, at Rockport, Indiana, Abe hired out at nineteen to a flatboat bound for the lower Mississippi, a tour that revealed to him the vast magnificence of American landscape and the pustulant shame of slavery. It was also in Rockport that he met John Pitcher, an attorney who opened his exceptional library to Lincoln, books that would return later dividends to the nation through the eloquence of addresses, proclamations, stories, utterances.

Pilotis suggested a stop in Owensboro, Kentucky, so we could walk to a lunch spot I'd been talking about, but the rising river apparently interfered with getting docks into the water because we saw no safe place to tie up. A year earlier in that luncheonette I'd met a man, now thickset but as a boy, said he, "skinnier than a tobacco stob." He'd not had a lucky life, but he'd been in jail just once. "I was bringen in hay bales and got the truck mired down in a wet field. Hell, I was nearly out of it onto the road too. I was in a hurry to see my wife — we was separated because she said I didn't keep my word or take things serious. God omighty! I had to get out of that slick fast and be on time. So I took off my overhalls and put them under one tire. All I had for the othern was my union suit, so I put it under too. Except for my boots and wedden ring, I was as nekked as man can be, but I drove her out. I wanted Mary to see I'd turned over a new leaf, so I took her some flars. I didn't have anywhere to buy them so I borried some off a fresh grave. Missus Chalmerses oldest boy, I believe it was. I didn't borry them all. They was big ol gladiolas. Then, hell, somebody come aholleren after me, but I got away. Being nekked was pretty nippy — and, a course, I was tense about visiten Mary like I was, but there weren't time to get clothes. So I come to take a couple of swigs on my bottle. Maybe it was three or four, just to ward off the cold. Anyway, when I got to her place and run up on her porch, I held them gladiolas in front of me. Thank god they wasn't roses. When I give her the flars — well, you can see how things was out in the open then. She looked down and said, 'Howard, you ain't never gonna change!' and she throwed them gladiolas at me. I went to whinen and beggen through the door to hear me out, when up comes a deputy, and he says, 'Hello there, neighbor. Where's your britches?' And I told him out in Peck's field, and he says, 'Well, I believe you, neighbor, but I'm agonna have to take you in for stealen off a dead man.' I said, 'I cain't go to jail like this!' 'Well then, neighbor,' he says, 'you'd better gather them posies up again.' Hell, they wasn't posies. Goddamnit, they fined me twelve dollars for stealen and six dollars for public nekkedness. I loved that woman, but I never could do anything right. When it come to her, I was just snake-bit."

Downstream from Owensboro, we entered a run among several slender islands, each a couple of miles long and giving a sense of the old Ohio and a choice of ways down through back chutes, but when the islands fell behind, the river was again just an expanse in the flatlands. More than any other mode of travel, rivering enforces a living in the present where the moment is nearly all, for to think too much about tomorrow or yesterday is to slip into a distraction that can endanger the boat. We had no wind, saw no tows, so I shut *Nikawa* down and let her drift, and Pilotis laid out a lunch of mozzarella, pumpernickel, roasted peppers, half-sour pickles, Kalamata olives, and a bottle of good cabernet. We sat at the navigation table, repast before us, and floated along at two miles an hour. I began figuring. Could we continue this speed day and night, traveling not on our terms but entirely those of the river, we'd reach the Pacific almost at the same time we were working for. I said so. "Sure, but for that thing called gravity — we're about to go contrary to it." Pilotis was correct. Tomorrow the tilt of the continent would be against us for almost three thousand miles before we might find this kind of ease again. But for now the Ohio carried us, demanding only buoyancy, and during that hour we went exactly as went the river.

I talked of the previous night when I tried to get to sleep in the hotel but succumbed to a fierce case of doubt, concerns that now seemed ludicrous as we sat idly on the silent and hasteless river, nothing more required than sipping a California red, all the while floating west. Said Pilotis, "The river's a clever sonofabitch. It'll make us pay for every minute of this." I said, And the price of life is death. So we toasted the old sonofabitch. Then it was time again to get behind the wheel and maneuver around Scuffletown Island and up to Newburgh Lock. We'd had our moment.

The outreaches of the river town of Newburgh, Indiana, gave us a ridge of large, recent houses and then, farther along, in floodlands, a string of trailers and shacks sitting atop twelve-foot posts, their bases plastered with waterborne trash. Seven miles below the Green River, we found a dock off the Ohio near Evansville, tied *Nikawa* in, and walked toward the city. On the big levee we came upon a middle-aged man dressed in a white suit and silver silk tie, sitting cross-legged and looking intently at the river. He glanced up and asked me, "Are you with the Postal Service?" I was wearing an Army surplus shirt, and over my shoulder was the satchel for my logbook. No, I said, but we're crossing the country at about the speed of a penny postcard. He said, "Look out there," and waved toward the Ohio. "Isn't it beautiful? Trees and nothing else. Greenery. Do you know Evansville is the only city in America with no other city on the opposite side of a big river?" I named a couple of others. Trying to rise, he struggled but was unable to get up. He was drunk.

When we reached downtown, we went to the sixth-floor bar of a hotel affording a lovely vista of the seven-mile-long finger the Ohio points at Evansville, and sat through the golden hour with beverages and watched the gleaming water lose the sunset. Pilotis said, "There's not another person up here so much as even glancing at the river. Only a drunk has the eyes to see it."

Down on the waterfront, the Ohio Ribber Barbecue Cook-Off was under way, and the evening air was savory with hickory and mesquite smoke, sauces and grilling meats, voices speaking of cookery. From five states they had pulled their big metal ovens fashioned from fifty-gallon drums, propane tanks, home-heating-oil tanks, a World War Two bomb container, and one from a boyhood-home coal furnace. Each carried a banner: OINK, CACKLE, AND MOO. SQUEAL OF FORTUNE. IF YOU HAVE A BUTT, WE'LL SMOKE IT.

Everyone had sold out of cackle, so we took some moo on bread, a moist brisket in a sauce that disappeared to leave only the flavor of hickoried meat, and we finished things with a plate of fried Vidalia onion rings. Then we walked around the heart of Evansville, once a lively spot where the Wabash and Erie Canal joined the Ohio, now turned barren and boring by so-called urban renewal — that is, parking lots — a place conceived by the sort of city planners whose most important design tool is a headache ball. Except for the old courthouse and post office, the town center was full of architecture memorable for its shoddy temporariness, a congelation of sameness, an obliviation of time-earned character, a grid to get away from, which indeed the people had done so they could go down to the fecund riverbank with the eccentric and vernacular cookers and ovens, down where traditions lived and histories clearly continued, where city engineers seem never to have walked.

Eyeless Fish with Eight Tails

A THUNDERSTORM had come in the night and rattled the river and razed trees along it; then a following fog, like a cool hand across a furrowed brow, smoothed the water, but visibility was poor as if we wore steamed-over spectacles. Sweeping up insects, martins and swallows sliced across our bow; there were many of the birds, and for hours they beat through the mist, and I could imagine their narrow wings fanning the air to clarity, but we still struggled to see the distant bends. Blown-down cottonwoods lay slanting off the banks into the muddied water, limbs broken, bark shattered, their leaves not yet withering. Then the wind rose, not strong, just enough to put athwart our course some shallow troughs that hid the storm rummage, logs splintered to wicked sharpness lying darkly half submerged like alligators. We could do little but go slowly, banging into those we failed to dodge. It was a morning of clunks and swerves.

The mist made the tows hard to distinguish from the perpendicular mud banks, and more than once a mass of barges seemed to materialize out of a field to bear down on us. I overtook one long tow and immediately came upon another, an unusual closeness since the boats normally give each other wide berth. We seemed to be gaining on it as though it were dead in the water, but its wake was churning up strange rolls of frothing river. Nothing looked right as the gap between us closed fast. What is this? I said, and then realized we were approaching not the stern of a towboat but the straight bows of oncoming barges. Because a downriver boat (like ours) has less control than one going up, it has right of way, but tows take precedence over small craft for several reasons, two good ones being a line of vision severely limited by several hundred feet of barges in front and a stopping distance of a mile or more. It was not the moment to weigh fine points of river practice. I tacked sharply to starboard, Pilotis went crashing into the bulkhead, and we cleared the monster somehow, but the captain came out to shake an arm at me. He thought I was playing one of those games of weekend boaters.

Below Henderson, Kentucky — where John James Audubon for a few years was an indifferent shopkeeper more interested in hunting, learning to draw birds and beasts, and keeping his pond stocked with turtles for his favorite soup — the Ohio becomes wider, a half mile across in places, and deeper, holes of sixty feet, and the high water created some boils, upwellings that made large shifting circles across the surface. Bean fields reached to the edge of the river, the plow furrows inches from the water, and with no stabilizing line of trees and shrubs to hold the banks, the edacious Ohio easily pulled the earth into it. Farmers, wanting to use each foot of rich bottom this season, would have less next year, and by not giving up a little now, they eventually would lose it all. But where a tree line protected the edges, nest holes of swallows filled the banks.

A bald eagle dropped out of a dead sycamore and took a course directly above the river, and for a couple of miles we followed its draft, on around Cypress Bend, up to Diamond Island, one of the largest on the river, past more low islands big and small, the wooded ones called towheads. Of the six states bordering the Ohio, Kentucky has the most miles of shoreline, and all the islands along its coast, no matter on which side of the river they lie, belong to it, a result of the federal government in 1792 setting the upper boundary against the north bank of the Ohio. Sixteen miles downstream from the courthouse and the industries in Mount Vernon, Indiana, we had speedy passage through Uniontown Lock, and two miles beyond *Nikawa* passed the mouth of the Wabash River and the Illinois line. Before our voyage began, I'd spoken with a couple of boat mechanics living two hundred miles up the Wabash, water they refused to set out on. One said, "The fish in that river got eight tails!" "Sure," said the other, "but can they swim! Now, if they only had eyes to see where they're going." The truth is, the entire Wabash, a biologist told me, "is under a fish-consumption advisory because of PCB and mercury contamination, and the lower river is dangerous to recreationists because of *E. coli* from animal wastes. It's going to be difficult to get improvement here because the Indiana legislature is deeply under the influence of the Farm Bureau and other property rights organizations. But there are seven states downstream from the Wabash, and that makes pollution here actionable by federal agencies." So when will the water get better? "When enough people speak out — as always."

The remnants of Old Shawneetown were hardly visible behind the levee; the best remaining building was the porticoed and pillared 1839 bank, once so close and open to the river a clerk could sling a half-eagle from the stone steps into the Ohio. That the bank still stands while the rest of the village has fled a couple of miles up the road is evidence of what an early chronicler called the citizens' "pertinacious adhesion" to river life as well as a levee that grew higher following each flood after 1884. In 1932 the townspeople built their ultimate dike, one five feet above the *highest* high-water mark, a margin of assurance everyone believed in; then the flood of 1937 topped that levee by six feet with such a show of power the villagers' pertinacity gave out and their adhesion yielded to the great brown master of the territory. At last they understood.

In Illinois, Hardin County is almost a descriptive name, for the place is hard ground indeed, an area of quarries as well as forested hills, a durable land that does what the ramparts of Old Shawneetown could not: keep people dry and force the Ohio four miles eastward. The underlying rock gives the last topographical relief, the final scenery of delight to the Ohio shores. Ledges of sheer striated limestone like seawalls reach down into the water, and where they have broken open, cedar and sycamores cling to crevices in a lovely manner unlike any other place on the river.

Along the south side of that big bend is Cave-in-Rock, a name with a nice ring to it although, as Pilotis commented, "Where else would a cave be?" Once called Robbers' Roost, the two-hundred-foot-deep chamber, opening directly to the Ohio, its mouth looking like a huge and flattened keyhole, lies only a few yards from the river. Scrawled on the interior today are the usual insipidities of the marginally lettered, but the most famous words ever were those on Samuel Mason's 1797 sign: LIQUOR VAULT AND HOUSE OF ENTERTAINMENT. The shrewd come-on, implying hooch and sex for sale, was an effective ruse to draw travelers and flatboatmen into a den of iniquity, although not the kind they expected. Inside, Mason's thugs robbed them, a scam so good it continued even after a large reward encouraged two of his henchmen to sink a tomahawk in his skull, sever his head, and carry it, wrapped in blue mud to prevent putrefaction, in a canoe to Natchez where they presented it as proof of capture. Also around here lurked Colonel Plug, a fellow who would pretend to be a traveler stranded on a remote shore; when a samaritan took him aboard, the colonel covertly pulled caulking from the innocent's flatboat, timing the leaks so the vessel would founder near his den where cohorts rowed out to rescue only him and the cargo. The thief, later known as Colonel Unplug, mistimed his last uncaulking and went down with his victims.

Nikawa passed through the wake of the small Cave-in-Rock ferry and on down beyond Elizabethtown and Rosiclare, Illinois, but neither afforded a mooring off the river away from the pounding of tows. At Golconda we pulled into a harbor built by the Corps of Engineers, and there we refueled. Tucked into a nearby slip and locked up was, inescapably, the *Dry Docktor*.

Pilotis called to find a room and managed to get a ride into town. When we climbed off the pier and went up to the road, we found waiting the longest limousine minus newlyweds, a mafioso, or rock musician I'd ever seen; in fact, it had once belonged to a country-and-western singer. I won't say that all of the village could ride in it at once, but I will allege that when the hood ornament left Golconda (named after the ancient city of proverbial riches in India), the rear bumper was just entering. Remembering our previous clunkers, pickup trucks, and shanks' mare, we rode preposterously to The Mansion, an old riverside house now an inn. Later, when we sat down to supper, in walked Cap and Mr. V—, smiling, full of good humor and bad tidings. Cap said, "We're not taking on the Mississippi. It's starting to back up the Ohio now, so you can imagine what's on out west. I heard the current is almost thirty miles an hour in places. Uprooted trees coming down fast. And then that damn Missouri? Not us. Forget it."

Pilotis and I, clearly, couldn't forget it, but we did try to ignore matters just then. Cap, hoping the spring rises would ease, planned to go home for a couple of weeks and then return to ascend the safer lock-and-dam Tennessee River, perhaps as far as Knoxville. I tried to persuade him at least to try the Missouri after his wait, but I failed; he'd set his course, and maybe he was right, considering that his destination was never the other side of the country but merely wherever he chose at the moment; he was free as we could never be. We put rivers aside and ate a good meal, poured out toasts, retold stories of watering westward, and Cap was jocund. Later, Schuyler Meyer and several students did ascend the Tennessee, and some months after that he fell gravely ill and died. He was seventy-nine. I never saw him or the *Doctor Robert* again.

The Great Omphalos
in Little Egypt

THE MORNING was warm, lightly muggy, but we felt not so much the air as our anticipation tinctured with apprehension about rising waters. We needed a day of things done correctly and occurrences falling in our favor, and naturally it didn't begin like that. The limousine mistakenly hauled our backpacks to the next town, so we had to wait for their return before we could go to the docks and board *Nikawa.*

We filled our fuel tanks and took aboard a young Erie canalman — handsome, thick hair to his shoulders, an accomplished bagpiper whom I'd earlier promised a few days on the big rivers — and set off, our musician on the bow to pipe us into action. We dropped south past the strung-out Sisters Islands, low and slender in the Ohio manner, then around chunky Stewart Island. The river ran smoothly, an assist on this day when gasoline would be a concern, so much so that I concentrated on steering the most direct course through the bending channels.

Descent down the lock of big Smithland Dam went easily, and just below there I resisted an urge to cross behind a mess of bars and islands to motor a ways up the mouth of the Cumberland River. Although the last fifty miles of the Ohio are its widest, the section is deceptively full of shoals; a smashing blow by an unseen something at Cottonwood Bar shook *Nikawa* but did not harm her and corrected me of trying to run too straight a course down the broad river and put an end to crew chatter about the difference between corned beef and pastrami.

Ten miles below the Cumberland, a long, needle-like bar angled out from the Kentucky shore to hide most of the debouchure of the Tennessee. It's a quirk of topography that these two major rivers, their sources far apart, enter the Ohio so close together, a detail that would seem to have made Paducah a bigger town than it is — after all, look what the Missouri, Illinois, and Mississippi did for St. Louis. We watched for a gasoline pump on the Paducah waterfront, found nothing open, and went on down to cross over the lowered wickets of Dam 52, an old barrier boats go right over in high water to avoid the lock.

At Metropolis, Illinois, where chances of shoreside gasoline seemed remote, I decided it was nevertheless our best hope for topping off the tanks, although the ramp was underwater. A couple of generations after the "birth" of Superman, little Metropolis, given its name, decided it might as well advertise itself as his home, despite the impossibility here of leaping tall buildings in a single bound (there aren't any); the local paper even changed its name from the *News* to the *Planet*. There is, however, genuine history on the east side at Fort Massac where I thought to make a landing on a slope of loose cobbles, a decision the crew took mumpishly. Pilotis said, "Even if we get up onto the rocks all right, there's still no gas there," but I believed we had no choice and that it was time again to test our luck. Our musician went to the bow to watch the bottom and then pipe us up some friends, but the wind pulled his notes back into Kentucky, and nobody noticed us, not even when we had to go overboard to pull *Nikawa* onto the stones.

The first Fort Massac, or Massaic, the French one of 1757, long ago fell into rot, as did subsequent British and American outposts, but in 1971 Illinois began rebuilding the 1794 Yankee version and thereby returned to the Ohio one of its formerly numerous wooden fortifications. It was there that Meriwether Lewis stopped for three days on his way from Pittsburgh to the Expedition encampment opposite the mouth of the Missouri; he purchased thirty-four gallons of whiskey for the soldiers' daily ration during the voyage to the Pacific from Alexander McNair, a young clerk who years later became the first governor of Missouri after being elected over a candidate running on a platform of an orderly rather than fast, greedy, and irresponsible development of the new lands — William Clark.

Pilotis stayed with *Nikawa* while the Piper and I walked up to the fort as if we were flatboatmen come ashore to inventory our cargo and pay duty. I found a groundskeeper, told him our tale, asked the Piper to play for him and a few visitors; the man listened, whistled along, then handed us the keys to his van. As we drove off for gas, the Piper said, "Does it always work like that? Always that easy?" Yes, I said, duck soup. We could find only two gasoline canisters, so we had to make the trip twice, lugging in sweaty silence the heavy cans down to *Nikawa*. As we stepped into the cool river to pull her off the rocks, our young friend remembered he'd left his bagpipes in the van, a recovery that took long enough to make me edgy about losing daylight before we could accomplish the last twenty miles of the Ohio and fifty more up the Mississippi to a presumed flood-safe berth at Cape Girardeau, Missouri. I said nothing, but I thought, He travels farthest who travels leanest.

Then we were on the water again, past the big gambling boat that plies a few miles of the Ohio, a tub from which no passenger has yet been known to look at the river. Not long after, we went over the lowered wickets of Lock and Dam 53, the last of the old-style barriers and the final one between us and St. Louis. For the next several days, we might be on floodwater, but it would be open river. In a few years, Olmsted Lock and Dam, under construction off to starboard, would replace 52 and 53, and another era of Ohio navigation would end.

Mound City, Future City, and Cairo, Illinois, are the original settlements of an area called Little Egypt after a St. Louis merchant and founder of Cairo (rhymes with "pharaoh") fancied a resemblance to the Nile delta, a place he never saw. The towns line up along a six-mile stretch of the Ohio where it joins the Mississippi, one of the great fluvial junctures in the world, a location seemingly perfect for a real river city — a Pittsburgh, St. Louis, or Kansas City. Indeed the waters are there, but otherwise the geography is an adverse peninsula of lowlands, a fact ignored when English speculators in the 1830s sold bonds in a town company. One of the investors may have been Charles Dickens who was outraged at what he found when he journeyed here by boat. Wrote Boz in the account of his 1842 United States tour, *American Notes:*

> At length, upon the morning of the third day, we arrived at a spot so much more desolate than any we had yet beheld, that the forlornest places we had passed were, in comparison with it, full of interest. At the junction of the two rivers, in ground so flat and low and marshy that at certain seasons of the year it is inundated to the housetops, lies a

breeding-place of fever, ague, and death, vaunted in England as a mine of Golden Hope, and speculated in, on the faith of monstrous representations, to many people's ruin. A dismal swamp, on which the half-built houses rot away; cleared here and there for the space of a few yards, and then teeming with rank unwholesome vegetation, on whose baneful shade the wretched wanderers who are tempted hither, droop and die and lay their bones; the hateful Mississippi circling and eddying before it, and turning off upon its southern course a slimy monster, hideous to behold; a hotbed of disease, an ugly sepulchre, a grave uncheered by any gleam of promise; a place without one single quality, in earth or air or water, to commend it — such is the dismal Cairo.

This outpouring of vitriol didn't drain Dickens, for the next year, in his American novel, *Martin Chuzzlewit,* his wretched fictional City of Eden is Cairo and the region Little Egypt:

As they proceeded further on their track, and came more and more towards their journey's end, the monotonous desolation of the scene increased to that degree, that for any redeeming feature it presented to their eyes, they might have entered, in the body, on the grim domains of Giant Despair. A flat morass, bestrewn with fallen timber; a marsh on which the good growth of the earth seemed to have been wrecked and cast away, that from its decomposing ashes vile and ugly things might rise; where the very trees took the aspect of huge weeds, begotten of the slime from which they sprung, by the hot sun that burnt them up; where fatal maladies, seeking whom they might infect, came forth at night, in misty shapes, and creeping out upon the water, hunted them like spectres until day; where even the blessed sun, shining down on festering elements of corruption and disease, became a horror; this was the realm of Hope through which they moved.

I submit these passages as challenges to those who hold the English to be practitioners of understatement, and I point out that Dickens's rancor is not unique among nineteenth-century British travelers in America. While the barren grid of Future City still seems to be waiting for its tomorrow, Cairo and Mound City did grow to see some fulfillment of this Golden Hope a generation after Dickens's expostulations, a rise driven by river commerce and industry, notably James Eads's gunboat shops that constructed several ironclads for the Union, craft that broke the Confederate blockade of the lower Mississippi and mercilessly shelled Vicksburg. I don't know whether profits from war machinery were part of the Golden Hope or Giant Despair.

Cairo still exists, a county seat surviving for a century and a half on its narrow peninsula between the big rivers and encircled by a levee, something like a moat in reverse. Perhaps Cairo is what Pilotis called an SBDB, a Seen-Better-Days Burg, even though it remains one of the most unusually situated towns in America, but its topography is so vast that the joining waters are almost impossible to behold from any view other than an airborne one. What Dickens failed to comprehend — but American Indians a millennium ago understood, as their ceremonial mounds attest — is the way Little Egypt sits at the center of what is probably the greatest nexus of grand watercourses in the world: within a crescent of about a hundred miles are the mouths of the Wabash, Cumberland, Tennessee, Ohio, Missouri, and Illinois, all merging into the Mississippi. At any time, but especially during flood, this is a powerful, overwhelming omphalos of waters.

We went past Eads's marine ways, yet visible, that launched his ironclads, then on under the 105-year-old railroad bridge, and two miles beyond we saw the Mississippi sprawling brownly out, yawning wide as all yonder, rolling menacingly down as if to Hell. We had done the Ohio, every flowing foot of it, and over its nearly thousand miles *Nikawa* had descended less than five hundred feet. Pilotis said, "Do you realize we didn't see a single shantyboat? What's the Ohio without shantyboats? Barbecue without sauce." I asked our musician to go to the bow rail, take a secure position, and pipe us around Cairo Point — where passes the downflow of half the states and two provinces — and on into the Father of Waters. He went out, blew the bag full, and cut loose. Now that my native state at last lay on the far shore, he opened with "Going Home," segued into a venerable piece Missourians claim, "Sweet Betsy from Pike," and then to "Old Man River," a song all but felicitous coming out of a bagpipe, yet with the skirls rousing us, we were ready for the great Mississippi, come hell or high water.

VI

THE MISSISSIPPI RIVER

COMMERCE, MISSOURI

ICONOGRAM VI

But what words shall describe the Mississippi, great father of rivers, who (praise be to Heaven) has no young children like him! An enormous ditch, sometimes two or three miles wide, running liquid mud six miles an hour: its strong and frothy current choked and obstructed everywhere by huge logs and whole forest trees; now twining themselves together in great rafts, from the interstices of which a sedgy, lazy foam works up to float upon the water's top; now rolling past like monstrous bodies, their tangled roots showing like matted hair; now glancing singly by like giant leeches; and now writhing round and round in the vortex of some small whirlpool, like wooded snakes. The banks low, the trees dwarfish, the marshes swarming with frogs, the wretched cabins few and far apart, their inmates hollow-cheeked and pale, the weather very hot, mosquitoes penetrating into every crack and crevice of the boat, mud and slime on everything: nothing pleasant in its aspect, but the harmless lightning which flickers every night upon the dark horizon.

For two days we toiled up this foul stream, striking constantly against the floating timber, or stopping to avoid those more dangerous obstacles, the snags, or sawyers, which are the hidden trunks of trees that have their roots below the tide. When the nights are very dark, the look-out stationed in the head of the boat knows by the ripple of the water if any great impediment be near at hand and rings a bell behind him, which is the signal for the engine to be stopped: but always in the night this bell has work to do, and after every ring, there comes a blow which renders it no easy matter to remain in bed.

Charles Dickens
American Notes for General Circulation, 1842

A Night Without Light
on a River Without Exits

OUR ROUTE drawn across a map of America strangely reflected the southern border of the United States from Florida to California, and we were now at the most southerly point, the place glaciers reached deepest into America. If you speak of north as "up" and south as "down," then we were as down as we'd get, and from there to Idaho we would be going up, up northward, upstream almost three thousand miles, up against the flow of half a continent. As soon as we left the curving course of the Ohio, its line of current most evident on the surface of the joining waters, we caught the downrush of the Mississippi and felt that American outpouring, forceful beyond anything we'd known, and it was thrilling to move in a land that could show such native power.

Nikawa rolled hard as if struck from below by some beast of the depths, her pilothouse leaning, and she yawed until I put her straight to the current, and then the Piper yahooed. "Steady," Pilotis said. "We're being taken downriver." I pushed the throttles forward, *Nikawa* shivered, began to inch upstream, her flat bottom rising enough to escape some of the pull of the flood, and we started to climb toward the Rockies. Everywhere huge boils broke the surface: the ones ahead we cracked into as if they were curbings, and those rising suddenly beneath us jolted the hull as though we'd ridden onto the back of a river kraken. The current beat at the channel markers, taking some cans underwater while the conical nun-buoys went into a thrashing dance, a mad tarantella, and Pilotis played the binoculars back and

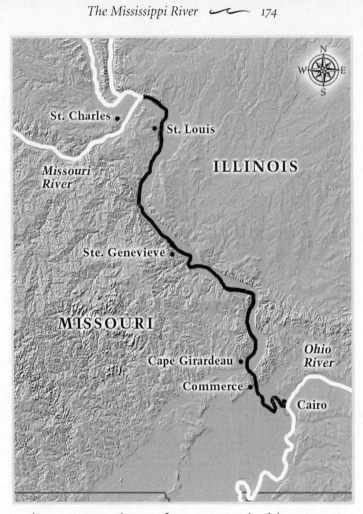

*The Mississippi, Ohio Confluence to mouth of the Missouri,
196 river miles*

forth to watch for any buoys torn free and turned into veritable torpedoes. The river ripped along in such tumult it seemed alive and foul-tempered, unwilling to tolerate the smallest error.

A big uprooted elm caught against a bridge pier shook violently, the Mississippi treating it as a terrier does a rat, and the tree was pitiful in its helplessness. Said Pilotis, "From here on, the logs will be coming at us. Head-on-collision country." Entire trees were bearing down, not just willow saplings but sycamores and cottonwoods sixty feet long; yet it was shorter pieces I worried about, ones small enough to be sucked under and kicked explosively back up by a boil into our motors. To lose props in this turbulence, to go abruptly powerless, was to be at the mercy of the Mississippi because one must move faster than the current to steer. Goodbye props, hello Memphis.

The young Piper said, "Do you think we ought to go back?" Go back where? "I don't know, but it's like we're the *Millennium Falcon* passing through an asteroid field." We were all watching for drift, struggling to distinguish big knots of dirty brown foam, hardened clots like little icebergs, from the floaters until the moment they hit the bow when all I could do was jerk to starboard or port in an effort to send them down alongside us rather than underneath where they would end up in the propellers. I kept thinking what the dark and torn bottom of the river must look like, kept remembering that Hernando de Soto ended up sleeping forever with the catfish in the Mississippi graveyard.

I caught Pilotis staring at me. "You're liking this." Only a little bit, I said. "Only a little bit of a lot." Once beneath the big Interstate 57 bridge, we entered a stretch where nothing reached the river except fields and bosky woods, and beyond, dirt tracks we couldn't see lying behind unbroken miles of levees, conditions that made our fuel and the dropping light of ever more concern. I guessed the river to be running at about fifteen miles an hour, and we were doing about twenty-five, to give us a true speed of ten miles an hour through the upper end of one of the most twisted sections on all the Mississippi, a narrowness that creates swift currents even when not in flood. At Missouri Sister Island we had to travel twenty-two miles around the big horseshoe bend to gain only three and a half along our real course. The contortions and currents and our jockeying through drift ate up the gasoline egregiously, and the light dropped faster than the fuel needles. To worsen things, a bank of dark clouds moved in from the west and took the sun and stole away another thirty minutes of daylight. To run that swollen river in darkness would be suicide. I had no idea, should the clouds pass over, what time the moon would rise, but I did know it would be nearly full, and that was the only positive thought I had. I spoke all this to the crew, not to make them more apprehensive but to prepare them for what was shaping into a nasty possibility: a night without light on a river without exits.

The low banks turned to flooded woods full of stumps and snags and swarming with mosquitoes. A try at mooring in such a place could be the end of the voyage, but I saw no other choice. "How do you know the docks aren't underwater at Cape Girardeau?" Pilotis asked, and I said I didn't know, but it was moot anyway because there wasn't enough light to make it. The Piper said, "If we hadn't stopped for gas we'd have enough light." But not enough gasoline. "Jeezis," Pilotis murmured, then, emphasizing each word, "This does not look good."

Nikawa neither rolled nor pitched, but she did yaw and shimmy as she worked to skate over the cauldron. The Piper studied the chart to take relief from watching the darkening water and in hopes of finding what would not be there, a haven. He said, "There's a little town ahead on the Missouri side, Commerce." Hell, I said, Commerce washed down the river two floods ago — Commerce is out on the bottom of the Gulf. "There's nothing else," he said. "Nothing as in zero." And there wasn't; even the sandbars were gone under. Pilotis looked at me. "Well, Noah?"

The sky lowering, I was thinking how two people had put their trust in me, and now I was endangering them, proceeding without knowing whether the way were open, working harder to reach the mountains than to provide for their safety. Oh yes, they knew the plan when they came aboard, but still, I had no right to put them in jeopardy. Pilotis was correct: my job was to set our little ark down along some proper shore. The miles went on, the river knocking at the hull, waiting for an opening, the banks nearly impenetrable. Finally I said, We've got about half an hour of light, half an hour to find a way off this river. And on we went because it was all we could do.

Then something began to rise from the treetops. I said, What the hell is that? Pilotis picked up the binoculars. "It's a cross." Cut the crap, I said. "It's a cross on a steeple!" And it was. "I hope you're going to take that for pure chance, mere coincidence." I'm taking it for more than that, I said, I'm taking it as an exit. "Where? There's nothing." Off at eleven o'clock, an opening in the trees. "There isn't." I slowed and went warily toward the gap, paused, then entered. What's that ahead, dead ahead? Pilotis squinted through the field glasses. "It's a dog pen. One beautiful dog pen and a gorgeous clothesline." The Piper said, "We're in somebody's back lot." The water became too shallow for the sounder to operate, so I raised the motors as far as I could and idled one in case of a hit; then the trees opened further to reveal a small house, and I ran *Nikawa* up into the yard not far from a little houseboat, and the Piper jumped overboard and planted our anchor in the grass.

A man came onto the stoop and stared at a dory sitting almost in his flooded pole-bean patch. Pilotis called, "Do you know where we are?" and he answered, "I know where I am," and went inside. I said, If he comes out shooting, all we'll do is duck because we're not going back out on that river. He returned, cradling something in his arms, and approached *Nikawa*. Pilotis said, "Please let us stay." He held up cans of beer and said, "Come on off, then. This is Commerce." He was Dariel Williams, the first name rhyming with "peril." Then we were popping open beers, our Piper played, and we laughed in deep relief and went up onto the stoop. I looked back at our river horse tethered in bluegrass as if she had never been anywhere but up a pasture creek.

We'd climbed two hours up the Mississippi flood and found in dying light the single good landing, the lone haven. Pilotis asked, "Would you have spotted that opening without the steeple?" I answered, You already said it — I'm treating it as a pip of a coincidence. Then we went into the house. We had covered forty-eight river miles from Mound City on the Ohio to gain only sixteen westerly miles.

The Ghost of
the Mississippi

IT WAS THE KIND of mistake I was happy to make: Commerce, Missouri, had not yet been entirely washed away. Other than the white church and steeple, there were several houses, a post office, and a small winery nearby, but the rest of what was once there — the name notwithstanding — was a motley few beat-up and shut-down buildings, and no one selling gasoline or anything else. Northward along a diminishing road below a wooded bluff was the Williams home, a small cabin added on to over the years so that it was a warren of dim rooms. Inside, the air lay compacted into a single scent of children, cooking food, and river-bottom damp; it was a heavy air, but one generated by breathing people, the very sort we were relieved still to be among.

Annie, Dariel's wife, offered us appetizers of bologna on white bread, to be followed by catfish — blues and flatheads — he had taken from the river; she battered the big chunks in cornmeal and fried them in an iron skillet. "Is there enough?" Pilotis said. "I mean, with all your family?" "It's hard to run out of catfish here," Dariel said.

While the dinner crackled in the skillet, we sat at the kitchen table. Dariel operated heavy machinery at a quarry, a dangerous job requiring him to move rock around the edges of the pit. The Piper took out his fife and played an old Erie Canal tune, and children, Williams's nephew and nieces, came from unseen corners of the house: a young girl just recovering from chickenpox, a ten-year-old boy, and his elder sister. The boy, Michael, sat absorbed in the music, the teenager trying not to be, and the little girl alarmed. Michael soon began pouring out questions. Where had we come from? Had anyone drowned? Did we think our boat would sink? When he heard Pilotis mention New York City, he stood up. "You saw the Statue of Liberty? I've only seen her in a book." We told our tale, the boy alight with fascination at one more strange thing the Mississippi had washed up into his life. His excitement grew until his questions turned into a narrative of his own. He had a slight speech impediment, the result of a perforated eardrum affecting his hearing, something a recent operation should correct, but still his words required attention. What I heard as "Thomas" was "Commerce," and "hatchet" was "statue." He reported the indignities his elder sister visited on him and his attempt to sell her up in Farmington once, a try that brought an alleged offer of fifty dollars. To that she said, "Quit it!"

He talked so much I said, Son, I think you'll run for governor one day. "No," he said, "I want to be an author." "It's about the same thing," Pilotis said. "Slinging the bull." Michael reached for a pencil. "I've got my signature ready," and he carefully demonstrated it for us. You need to write a book before you can sign one, I said. "I'm about ready," he said. "My first title will be *An Outline of Missouri*. You think that's history, but it's not. It's about a ten-year-old boy who has no sisters and walks around the border of Missouri with his dad. They cross the Missouri River okay, but when they get to the Mississippi the father drowns, so the boy has to go on by himself. After he reaches his starting point, he goes to see the governor who gives him a million dollars, and the boy becomes a legend."

Nodding toward me, Pilotis said, "Watch what you give out in front of him. He's been known to appropriate a story or two. That's probably why his pen's working right now." "He can have it," Michael said. "I've got more. Like *The Ghost of the Mississippi*. It's about this ghost with pale blue eyes, no nose. Long, bony fingers that can claw girls' necks."

At that point, the room went dark. After surprised exclamations from around the house and a shriek from an elder sister, Dariel guessed the flood was responsible, and Pilotis said to the boy, "I think you'll be an author all right because coincidences take to you. That's how our skipper gets by."

Annie pulled out a kerosene lamp. By its lambent wick and the flickering blue flame under the skillet, we began to eat while she kept the catfish coming, crisp and moist and sweet, and the talk rolled along. The boy told how river people when they really needed food "fished intelligent," if illegally, by cobbling together a simple battery-powered device inside a snuff can that could make a catfish dance on its tail and sometimes even jump into the boat. The little shock boxes were almost better than food stamps.

The house got so close in the warm darkness we all went onto the porch and stood looking out at the river, now agleam with moonlight, more lovely than lethal, and Dariel said, "The current's bad in this section because the river's narrow and it goes over hard bottom. To-morrow you'll catch it pretty good from here on up past Cape, and the river's still rizen. And the Missouri's worse."

Honeysuckle and tree frogs and mosquitoes drenched the muggy night, and our conversation was a staccato of slaps and sentences until someone said, "Oh my god, look out there!" Down through the thick moonlight came a single barge, twisting in the currents, a juggernaut broken free and in search of a collision to stop it. "If there's one loose barge, there's six more," the boy said, and a few moments later came a horrendous thud, a deep and ominous sound, and Dariel said, "That's another one hitting the railroad bridge at Thebes, three and a half miles upriver." When Pilotis and I went aboard *Nikawa* for the night, I lay swatting at mosquito whines and listening to the awful thuddings of berserk barges roaming the dark.

Of Swampsuckers
and Samaritans

HAVING SLEPT with mosquitoes that entered a pilothouse that seemed to have only imaginary bulkheads, we got up as if we had chickenpox (two weeks later, the Piper did come down with it), but an early breeze blew the insects back into the woods, and the sun so struck the flood in its rush for the sea that the water seemed to throw off sparks like another ancient element, hard earth: corundum against iron. The river overnight had risen eight more inches. We set out on it, engines pushing us among the usual accouterments of flood: drift, foam, boils, steel barrels, a propane tank, barges askew in the trees, and bobbing nun-buoys playing peekaboo in the current. We were no longer much concerned about fuel, assured by Dariel we'd find it at Cape Girardeau. So the Monday morning was good, even as we passed under the old Thebes train bridge, one that bargemen detest, its position noted on the chart as "an area typically more difficult to navigate," a warning especially to long, down-bound tows that must execute a sharp turn and then a broad one before realigning quickly to clear between the stone piers. Early towboatmen claimed that railroads, competing with paddlewheelers for freight, deliberately placed some bridges at angles to encumber and endanger vessels.

That section of the river breaks through a distant outreach of the Ozark Mountains at the top of what was once the Mississippi Embayment, a very long arm of the Gulf of Mexico. When the great sauropods and forty-five-foot crocodiles were in their last days, this former mouth of the ancient river probably poured over a three-hundred-foot-high precipice, a massive cascade twice the height of Niagara, to enter the Gulf. Had Commerce been around, it would have been a seaport.

At Cape Girardeau, we looked for gasoline but found the flood had either closed or damaged two different fuel docks. We couldn't risk going farther, so I turned *Nikawa* downstream again and pulled up on the inside of a big Corps of Engineers floating dry dock. I climbed the ladder and walked into a small lounge. Workers sat drinking coffee, and I asked whether we might tie up there for an hour till we found gasoline. "No, you can't! Get out of here!" a bloated man said. "Get your craft out of here!" I said we were in a real pinch, what with this flood. "I told you to get your damn boat off this dock!" Okay, I said, just direct me to some other place to tie up. "I told you all I'm gonna tell you except this — you aren't going to stay here!" I said, leaving, Thanks for your help, you swampsucker.

We prowled along the high floodwall. There was but one possibility, an inundated concrete ramp, or what looked like a ramp, a thing useless except for a boat trailer, where four men stood staring at the flood. With no idea what was under us, I edged through the rough water on one motor, Pilotis giving me the sounder readings until we were close enough to ask the men about the ramp. "It's not a ramp!" one yelled, and picked up a piece of drift and plunged it in to show the depth. "It's a straight wall!" Good news. We approached slowly, got our fenders down low enough to ride against the ledge, and tossed a line to them to hold *Nikawa* steady in the barge waves threatening to slam her onto the concrete.

The men were down-and-out, had no vehicle, and the gasoline was up on the highway, too far to walk, so I stood bewildered. Pilotis asked, "Waiting for a coincidence?" It's all we've got, I said. "Again." So we passed the time: took snapshots, counted trees coming down the river, someone told a flood joke involving a chicken and pig. Then a man carrying his daughter on his shoulders walked up to show her the bad Mississippi misbehaving. He asked about *Nikawa*. I told him about her, spoke of our voyage, and his expression became intense. His name was David Keiper, and he once had sailed a trimaran from San Francisco to New Zealand. He understood exigencies. "So you need some gas?" Indeed. While I checked the fenders, Pilotis said, "There's one person in the entire state who's sailed across the Pacific, and he's the one who strolls right up to us." And the Piper said innocently, "Duck soup." I quoted Ernest Hemingway after he walked away from an airplane crash in Africa: "The luck, she is still running good."

In an hour I had canisters of gasoline, and we were under way again, waved onto the flood by our benefactors, and I said I was glad to have come across the swampsucking orzizzazz — his role made for better drama. "Yes," said Pilotis, "but your Pacific *deus ex machina* was too much. The audience won't buy it." Given the pressure, it was the best I could do, I said.

For lunch we ate peanut-butter-and-preserves sandwiches on sourdough bread, mine with sliced sweet pickles. The twenty-eight miles up to Tower Rock was a generally straight run full of low swells that impeded us on the upside and rocketed us forward on the downslope, and driftwood formed into floating islands, some so large we could only tractor through as if we were in a small Sargasso Sea.

South of St. Louis, the Mississippi is somewhat lacking in exceptional scenery, but much of the best of what is there occurs between Cape Girardeau and Ste. Genevieve, Missouri. In that stretch the most celebrated landmark is Tower Rock, or the Grand Tower, the latter name not really accurate in either word, although the stony outlier is distinctive with its creviced striations of yellowed limestone capped by oaks and cedars, a thing even jaded towmen like to look at. From the late seventeenth century on, travelers — Marquette and Jolliet, Lewis and Clark, explorer Stephen Long, ethnographer Prince Maximilian and his artist Karl Bodmer, John James Audubon, Mark Twain — have noted or sketched the Tower, the earliest accounts speaking of the fear and reverence Indians held for the rock and its swirling waters. Meriwether Lewis wrote in his journal:

> This [Tower] seems among the watermen of the mississippi to be what the tropics or Equanoxial line is with regard to the Sailors; those who have never passed it before are always compelled to pay or furnish some sperits to drink or be ducked. . . . These strong courants thus meeting each other form an immence and dangerous whirlpool which no boat dare approach in that state of the water; the counter courent driving with great force against the East side of the rock would instantly dash them to attoms and the whirlpool would as quickly take them to the botom.

Concerned not about hard water but rocks, we approached only closely enough for photographs and then went on.

If you've seen the movie *In the Heat of the Night*, you may remember the high, slender bridge the police captain uses to overtake a fleeing man suspected of murder. The span links Missouri to Chester, Illinois, atop the eastern bluff, with a state prison below it and northward a plainly handsome French-colonial house Pierre Menard built in 1802 on the low bank of the Mississippi, elevated just enough to stay dry. Menard, a merchant and legislator, was an alert immigrant who troubled himself to study the territory and adapt to its ways. During muggy summers, he piped chilly drafts from his springhouse into his home to make it one of the first air-cooled places in America; there he comfortably entertained Lafayette and Indian chiefs and became wealthy by understanding and respecting two native forces: the Mississippi and the aboriginal people.

Among those not giving the river or the Indians their due were the priestly founders of Old Kaskaskia, platted in 1703 on the floodplain just below the spot the Kaskaskia River issues into the Mississippi — a bonehead location that nevertheless managed to last almost two centuries before the rivers sent south this once most important river village above New Orleans and, for a couple of years, the first capital of Illinois. On the bluff above, earthen ramparts of Fort Kaskaskia remain, overgrown in large trees, a haunting place where John Dodge, an acquaintance of George Washington, took up despotic rule from the abandoned fort in 1784. He tyrannized the wilderness residents and murdered messengers sent out for help. A priest, Father Gibault, wrote of the iniquity: "Breaking of limbs, murder by means of a dagger, sabre, or sword (for he who will carries one) are common, and pistols and guns are but toys in this region. The most solemn feasts and Sundays are days given up to dances and drunkenness, with girls suborned and ravished in the woods, and a thousand other disorders which you are able to infer from these." It took troops under George Rogers Clark, William's elder brother, to set things right.

Four miles around the big bend upstream from these troubles, we found a small dredged-out harbor near the old French village of Ste. Genevieve. Despite some of the boatworks lying underwater, we pulled in for the night and, for the first time, broke out the kayak to get us to shore to a small bar — not one of sand but rather the other kind — and we ordered a round of quenchers and toasted our surviving another day. I coaxed the smiling bartender to take us across Bois Brulé Bottom into Ste. Genevieve when she got off work. As she drove us into one of the first towns west of the Mississippi, she said, "So you're on a little ol excursion trip?"

People revere Ste. Genevieve as they do a Queen Mum — for her dignity, quaintness, and for having seen so damn much history. Yet in her early days of frontier hardship, residents of rival Kaskaskia, "the little Paris of the Wilderness" now gone downriver, called her Misère ("misery" or "poverty" or "shabbiness"; St. Louis was then popularly Pancour, "short of bread"). We took lodging in the attic of the Main Street Inn, an excellent antebellum house. Our hosts invited us onto the garden porch for wine, popcorn, and conversation. Pilotis, relaxing in the late sun, said, "When this little ol excursion trip isn't beating our brains out, it gives us one sweet and grand tour." And the Piper said, "On the river, it's like there's no Mondays — every day feels like Saturday." I said, Except for those Saturdays that feel like a week of Mondays.

To the Tune of
"Garry Owen"
We Get Ready

T HE MISSISSIPPI at Ste. Genevieve was ten feet above flood stage and still rising, and we'd heard that the Missouri, only seventy-five miles away, would crest about the time we reached it, a concern because the Corps of Engineers might "shut down the river" — not its flow but navigation on it. I'd become confident *Nikawa* could handle the flood, but would the necessity of catching the spring rise in the Far West allow us to accommodate regulations two thousand miles east?

As I oiled the engines and refueled, I talked with a man who had arrived a couple of days earlier from Florida, on his way to Chicago in a fifty-foot motor yacht, a boat bigger than its length alone suggests. He had used 450 gallons of diesel to run the 122 miles from Cairo to Ste. Genevieve, at a cost of seven hundred dollars. He said, "That damn current ate my lunch." I told him we'd come almost two thousand miles from the Atlantic Ocean on only a third more than that. "Sure," he said, "but you're in a toy." The eye of the beholder: I'd considered boats like his the toys.

The weather was about to turn again, and already the wind was reaching twenty miles an hour, but it was generally blowing upriver to give us a push against the current. Every few miles we had to stop and raise the motors to clear the props of drift while *Nikawa*, indeed, bounced like a toy. We took one hard hit that knocked off a piece of propeller first damaged in Lake Chautauqua, but it wasn't enough to stop us. When people asked, as they often did, "Is it fun?" I remembered the perpetual threats, a sure depressant of that so American thing called fun. I thought, Toys are fun — cross-country river trips are something the hell else.

Above the Ste. Genevieve ferry, rocky bluffs come down to the river along the Missouri shore, and where quarries have not destroyed them, the cliffs are lovely, seated in maples and cottonwoods, topped with cedars and hickories. On the Illinois side a long line of levees protected a bottom cropland of grains and legumes. For more than a thousand miles, the Mississippi from above St. Louis to below New Orleans runs as an engineered conduit with either levees or bluffs penning the river, a circumstance that makes the roll of a flood faster, deeper, meaner. Like the Missouri, the Mississippi can no longer significantly spread high water full of silt into lowlands to diffuse the flow and enrich the soil. Of the hundreds of uses of this river, the Army Corps of Engineers for years tried to operate it for only one — barge navigation. The old steamboats, of course, hauled freight and people when the Mississippi was still nearly a wild river, but then those boats and cargoes were smaller; today, shipping companies speak only about economies of scale, and well they can, since on the broad Mississippi a full fifteen-barge tow can carry as much as 870 semi trucks.

The river has been not just caged, it has also undergone considerable straightening — channelizing — another element adding to the severity of a modern flood. And sometimes the Father of Waters takes things into his own hands. Mark Twain wrote in *Life on the Mississippi*:

> In the space of one hundred and seventy-six years the Lower Mississippi has shortened itself two hundred and forty-two miles. That is an average of a trifle over one mile and a third per year. Therefore, any calm person, who is not blind or idiotic, can see that in the Old Oolitic Silurian Period, just a million years ago next November, the Lower Mississippi River was upwards of one million three hundred thousand miles long, and stuck out over the Gulf of Mexico like a fishing rod. And by the same token any person can see that seven hundred and forty-two years from now the Lower Mississippi will be only a mile and three quarters long, and Cairo and New Orleans will have joined their streets together, and be plodding comfortably along under a single mayor and a mutual board of aldermen.

Villages and towns along this portion of the river, unlike on the Ohio or the Allegheny, do not commonly sit right on the edge of the banks; rather, they're behind a levee or a natural rise, frequently some distance away, so for hours the traveler may have little relief from the miles of willows and maples, shrub and bush, with no main drags — often named Water or Front Street — to offer a pause to body or a boost to imagination. If you want to know you're passing, say, old glass-making Crystal City, population 4,000, you have to look at a map. Despite these drawbacks to the journeyer, the Mississippi, of all our waterways, has spawned a greater number of river narratives than any other, a happenstance brought about more by the spell of Twain than any magic in the lower Mississippi itself. I had a couple of years earlier traveled it from New Orleans to St. Paul, and below St. Louis the river isn't by any means one of my favorites, so I moved along that day with a near eagerness to get off it and take on the longest river in America, of which an old pilot once said, "We used to separate the men from the boys at the mouth of the Missouri. The boys went up the Mississippi and the men up the Missouri."

The day became progressively darker as we banged on north, and by the time we passed the mouth of the Meramec River, the sky had turned oppressive and the industry of St. Louis started showing itself. A fourteen-year-old boy, Auguste Chouteau, began the construction of the city named to honor Louis IX of France and, indirectly, pay regard to the boy's current king, Louis XV, that self-indulgent, lecherous profligate who inherited the mightiest monarchy in Europe and proceeded to give up much of it while he pursued, among others, Madame Pompadour, a woman whose counsel almost made him into a good king. It was this Louis who purportedly said, "After me, the flood," words that often have an ironic ring to them in St. Louis. In fact, the day we arrived there, the Mississippi was inching its way up to the foot of the great Gateway Arch, the tallest national monument in America.

Three miles below the heart of the old waterfront where the teen-aged Chouteau first put saw to timbers, hammer to pegs, we searched out a moorage Pilotis had recently arranged with the Corps of Engineers on the inside of its big dredge *Potter* and two service barges. Tethered off the bank, the boats formed a narrow chute free of the roiling water on the channel, a safehold further quieted by a driftwood dam beavers had built between the *Potter* and the shore. We were only twenty feet from the open Mississippi, but the chute was gentle enough to shelter a dozen black-crowned night herons giving out their guttural *quok! quok! quok!* at our arrival. I once heard the birds called river ravens, and assuredly the evening fit their dark plumes and mournful quothings.

We phoned a friend to ask for a lift from under the actual shadow of the second-largest brewery in the world to a small pub serving its own cask-conditioned ales and a potently spiced white-bean chili. I called on our musician to play. As he blew his bag full, the windy night began to rattle the windows of the St. Louis Brewery, lightning flashed, and rain got dumped everywhere, but he merely glanced into the blackness and piped away, and women rose to dance to "Garry Owen," lifting their smooth knees high, hands clapping above their heads, and inspiration flowed like the sky.

When we returned to *Nikawa,* she was low in the stern from rain in the welldeck, and a young man from the Corps lent me an electric bilge-pump to empty her. Off and on the rain came down through the thunder-and-fire-rent night, a storm to extinguish the flames of Hell, and I had no doubt that the great Missouri, which would hold our lives for at least the next six weeks, was announcing itself, already testing our mettle.

VII

THE LOWER
MISSOURI RIVER

NIKAWA NEAR ROCHEPORT, MISSOURI

ICONOGRAM VII

[September 10, 1840] For the last 2 or 3 days we were steaming up the Missouri. Being confined to my berth, I saw but little of the scenery, but it appeared to be the same kind the whole way. The river itself is the most peculiar feature: the steamer was continually winding & twisting about among the enormous snags & sawyers and masses of trees & bushes laced together with which the course of this extraordinary stream is constantly interrupted, while in some places the whirlpools, eddies, currents, rapids & sandbanks (covered with thousands of Canada geese) together with the tremendous violence of the waters, form a spectacle the grandeur of which I have never seen at all approached except in the rapids above Niagara. Very often the whole power of the engines was barely sufficient to resist the impetuous fury of the stream and every now & then we would drop down, till, gathering new way, & *vires acquireus anudo*, we would slowly work past the contested point, which was usually some immense snag which formed a "hell of waters" boiling & hissing around it. We saw few settlements, the villages generally being 2 or 3 miles back from the river with roads leading down to small wharves on the waterside called "landings." . . . The numbers of boats that go up this immense stream is astonishing considering the difficulties of the navigation & the comparatively wild state of the country.

William Fairholme
*Journal of an Expedition to
the Grand Prairies of the Missouri*

We Start up
the Great Missouri

HAD HISTORY TAKEN a slightly different turn, the Missouri would be the longest river in the world. From its *true* source to the Gulf of Mexico, its length was more than five thousand miles before shortening by the Corps of Engineers, a thousand miles longer than the Nile or the Amazon. Because of a few interpretations, arguable ones, the Missouri has not been so recognized, but in the early days of white exploration and settlement many travelers and rivermen considered the Mississippi to be the tributary of the Missouri. Before the engineers and their dams and before dryland farmers and their pumps, the two rivers at their juncture fifteen miles above downtown St. Louis had a similar width and average flow, both figures common measurements to determine a tributary; even today, from its highest waters just north of Yellowstone Park, the Missouri is a couple of hundred miles longer. Nevertheless, the Mississippi claimed the lower river for two key reasons. The first is that the Missouri, in keeping with its character, changes its course at the confluence to assume the more regular overall due-south direction of the Mississippi. A straight line between St. Paul and Baton Rouge shows the deviation of the Mississippi to be never more than about 160 miles east of the mark and twenty-five west; but along a line between, say, Helena, Montana, and the confluence, the Missouri has a deviation of 250 miles on one side and a hundred on the other. In ways beyond distance, the Big Muddy is the most changeable large river in America, perhaps on the continent, a quality inimical to early explorers and merchants.

But the major reason for calling the river below St. Louis the Mississippi is that when names first got set onto maps, it was an almost familiar waterway ready for commerce, while the Missouri was still an unknown thing coming from an unexplored country and only a remote possibility as a route to the western sea and the wealth of the Orient. Explorers found the Mississippi more comprehensible, workable, and even predictable in both its topography and its nature, a river lying conveniently about halfway between coasts, one that could rather tidily set a western boundary to the new nation and provide the longest and most direct natural route north to south, nearly border to border. If you draw a square between the Appalachians and the Rockies and then divide it into equal quarters, you almost have a map of the courses of the Ohio, Mississippi, and Missouri, a basin full of other tributaries once having no compeer on the globe for navigable waters.

Below St. Louis the Mississippi takes on the character of the lower Missouri — color, turbulence, aura, its native life. The pallid sturgeon, for example, inhabits the Mississippi from Louisiana only up to the confluence but then follows the Missouri all the way into eastern Montana. This oldest species of fish in these waters, in other words, recognizes the upper Mississippi as a different river.

To call the Mississippi the Big Muddy, as the press routinely and incorrectly does, is to acknowledge the Missouri as the major river, for that sobriquet properly belongs solely to the latter, as early travelers attest in their accounts, virtually all of them commenting on the heavy sediment. William Clark, for example, wrote in 1804, "The water we Drink, or the Common water of the missourie at this time, contains half a Comn Wine Glass of ooze or mud to every pint."

I submit my last thought on the matter: given the American mania for rankings, the United States could still have today — even after the shortenings — the third-longest river in the world simply by dropping three letters and changing three others to make Mississippi spell Missouri. Failing that, then perhaps a grand compromise: the Missourippi. Try it: Mizza-rippi.

After the storm of the previous night, I had hoped for propitious weather to start us out on our lengthy climb up the continent, our entry into the Louisiana Purchase, but that Wednesday was nearly as ominous as the evening before. Until then, I'd not seen on the voyage

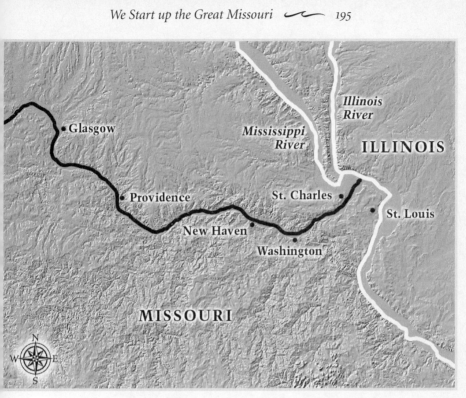

The Lower Missouri, mouth to Glasgow, 227 river miles

a morning I less wanted to venture into. My interior was strung with gloom as if I'd inhaled the weather, a day with neither the adventure of storm nor the romance of the moody dismals; it was merely drab and drizzly; like a poor novel not bad or outrageous enough to be remembered, it was memorable only for what it wasn't. Absence defined the morning in another way too, for Pilotis had to leave to handle affairs at home and would rejoin me upstream in a few days. Our young musician became a midshipman and assumed copilot duties, yet I much felt the absence of my great friend.

We heard that rain was coming down along the Missouri Valley out of eastern Kansas, causing the river to continue to rise, perhaps higher than the record flood of 1993, the most costly American alluvion ever. By departure time, a lone piece of good news — but an important one — suggested our route over the Great Plains at least should be well watered.

We pumped nearly four inches of rain out of the afterdeck, tightened down the canopy and kayak, set out onto the Mississippi, and
headed toward the landing where began St. Louis, obscured that day in
a rise of vapors, and on beyond the high Arch, the symbol of the city
and the Missouri as Gateway to the West. Passing tows tore up the
water, and *Nikawa* went into a violent rocking — pitching, yawing,
rolling all at once — a varied chaos even Lake Erie had not worked
upon us. We dodged drift and barges, jangled ourselves north through
the hullabaloo morning, passed under the great Eads Bridge of 1874, a
piece of engineering above all others that made St. Louis what it is. To
the northwest on the Missouri ridge of Bellefontaine, "beautiful fountain," sleep the bones of William Clark; had they eyes, they could look
across the river toward the place where the great Expedition began. We
reached quiet water behind Gabaret Island on the dug channel that
leads to the Chain-of-Rocks Lock, the final — or first — on the Mississippi and our last one for almost three thousand miles.

While securing our line in the chamber, the Piper fell hard enough
on the drizzled deck to stun himself before he could recover and
execute the mooring. In the lock with us was a big towboat. The pilot
apparently saw the fall and took it as evidence that we were novices,
and warned over the radio, "In this high water, you boys better know
what you're doing or you'll find yourself in a tree." His tone was not
one of concern but superiority. I radioed our thanks and said we'd
had to chainsaw our way out of treetops only twice since leaving New
York City.

We returned to the Mississippi a little below the mouth of Wood
River from where the Lewis and Clark Expedition embarked in 1804
on another day in May of similar wet and cheerless weather. We
crossed the Mississippi, and there before us opened the great Missouri charging down fiercely a flood that bulled into the other river, hit
Nikawa, shimmied her, bounced her in the confusion of waters, a
violence that fulfilled my long wish for such an assertion of force. The
moment had come, and my excitement to see our ascent begin quite
purged my glooms. Facing the river that more than any other would
decide whether or not we would make it to the Pacific gave me so
much adrenaline and exuberance, quickened further by apprehension,
I felt almost as if we were starting afresh. Herman Melville wrote, "He
who has never been afar, let him once go from home to know what
home is. For as you draw nigh again to your old native river, he seems

to pour through you with all his tides, and in your enthusiasm you swear to build altars like milestones along both his sacred banks."

I'd waited for this moment not just since Elizabeth, New Jersey, but since I was ten or eleven years old when I wanted to know what it felt like in a small boat to enter the maw of the Missouri, the ruction of rivers, and I was glad for the high waters because I wanted it to deny us nothing. At last the river I grew up near, the one whose water I drank from birth until I went off to the Navy. The Big Muddy was in me, the source of my first blood, the humour in my bones, my definition of a river, a winding trickery that once nearly took me down, a flowing whose farthest stream is Hell Roaring Creek and which leaves the mountains under the shadow of a peak named Nemesis. We were about to go against it all the way to the mountains, to that place nine thousand feet above the sea where we could stand astride it and drink straight its native purity.

In 1841, the Reverend John Clark passed by the confluence and wrote in his book *Gleanings by the Way:*

> We witnessed one of the most interesting sights in all our journey — the meeting of the waters of the Mississippi and the Missouri! I cannot attempt description. The imagination alone can conceive it. If I ever had feelings of sublimity waked up in my bosom, it was when our boat stood off just abreast the Missouri, and I looked up its mighty channel, and thought of its source between two and three thousand miles distant, amid those mountains whose tops are covered with eternal snow.

Befitting its nature, the Missouri comes snaking into the Mississippi on a bend five miles long before straightening perfectly into a reach that leads to another set of big bends. To hold in place this particular configuration at the confluence and to create a stable navigable channel, engineers have built along the first four miles thirty-five rock wing-dikes, structures that usually force even small boats to keep to the winding channel, but the stones were now well below the surface, and we were free to go nearly anywhere we saw wetness. The Piper took a position on the bow and played "Mist," "My Home," and, to make sure I was truly stirred to the challenge, another round of "Garry Owen," the Irish quickstep Indians like to whistle, the one that led George Custer's Seventh Cavalry into the tombs of history.

The Missouri is one of the fastest navigable rivers of length in the world, but as historian Stanley Vestal wrote, "The trouble with going up the Missouri River in a boat is that you have to take the boat along." For years a certain popular recreational cruising guide dismissed the river with the curt warning that it was "very hazardous to all boaters," but in the year of our ascent, the book at last included it, toning down the direful to a mere grousing "navigation [on the Missouri] is more a game of chance than a skilled profession." Reading that caution a day earlier, Pilotis had said, "Sounds like a perfect match for your brand of skippering."

The Piper had just come off the bow when *Nikawa* dropped into a virtual hole with a banging that shook our jawbones. It wasn't a true whirlpool but a large and ferocious eddy turning water, something a little less common than the numerous boils pushing currents upward, a less unnerving direction. I knew then, whatever else the Missouri did, it was not ever going to disappoint us; we could expect it, like a cross-grained grandfather, to do anything but bore us. We had the wind on our nose but only enough to ripple the water and leave the jouncings to the erratics of currents. And that's the way we started up the Missouri.

We passed through the extensive inundated flats called Spanish Bottoms where Hispanic troops in 1767 built facing fortresses, both long ago taken by the Big Muddy, a river that has always, given how it sweeps away the works of human hands, seemed to want its past written as myth rather than history. That morning I'd made arrangements to meet friends at the bankside park near the big gambling boats and below the hills of St. Charles, Missouri, once the western-most white settlement, the last stop in "civilized" territory. If the Mississippi kept to its southerly course just north of town, the great confluence of rivers would happen below Main Street, and St. Charles might now be the city with the Gateway Arch and a statue of Stan Musial. When we arrived, the park and casinos were empty, evacuated because of the flood.

I circled *Nikawa* awhile, then pressed on as the western sky slowly worked itself into ever more darkness. We rounded the big turn at what was once Catfish Island before engineers attached it to the shore, and then we passed under the paired bridges of U.S. 40 where the river even in its darkening became a fine stretch of heavily wooded hills, many of them sheared into rocky exposures by thousands of years of scouring water laden with grit carried down from the far granites of the Rockies. We were in the quiet territory of mid-nineteenth-century German immigrants who, using an excellent native grape, the Norton, made the area the preeminent wine country in America, an enterprise that Prohibition and California finally wiped out. It was from those hills that rootstock went to France to help restore louse-devastated vineyards; to drink French wine today is to take in a little of the Missouri Valley. For a hundred miles along both shores were roads running the green hills of woods and, once again, wineries. We continued beyond Defiance where, on a low rise above the bottomland, Daniel Boone built his last home, this one a solid stone place still holding the bed he died in, his chamberpot yet beneath.

As the weathery western sky drew in the last light, *Nikawa* went around the most southerly point of the long river and approached Washington, Missouri. At the edge of the flooded waterside park, a couple of dozen people under bright umbrellas watched our little white boat emerge from the drizzle, and we heard shouts. We were in serious need of a safe landing for the night. The musician went forward to pipe them a tune, and I moved in close to search out a berth near the shore. From the crowd we heard *"Nikawa! Nikawa!"* It was friends pointing toward a small assemblage of docks now cut off from land and exposed to the open river. I didn't like the precariousness of them, but the other choices were even poorer, so I picked out one protected by a few trees, and my midshipman tied us in. We took down the kayak, attached a long line for retrieving it, and paddled ashore one at a time, and from among the curious strangers came our friends to clap us on the back, their worry gone. A woman, who seemed to steam in the cold rain, approached and scolded, "We heard there was a boat out there! I was ready to call the sheriff about two wacko drunks out on such a flood!" Madam, I said, we may be crazy, but we're not crocked.

Washington is one of the good places right on the Missouri, the lower town still possessed of much of its past, its streets coming down like creeks to the water; because of judicious location, it is without a blockading levee or floodwall. By the old corncob-pipe factory where a worker once could light up a bowl in full view of passing steamboat decks loaded with tobacco, whiskey, and hemp, cobs lay strewn on the sidewalk. Next door we took supper, an occasion for toasts and stories, a rousing time, and then in *he* walked.

I Attach My Life to the Roots of a Cottonwood

OUT OF THE WET NIGHT he came, blown into the cellar café where our meal was, blustering in like an actor overplaying his entrance, a soggy cap on his head, oilskin pants and jacket, a cigarillo clenched under his white mustache, and he rasped out across the room, "Where's the captain? The one crossing the country. Where is he?" Surprised, thinking him perhaps unstable, no one spoke, the diners silent and guarded, watching. He scanned the place, approached our table, the several of us, and settled on me. "Are you him? You're the man? It's your boat?" I said it was, and who was he? "I can help you. You're tied out on that dock. That's no good in this bad water. You come up to my dock — it's a good dock — gas, everything you need. It's no good here. I'm your man on this river."

Maybe tomorrow, I said. "Hey, Captain! Captain! Trust Nick. I know this river — no one here knows it. You're down here, and you'll have problems." Maybe tomorrow. "Maybe, maybe! Captain! There's no gas on this river till St. Joseph — five hundred miles! Come up to New Haven, up to my dock. You think maybe, maybe, so maybe tonight your boat gets loose and you never see it again. There're punks on this river — pirates. They find a loose boat, and they strip it. You want a hull? Just a hull? That's what they'll leave you. Take a hull across the country! Try it! Scavengers are worse than the flood. Or maybe your boat just floats off and hits a bridge pier and damages it. Who's responsible? The captain has to maintain control of his vessel at all times. You got a lawsuit. But up at Nick's nobody bothers anything.

And this river, it ain't through rising. I'm a Greek — I know water." He was a small man, in his late sixties. He stood too close, talked too loud, too relentlessly, pointed his index finger too often, but I liked Nick Kotakis. Maybe tomorrow, I said.

The next morning after a big breakfast we learned the Corps was going to close the river to boats, and the Piper announced he wanted to leave a few days early. I felt the voyage starting to unravel. Next to me stood the Reporter, my newspaper friend from the *Kansas City Star* who had just been speaking of his time of terror on the Hudson River when he kept storm watch aboard *Nikawa* while Pilotis and I explored Pollepel Island. He had returned for an update to his story, and now he was going to get one as a shanghaied sailor. The Piper, in youthful haste, failed to proceed until the sky opened and insisted on getting gear from the boat just as black clouds rumbled in, and, helping him, the Reporter and I got soaked in the rain, then took shelter in town until the weather passed, and it was afternoon before the two of us could set out.

The truant Missouri sprawled everywhere, flaunting its mastery of the valley, and we had to follow tree lines that delineated the river from the inundated everything else. *Nikawa,* as if recognizing her baptismal stream, ran atop the boils and eddies so slickly I had to restrain her, hold her back since the current wasn't doing it. No boat can be built for all waters, but I was beginning to see that *Nikawa* — although she was almost certainly the first C-Dory ever on the Missouri — might prove herself a match for this most cantankerously challenging of American rivers, a good thing because the long Big Muddy was *the* key to reaching the Pacific.

New Haven, Missouri, only thirteen miles from Washington, sits behind a modest levee, and in front of it was Nick's barge-dock, the *Penelope,* a simple contraption — two fuel drums at the rear, a sodapop machine, a withered potted plant, a television antenna — the entire rig secured at the edge of the roiling channel by nothing more than a slender cable wrapped around an old cottonwood and another tied to a skinny post, both of those stanchions in ten feet of moving water. "That's it?" the Reporter said. "Somehow he made it sound better. Can that thing hold?"

The current put the mooring lines under a keen tension, enough to make me wonder how long the roots of the cottonwood might keep their grip in the saturated bottom. I could hear Pilotis speaking of "the prudent mariner," but I couldn't think of an alternative. Nick came out, hailed us, and I asked, Is that tree going to be there in the morning? "Captain! Captain! It held *Penelope* through the 'ninety-three flood, the big one. Bring your boat in!" I knew of no means to test the cottonwood, and once again I had to give us over to chance. We secured *Nikawa* on the inside of the dock, out of the way of direct hits by floating trees, barges, chicken coops, oil drums, or any of the freak debris that floods bring down. *Nikawa* would remain as long as the cottonwood, and for the next hours our trip would depend on tree roots; if they pulled loose, so would our voyage.

When's the crest supposed to hit? I asked. "Maybe tomorrow," Nick said, "maybe later, but when it does, the dock will still be here." The Reporter said, "How do you know that?" And Nick: "Hey, my friend! How do you know you'll be here tomorrow? Hey! I got more crucifixes inside than a church." I muttered, Now I'm reassured. I could only hope that his *Penelope* was as steadfast as Odysseus's.

Nick ran us to shore in his johnboat, and we walked along the levee to a two-storey bed-and-breakfast, a clean and pleasant house sitting at the base of the dike and affording a good view of our boat. The caretaker answered the door but tried to turn us down, saying conditions were too dangerous to stay there overnight, what with the river only fifteen feet away and rising and now actually above the ground floor. I pointed to *Nikawa* and told her we'd come from the Atlantic Ocean in that thing, so a house seemed a citadel to us. She studied the little dory, then said, "If this is what you really want." I took the upstairs room so I could lie abed and look out onto the cottonwood holding everything that then constituted my life.

After dinner, the Reporter and I walked along the levee, the Missouri only a few feet from topping it, and we tried to estimate the awesome weight rolling past the village, by our beds, under our boat. The windless night had filled with stars, and the river — you must understand this — although capable of sweeping away a town, the river made no noise whatsoever. The water moved hard and fast and in utter silence as if nothing were there, nothing at all.

A Language with
No Word for Flood

T HE TORNADO was bearing down fast with terrific noise, and the Reporter had us on high ground. I yelled for him to get the tow wagon to the creek, and he did as I awoke to find a blank wall inches from my nose. Then I remembered where I was and whirled in the bed to face the window. In the early sun the cottonwood still stood, and *Nikawa* rode securely against the little dock.

The Reporter heard me come down the stairs. He sat up in blinking astonishment, bigger eyes I've never seen, and pointed beyond the window. That's called a river, I said, and he, "I couldn't see it from the bed yesterday. It was too far below the levee." He hurried himself ready as if about to be swept away, and we went outside. The Missouri was up considerably, and by seven A.M. sirens called citizens to the shore, trucks were hauling in sand to be hoppered into bags, and soon people began arriving to form a long line on the levee and start laying down several courses of bagged sand only recently, and ironically, sucked from the river bottom. They hoped their two-foot barrier would be sufficient to thwart the rise. Hand to hand the sandbags went along, and the barrier rose only slightly faster than the river. A boss called out, "No slackers!" and they laughed at him, paused when the town siren sounded again, returned to their good humor, one woman saying, "Two years ago we had to do this in the rain. Today this is picnic weather." I walked the line, filled in when the brigade got stretched thin, listened to the talk. There were as many women as men, but the females, perhaps revealing some innate affinity with water unknown among males, treated the occasion as if it were an annual festival of spring: jokes, queries about so-and-so's divorce, what was wrong with Lendon's elbow.

Our man Nick arrived, nervous, less assured of his dock, tired, and he grew vexed when I asked again about the cottonwood holding on. He said national television networks were now showing the "raging Missouri" and announcing the month likely to become the wettest May on record. His agitation caused everyone to avoid him, but I couldn't shake free for some time. He pointed to the river gauge, a plain wooden post inscribed with numbers and notches, and he said it might go under, something it had not done in the record flood of 'ninety-three; if it did, the river would top the sandbags soon after and begin pouring into New Haven, first filling the cellars of the buildings on Front Street a block away before doing the real damage.

Trucks backed up to the stores as merchants selected which goods to haul out. I found their decisions unaccountable: a broken desk, a box of cheap dolls, two pieces of stained plasterboard. One man said he knew things were serious last night when he found mice moving to high ground, in that instance up into cabinet drawers.

The proprietor of The Christmas Shop, a woman in her seventies and noticeably bent in the upper spine, refused to move this time after shuffling items out two years earlier; frail and indomitable, she sat steady on her stool behind the cash register on the off chance someone might need a festive decoration just before the deluge. She said, "Why else do I have flood insurance? It's expensive, you know." The old barber in the old one-chair shop snipped away at old heads who had no fear of the old Missouri, and he talked about old topics, old Edna's old limp, the squirrels bagged that time in 'forty-eight, the durn price of corn. The beverage distributor, the richest man in town according to several reports, hurriedly wheeled soft-drink machines onto a flatbed; unlike the others, this younger man worked with little equanimity. With even less composure was he who most required it, the town Emergency Management Director, a loud, cigar-gnawing bantam who fretted his way around, relished his moment of authority, barked at his neighbors; people mostly humored or mocked him because they already knew what to do, one of them saying, "For us, this is a 'Been there, done that.'" The martinet's temperament grew fouler as the baggers, toiling hard in the sun while he strode about accomplishing nothing, responded to him with hand gestures and recommendations on where his despotic lips might be less annoyingly and more usefully employéd.

New Haven, population 1,500, sits just below a narrow bend, a curving stricture that even in low water creates strong currents against the forty-year-old levee. In its first century and a half, the village never saw the two lower streets flooded because the river had room in the miles of wide valley upriver to spread out and get absorbed. But as the Army Corps of Engineers gradually turned the once richly twined river into a trough and eliminated a half-million acres of meanders below the South Dakota line, and as the Army and farmers built more and more levees, the Missouri lost an innate capacity to absorb its frequent excesses, and floods became more virulent. (An Osage man, a descendant of the people who lived here at the arrival of the whites, once told me that in the native tongue there was a word for "great flow" but nothing really for "flood." He said, "Floods are white man's things.") That's why New Haven, like other intelligently situated river towns, for a century remained dry without floodwalls or levees. But now, after the big rise of two years earlier, bottom farmers near Treloar (rhymes with "Seymour") across the river had raised their earthen dike several inches, making it slightly higher than the one at New Haven; an inch difference, of course, is all it takes to top a neighbor's levee.

The jolliness along the bagging line ceased only when a new river-gauge reading was passed along: "It's up another notch!" The people would pause, look out at the Missouri rolling past and quietly carrying down trees like doomed pinnaces, and the workers' sweating brows wrinkled, but I heard no one execrate the river; each just went back to passing along stories and sandbags. No one said so, but I think they understood the Missouri provided purpose to certain idle days, excitement to a place where such was rare, a chance for community and contribution in an era of self-servers. The river invigorated them, renewed them, gave of its power and life, and that was the reason they did not curse it but chose to live beside it.

When, about noon, word came that the gauge was at a record height, a man told me, "If the Treloar levee doesn't give out, somebody'll blow it to save our town. What are fields compared to buildings?" Another whispered, "Better do it soon." There was the rub:

damaging a levee carries a long prison term, so destruction must happen after dark, probably too late to save New Haven.

I spelled a bagger here and there. A woman said to me, "Are we providing enough entertainment for you here in little old New Haven?" She looked out at *Nikawa* still clinging to the cottonwood and dock, and she said, "You couldn't pay me enough to go out on that river." I said we'd learned that morning the Corps had closed the Missouri to all boats, and I'd called a friend to bring our trailer down so we could get *Nikawa* off the water. It was lucky my home was only ninety miles away.

Bumblebees buzzed garden blossoms blithely, and swallows slipped back and forth over the river as if things were just as they ought to be, and, of course, they were. It was only the foolishness of trying to control the Missouri that was not as it should be. A man said so: "Our life would be easier if we'd grant the river its rights." And a woman next to him said, "What in hell are you saying?" And he, "I'm saying there isn't any way to manage the Missouri because only *it* can manage itself. In ten thousand years, who do you think'll be managing the river? Taxpayers have spent billions so we can stand out here and sandbag. My grandfather never had to do this, and old What's-his-name over there at Treloar never had to fertilize that bottomland — the river did it, and with no chemicals to get into our drinking water. So now we got levees and rock dikes and we've seen two five-hundred-year floods in two years. Just tell me how any of that makes sense." "I can't," said another, "but I think it makes us a thousand years old."

Along came an admonishment: volunteers in one section had laid bags with the open ends upriver, a flaw the Missouri would likely discover soon, but there was no time to correct it. Already water was finding ways into the levee through small rodent burrows now turning to trickles that for the moment a finger could plug, but in two hours even a sandbag couldn't stop. Should there be any woodchuck or muskrat dens and tunnels, the consequences would be more immediate. Then a new gauge reading — "Up another inch!" — and a fellow said, "Go down, Treloar! Go down!"

Nikawa rode only inches below the height of the levee, and I could but guess at the force the river was exerting on the cottonwood. I'd never before thought so much about tree roots. Where was our trailer? At three o'clock, the last message came down the line: "We can't keep up. Everybody go home. We've done what we could do." The Missouri was eleven inches above the record high-water mark. The citizens, tired and hungry and demoralized, looked over the low sandbag wall to see the brown water against the first course, the river creeping innocently, invisibly against the sacks, clover heads and grass stems wafting gently as if in a puddle, and there was nothing threatening or sinister whatsoever in the way it rose; it was utterly mild; only the uprooted trees sailing toward the Gulf gave indication of what loomed. The volunteers went slowly off the levee, no longer talking, futility saying it all.

I thought, If I hear *Nikawa* break loose, I'll swim for her. Can I make it? Futility indeed. This was the river that denies a drowning person the usual allotment of three times up and down. We all were caught in a village no longer a haven. The Reporter and I walked toward the Levee House — there'd be nobody in it tonight other than Old Man Muddy — and gathered our gear. A neighbor came out to greet us; as we stood talking in her yard she said, "Well, look at that!" I wheeled around toward the boat. *Nikawa* was still there. The woman reached down into the grass and pulled a four-leaf clover and handed it to the Reporter. "I don't know who needs it more, you or us," she said.

We walked onto the ramp to wait for the trailer. The emergency martinet, cigar clamped in the corner of his mouth, came up and shouted for us to leave. I told him the dory out there was mine and we were about to pull it off the river. "No you're not!" he yelled, although we were standing next to him. I most certainly am! "You do and you're going to jail!" There's no danger whatsoever to the levee by bringing her in! None at all and none to the ramp! He pulled out his radio like a weapon and spoke into it, "We may have a violator problem down at the pull-out!"

As timing would have it, my friend just then arrived with the trailer. I was losing my capacity to reason with the man, and the Reporter said, "Step away. Let me try." So I did, but it was no good, and from that point the conversation continued in volume between stage voice and bar shouts. I said, The Corps is closing the river, and you're closing this ramp, so where does that leave us and my boat? "Right where it is!" And for how long? "That's not my problem!"

Seeing our expedition, all our months of preparation, our weeks of hard miles suddenly going under because of one man's senseless and baseless exercise of egomania, I went into a fury and shouted in his face, If that boat goes down, I'm going to enjoy my jail time for beating the hell out of you! "Easy," the Reporter said, "he's just a man under pressure." No, I yelled into him, he's a tyrannical little turd under pressure!

We took the trailer up the hill to park it, and the whole time I planned my rescue of *Nikawa*. I would swim to her if I had to. She was not going to go down. On Front Street, the sirens blew, and a police car cruised by twice, the speakers telling the last merchants to get their vehicles to high ground. A man hurried past: "They've hauled all the post office out!" We walked on toward the upper end of the levee, where we heard a hubbub. "It must have breached!" the Reporter said, and we rushed forward. "What happened?" he called out, and a fellow turned: "Treloar's broke open!" We stood and watched the river gauge, the notches slowly emerging into the afternoon light, the water withdrawing from the sandbags that had held just long enough. For now New Haven was safe again, and, for a few more hours, probably *Nikawa*.

That night, in the Hilltop Lounge, some of the citizens celebrated with us, and the Reporter showed them the four-leaf clover and asked whether they believed in such things. "You bet your life," a fellow said sarcastically. Three weeks later a tornado hit New Haven, just as one had done after the last flood. When we heard that news, I said to the Reporter, We shouldn't have accepted the town clover.

Looking the River
in the Eye

W E HAD NOTHING but hearsay that the Corps of Engineers had closed the Missouri to tows and perhaps small boats too, so, the trailer ramp forbidden, I decided to treat the shutdown as only rumor and make a run upriver to my home country where I could protect *Nikawa* and get better control of our fate. That sunny morning we found her secure at the dock, the cottonwood holding strong. Nick gassed up our tanks, and we, hoping the way was open, proceeded on west.

The Missouri was everyplace a wide and weird deep, a maze of tree lines where the river afflux turned the bottoms into itself, and I struggled to distinguish the channel from the rest of the water. Once under way, I immediately headed into a broad flooded field before I realized my error and regained the river proper. *Nikawa* again rose to skim the current, but boils banged her repeatedly, some of them forcing up large gelatinous bubbles, yellow bulbs of methane that slowly broke open in the sunlight. The Reporter took up a drift watch and learned how to tell a wind riffle from a floater and where to find the navigational day marks among the trees. Other than dodging drift, *Nikawa* almost steered herself, as if she were a horse that knows the way home. Without minimizing the dangers of the Missouri, especially when in flood, I was coming to see it as a river given to intimidation yet yielding good passage to those who look it in the eye, and I had to admit that the engineers in their elimination of the braidings have made ascent of the lower Missouri an easier undertaking than it was ninety years ago.

Hermann, Missouri, an old German wine town between the bluffs, is one of the most famous on the river and of inviting access to a boat traveler, its steeples, courthouse, nineteenth-century White House Hotel marking it well, its Wharf Street open to the water in an agreeable way, but we dared not stop and again risk being prevented from continuing. I'd visited Hermann many times, and told the Reporter about the night I was having dinner in a little place there. At the next table, a young man talked loudly and unceasingly about himself and his greatness to come; finally his wearying audience, a woman so Teutonically fair her eyebrows were transparent, said, "Kevin, love thyself not too much, lest thou make others puke."

The country was rocky bluffs marking the river valley, their tops sprinkled with small burial mounds of the first people, most of the tumuli at cliff edges to give a long view down the water that may have represented the way into their next realm. Almost entirely free of industry and sprawled housing, those miles go among terrain lovely as any we'd seen, but it is, even today, something of a terra incognita because the wide floodplain typically keeps highways distant from the Missouri, and boating, other than fishermen's johnboats, is virtually nonexistent on the 365 river miles between St. Louis and Kansas City. The territory is not actually isolated, but the wooded hills circumscribe one's line of sight to create frequent impressions of a land only recently discovered. Yet it was up this lower Missouri that the vanguard of Europeans and Americans came into the West. I've found more than a hundred antebellum accounts of explorers and travelers describing the region, from the 1714 voyage of Étienne Veniard de Bourgmont to the 1861 trip Mark Twain briefly mentions in *Roughing It*. In between are narratives from many of the great figures in American western history: Lewis and Clark, Edwin James on the Stephen Long expedition, George Catlin, Narcissa Whitman, Alfred Jacob Miller, Pierre-Jean De Smet (six trips), John Charles Frémont, John James Audubon, and young Francis Parkman on his way to the Oregon Trail. From these hands famous and less so, one of the fullest accounts is hard to find and read by only a few, that describing the 1833–34 journey of the German prince Maximilian with his illustrator, Karl Bodmer, who created the most exquisite watercolors of the lands and peoples of the Missouri country ever made. The prince, perhaps the earliest ethnologist to visit tribal Americans on both continents, described meticulously what he saw, heard, and ate, creating a rich mosaic of the upper Louisiana Territory in its last days of Indian dominance.

The Missouri we saw on that May afternoon was little like the one those hundred chroniclers recorded, for the Army engineers have changed it from a river of ten thousand channels, chutes, islands, towheads, meanders, marshes, backwaters, slackwaters, sloughs, sandbars, and wrenchingly tight bends into a mildly curving conduit. The 750 miles of the lower Missouri — that portion below the last dam — is today essentially a single channel with hardly an island deserving the name. Instead of those features there are rock wing-dikes, five to ten for every mile, that straitjacket the river and force its current to scour the bottom to self-maintain a barge-navigable waterway. There is, however, little commercial navigation on the Missouri, unless you call Corps service boats or private sand-dredges navigation. The most heavily subsidized segment of the transportation industry, barge companies pay only about thirteen percent of the cost of operating and maintaining eleven thousand miles of major commercial waterways in the United States. Yet for a century the river has been manipulated for the nearly exclusive benefit of barges, a scheme that also opened expanses of valley bottoms to agriculture; according to state law, these "accreted lands" become the possession of adjacent property owners, largely farmers who can then demand federal protection from flooding into areas that were only recently towheads and shoals. Today the lower Missouri occupies about half the surface area it did before the engineers arrived, and of 160 large islands comprising 65,000 acres once in the river, only eighteen remain. Channelizing destroyed thousands of acres of natural habitats, removed spaces that formerly absorbed high waters to lessen the impact of floods, and forced Americans to pay millions of dollars to benefit a few companies and bottom farmers and people who should never have built houses and businesses in the altered floodplain in the first place. After the massive inundation of 1993, federal and state agencies started trying to give the lower Missouri back some of its escape valves by purchasing bottomlands that currents, engineered into violence, had alternately scooped holes into or covered with sand. What the government *gave* to farmers a few years ago, it began buying back to mitigate an impossible and destructive human design.

For the river, such schemes are but another moment in its long and ancient life; after all, what is a mere levee compared to the mile-high wall of ice that lay along the north bank three hundred thousand years ago? When our civilization is nothing more than disconnected pieces of half-buried things that don't decay, the river will already have remade itself according to the grand natural arrangement where everything answers to harmony, and the Missouri will have rebraided from the Rockies to the Mississippi.

We passed the mouth of the Gasconade, "the boastful river" although no one any longer knows why, and twenty-five miles farther the Osage entered, both rivers formerly steamboat navigable during high water for a hundred miles upstream. At the debouchment of the Osage once dwelt the people who gave the river its name and whom Audubon described as "well formed, athletic and robust men of noble aspect" capable of walking sixty miles a day. Chief Big Soldier, before his nation was dispossessed of Missouri, told a white friend: "You are surrounded by slaves. Everything about you is in chains, and you are in chains yourselves. I fear if I should change my life for yours, I too would become a slave." The Osage no longer lived on the shores of their river when white men fulfilled the old chief's words by massively enchaining the once freely flowing water to spin turbines to run bumper cars and light billboards around the Lake of the Ozarks.

Then, atop a long limestone bluff at Jefferson City, rose a veritable image of the United States Capitol, the Missouri statehouse, perhaps the most eminently situated one in America. The architects placed atop the dome a bronze Ceres, goddess of fecund corn fields, yet turned her back to the river and the valley it once kept deeply and naturally fertile. For a couple of millennia the ancient goddess has seen civilizations come and go and has watched the effect of hubris on nations that can dream up divinity but not accord themselves with natural force.

Around the broad bend beneath the purview of Ceres, we ascended another twenty miles to reach the mouth of Perche Creek (usually pronounced PURR-chee), its lower miles formerly the course of the Missouri until the river moved itself across the valley before the engineers could. Half a league up the stream is Providence, population 3, formerly the steamboat landing for Columbia. Waiting was my friend with the trailer. The current in the creek rushed hard against us, turned *Nikawa* around, and we had to winch her into the cradle, and then we hauled her up the narrow bluff-road.

I arrived home one month and one day after leaving the Atlantic Ocean, now just over two thousand water miles behind us. When the flood and regulations might permit us to resume the voyage I had no idea, and I was concerned not only about losing time against the snowmelt in the West but also that the forced layover in my homeport, the ease of the familiar, could make my return to the river nearly impossible.

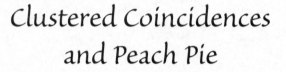

Clustered Coincidences
and Peach Pie

I T RAINED OFF AND ON for two days, but the Missouri neither rose nor fell appreciably, nor did the Corps open the river. I watched the calendar as a mill hand does the shop clock, and the Rocky Mountain Snow Imperative loomed greater than ever, since rain in the Far West could speed the melt. I wondered whether we should risk the tricky water, arrest, and maybe an angry farmer who might take a shot at us, even though the small wake from our boat would endanger no one's levee.

During that forty-eight hours, the Photographer and I replaced the propellers and made changes in our equipage to ready us for the western rivers and Great Plains and mountains we would pass through. After all the days and nights with someone only inches away every moment, I found the solitude of keeping bachelor's hall disconcerting, so each evening I went into Columbia to the Flat Branch brew pub, the creek an indirect tributary to the Missouri and our voyage, and the pub a direct contributor — writing being an insular occupation — to my social health. The Branch is a place of excellent ales and pilsners, with a dictionary and world almanac behind the bar to settle wagers. The second night, I joined friends at our favorite restaurant, Trattoria Strada Nova; they could see my resolve to continue fading in their glow, and I found on the table a note — ADMIT NO IMPEDIMENTS, ALLOW NO SKID DEMONS — to remind me that for many weeks yet the easy life was a hindrance and, for now, my true home was on the river. The message awoke me, and some time later, above the table that helped send me out again, I carved into the wall a map of our route.

I phoned to announce the departure to my great friend, who took the usual cautious Pilotis position: "Did you know I joined the Church of Procrastination?" What's the doctrine? "Procrastianity." Meaning what? "I don't know — I'll figure it out later." Time and tide — , I began, but my first mate interrupted, "Is the way open?" You know the answer to that. "Not long ago," said Pilotis, "I broke into a fortune cookie and found it empty. A metaphor of my life." I said, Tomorrow the river is in your cookie.

The next day Pilotis appeared and we went down to the creek, launched *Nikawa,* and again took aboard the Reporter. A few other friends waved us back onto our little ol excursion trip, and I soon felt safely under way once more and was no longer afraid of home. When we entered the Missouri, it thumped us hard, leaned *Nikawa* downstream before I could wheel her into the current, level out, and let her run. Black terns, in a signal welcome, accompanied us for an hour. Of all our long route, those next thirty miles I knew best, and I talked for much of the way, pointing out a particular creek, a special eddy, a goose nest, all the time Pilotis saying, "Where? Where?"

Item: Doug Elley, former mayor of the village of Lupus, invented a two-storey outhouse jocularly called the Sky Crapper that employs solar energy to turn human waste into desiccated and odorless crumblings, an innovation to reduce sewage in the river and one that will surely have its day, even though a senator from Wisconsin, William Proxmire (who spent only $145.10 on his 1982 reelection campaign), cited the thing as a fleecing of taxpayers.

Item: Plowboy Bend bears the name of a sternwheeler sunk there in the mid-nineteenth century, one of more than four hundred steamboats to go down in the Missouri, half of them from hitting snags. The average life of a nineteenth-century paddlewheeler on the river was less than two years.

At Rocheport, a village of singular charm, we turned up Moniteau Creek, and while Pilotis held *Nikawa* to the old railroad bridge, the Reporter and I ran for sandwiches. It was near the mouth of the Moniteau (the name is a Frenched-up corruption of the Algonquian word *Manito,* "Great Spirit"), the winter I was twenty, that I got the idea of crossing the Missouri on ice floes just to see what it was like.

One warm February Saturday, I started over the frozen chunks about the size of bathtubs, crusty and jagged pieces loosely locked together. Several yards out, I heard a rifle shot, and another, and I paused. Then I realized the reports came not from a gun but the ice itself as it snapped under stress from the current. I could hardly believe how loud the sound was. I felt the floe I stood on begin to shake, then wobble, and before me the ice parted to reveal the cold, muddy swirl twisting below — a more fearsome thing I'd never seen. The frozen river wasn't locked in place as I'd supposed but was being forced slowly downstream, buckling, snapping, opening, closing, ready to swallow whatever came onto it. That's when common sense and terror hit and I headed for shore, unsure whether to go gently and slowly or hard and fast. How did Eliza do it? When I reached land, I looked back, incredulous that I'd thought I could actually make it across. After I finished recounting that imprudence, Pilotis said, "The way closed by opening and saved you."

About twenty-five years later, almost exactly at that spot of my near demise, I encountered a thing of another sort. I was hiking along the old M-K-T Railroad, today the beautiful Katy Trail, in search of ancient pictographs William Clark mentioned on the way west in 1804. He wrote, "A Short distance above the mouth of this Creek, is Several Courious Paintings and Carveing in the projecting rock of Limestone inlade with white red & blue flint of verry good quallity," and between the lines in his journal he drew three of the figures. Over the years, steamboat travelers continued to note the numerous pictographs so close to the river, but railroad construction at the turn of the century blasted most of them away. I walked along in search of what might be left, and from time to time glanced at the river and wondered whether I'd ever discover a water route across the country that would allow me to ascend the Missouri to its farthest source. I finally gave up on finding any figures and stopped to watch the darkening water roll past. When I turned to take a last look at the rocky bluff in the falling light of that July evening, my gaze, as if it were an arrow put in flight by an unseen archer, landed directly on a rust-colored image, and I froze in disbelief, my skin crawling. There was a pictograph, but not just any pictograph — that one was the precise image Plains Indians drew to indicate the seventh lunar month, the Blood Moon, or the Moon of Heat. On that eroded limestone was a drawing of my name. I realized

William Clark and Meriwether Lewis, whose names I also bear —
William Lewis Trogdon — had seen it, the only piece of Indian "picture writing" all of us — red, white, mixed — ever encountered.

A few months later, I moved to an old farm near the river bluffs, and
I began seriously hunting a water way across America.

"Is all that true?" the Reporter asked. I pulled *Nikawa* close to shore,
handed him the binoculars, and pointed to the bluff twenty feet up. He
lifted the glasses, searched, then, "Whoa!" he murmured, and Pilotis,
who knew the story, said, "Treat it as remarkable but don't encourage
his belief in coincidences." Clustered coincidences, I corrected, and
then I told a third story.

The final anniversary gift my spouse made me, a few months before
she went on to another life and I to the rivers, was a big Hopi rainstick. For several days, I often turned it back and forth to listen to the
pebbles trickle down like droplets inside the hollow cholla limb. By the
end of the week, a serious dry spell broke, and the rain and snow fell
throughout the winter, not just along Perche and Moniteau creeks but
across the entire Missouri Valley well into western Montana to end an
arid decade and create just the kind of snowpack a cross-country
voyage would need.

The Reporter said, "You're taking liberties with this story." I answered I was taking nothing, every detail verifiable. Call it all clustered
coincidences, luck, or what have you, I said, but fabrication it is not.
"Well," he mused, "we *did* escape New Haven a few hours after the
woman gave us the four-leaf clover." Pilotis, who admits no gramarye
into anyone's philosophy and grows vexed with those who might, said,
"What? Not again!" and scowled at me. "Where's your native Missouri
skepticism? This is the land of Show Me." I said, Done been showed.
Then we reached the Boonville Bends.

Item: Near the north bank once was Franklin, briefly an important
village and, in 1819, the destination of the first steamboat to ascend the
Missouri which washed the settlement away soon after it became the
head of the Santa Fe Trail in 1821, a starting point that moved progres-

sively west with the years, finally ending up almost halfway across Kansas.

Item: Arrow Rock, a village vying with Rocheport for historic quaintness, sits too high for the river to flush away, so the Missouri pulled its other trick, abandoning the place for the opposite side of the valley. Indians mined chert from the bluffs there for tools and weapons, and it was in Arrow Rock that Dr. John Sappington developed anti-malarial quinine pills, and in 1844, relinquishing a fortune, he published his formula for the world to use.

Item: Not far away in a barbecue joint, a place of excuses and poor food, two friends and I ordered sandwiches. I wanted a truly hot sauce, Jim wanted medium, and Bob mild; when I asked for the three, the ornery waitress pointed to a small squeeze bottle on the table and said, "There it is." We need three, I said, which one is this? "All of them," she glowered. "You want hot, put more on."

Under the Glasgow train bridge, on the site of the first all-steel railway span in the world, the later one knocked loose from an abutment by the previous flood, the current was fierce enough to put us on alert, our edginess compounded by an approaching storm. I searched the riverfront for a tie-up, but everything lay horribly exposed to current and drift, so I doubled back to look again. "Rub that clover," Pilotis mocked. Above Stump Island, although it is one no more, I eased in behind an earthen bank, where the flood had turned a sunken spot into a shallow, quiet pond, and we moored to a dead tree. Ever circumspect, Pilotis said, "If the river drops, we'll be high and dry in the morning," and I answered, As a novitiate into the Church of Procrastianity, I'll think about that later. The Reporter, staring out the window, said, "Are we going to walk through that muck?" *Rule of the River Road:* When you have a choice, it will be Hobson's.

We rolled up our pant legs, debated another Hobson's — muddy shoes or feet — then went over the bow and into six inches of classic Missouri-bottom gumbo, stuff that adheres as does guilt to a novice sinner. Not happy with such rank adventure, Pilotis spoke in Henry James: "There's a constant force that makes for muddlement." We slogged to a road and up to little Glasgow and into a farmers' tavern, Hartung's Inn, widely called The Hard Up Inn, and ordered plates of broasted chicken and peach pie. When dessert arrived, so did what may prove to be the acme of Pilotis's empty-fortune-cookie existence, a moment my friend had waited for since first hearing an old Yiddish joke years earlier. Noticing the cutlery had disappeared with the chicken bones, Pilotis said to the young waitress, who had humored and charmed us, "Taste my pie." Surprised, she answered, "I cain't do that." "*Please* taste my pie." She looked at the table and said, "Cain't — they ain't no fork." Raising an index finger, Pilotis crowed, "Ah ha!" To ease her embarrassment, I turned to her and offered, You just made someone's evening. Said Pilotis, "Evening? No! My life!"

Gone with the Windings

To make sure an ebb in the river would not leave *Nikawa* stranded on the mud, I Tom Sawyered the Reporter's cameraman — he liked to be called a "shooter" — into sleeping aboard. Of course the Missouri, hearing all that happens along its shores, behaved with expected contrariety and helpfully rose four inches from the rain that came down without surcease through the night. Of the past thirty days, it had rained on all but two. The Shooter had bailed the afterdeck three times, and slept poorly in the cramped pilothouse even after he found my full bottle of rare sourmash, but he was young and pleased to join the expedition for a few hours. The Reporter, Pilotis, and I slept passably well in quarters large enough for us, and we brought the night-watch breakfast and told him of our café conversation with a retired farmer who had seen *Nikawa* tied to a tree in a place he usually parked his truck while he fished. He asked, "How far you going? Up to St. Jo?" I said the Pacific Ocean. "Well, that's a piece futher," he said, "but why would you want to do that?" Pilotis, having the gift of summary, answered, and the man, perhaps thinking of the many crops he'd taken off the bottoms, said, "I could do me a book about the Missoura, and I'd call it *That Dang River*, but I don't spect I will, so if you want that name, you go ahead and take it. If the wife would let me, I'd even call it *That God-dang River*. Take that one too." Said Pilotis, "It sounds like something in China."

We went down to the river Dang and bailed out *Nikawa* and struck off into the alternations of drizzle and mist, the Missouri full of drift that gave us *something* to watch since the shores lay hidden behind the gloom. We'd heard more rumors of the river being closed, but I

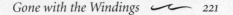

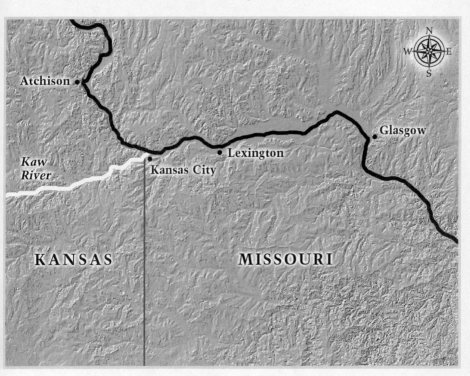

The Lower Missouri, Glasgow to Atchison, 197 river miles

believed if we could reach Kansas City and get beyond the mouth of the Kaw then pouring in tons of floodwater, we would be able to proceed without further legal let or serious fluvial hindrance. Should the rain continue along the upper Missouri Valley, the engineers upstream would have to begin releasing water from the six immense reservoirs nearing record capacities, and when the overflow came down, we'd be driven from the Missouri for days without a chance of reaching the West Coast that year.

"What are you going to do if an Army patrol boat stops us?" the Reporter said. I mumbled I'd try to persuade them with the romance of our voyage. "That's it?" No time for supporting letters from senators, I said. And on we went.

We passed by without seeing the mouths of the channelized Chariton and Grand rivers, wedded as they were to the wet air. To relieve ourselves of the drudgery of keeping watch for drift bearing down on us, we spoke of things having nothing to do with our situation. Pilotis, who had recently completed a draft of a novel not yet satisfying, said, "I wish I were blessed with the language of Shakespeare, the theme of Tolstoy, the plotting of Dickens, the humor of Twain, the industry of Balzac, the precision of Dickinson, and the swing of Babe Ruth." Said the Reporter, "If you had the last one, you wouldn't need the others." Just then I veered hard to miss a nasty dark log, broken and worn into an uncanny likeness of a shark — tail, eye, dorsal fin — and everyone went silent in the alarm. Then Pilotis added, "And the longevity of Shaw."

We passed below the bluffs of Miami, Missouri, where, during highway construction, archaeologists found a mastodon skeleton they dated to be 36,000 years old. Nothing unusual in that, except the bones — lying fifteen feet below the surface in undisturbed loess, a rock-free soil deposited only by wind — had been carefully arranged and with them lay crude stone scrapers and knives, and one *cut* tusk. Because of the construction, the dig had to be hurried and a later fire destroyed the bones, so the discovery could not be documented fully, a find that might have proven human presence along the Missouri 24,000 years before the currently accepted date.

A little west of Miami, the Missouri runs about as unbendingly as it can, and we hummed along when the floaters allowed it. A mallard winged past us, and I said on our best days we were crossing the country at half the speed of a duck in flight. Things seemed slow because the weather limited our view and made the misted Missouri an almost featureless and claustrophobic tunnel. But had the sky lifted, the towns still would have been hardly visible, since they are typically too far off a river they no longer depend on.

Every turn of the lower Missouri bears a name, although straightening it has made some bends almost unidentifiable as curves; I said, Many of the old names are gone with the windings. Pilotis, as intolerant of punning as a preacher's wife of off-color tales at the Sunday table, tried to stop any follow-ups, the natural fruit of wordplay, by reading names aloud from the chart: Bushwhacker Bend, Teteseau, Tamerlane, Cranberry, Baltimore, Tabo, Sheep Nose, Bootlegger, Sni-a-Bar, Jackass. I knew of no history of the bend names, but such a work would be a gladsome thing, especially to three cramped jacks-afloat on a drizzly morning.

As we approached Waverly, Pilotis said, "Give us a Lafayette County anecdote." Can't think of one, I said. "Make it up." The weather and miles were turning the crew restless. Trying to pull out a true story, I fumbled, There was this woman — "Heard it," the Reporter said. Then I told an elongated version of this: She wasn't poor, but she hated to spend money on clothes, so she bought apparel at church thrift shops, and in warm weather she went to bed nude to save on sleepwear. Quite a pretty woman. One business trip required her to share a room, so she found a garage sale and bought a frumpy, speckledy nightgown for thirty-five cents. In the hotel — a fancy one — the nightdress apparently got entangled in the sheets and tossed down the laundry chute. The next day she reported her loss at the front desk; when she later returned to her room, on the bed was her gown, laundered and neatly folded. Pinned inside was a ragged note in a hand barely literate:

My mariners stared at me. "We ask you to make up a story, and you give us that?" I didn't make it up, I said, I just changed the location. There was grumbling and shaking of heads. I relate the incident here to try to give a true picture of how things could be on long river days; I had kept them occupied for a couple of miles in expectation of some libidinous turn of events and then for another mile with the complaining. There are sacrifices a skipper must make for the welfare of his crew.

The mist began to lift, and soon after we passed Lexington. One morning in September of 1861, Union troops entrenched at the edge of the village looked down in astonishment at a peculiar wall of big bales of hemp slowly and mysteriously rolling over the slope toward them. They soon realized that Confederates were levering forward the heavy, water-soaked bundles that even heated cannonballs could not penetrate, men firing from between the crevices with the advance, an immense labor that eventually brought the Southerners close enough to the Union breastworks to engage in hand-to-hand fighting. By midafternoon, the attackers had forced the surrender of the river-view position, one they abandoned ten days later. Wrote Union commander James Mulligan, "All is destroyed, even the rails and trees, fencing of every kind, bushes and shrubs, nothing left that would hide a chicken."

Twelve miles beyond Lexington is the village of Napoleon. The Frenchman's nineteenth-century legend has left many related names across America, but, for reasons I don't comprehend, perhaps nowhere more abundantly than in Missouri. Just down the road from the village is his archenemy, Wellington, and halfway between is what's left of Waterloo. This latter name was working on me in a special way that afternoon because the Army Corps of Engineers has a station at Napoleon, and I was considerably concerned with being put off the river. I took *Nikawa* to the opposite side and, as best one can on open water, tried to slip invisibly past the outpost. Pilotis, keeping the binoculars on the place, watched for the modern equivalent of a warning shot across our bow, and I complained the miasma had lifted only moments too soon. Once we were again out of sight, the Reporter said, "I think we made it," but that was still far from assured — a patrol could be waiting for us anywhere upstream. Pilotis: "Here's one more version of proceeding as the way opens."

We reached Fort Osage, established by William Clark two years after his return from the Pacific. Once, and only briefly, the most important trading post in the West, it had a life of less than two decades before it fell into ruin. Almost under the brow of the recently rebuilt fort, we pulled up to a gentle clay bank so the Reporter could leave and the Shooter come aboard. As I backed off the slope, the Reporter called out and held something up. I asked Pilotis what he was yelling, and the Shooter answered, "He has the four-leaf clover." We'll get it later, I said and turned upriver. Within two minutes a resounding crack came from the stern. I cut the motors and raised them. A bough, only the size of a girl's arm, was caught between the bent and chipped props. I looked to shore to hail the Reporter, but he was gone with our clover. No one said a word, not even Pilotis.

Nikawa limped on, past the Little Blue River, scene of fierce fighting during the Civil War and one of the most westerly of its battles. On beyond Sleepy Branch and around Liberty Bend, the town a few miles north, with an 1833 calaboose oxymoronically called the Liberty Jail, a name Pilotis thought expressive of the human condition; it was there the founder of Mormonism, Joseph Smith, sat incarcerated four and a half months and had more revelations than a televangelist the night before a pledge drive.

The industrial bottoms of Kansas City, punctuated by big gambling boats, began appearing port and starboard. Through the gray but drying afternoon, the city towers rose from the river bluffs like Oz and gave us a remarkable riverscape impossible from any road. We went under seven bridges, including the 1886 Chouteau, the oldest on the river but soon to come down, and then beneath the Hannibal railroad bridge of 1917, which replaced the one of 1869, the first across the Missouri and the span that helped the Town of Kansas become *the* city of the American heartland.

Near the mouth of the Kansas River, commonly called the Kaw, Thomas Jefferson's Corps of Discovery camped for three days in 1804, saw large numbers of Carolina parakeets, a brightly beautiful bird hunted to extinction, and there William Clark, in one of his more solecistic sentences, wrote, "The waters of the Kansas is verry disigreeably tasted to me." When we entered the mouth of the Kaw, it disagreed with us in a different way: its formidable outrush of floodwater was sending down a small forest and enough human scourings to stock a salvage yard. We found a commercial excursion boat tied to an old barge where we hoped to lay up for the night, along the Kansas side in the Fairfax Bottoms. The owner, Ted Chapman, a burly fellow in his late fifties, directed us to a mooring on the outside of the old tender, an open spot under assault by the fast current and charging, ramming debris.

Trying to be a prudent mariner while not challenging his experience or abusing his hospitality, I ineffectually refused such an exposed berth, and he insisted, I resisted, insisted, resisted. At last he let us move to a quieter location between the barge and shore and behind his big tourist boat made to look like a sternwheeler. In the forbidding current, we donned life vests and worked tensely to get *Nikawa* as secure as conditions would allow. Then we climbed onto the tender and walked it to the gangway sagging into the floodwaters. We took off shoes, rolled up britches, and waded the swaying thing to shore. We had accomplished 140 miles, our farthest day yet, and we went off to Eighteenth and Brooklyn, once the nave of Kansas City jazz, for barbecued chicken and a real choice of sauces. Not once during the meal did I forget the way the Kaw, as if hating them, was sweeping trees out into the Missouri.

Pilotis's Cosmic View
Gets Bad News

KANSAS CITY, MISSOURI, is the preeminent city on the longest river in America, but you would never know it from talking to the inhabitants, not because of their usual modesty but rather their forgetfulness of the Missouri. In the self-proclaimed City of Fountains there is no spiritual link between them and it and only a distant awareness of its connection to their iced tea, potted geraniums, and baptized babies. Living in such a topographical Land of Nod, they are little different from most other Americans, who nevertheless seem to awaken when properly nudged. One day, perhaps, even their pastors will come to and dare to proclaim God dwelling not only in the hearts of humankind but also in the actual lands and waters from which those fleshly pumps derive. But Kansas City, born of the Missouri, has turned away from its great genetrix more than almost any other river city in America. If you want, for example, just to see the Missouri here, you have to cross a bridge at breakneck speed or take an elevator in a downtown skyscraper.

The view is important because the river makes one of its two grand changes in direction (the other, near the Canadian border, keeps the Missouri from leaving the country, which it did thousands of years ago when it flowed into Hudson's Bay). If the river did not turn at Kansas City just where the Kaw enters, it would by a shorter route — were the Ozark Mountains not in the way — enter the sea coincidentally at the place the Mississippi does. To look from atop an office tower is to witness one of the great facts of American topography, a detail that has made a decided difference in the way the West got peopled.

That Thursday began in one wise and ended in another. Perhaps because I grew up here, I couldn't escape a bedful of dreams about my recently dead father and my infirm mother's incapacity to realize he was gone; it was a night of sorry sleep turning every incident into loss. On waking, I recalled the words of a fellow a few days earlier: "The Army's going to pull you off the river." Then I remembered our misshapen propellers and nearly empty fuel tanks. For some moments I felt I couldn't do another mile, believed I was too weak a man to continue, and knew now was the time to admit it. I seemed to hear, *Face it, the voyage is finished — you're flagging, and you've come only halfway.* Then that last word hit and got me out of bed: halfway. A midpoint in any venture is difficult because that's the place where days gone and miles done equal those ahead, and the result is equilibrium, stasis, inertia. A rollercoaster nearly stops just before the last drop to the finish. In some ways, the first mile of the second half is the most crucial because it's the one that propels the traveler down the slope of endurance to destination. While we were still some miles shy of being exactly halfway, I knew I had already emotionally arrived there. So I dragged up onto my feet, doleful, depressed, dejected, disgruntled, dissatisfied, dissipated, discouraged, disheartened, downcast, and otherwise down in the mouth, and I went into the damp, dreary, dismal day drooping, despondent, disconsolate, and damnably in the deep doldrums.

Pilotis chirped about, whistling, but I couldn't find a blunt instrument smaller than the bathtub. The Reporter appeared briefly to bring us bagels and the New Haven clover, and then Pilotis and I went down to the river. *Nikawa* was steady and riding out the malign Kaw, but two entire sycamores had washed in to lodge between the barge and the bank to trap her. Okay, I said, that solves that: a boat that can't move doesn't need propellers or gasoline. I sat down and stared at my shoes. Pilotis let things be, but I could almost hear "Rub that clover."

Soon our host appeared and said his crew had gone for chainsaws and would take to the johnboat and try cutting up the trees so they could float on downstream; that left me again with broken props and empty tanks. The nearest gasoline on the river was eighty miles away, too far. We'd have to haul some in, a lot of it, and we had no transport and no good containers, a serious oversight. Pilotis mentioned a man I'd met only days before leaving on the trip, a fellow who volunteered help should we need it. Hoping for the unlikely, I phoned Barth

Kleinschmidt, actually found him, and he was happy we'd arrived, pleased to help, and, "By the way," said he, "it's a big city, but my warehouse happens to be only a couple of blocks from you." I hung up the receiver and said to Pilotis, I'm afraid I've got bad news for your cosmic view — we have another coincidence happening here.

Kleinschmidt arrived in his truck to drive us to the big warehouse full of his business — unclaimed freight — and he helped us comb through the eccentric place stacked with the draff of our times: chef toques, reams of copy paper, deodorant-stick rollerballs, toy swords, carnival tickets, chinchilla pelts, lampshades, microwave ovens, wet suits, a snare drum, football bladders, bookends, a gumball machine, and thirty thousand other things. Within minutes I found some five-gallon containers, and Pilotis said, "I'm only surprised that you didn't find them already filled." We took them to a gas station and pumped them full, ate a good lunch, and returned to the river to see the last log drift away from the barge. Pilotis: "We're down to props. It's going to be hell or impossible to change them in that water." Pedro, our host's mechanic, overheard us, and said, "Come, amigos." We got in the johnboat and motored up to the stern of *Nikawa* and, from his boat, replaced the props.

Twenty minutes later, under a lifting sky and light breeze that pushed away the dampness, we backed *Nikawa* into the Kaw, let the current turn her, and went again into the Missouri to start our ascent toward the next great bend, the one that would take us nearly into Canada. We pushed up along the Quindaro Bottoms, past the Kansas City water intake sucking in nine thousand gallons a minute to fill their fountains and make it easy for citizens to forget the river. Above the Kaw mouth, the Missouri was much less flood-struck, and we unconcernedly went up among the green hills. Park College sat atop its bluff, marked by the tower I used to visit in 1965 to look at the river and try to write poems about it; the reminiscence gave me confidence that I'd safely passed a point of no return in the heart. Then came Weston, a delightful old tobacco and whiskey town the river moved away from, leaving it high and dry ("Divine justice!" a preacher once stormed). Even with frequent stops to clear brush from the propellers, we moved easily through the peaceful afternoon, a calm enhanced by our having heard that the crest of the flood was now below Kansas City. The Army would not have to close this section.

We followed a broad curve of river and went under the long Kansas bluff that holds Fort Leavenworth, the preeminent post in the West after it replaced Fort Osage in 1827 and still today the place where the military writes its doctrine and incarcerates the most nefarious federal prisoners. In the first five years of the cantonment, disease and alcohol so troubled it that General Winfield Scott issued an edict:

> Every soldier or ranger who shall be found drunk or insensibly intoxicated after the publication of this order will be compelled, as soon as his strength will permit, to dig his grave at a suitable burying place large enough for his own reception, as such grave cannot fail to be wanted for the drunken man himself or for some drunken companion.

And it was at Fort Leavenworth that a young officer, F. Scott Fitzgerald, wrote the initial draft of his first novel, *This Side of Paradise.*

Dividing Missouri and Kansas, the Missouri River valley is a rather uniform two to three miles wide. Channelizing by engineers, coupled with the inconstant character of the river itself, have filled the bottoms with horseshoe and oxbow lakes, old meanders of the Missouri that create an abundant chain of pollution-cleansing wetlands underneath the Great Central Flyway used spring and fall by millions of migrating birds: bitterns, godwits, dowitchers, phalaropes, terns, grebes, widgeons, buffleheads, coots, herons, rails, soras, plovers, snipes, willets, ibises, sandpipers, dunlins, yellowlegs. Three quarters of American bird species depend on wetlands for rest, food, or nesting, but over the past two centuries Americans have destroyed sixty acres of wetlands every hour.

With the floodcrest downstream, *Nikawa* could no longer simply follow the curve of the river, so to avoid tearing her open on a wing-dike, we had to observe the navigational day marks attached to trees and poles; we tacked northerly along zigzags that are the hallmark of piloting on the Missouri, a procedure Mark Twain would recognize. It became necessary on bends to keep to the outside, often only a couple of feet from the bank, where the deepest water is, and everyplace we had to watch ripples to see whether they foretold merely wind or a rock dike or something worse. There is nothing more challenging or necessary than reading the surface of the water, and no pilot does it flawlessly all the time, for the only thing more fickle than wind is a river. An auto rides on top of a road, but a boat rides *in* a river, down in the usually invisible heart of it. People who do not like to swim in water that obscures their feet do not make for jolly river boatmen.

As we approached the old railroad pivot bridge at Atchison, Kansas, Pilotis stiffened. "Can we get under that damn thing?" I slowed, my mate went to the bow as we crept forward, nosing beneath while Pilotis called out the clearance. "Ten inches! Seven! Easy, easy!" I waited to hear a scrape or collision, but all was quiet except for the aerial soundings. "Six! Okay! Seven! A foot! Clear!" Had we arrived two days earlier, had I not been forced to lay over in my homeport, we would not have made it under that bridge. During the months planning the voyage, I'd forgotten to consider this lowest span on the navigable Missouri, and I wondered what others I might have overlooked.

At half past seven, we found at Atchison only the second dock since Kansas City, a small, friendly float although quite exposed to river drift. There wasn't enough daylight to continue. Another Hobson's. But for once the drift gave us something beyond consternation and broken props: a massive tree trunk, an ancient thing the river had pounded down to a heavy forked log, lay hooked under the front of the dock to form a V-shaped breakwater against the platform. After some shoving on the trunk, I slipped our horse between as if putting her in a stall. Could the timber hold, *Nikawa* had a chance to lie during the night safe from marauding drift. Pilotis: "What would we do without that tree?" Toss here sleepless or wake up in Kansas City.

The dock gangway was underwater, and we were not in the mood to get out the kayak, so we stayed aboard, but people came down to call their questions: "Why are you out there? Where you going? Aren't you scared? Need anything?" Pilotis set up a small supper of smoked herring, Kalamata olives, pepperoncini, Branston pickle, and sourdough bread, and by the light of a candle I poured out glasses of merlot. We toasted, and while the Missouri rocked us softly by the Kansas shore, we sat in the little pilothouse, now our dinner club, and supped and said we'd not gone far on that day fraught with hindrance, but nevertheless we'd done the important thing — we had gone. Now we could hope to be above the worst of the flood. I relished how such an atrabilious morning led to the sweetest evening aboard we'd yet found. Months earlier, in my hopeful innocence, just so I'd dreamed of our voyage happening. The best part of that day was the night.

The Dream Lines of
Thomas Jefferson

WE BROKE OUT the kayak that morning to get to shore, learned we had slept under the bluff on which Amelia Earhart spent most of her childhood, and found a man willing to take us into town to fill our gas canisters. Then we went to eggs and hash browns in a building not far from where Horace Greeley, on his great tour in 1859, ate his first dinner in the West. We found conversation with a fellow who had put his twenty-four-foot boat on many different American waters but had never succeeded in getting it up the tricky sixty miles of the Missouri from Ponca, Nebraska, to the first dam near Yankton, South Dakota. I told him we were determined to keep river under us, and he said, "In the right conditions, I hear some of the natives do it, but your boat will be at risk."

When we returned to *Nikawa*, I laid out plans for our last miles on the open Missouri before we would encounter the Fort Randall Dam, and Pilotis turned to on the bow and afterdeck to make things ship-shape. By noon we were under way, the sky clouded but the river smooth yet still full of debris, a sign the water was not dropping, since a rising river flushes out flotsam and a falling one clears itself by beaching floaters. We stopped often to unclog the props and motor stems, glad each time we found only entanglements rather than re-designed blades.

At St. Joseph, Missouri, one of the great jumping-off places of the nineteenth century, *Nikawa* crossed the route of the 1861 ferry that

The Lower Missouri, Atchison to Sioux City, 310 river miles

hauled the Pony Express over its first barrier; the little city has replaced expressmen with expressways in a web of ugliness that made it impossible to imagine the riverfront of pony days, but the opposite shore, grown up in a verdant line of trees, we could better picture as once the edge of settled country, the start of Indian lands. For the next week we would follow the great coast of the West lying on our port side, the East to starboard — a long skirting of the rim of the Great Plains before entering them in South Dakota. Onward from an old channel of the Missouri called Lake Contrary, we saw numerous beaver-gnawed tree trunks, an imprint returning to the valley after years of near extermination. The pair of stout ten-foot poles I carried along to use in sounding shallows and pushing off from shoals were lengths of ash sent into the river by beavers, the ends bearing marks of their chisel teeth. Pilotis said, "The symbol of the Army Corps of Engineers is a castle, but a more appropriate one would be a beaver." Yes, I said, the first engineer on the Missouri, the creature that knows how to dam without damning.

The overcast became mist, became drizzle, became downpour, and then reversed as the wind rose and churned the river to chopwater, and we seemed to make slow headway north. The Missouri gave gentle turns and a narrower width, creating beauty and a kind of cozy comfort. Said Pilotis, "I've heard that cattle being driven to slaughter calm down in a narrow chute with a curve in it. Maybe it's the security of not seeing ahead, not seeing your doom." The Blind Bend of Happiness? "Why not?"

I stopped in midriver, let the current work its will and take us in its nearly invisible grip, while I put into my logbook a sketch of the Mount Vernon Bends. Pilotis: "It's one of the most captivating sensations a traveler can know, drifting on a river." And then, watching us lose the mile we'd just gained, "We keep hearing about this guy or that coming down the Missouri last year or some other year, but nobody talks of anyone going up it. I see why now." When I finished drawing, I heard, "So why aren't we going these twenty-five hundred miles downstream?" It was a rhetorical question of weariness, for Pilotis knew we couldn't ascend the westward-running Salmon River in Idaho without a jet boat, hence its name, River of No Return. I said, This is America — who ever heard of eastering explorers?

I spoke of recently reading an account by a Washington newspaperman who made a quick two-week trip across the nation and came to believe America was "a big country that impresses one most when experienced overland." Pilotis growled, "Let me make a note of that profundity." It's true, I said, *until* one does it by water — then America isn't a big country but hundreds of smaller ones. I meant, moving as slowly as we were enunciated differences that scarcely matched the political geography west of the Mississippi. Indians developed their concepts of the land by going afoot and carrying away in their heads detailed images like maps, yet that wasn't how Thomas Jefferson went about it: his map was one of imaginary grids, of true latitudes and longitudes free of the rise and fall of the territory. Indians dreamed rivers and mountains, Jefferson dreamed township and range, things necessary to ownership. Traveling rivers and lakes as we were, only rarely did we see the manifest evidence of the Great Jeffersonian Plat — section-line roads and fields. I said, I'd love to see how William Clark might have laid out the West.

We proceeded on. To our port side lay the eastern boundary of our first Indian lands, the Iowa Reservation which abuts the Sac and Fox reserve extending a few miles north into Nebraska. Just below the state line is the village of White Cloud, Kansas, named after an Iowa chief whose wife was Strutting Pigeon, both of whom George Catlin painted and described. The artist wrote at length of the year-long tour in England and France that fourteen Iowas made. In the fall of 1845, when pressed by a roomful of London preachers — "black-coats" — to take up the white man's vision of the sole way to salvation, Chief White Cloud, not feeling well, perhaps from the merciless sermonizing, called on his war chieftain to respond. Neu-mon-ya (a name that does not mean what it sounds like), who had puffed hard on his long pipe throughout the lecturing, stood and spoke carefully so the translator could get it right:

My friends, you have told us that the Son of the Great Spirit was on earth, and that he was killed by white men, and that the Great Spirit sent him here to get killed. Now we cannot understand all this. This may be necessary for white people, but the red men, we think, have not yet got to be so wicked as to require that. If it was necessary that the Son of the Great Spirit should be killed for white people, it may be necessary for them to believe all this. My friends, you speak of the good book that you have in your hand; we have many of these in our village; we are told that all your words about the Son of the Great Spirit are printed in that book, and if we learn to read it, it will make good people of us. I would now ask why it don't make good people of the pale-faces living all around us? They can all read the good book, and they can understand all that the black-coats say, and still we find they are not so honest and so good a people as ours. This we are sure of. Such is the case in the country about us, but here we have no doubt but the white people who have so many to preach and so many books to read are all honest and good. In our country the white people have two faces, and their tongues branch in different ways. We know that this displeases the Great Spirit, and we do not wish to teach it to our children.

Few small-boat facilities lay along the lower Missouri, and most of the ones we did encounter were closed, flooded out, or their docks pulled off the river altogether. We began to lose the afternoon once again to deep overcast in the west, and the prospects for a good mooring within reach of daylight were poor, and I said, Here the hell we go again. "Rulo, Nebraska, is just ahead," Pilotis offered. I said, You could put little Rulo in a boxcar — we'd better start looking for a deep creek. The other choice (and an excellent one it could be), beaching on the inside of a shallow chute of a big sandbar, was impossible because all the bars, those few yet remaining in the channeled river, were under the high water. With the binoculars, Pilotis scanned the banks ahead, up and down, up and down. Desperation time? I said. We continued until, "Hold on! Hold on! Off to port, at eleven, isn't that a dock?" Indeed it was. In front of a cabin bobbed the smallest dock we'd seen, not even the length of the kayak. Our Hobson's for that day. I warped into the thing tied tenuously by slender ropes to a pair of cottonwoods well chewed on by beavers. When I said we could put our own line from *Nikawa* to the trees for safety, Pilotis said, "Do beavers gnaw rope?"

I snubbed the boat to the dock while my mate tiptoed across a narrow, bouncy plank to shore and went up to the cabin. A man in his forties stepped out with a rifle in one hand. There was an exchange, and the fellow laughed and came up to me. "I'm just putting the gun away. I was shooting beaver last night, literally. Got nine of them in four hours. You can see they're taking my trees." Other than toward beavers, Ron Hoagland was an amicable man who was stripping and refitting the old cabin; he couldn't stay the night but was pleased to let us use it. When he left, he said, "There's a bounty on beavers here because they burrow into levees." Pilotis said moments later, "Nature knows best," and we talked of how the bucktooths were the teeth of the river, the gnaw of creation to return the Missouri to its native condition, a sprawling of nurturing waters. I said, If nature undoes immediately what we work years to do, then we're not doing it right.

The drizzle came on again, but robins took up their melodious evensong anyway, apparently no longer able to wait for a proper spring evening to arrive, their territorial courtship born not out of a pleasant dusk but from mere genetic necessity, and it seemed their hearts were not in it. That night a farmer told us rainfall around the Big Nemaha

River was 120 percent above the yearly average: "We're starting to call our chickens field perch."

The heavy sky pushed Pilotis into the thrall of a spiritual skid demon like mine of two days earlier. Following the lead of Captain Meriwether Lewis when his Corps felt low, I issued an order for grog, and we walked a few yards to Club Rulo for a brace of ardent spirits, a pass at the salad bar, and plates of fried carp. We took up a position of good vantage by the Missouri, perhaps an error of judgment, and I continued to speak of the river, another error. I should have talked about prairies, or mountains, or baseball, or our Atchison morning when I heard a man ask a young woman, "What's going on with you?" "Oh," she answered tiredly, "I'm just doing life." It sounded like a judge's sentence. Then the waitress, who queried us while dispensing motherly care, delivered the fish and said, "Do you want some water, or have you seen enough of it?"

A Water Snake
across the Bow

B Y EARLY the next morning, we'd seen enough water of a certain kind. Accepting Ron Hoagland's offer to put our sleeping bags on the floor of the cabin, I woke at seven to a thunderstorm, dozed on in the sweet rumblings and patterings until I became aware of an icy flow creeping along my outstretched arm. We grabbed up our bags and manned mops and swabbed for an hour before the storm ceased and the flow under the doorsill stopped. We went to *Nikawa* to bail out the welldeck and make logbook entries, then resumed our quest under a grand cumulonimbus sky pried open by long shafts of sunlight.

The way was beleaguered by drift, much of it large stuff different from the whole trees we'd been dodging earlier. Now old timber, fat trunks smoothly shorn of limbs and turned into waterlogged submarines just barely visible and weighing a half ton or more, moved down at us in the potent current, and at every moment they jeopardized the journey. A following wind pushed us upstream as it beat against the down-bound current to raise a rough river, but black terns came up and formed a vanguard to break us through the weather.

Pilotis said, "Have you noticed when river people learn we're not Sunday boaters, their attitude changes and they're ready to help? It's good *Nikawa* doesn't look like a runabout. She's a workboat, a vessel of passage. She's our ambassador." I suggested our wayworn faces also set us apart from weekenders.

We were in almost isolated country, the river a uniform breadth of about three hundred yards, bound in by willows and maples punctuated by tall and wonderfully irregular cottonwoods that made a straight trunk seem a deformity. As elsewhere on the lower Missouri away from cities, there was virtually no industry other than an occasional grain terminal or even less frequently a power plant; the route did not appear like wilderness but neither did it look settled like the farm-and-village landscape lying beyond us. The most removed way to cross America is by her rivers; usually secluded and often sequestered, they give a sense of an untrammeled, peaceable nation, even when they themselves are in turmoil.

The Tarkio River, really a big creek, poured in its muddiness from overcultivated fields, and Pilotis said, "What in hell did you do that summer you lived up along it in that college town?" I said, Taught my classes, played tennis every evening, ate ten-cent boxes of popcorn, sat on the porch to read or watch the elm-lined street. I told Pilotis about the elderly woman living on the corner in a big Queen Anne house: each morning she came out to sweep her walk to let neighbors know she was still alive. Some eighty-year-olds phone a friend once a day, but this one just appeared with a broom. Always she said something to people passing by — locals or strangers — and often all she could come up with was churlishness. She didn't want friendship; rather, she was simply staking out the territory, claiming a corner in our memories so that after she was gone it would be years before anyone could pass without remembering her and perhaps telling a grandchild how the broom lady used to toss off her scoldings. One afternoon a boy sassed her, and I heard, in tremulous response, "Ohhh, mustn't get saucy, young chum!" In all her life, I'd heard, she had done nothing worthy of recognition except her objurgations, and I came to believe she was trying to turn that quiet street corner into her living epitaph. Said Pilotis, "I guess it worked."

The nuclear power station outside little Brownville, Nebraska, had a concrete floodwall plastered with mud-jug nests of cliff swallows, and the river was aflitter with their wings climbing into long ellipses, scimitar swoops down and around *Nikawa,* sunbeams gleaming off their iridescent heads as if that hot avian blood were radioactive. Brownville is an old steamboat village that wanted to become the state capital but couldn't manage to hold on even to the county seat. Pilotis, looking as we passed: "Speaking of epitaphs."

About three leagues above the Nishnabotna River (a Siouan name with several lively meanings but no certain one), we crossed the Iowa line after more than seven hundred miles along or inside Missouri borders, the most, with Montana, we'd see of any state. I use the word "see" advisedly because a river isn't a place of wide or deep vistas; its valley and usual border of trees and its ceaseless bendings so confine the view that we never saw more than a couple of miles at a time. The prospect of an ocean, a lake, a mountain, those you can gorge on, but a river you take in piecemeal. Of the twenty-five hundred miles of the Missouri, we could see in the longest reaches no more than about a thousandth of it; since a river is continuous in a way few things in nature are — its beginning is soon its end, its source water becomes its mouth — it can defy comprehension even more than an ocean. At sea, the North Atlantic looks much like the South Atlantic, but the Missouri in western Montana looks nothing like the Missouri in Iowa. Yet, as with an ocean, most of a river lies beneath, out of sight, crawling invisibly to disappearance in the sea, that ultimate source of its source. We were looking at only the top half inch of the Missouri, and, had that been all we wanted to view, we could have anchored at its mouth and watched every bit of it pass before us in about a month, the time it takes in average flow for a drop of it to get from the Continental Divide to the Mississippi, one of the quickest, long river journeys in the nation. The mountain may come to Mohammed, but stay-at-home travelers can have a river come to them.

At Nebraska City we would have appreciated a restricted view to cover some of its riverside ugliness, or, had we arrived a few minutes later, the weather would have blotted out the scene. A fat water snake crossed in front of our bow, an Osage portent of storm, and the sky fulfilled the reptilian forecast by occluding, the wind rising, and on farther, near the mouth of Weeping Water Creek, the river turned turbulent and muddy, full of natural debris, so that *Nikawa* banged along and silenced our conversation.

Every few miles I had to stop and go back to the pitching stern to clear the propellers. Minutes after one untangling, a cannonade of water shot forward from the motors and into the pilothouse window, wetting us and our sandwiches, and I stopped and cussed my way aft again to unwind a plastic trash bag. On we labored, beyond the mouth of the Platte, just about the last braided river of length in the West, the one Oregon Trail pioneers followed across the Great Plains so they would have water and forage. At Bellevue, its name right then ironic, we came upon the first riverside billboard we'd seen since the Atlantic Ocean. "Damn!" Pilotis yelled in the banging. "Suddenly things have gone to hell!"

It was true. Nothing had given a sense of beautiful passage as had the absence of signboards; without them, long stretches of the country appeared to us, if not pristine, then at least no worse the wear for half a millennium of explorers, settlers, descendants. The bullboard boys and others who see landscape only as a means to grab a fast buck without returning anything but ugliness have so degraded the view from so many American highways and so numbed us to the blight that we, especially the young, often silently accept the unsightly as a requisite of our economic lives and do nothing more than turn a blind eye to it.

As if to purge the hellacious miles, the sky blustered in rain so thick we could see little past our bow, and things became worse when hail drummed *Nikawa* hard and smote the waves flat, turned the surface white, and knocked the daylights out of the afternoon. But the downpour didn't bother me so much as the lightning. Our bow rail was a conductor supreme, so I moved us close to shore, where cottonwoods stuck their wet branches high into the fulminations. We thought falling limbs less deadly than ten thousand volts. It was a storm to appall the devil.

By nature, prairie storms are sprinters, coming on fast, exploding with often dreadful energy, then soon spent. After some miles, the weather changed again, and by the time we reached the sunlit outskirts of Omaha, the western sky made it seem we had dreamed the water snake and its consequences, and Pilotis was laughing and pointing out our location on the chart, a curve labeled Florence Bend Lower, and I said I'd always heard old Flo was a tall woman.

It was at about that place where H. Hussey Vivian, who only *crossed* the river in a Pullman car, complained in 1877: "The Missouri is the dirtiest, ugliest river I ever saw in my life. Its valley is a wide dreary mud flat with which it plays all kinds of tricks, altering its course for miles at a bound." Later in his trip, this member of Parliament, his ill humor surpassing even the measure usual to the British traveler overseas, wrote, "Two hideously ugly Indian squaws are looking in at the [train] window as I write, for we are now halting at a station, and I will be revenged by describing them." On behalf of the women — and perhaps the river — I hope recitation of his own words reveals where true ugliness lies.

The Missouri separates Omaha from Council Bluffs, Iowa. In the quieting water between the two cities, a Coast Guard Auxiliary patrol boat pulled alongside us, and Pilotis whispered, "What did you do?" I didn't know. From the patrol came, "*Nikawa,* are you all right?" Through the river grapevine, a surprisingly efficient system, the Auxiliary had learned of our approach in the storm. We talked rail to rail for a few moments, then followed the patrol to the north side of Omaha and into a good slip in the dockyards at Dodge Park where we found waiting for us two reporters who also had tapped into the grapevine.

They drove us into the city to a long-established Italian restaurant, Mister C's, that grew room by room over the years, slowly filling with a sediment of brummagem: plaster statuary, plastic flowers, ceramic figurines, vinyl-padded doors, and enough Christmas mini-lights to rig out the Brooklyn Bridge. We ordered up martinis, the best ever to touch my palate, but the bartender declined to divulge the formula. Salvatore Caniglia, the proprietor, asked how we liked his place, and Pilotis said, "We've come all the way by boat from New York to eat here." He said, "That's nothing on me. I came all the way by boat from Italy to New York," then took us into yet another room, this one with a diorama covering an entire wall, a re-creation of his village piazza peopled with little figures painted with faces from his boyhood: his five brothers idling, his aged mother bent to fill her urn at the village fountain, the mayor politicking down from a balcony. "The Eighth Wonder of Nebraska," one of the reporters said. No, I said, that's the martinis, but the bartender won't reveal the secret. "Tell him," Caniglia called to her. "It's okay to tell him." She looked hard to make sure, then answered, "There *is* no recipe. Just a straight gin called Barton's, an inexpensive one you can get at about any store around here."

That night we sought out a wet grocer to stock our lazarette for those stretched miles ahead through the Great American Beer Desert where we'd find nary an extra-stout or pale ale or genuine pilsner. I had read my Lewis and Clark, and I knew the importance of a ration at the end of a river day; for the Corps of Discovery, it helped maintain morale *and* discipline. My chum, I thought, was becoming a bit saucy.

Sacred Hoops and
a Wheel of Cheddar

IT WAS OUR LAST DAY on the lower Missouri, those bottom 750 miles the Corps of Engineers maintains for a virtual ghost fleet of barge traffic. By comparison with the nearly eighteen hundred miles of the upper portion, the lower segment was likely easy. Because of changes in this century, the Missouri is at least three different rivers: the navigable end, the giant reservoirs behind the giant dams in the Dakotas and eastern Montana, and the mostly free-flowing sections of the Far West. We did not really know then of a fourth river hidden among the others, one hardly recognized these days, a secret one that can spell the end of certain transcontinental aspirations.

Because there are no locks through the fifteen dams on the Missouri, we would have to portage *Nikawa* a few hundred yards around them; to help us along, I arranged a team of three, a for-the-nonce Order of Tri Pi's — Pilotis, the Professor, and the Photographer. They would support the expedition as a tripod does a telescope. Pilotis and I would be on the river every day, while the others alternated moving the boat trailer and canoe toward the next dam. That morning, under overcast and a stiff north wind, we assembled, with the Professor ready to come aboard. Pilotis went to the dock to unknot us but stopped and stood staring in front of *Nikawa*. I looked down to see what was the matter, and I too stood in silence. "What is it?" the Professor said. There, carefully aligned with our cutwater, was a small thing, a circle with four spokes — red, white, blue, yellow. It was the Plains Indians' ancient emblem of the sacred Four Directions, a symbol of the Great

Mysterious, a token reminder of how we can proceed through the journey of our days. It was almost the size of a silver dollar, made of dyed porcupine quills; when I picked it up, I found it was a broken earring. The famous Lakota holy man says in *Black Elk Speaks:*

> Everything an Indian does is in a circle, and that is because the Power of the World always works in circles, and everything tries to be round. In the old days when we were a strong and happy people, all our power came to us from the sacred hoop of the nation, and so long as the hoop was unbroken, the people flourished. The flowering tree was the living center of the hoop, and the circle of the four quarters nourished it. The east gave peace and light, the south gave warmth, the west gave rain, and north with its cold and mighty wind gave strength and endurance.

I said, If someone lost it right smack in front of our prow, it's a remarkable coincidence — if someone placed it here, it's an Indian blessing. I liked either idea because tomorrow we would enter the homelands of those people now commonly lumped together as Sioux but who prefer their tribal names: Yanktonai, Teton, Dakota, Lakota, Assiniboin, Hunkpapa, and more. Pilotis said, "At our exact halfway point, I really can't believe the timing of this." I took the little hoop into the pilothouse and affixed it to the forward plaque, Proceed As the Way Opens, for the Great Circle is very much about proceeding, ways, and openness.

We set off upstream into a wind that moved with the current to smooth it but forced us to buck the air. We left Omaha behind, the last real city we'd see until Portland, Oregon, almost three thousand river miles distant. The bluffs were now lower and farther away, often blocked from view by trees, and the tilled bottomlands steadily came closer to the water until they eradicated the green margin to expose low banks of soft brown earth that today require miles of stone revetment to withstand the engineered current. We might as well have been in a wide canal (a term some Corps employees still use on the river), the impression heightened by old wooden markers giving mileage to the Mississippi, figures more than fifty miles greater than the distance these days, a difference made by channeling the Missouri and cutting out meanders. A shorter river, of course, is a less abundant river.

One of those abandoned oxbows, the eight-mile curve of Desoto Bend, was now a wildlife refuge, a place of exceptional diversity — singing birds, calling frogs and toads, and greenery rustled by mammals we couldn't see. In 1865, a week before the Civil War ended, the packet *Bertrand,* built on the Ohio River and described as a "nice trim little steamer, neat but not gaudy, that sits upon the water like a duck," started off on her maiden voyage up the Missouri from St. Louis to Fort Benton, Montana, only to hit a snag and go down in the bend. Years later, engineers straightened the river, leaving the flat hull of the boat thirty feet under what became a field. Then, more than a century after the vessel sank, treasure hunters appeared, excited by accounts like one in the *Omaha Weekly Bee* in 1896: "For the amount of traffic that has been carried on it, no stretch of water on the globe has swallowed up as much wealth as the Missouri River." Hoping for a share of its legendary gold, the searchers at last found the boat and, surprisingly, reported it as law requires.

Archaeologists excavated the *Bertrand* and discovered not gold but something even more rare — one of the most abundant and diverse lodes of artifacts, almost two million items, ever to come to light in America, things instantly preserved in the anaerobic world of Missouri muck, much like household goods buried when volcanic ash covered Herculaneum. Diggers brought up object after object, conserved and displayed them in a new museum near the site of the wreck. Behind the glass cases today is a three-dimensional inventory of common life on the northern frontier, goods still seeming to be on the way to Montana, things just waiting for use: bottles of ale, Drake's Plantation Bitters, bourbon whiskey cocktail, ketchup, brandied cherries, cod liver oil, horseradish, pepper sauce, and lemon syrup; maple sugar candy, flour, butter, lard, olive oil, canned oysters, sardines (soda crackers also, of course), pickles, and tamarinds; boots, brooms, candles, hats, clocks, ink, pen points, pencils, skillets, teakettles, churns, cutlery, goblets, griddles, coal-oil lamps, matches, dye, mirrors, shoe polish, soap, starch, washtubs, pickaxes, plows, sleigh bells, axle grease, bullwhips, cut nails, keyhole facings, tar paper, black powder, tobacco, and snoods.

Above Desoto Bend, the river valley widens in places to sixteen miles, an area gridded with roads and cut with diversion ditches to drain it and give it over to soybeans. Had the Missouri not created such a rich and level bottomland, it might have been spared to keep some of its native character, but its fertility undid it. Paraphrasing, I think, Kurt Vonnegut, I said, If only God in his infinite wisdom had made it worthless. To hold the river thereabouts in its single artificial channel, its chains, commonly requires ten wing-dikes to the mile on one side with three miles of rock riprap opposite; yet, over the last 350 miles above Kansas City, we had not seen a single tow under way. I said to my mates, These last couple of days *Nikawa* has been the only boat on the river, so, to put it bluntly, engineering this river has served today no other purpose than to get us upstream. Pilotis said, "I've heard that all the channels in the old river allowed pioneers at certain times to cross it in wagons."

We passed beneath a big loess bluff covered with cliff swallow nests. Loess, the emblematic earth of the lower Missouri Valley, is a soil made from the fine grindings of glacial dust blown off exposed bars of the ancient braided river and commonly deposited near the shore. In its natural state, the soil has a peculiar and powerful adhesion that allows it to be sliced across like a big wheel of Cheddar and still stand vertically through years of rains and freezes; children dig shallow caves in it and, along highway exposures, carve in their names. But once loess is disturbed, it returns to its original powdery condition — good for farmers, useless for ten-year-olds — and the magic quiddity that Aeolus added to it fifteen thousand years ago is lost until the next glaciation.

Between Decatur, Nebraska, a town that used to be moved like a traveling tent show to follow the erratic Missouri, and Dakota City (as much a city as Kansas City is a village), we passed the Omaha and Winnebago reservations, further reminders that the Missouri once marked the edge of Indian country, the end of total white domination. These tribes, in a significant accomplishment, have held on to their reserves despite the increasing value of the land, but holding on to native things cultural and spiritual has been more problematic.

Rising high to starboard was the bluff containing the grave of Sergeant Charles Floyd, the only member of the Lewis and Clark Expedition to die en route, probably from a ruptured appendix. Clark, in one of his finest expressions, wrote in August of 1804: "We Came to make a warm bath for Sergt. Floyd hopeing it would brace him a little; before we could get him in to this bath he expired with a great deel of composure, haveing Said to me before his death that he was going away and wished me to write a letter — we Buried him [in] the top of a high round hill over looking the river & Countrey for a great distance."

The grave was so close to the edge of the bluff that, by 1857, the

Missouri had undercut the cliff to spill some of Floyd's bones into the muddy water. Citizens removed the remaining ones, made a cast of his skull, and reburied them; in 1895 the sergeant was again reburied farther from the precipice, a site now marked by a tall stone obelisk designed by Missouri River engineer *and* conservationist, as well as historian, the inimitable Hiram Chittenden.

At Sioux City, Iowa, we found a new shoreside park, and within its sheltered waters we lay to in a slip that would let me sleep without nightmaring about *Nikawa* being washed away like the bones of Sergeant Floyd. Our crew took a meal in a place overlooking the water, and from them I drew out all the advice and rumor each had recently gathered about our chances of farther ascending the Missouri. The opinions were one: the first miles on the upper river were going to test us in ways we'd not yet seen. I phoned a local boatman whose most positive comment when I asked whether we could make it was, "It's dubious." He thought I should call a steakhouse twenty miles up the road, a hangout of watermen ("river rats" was the actual term). There, a fellow considered my questions about the route up to the first dam eighty miles away, a braided stretch of old river full of shoals and sandbars and snags — the classic impediments. "I don't know whether you can make it or not. I don't know your boat, I don't know your skill, but I do know this — the water is up, way up. If ever there's a time to get through that section, you'll be able to do it tomorrow." He paused, then, "The best thing would be to get Billy Joe Conrad, the Indian. He's the man. He lives alone out somewhere, but this time of year he's probably sleeping with his dog in the bottom of a johnboat up some creek. I can tell you, getting up the river will be easier than finding him."

I began calling Cedar County cafés and taverns near the Missouri but could come up with only traces of Billy; at each place he was just beyond my grasp. It was as if I were tracking him over rock. I returned to the crew and said, The kiddie party is over — tomorrow we meet the real river. "Good," said Pilotis, "I'm tired of this fake one we've been on for seven hundred miles."

VIII

THE UPPER MISSOURI RIVER

NEAR FRAZER, MONTANA

ICONOGRAM VIII

The Missouri is, perhaps, different in appearance and character from all other rivers in the world; there is a terror in its manner which is sensibly felt the moment we enter its muddy waters from the Mississippi. From the mouth of the Yellow Stone River, which is the place from whence I am now writing, to its junction with the Mississippi, a distance of 2000 miles, the Missouri, with its boiling, turbid waters, sweeps off in one unceasing current, and in the whole distance there is scarcely an eddy or resting place for a canoe. Owing to the continual falling in of its rich alluvial banks, its water is always turbid and opaque, having at all seasons of the year the colour of a cup of chocolate or coffee with sugar and cream stirred into it. To give a better definition of its density and opacity, I have tried a number of simple experiments with it at this place and at other points below, at the results of which I was exceedingly surprised. By placing a piece of silver (and afterwards a piece of shell, which is a much whiter substance) in a tumbler of its water, and looking through the side of the glass, I ascertained that those substances could not be seen through the eighth part of an inch; this, however, is in the spring of the year when the freshet is upon the river, rendering the water, undoubtedly, much more turbid than it would be at other seasons; though it is always muddy and yellow, and from its boiling and wild character and uncommon colour, a stranger would think even in its lowest state there was a freshet upon it.

For the distance of 1000 miles above St. Louis, the shore of this river (and in many places the whole bed of the stream) are filled with snags and raft formed of trees of the largest size, which have been undermined by the falling banks and cast into the stream, their roots becoming fastened in the bottom of the river, with their tops floating on the surface of the water and pointing down the stream, forming the most frightful and discouraging prospect for the adventurous voyageur.

Almost every island and sand-bar is covered with huge piles of these floating trees, and when the river is flooded, its surface is almost literally covered with floating raft and drift wood which bid positive defiance to keel-boats and steamers on their way up the river.

With what propriety this "Hell of waters" might be denominated the "River Styx," I will not undertake to decide; but nothing could be more appropriate or innocent than to call it the River *of Sticks*.

George Catlin
Illustrations of the Manners, Customs, and
Condition of the North American Indians, 1841

We Find the
Fourth Missouri

I HAD FEW FEARS greater than discovering that big portions of the upper Missouri would be impassable to *Nikawa*, forcing us into the canoe long before I planned to use it many miles farther upstream from Sioux City. Too much time in the small boat would cause us to miss the June rise of snowmelt and thereby doom our reaching the Pacific that year. For months I'd studied maps and aerial photographs, queried anyone who might know the river, continually played the draft of *Nikawa* against the shallows, speed and time against miles and obstructions, hope against ignorance. During my research I came across this chilling sentence from paddlewheel days: "Navigating the Missouri at low water is like putting a steamer on dry land and sending a boy ahead with a watering pot."

All that searching decided what types of boats would have the best chances of making the ascent in the brief rise the river would likely give us. The upper Missouri determined nearly everything on the voyage, from hulls to departure dates, because no other portion of our route would demand so much. That morning in Iowa, the time for answers arrived, and I was eager for resolution, animated by expectation, and fidgety from the possibility the river would entrap us, ensnare the entire venture, and send me home broken in ways I didn't want to think about.

Elevation Report: 808 feet above the Atlantic, twenty-seven hundred miles distant from it.

I couldn't find Billy Joe. Under a cloudless sky and light wind, the

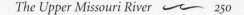

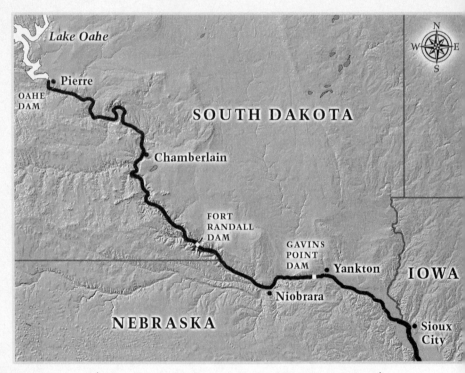

The Upper Missouri, Sioux City to Pierre, 333 river miles

kind William Clark called a "jentle brease," we set out north beyond the mouth of the Big Sioux River, the demarcation between Iowa and South Dakota, where the Missouri changes from almost due north to considerably more westward, a pleasing direction since we wanted the Pacific Ocean, not the Arctic. For the next many miles, if we could accomplish passage, we'd gain about one degree of longitude each day. Despite American geographers' insistence that the hundredth meridian marks the beginning of the West, the country now looked different; although still four degrees east of that famous demarcation, we were certainly in the Near West, the land between Middle and Far, the country where Lewis and Clark killed their first bison, an animal they'd never before seen.

For twenty miles the riprap and wing-dikes continued to make an easy channel, but just below Ponca State Park they ceased, and 752 miles above the Mississippi, the Missouri at last showed us its native face, a thing I'd both longed for and dreaded. I set *Nikawa* onto a sandy beach, and the crew took an ambulation while I asked a fisherman about the next thirty-five miles. He did his best to describe them as I translated his words into a charted sailing line through the strands of channels and backwaters. The problem would be not so much shoals but snags (trees caught in the bottom) and stumps (still rooted trunks). He said, "The Missouri eats props the way a baby does cookies — just chews them into a mess. Are you sure you don't want to use your canoe?" The poor quality of the Corps chartbooks and its badly printed sets of aerial photos fifteen years out of date further hindered us, but all our maps were the best I'd been able to find.

We went on a couple of miles to below the first real islands we'd seen on the Missouri and stopped at a ramp where we were to meet the Professor hauling the trailer and searching for Billy Joe. Our colleague had not found Conrad but did come up with another man who had run a tour boat in the navigable section and was willing to try to direct us through the invisible maze, so he came aboard, Pilotis made sandwiches, and we shoved off. Almost immediately we hit something that deformed a propeller. I was able to wrench it back into service; stainless-steel props can take harder hits, but once bent, you can't straighten them without a forge. The guide dropped his sandwich, the chart twice, broke the clasp on the forward hatch, and laughed when he didn't know the way. Still, he was a man trying for responsibility, and we liked him, but I repeatedly struggled between his recommendations and my reading of the river, and it concerned me that he readily gave in to my intuitions. We went forward slowly and had time to take in the new river reshaping itself according to ancient natural law, the fourth Missouri, the one hardly known because it endlessly remakes itself.

Islands of low vegetation and clean-swept sandbars became prevalent as the river took up its braiding and, in places, gave us four or five channels to choose from. Because a boat bound downriver can be carried deeply into a dead-end chute and struggle to get out, I was glad for once that we were running against the current; when I chose a wrong channel, I could wheel the nose of *Nikawa* a few degrees to let the river catch her bow and turn us back downstream. The trick was to avoid driving her too hard into the sand.

Off to port, below a ninety-degree bend, we passed Volcano Hill, about which William Clark wrote, "Those Bluffs has been lately on fire and is yet verry Hott." For years geologists believed the formation was a genuine volcano that erupted whenever the Missouri dumped flood-water into subterranean caverns of molten rock, but in fact the heat came from carbonaceous shale oxidizing as it eroded. Nevertheless, if there's a river in this country that can set fire to rock, it is the mysterious Missouri.

Above the mouth of the Vermilion, our river became broad enough to slow the current to invisibility except where it crossed an extreme shallow. After a string of islands and bars, the water narrowed to turn sharply north at Mulberry Bend and then spread out again into a veritable lake only inches deep and splotched with snags and stumps, ugly and dangerous things, just the kind painters like Karl Bodmer depicted in early-nineteenth-century riverscapes. Up there, people sometimes call those broken trees rampikes, a name as nasty as their threat. The nearly mile-wide water lay like a sheet of imperceptible flow, and I had no idea what course to pursue. I looked at our guide who laughed again. "I don't know," he said. "It's your boat."

I did what one does on the Missouri: go slowly into the outside of the bends where the current is supposed to be, even though that out-curve was full of snags. I wove a deviant sailing line among them, then ran out of water. I said, How the hell can a sandbar run athwart the channel of an outside bend? Our depth finder was below the transom, a place of some protection from drift, but its readings were always of the bottom behind us. Pilotis went forward with the sounding pole, and the Photographer watched at the stern for the amount of sediment we stirred up. The place was too narrow to turn around in, so before I could come about, I had to back us down, props dangerously first. I tried another strand of dark water. There too we grounded out and had to rock the little dory to get her free. I essayed one more. Creepingly we went forward until I heard the hull grate into sand. Of sounds a riverman can encounter, that's one of the most sickening. *Nikawa* refused to be wallowed free, so we took up the poles and shoved and pushed and cursed, and she slid off the bar. "What would we do if she had a vee-shaped hull?" the Photographer said. Pilotis: "Turn her into a duck blind and go home."

I must say here, in unabashed self-defense, that cursing is part of a Missouri River pilot's proper and honored method of ascent; to go upriver without it is simply unhistorical, probably unhealthy, and certainly unlikely, so much so that even devoted Southern Baptists and Missouri Synod Lutherans deem it less than a peccadillo.

I went atop the pilothouse to try to discern a route, but all I could see was a big sprawl of wetness spiked with snags and glistening riffles, every place looking equally passable, even where we had shoaled out. I had no idea what to try next. Three faces turned to me expectantly, confident the man who had studied things so long would have the answer. I looked again, hoping for a hidden route, this time seeing not the river but a most evident truth. My months of speculation now had answer: *Nikawa* could not get through. I was overmatched, and the Pacific was too far away for that year. That was it. The trip was done for.

As despair crawled up me, our guide came out with the lore that the east side of any river will always be deeper because of the rotation of the earth. I didn't point out that we were *on* the east side, but I did say, This goddamn Missouri River doesn't answer to the goddamn spin of the planet — it answers only to itsgoddamnself.

Pilotis said, "Two choices, skipper. Try again, or go back downriver." Standing atop the pilothouse, I yelled out into the wide empty space, I am not going the goddamn hell back down this goddamn bastard river! I jumped to the deck and went to the wheel, cranked *Nikawa* around hard, and rammed her across a narrow shoal and turned her violently upriver. I was losing the voyage, and I didn't give a damn that I was failing to avoid irritation at the way not opening, a small thing compared to despondence. "The props! The props!" Pilotis begged as I jammed us toward the other side. "Steady, Captain! Please! Please!"

The Photographer pointed upstream. "Look at that crazy monkey!" Coming down was a small boat, going fast. I hated his insane speed. Pilotis: "Maybe he's not crazy. Maybe he knows the way." Hail the bastard, I ordered, and Pilotis went to the bow and waved both arms, but the boat continued its course, then suddenly veered toward us. The Photographer put the binoculars on it. He said, "Somebody's signaling. I think he's warning us." I'll warn the goddamn hell out of him, I said.

As the boat approached, our nominal guide announced, "That guy standing up — I know him." Marvelous, I said, we'll just have us a little old fuckin fish fry out here on this pissant of a goddamn river —

who is that peckerwood anyway? "Billy Joe Conrad." I threw the motors into neutral and coasted to a stop. Say again? "Hell yes, that's Billy all right."

Said Pilotis to the Photographer, "I just can't believe this. We're in South Dakota, sitting alone on a sheet of nowhere water, the trip finished, and out of the blue comes the one man who knows the channel." Then to me, "If you write about this, you better include affidavits from us that it actually happened." I knew things did look a bit too miraculous, but all I said was, I do believe the way just opened.

When the other boat pulled alongside, our guide and Billy Joe changed places. Under his arm was a twelve-pack of beer. He was forty years old, solidly and broadly built in the Siouan manner, a large belly, but not tall. His eyes were slightly reddened, I hoped only from a morning on the water, and his speech had the slight lilt of Indians of the West. He said, "I don't like to run the river when it's high like this — it's tricky." There's good news, I said, which way? "Straight on for now," and he opened a beer. He told us the Professor had stumbled onto him upstream and told him to keep an eye out for a little tugboat with green trim. I moved us forward slowly, and he said, "No, no. Speed her up, get her up out of the water." She's got a flat hull, I explained, she doesn't really get up out of the water. "That's okay," Billy said, "give her some speed." I pushed the throttles forward, and he said, "More." The Missouri clicked underneath us in a way that could spell disaster.

"Maybe you can teach us your secrets," Pilotis said, and Billy answered, "Sure. You just got to look ahead, see what's ahead." He spoke that while staring toward the stern, watching where we'd been, and Pilotis said, "Is it good to look back at the river?" And Billy, "Why would you do that? You got to see ahead." He worked on the beer, occasionally calling for a change in our course. He said, "I'm blind in one eye." Blind? I reached for the throttles. You've got only one good eye? "It works. You've got two eyes, so you should see real good. You just got to learn to look ahead. Don't slow down. You want a beer anybody?"

Ripples lay dead ahead, and I asked, Which side? He turned to glance upstream. "That's nothing, but when you cross them, get over against the bank, right against it," and he turned again to face downriver. "You know, I'm not responsible if you hit something." The Photographer asked what a certain agitation in the water meant, and

Billy, not even turning, said, "That's nothing." We had a nasty hit this morning, I added, to alert him. "Yeah, you weren't looking ahead good. Okay, now come on over right, not too far. If you don't look ahead, it's hard." I said, I know — looking backward has made these last two thousand miles from the Atlantic hell. "Where?" Billy said. "I never been there. Okay, go back left and get against the bank so I can pick the daisies," and he swigged. "I don't like it when the river's up." If this is up, I said, I'd hate to see it down. Then I realized: Of course! The river is easier when it's low, because that's the time you can see the pools and through channels; everything else, the mirage river, is dry. Imagine a parlor filled with six feet of sand; take half away and *then* you can find yourself a chair.

Pilotis asked, "How can you navigate looking backwards?" Billy said, "It's the same river." I told him of our friend, old Ed Miller, who once answered when I'd asked whether he returned the same way he'd gone to Colorado: "No, I came back on the other side of the road." "Sure," Billy said. "Get closer to the bank."

I asked him what his tribe was. "Santee. I'm part Santee. Santee and white." His work was delivering diesel fuel to farmers in the field. "I used to box," he said and turned forward for a glance. "Cross over now and don't slow down. I couldn't be beat. Nobody."

When we reached Goat Island, three and a half miles long in high water and even longer in low, I pulled up at a small tavern, a spot, to my surprise, I'd phoned the night before. The Professor was waiting to change places with the Photographer. Billy said, "I'll get out here." Whoa! I called, we've got twenty more miles of this. He shrugged. "Okay, but I don't know the run up to Yankton so good. But, you want to try it, I'll try it." Off we went. "Faster! You got to get your boat up." She's as up as she gets, I said. "Sure." Billy nodded. "You want a beer?" Not too thirsty right now, I said. "Anybody thirsty?" Billy whispered, "I'm ninety-nine percent drunk myself, but I'll get you through. Come on over left. You know, I'm not responsible if we hit something up here."

Hey! I called to Pilotis and the Professor, help Billy with that beer — we'll buy him some more when we get there! I motioned for them to drink a couple fast, and I took one and faked sipping it. "I'll get you through," Billy said. "See that ripple up there? That's nothing. But that other one, stay off it." Pilotis said, "They look the same to me. What's the difference?" "Sure," Billy said, "they're different. Better believe it."

His voice became so soft I had trouble hearing him, and I began saying loud, pointless things to keep anyone from nodding off, and Pilotis helped with, "Tell us about your boxing." Billy, slurring, almost inaudible, "I couldn't be beat. Nobody. Cross over now." Pilotis, fortissimo: "Boxing's a great sport!" Billy: "Not if you get beat." Then he turned forward and stood up so he could see past the mouth of the James, and he motioned me to stop. "I don't know this up here so good, but I know that way there is stumps and that over there is rocks. Take your pick." I stared too, then headed for stumps and said, This one we'll do slow. Pilotis went to the bow to watch for trees. Finally Billy said, "Okay, we're through it," and I throttled forward and the props banged something hard. Within sight of Yankton luck ran out. I raised the motors, and the Professor went aft to look and shouted that the blades were still sound, so we went on, past a shore lined with junked cars used for revetment; otherwise, Yankton showed well from the river. Four miles farther we reached Gavins Point Dam, and below the spillway was our man waving the orange flag to direct us to the ramp. When we had *Nikawa* on the trailer, I looked at Billy, and he said with pride, "I got you through." You did indeed, I said, you're one terrific guide, the best I ever saw. I pressed on him our thanks but he declined it, so I put it in his pocket and said, This isn't for you — it's for your dog. I gripped his hand. "Sure," he said, "but you better remember to look ahead."

The Phantom Ship
of the Missouri Reeds

O F SEVERAL IMPEDIMENTS I evaluated from the wrong end, the great staircase of reservoirs on the Missouri was paramount, but when I was planning, my concern lay with their lower sections, the downriver ends where the dams are, and how to get around those massive pilings of earth and concrete without losing any significant water mileage. I neglected to consider that a dam on a river like the Missouri causes it eventually to remake itself into what it once was — a broad and shallow and frequently changing braided flow. Like a living being, an impoundment has a lifespan, and it starts moving toward its demise the moment it begins; when the currents of a silty river get slowed, they start to release sediment, and few things impede a river more than a deep lake, especially one behind a dam that can be closed to stop the flow altogether. The Missouri "mainstem lakes" are filling in from upstream down, and the time will come when the reservoirs will have to be massively dredged (at an economic and environmental cost beyond calculating) or removed. Left as they are, the Missouri will one day wash them away or turn them into spectacular cascades. This is another problem our era — we who believe in the mastery of nature and the supremacy of human desires — is bequeathing to another generation, not to some distant one, but possibly to children living now.

Sitting at supper in a place just behind the Gavins Point Dam, we began hearing about heavy siltation at the upper end of the impoundment blithely called Lewis and Clark Lake. One fellow told of Niobrara, Nebraska, our next stop, being flooded from time to time after the closing of the dam thirty-eight years ago and of a mass of silt that "backed up into town like one of those big-blob science fiction movies." But the news that concerned us was about the reed beds. Said he, "Did you see that *African Queen* movie when Bogart and Hepburn get lost in the tules and give up? That's what's there for you below the Niobrara River. If you don't know the place, you could spend days finding your way out."

I liked the notion of discovering a hidden passage, and I'd learned weeks ago to listen to and then largely discount difficulties residents described. *Rule of the River Road:* The more authoritative the adviser, the less reliable the advice. I expressed as much to Pilotis who said, "You're too cocky. No, not cocky — too assured. Assured of your luck." I'm not that assured, I said, but most of the time I do believe in the way opening. "All well and good," Pilotis said, "but let's get some reassurance." The Professor agreed, so he went off to find a man I'd heard about who knew the thirty miles up to the Niobrara.

The next morning at a café we met Jim Peterson, a retired teacher of business law who had spent most of his life around the Missouri and its people. I tried to glean from him everything he knew about the reed beds. He was articulate and informed, and I invited him to join us for a day. We stopped by the Corps of Engineers offices to ask questions all over again, and the words were disquieting. The next dam, at Fort Randall, sixty-nine miles upriver, was keeping back its water, letting little pass, to avoid exacerbating the flood in Missouri. The river above the mouth of the Niobrara, a natural section, was virtually dry but for pools. I asked whether our canoe could carry us through, and the Corpsman said, "Yes, if you want to drag it between wet spots and then risk tearing it open. There's a lot of Detroit riprap up there, junked cars that have washed off the banks into the water. That run is just damned dangerous." We can undertake danger, I said, but a stove boat is something else.

I disliked losing those river miles, few as they were, and I said, I love when engineers rebuild nature — in this year of near-record high water, a section of the Missouri is impassable because it's dry — since I want to do every mile of it, I guess I'll have to come back during a drought. Then, in a couple of sentences more laded with river language than necessary, I said something that boiled down to this: That engineers could build such colossal dams credits their intellect; that they actually built them discredits their foresightedness.

"You think you're miffed?" the Corpsman said. "Go to the tailwater below the dam and watch the fish swarming. Their gonads are telling them to swim upstream to spawn, but all they can do is beat their heads against the concrete. It's heartbreaking to see them massing up. Projects like this turn a natural system ass over teakettle. It was just imbecilic to think we could dam off one of the biggest rivers on the planet in fifteen different places and not upset balances."

Never before had I encountered, face to face, the heralded greening of the Army Corps of Engineers. He knew that many old mossbacks, like those who still called the river "the canal," did not agree with him, and he spoke at some risk to himself, but he was young and smart, and I told him I hoped he was the future of the Corps.

"With every flood," he said, "views like mine become less heretical. I'm not really an enviro, but if I were, I wouldn't be running scared. Green thought has the whole natural system on its side — that's about three billion years of trial and error posed against a couple thousand years of human engineering."

We went down to *Nikawa* and set off in fine weather, Pilotis and Peterson aboard, and headed up the long and "temporary" impoundment, fifty feet deep behind the dam and at that moment within twelve inches of the top of the spillway. Those inches were now critical because the snowpack in the northern Rockies was as much as 150 percent above normal, melt-off that would soon be on its way toward the oceans. Pilotis said, "Too much water above us and too much below, and in another few miles we're going to run out of it in the middle."

At first we took a due-west course, ignoring the old river channel at the bottom of the reservoir, but after ten miles of smooth running we began using the charts to try to follow the submerged Missouri and avoid shallows full of upright and broken trees that, within memory, stood living along the river. The reservoir has some beauty to it, largely because the Corps controls developers and requires them to cluster their buildings and leave miles of green and open shore.

Pilotis: "A tree at the edge of a river is a thing of elegance, but one *in* the water is a potential boat eater." Looking at the map and counting aloud, the first mate said, "Over these twelve miles of river, there are fourteen hazard areas marked on the chart." That was the reason we were winding our course over seemingly open water. Peterson said, "Fishermen love those fourteen places. The good aspect about snags, besides fish, is you can see between them and find your way through, but they'll break your props. The reeds won't likely break anything, unless it's your will to go on because you can't see the way out."

He talked of the Missouri he remembered from his childhood, before the dam. "Back then, the old river would take a farmer's land, but there was a fifty-fifty chance he'd get it back in his lifetime, and a hundred-percent chance his descendants would, and what they got back was fresh, rich topsoil ready for bumper crops. Now, the river here puts the topsoil underwater, where tractors and combines don't run too well." He paused, then said, "I have two photographs taken below the dam fifty years apart. The first is of my dad standing by a chute of the Missouri flowing north to south. The other is of my son in the same place, and the chute goes east to west." He paused again. "And my great-great-grandfather's homestead was a mile from the river — now it *is* the river."

The Santee Reservation lay along the south side of the impoundment and extended to the tail end of the lake where the water went from two and a half miles wide to just a half mile. Above Springfield, South Dakota, we reached the freshly remade ancient river and began twisting out a course among the stumps and sandbars, a piloting exercise to stir us alert. The Missouri became progressively shallower until the depth finder was useless, and I looked to our guide, and he said, "I can't believe how much this end has filled in. It all looks so different." His directions at first proved sound, and we moved through expeditiously until the reeds became heavy and the strands of water numerous; then we had to slow and guess. Because that section was more swamp than river, the current was again imperceptible. Our charts, older than the reed beds, proved nearly worthless, and the winding channels turned compass bearings to nonsense, so I tried to steer a course ninety degrees off the angle of the sunlight to avoid getting turned around and going back downstream. If a boat could be said to stumble, that's how we went. Jim shook his head. "I'm sorry I can't remember all of it, but the reeds are so much bigger than the last time I saw them. Maybe a good flood would scour them down."

We guessed onward, surmising here, conjecturing there, and sometimes *Nikawa* advanced, usually circuitously, and other times we had to retreat. The way became harder, and we began running aground, poling off, trying somewhere else. We were simply too low to see a route, and I said, If only we had a hot-air balloon and a thirty-foot tether, you could send me up to spy out the way.

The bewilderness went on. Then I made a mistake by proceeding too quickly and had to throttle down fast in front of a narrow shoal, and a splendid thing happened: our wake rolled under *Nikawa* and carried her over the sand. Asked Pilotis, "Did you do that deliberately?" Just an old riverman's trick, I said. "Well then, do it again and get us the hell out of this labyrinth." Flushing over the small bars was fun, and I would have enjoyed it more if I'd been certain I was flushing us in the right direction. The nightmare of reed beds is that we could travel miles up a dead end, then have to return to an entry point we were unlikely to recognize. I thought it possible to make the same mistake again and again, never to escape until we became the Phantom Ship of the Missouri Reeds, celebrated in story and song. We tried to memorize the stalks, attaching imagined resemblances to the bend of a leaf, the twist of a cattail, but it was like attempting to commit to memory ten million sticks of spaghetti standing on end.

Pilotis, working to match the charts to the distant hills we could see in places, said, "I think we just passed Lost Creek," to which I grumbled, Even the damn creeks around here can't find the way. And Pilotis: "I don't remember how Bogart frees the *African Queen* from the tules." A storm washes them out, I said. "What's the forecast? Where's your famous rainstick? Or maybe we can get the engineers to irrigate the Missouri."

At what I guessed to be the ninety-eighth meridian, the reeds began thinning, thinning, until we had open river, and we went on more easily, the water deeper, the current apparent, all the way to the mouth of the Niobrara (Ponca for "river spreading," oh yes), above which lay only the parching bed of the Missouri. The boat ramp nearby was a mudhole, so we radioed the waiting Professor to meet us back downstream at the old Running Water ferry crossing. That ramp was gravel and mud, and the current swept past so swiftly the Professor had to wade in to hook the hand winch to our bow so *Nikawa* could swing around and climb onto the trailer for the portage to Fort Randall Dam. I was equally relieved at being off the river and displeased with giving up those thirty-seven miles, but I vowed to return one day and canoe that section.

We hauled up to Niobrara, Nebraska, the one that recently moved out of the floodplain to higher ground but still saw almost half of its residents give up on the place altogether. The new Niobrara had a chance to lay out an innovative village plat, but the citizens only put down another grid and built a string of mock Old West false-fronts. I groused about it, and Pilotis said, "Is a mock false-front like a double negative where you end up with a positive?" Since the real West was full of false-fronts, perhaps Niobrara had to fake it to be real.

The reeds may have turned our wits to swamp muck, because such embrangled conversation continued in the Two Rivers, a new Old West saloon, and Peterson also fell into the bibble-babble of tired travelers. He said, "See if you can make sense of this sentence," and he wrote: Is that that that that that that that that person meant? We sat numbly until the Professor said, "It makes sense if you can hear it with the right inflections." I remembered a sentence grammar teachers used to inflict on students to punctuate: Hadley where Haddam had had had had had had had had had had had had a better effect on the instructor than had had had. Pilotis said, "I've done had had it. That that-that-that sentence is just like that reed bed — a damn tangle of sameness."

We went out and pulled *Nikawa* up along flooding Ponca Creek, left Nebraska, reached the Missouri again at Pickstown, South Dakota, and took a big room in the hotel of the Fort Randall Casino owned by the Yankton tribe. About those people, William Clark wrote (the passage corrected by his first editor):

> These are the best disposed Sioux who rove on the banks of the Missouri, and these even will not suffer any trader to ascend the river if they can possibly avoid it; they have, heretofore, invariably arrested the progress of all those they have met with, and generally compelled them to trade at the prices, nearly, which they themselves think proper to fix on their merchandise; they seldom commit any further violence on the whites.

We were about to see how the old commentary was holding up.

How to Steal Indian Land

SEVERAL YEARS AGO in Seattle, I was walking along the water-front to see up close the business of Puget Sound when a man approached me for a handout. He was tired, possibly ill, and probably younger than he looked. His T-shirt said HOKA-HEY, an Indian greeting, and I asked what his tribe was. He said, "Sioux." Does that mean, I said, that you're a Lakota? He looked stunned, awakened, and his eyes filled with tears, and he said more confidently, "Yes. Lakota. Oglala Lakota," and he smiled.

On the thirty-first of May, *Nikawa* entered what was once known as Sioux Country, a vast region covering nearly all the northern half of the Great Plains, the home of peoples who gave to most of the world the current perception of what an American Indian is. Even in the United States today, tribes with no connection to the Siouan nations have taken up certain elements of their nineteenth-century culture and apparel. Until we reached the mountains some weeks hence, the Indians we met would be Sioux, a name their ancient enemies the Chippewa put on them: "adders."

I reminded the crew that for the next fifteen hundred miles we'd be passing through Indian lands, reservations where we'd be foreigners, and I suggested they avoid the word "Sioux." I asked them to remember the four branches of those inhabitants of the northern Plains: Teton, Santee, Yanktonai, and Yankton, with each except the last having several bands, such as the Oglala, Hunkpapa, Assiniboin. Even better, I said, call the Tetons Lakotas, the Santees Dakotas, and the others Nakotas — if you wanted to make friends with someone from London, would you call him a limey, a European, or an Englishman?

We talked of that matter in the breakfast grill of the Fort Randall Casino and Hotel while a young Yankton waitress needled us about our losses (but for the Professor who had won twenty dollars) at the slot machines the night before. Pilotis said, "Consider the money reparation." And she: "You've got a long way to go then."

In the mid-nineteenth century, the Yanktons, under the usual pressures of white encroachment, were forced to sell most of their land for about thirteen cents an acre, although they had long demonstrated an amicable disposition to whites with their world-changing enterprises. In 1862 the Yanktons even sent warning to settlers about an impending raid by other tribes. From the earliest traders on, for the next half century, Yankton land marked a traveler's entry into Sioux Country, and those people were often a white's initial encounter with Indians still living their traditional ways directed by the ancient visions. In short, Yanktons were frequently the first full-fledged aboriginals Missouri River travelers met, and such meetings typically began with trepidation. Had an intractable and bellicose tribe, say, the Tetons, lived along here, the Anglo opening of the West would have gone more slowly, more bloodily. Despite the significant negotiations Lewis and Clark conducted with the Otos and Missouris downstream, it was the captains' parley with the Yanktons at Gavins Point that first began to reveal to them how insufficiently they understood the red world about to encompass them.

The adventure and romance of the great Expedition have blinded many Americans to its central aims which were more political and economic than scientific. A key duty of Captain Lewis was to inform people who had dwelt in the land for twelve thousand years and probably more that they were now "children" under the hand of the great and distant White Father. That is an act of conquest, not science. (The American West is today, of course, a bastion of resistance to anything emanating from Washington — except subsidy checks — and those who yelp the loudest about federal "intrusion" are the grandchildren of those who overran aboriginal lands. Right-wing militias are an ironic amusement to Indians.)

The world of the Plains peoples was considerably more complex and independent than any other native realms the Expedition had yet encountered, but relations began happily when the Yanktons welcomed two scouts Lewis sent ahead by carrying them into the Nakota camp on a bison robe, a sign of honor, although later one of the chiefs, Weuche, made it clear his people wanted more than words, peace medals, and American flags. When he learned the Expedition was not there to trade, he asked permission for his warriors to stop the next merchant boat and help themselves. Another chief, one of fine name, Half Man, prophetically warned that Indians farther upriver had ears harder to open. Indeed, in the next encounter, the Brulé Tetons so troubled the Corps of Discovery that Clark wrote words (again corrected by his editor) of uncharacteristic vehemence: "These [Tetons] are the vilest miscreants of the savage race [and] must ever remain the pirates of the Missouri until such measures are pursued by our government as will make them feel a dependence on its will for their supply of merchandise." Some history buffs prefer to ignore that sentence, just as they ignore the overt imperialism of the Expedition, as well as the words of its father, Thomas Jefferson, in of all places the Declaration of Independence where he speaks of "merciless Indian savages, whose known rule of warfare, is an undistinguished destruction of all ages, sexes, and conditions."

Among us latter-day ascenders of the Missouri was a notion the next morning that our night at the Yankton casino was but a permutation of the history there for the past two centuries, even if the only warriors we saw were the man-mountain security guards, today mustachioed, badged ("metal breasts"), wearing photo-identity cards, and on their sleeves little American flags. Our relationship with the Yanktons was recapitulated, if reworked, history: the night before, when the Professor began his winning streak, several Indian employees gathered around the slot machine, the thing gleaming like a campfire, while he dropped in coins perhaps like Clark tossimg out twists of tobacco and ribbons. It seemed our crew and the Nakotas were very much the descendants of old rivermen and chieftains. When the luck ended, a young Yankton asked where we'd come from, Pilotis answered, and she said, "Are you redoing Lewis and Clark through here?" To this question we'd heard before, I said, Yes, but only because it's the best water route west. She shook her head. "I mean, are you reliving a little of the history?" Until that evening, I would have said no.

Down the hill from the casino, Fort Randall Dam lies along the edge of the second fort, of 1870, where only foundations and a ruined chapel remain. Randall was part of a catenation of outposts built in the middle of the nineteenth century to help open the upper Plains for the taking. In 1881, Sitting Bull was brought to the fort after his surrender and imprisoned for two years; the soldiers, tired of tourists come to see the great chief, were glad he later was sent on up the Missouri to Fort Yates.

After we did work on our engines and propellers, we pulled *Nikawa* down to a narrow arm of Lake Francis Case (named after a South Dakota senator who supported anti-Indian bills President Truman vetoed) and launched under a blue sky holding big round clouds as the sea does islands. I took us in close to the dam, then we turned upstream and struck a course atop the old bed of the Missouri 120 feet below, heading west, passing over the site of the first Fort Randall of 1856 drowned by the impoundment like so many other historic places here. After all, Great Plains history often happens in watered valleys.

I kept an eye on the chart to keep us above the former riverbed, not because of surrounding shallows but because I wanted the Missouri to know we respected its ancient path to the sea. Just after we crossed the ninety-ninth meridian, the Professor, a teacher of writing whose pate was coming into the years of high polish, said as if thinking aloud, "There are no angles in water. It's an angleless stuff. Mountains have angles, and canyons, forests, the sky on a clear night." Pilotis said, "That's probably why fish have been so slow to take up geometry." The Professor, still to himself: "A big spread of lake like this just seems to *be,* as if it does nothing more than exist. It doesn't grow like a tree, or erode like a canyon or mountain. On a quiet day it's just here, with no more apparent life than a big old lichen on a rock." And Pilotis: "It's ruminating."

From my first day on the great river, I had learned to be cautious of what I said in its presence, for it has great ears. The Professor was yet a gosling on the Missouri, so I warned him how Loose Lips Sink Ships, not just in war but also on certain rivers. I said, For example, speak of a day going easily, and some waters we won't name will set your boat on her gunwales. He looked to see whether I was serious, and I said, If you must comment about smooth passage, then say it upside down. He thought, then whispered, "Well, the old Missouri, she's putting it hard to us today." Yes, I agreed, around the next bend we're likely to catch it even worse. Pilotis told the Professor, "The coincidences on this voyage have coincidences." I was just thinking that very thing in those very words, I said. And the Professor: "So was I." A mile farther, we banged into a low rider, a waterlogged timber showing almost nothing above the surface, but we escaped with no worse than pounding hearts. Said Pilotis to the Professor: "He may have hit that deliberately to indoctrinate you. His former spouse claimed he wasn't very smart, but he was lucky as all get-out." I said, You don't need to be smart if you're lucky. Just then we struck another low rider, this one an unnerving thunk. Again we got away with it. Pilotis: "Will you the hell stop doing that? He believes you." I said, It was pure coincidence.

I have not mentioned that, a year earlier, I gave consideration to making the voyage alone in a motorboat, because, for a journeying writer, companions human or otherwise are distractions. I've often thought how much better *Travels with Charley* might have been had John Steinbeck left at home that eponymous poodle. Isolation is more than a boon to a writer's effort — it's a near necessity. However — *however* — the great enemy of long-distance solo travel is, as Steinbeck understood, desolation. I've covered thousands and thousands of miles alone, but for this venture I came to believe the isolation might turn into a desolation that would sooner or later doom the voyage. That spring afternoon as we rolled along between the great bluenesses of the Dakota sky and the Missouri lake, I relished my companions — their voices, their laughter, their very distraction — and I understood they were as necessary as my eyes, my hands, and they were indeed my good hands.

The Professor brought along a small library of Missouri River books, and from these he read to us in quiet moments or sometimes just paraphrased a page or two, words always linked to our location or experience. As I sat back listening, steering *Nikawa* with my stockinged feet, taking in the greatness of the undulation of plains, he was saying, "South of here Lewis and Clark poured five barrels of water into a prairie-dog burrow to flush out a specimen to send to President Jefferson. They dug six feet down into another den only to discover they weren't halfway to the lodge, but they killed a rattler in a tunnel and found inside the snake a freshly swallowed prairie dog." Then he read a passage, changing a few crucial words to turn it into pornography, which may explain why the note I was making at the time about a west butte later appeared on my pad as "wet butt." My good hands, my sweet distractions.

Somewhere along there in 1843, on about the same date in May, Indians waved their request for the little steamboat *Omega* to make a landing and engage in trade, but the vessel chugged on upriver as the Indians stood disappointed before picking up their firearms. Passengers along the rail heard bullets striking the chimneys and piercing the cabin bulkheads, and a sleeping Scotsman had a bullet cut through his pantaloons before bouncing off a trunk to fall to the deck, and another traveler, John James Audubon, picked up two lead balls and put them with his collection of bird specimens.

We passed the mouth of Whetstone Creek, and three miles farther made a perfect ninety-degree turn back westward, and then, after sixteen miles, went under the Winner Bridge. From that point on, we'd be traveling farther north than we'd yet been. For years I've loved bridges — their designs, histories, function — but being on rivers made me see them as something even greater: they confirmed our position; they gave us hope that, were one of us to fall to injury or illness, we could find help; they reminded us we were not so alone as the vast openness often made us feel.

Near Snake Creek the sounder showed a depth of 240 feet, and Pilotis said, "The river Audubon or Maximilian or Captain Lewis knew is twenty-four stories below us," a comment that likely would have sent me into one of my bottom-walker reveries had not the inconstant Missouri suddenly shoaled out and put us into an increasingly twisted section of submerged trees on islands and sandbars then just inches beneath the surface, and I asked my mates to take up a deadhead watch. We'd gotten away with two hits that afternoon; even a dull-wit pilot knows when not to push luck too far. The compass headings rolled from west to west by north, to west-northwest, back again, west by south, west-southwest, and started all over once more, then we ascended past the inundated mouth of the White River pouring a long streak of muddy water into the blue lake.

Soon we came up to the old Milwaukee Road railway bridge, and then to a big, broad span. I asked, Do you know what that is? The Professor: "I've customarily called it, or ones resembling it, a bridge. What is it in your tongue, Tonto?" Interstate Ninety. In sarcasm, Pilotis took up the copilot's log and pretended, with manifest flourish, to make a note of it as if we'd spotted something rare, like a lost leg of the Oregon Trail. When sailors must suffer under a monomaniacal captain, they are prone to such mocking sport to relieve their repressed vexation. Just so, my hearties, said their Ahab, but where did our ship first cross Ninety?

Their *jeu d'esprit* turned to curiosity, then to sorry lubberly guesses, then to a mad riffling through the road atlas. Said the surprised first mate: "It was the Hudson, a hundred forty miles above New York City," and then more turning of pages and, "This is the fifth time we've gone under it." I asked, And where will be the last? — Don't look it up! — Just guess and wait. And they, macaronically, smartly, "Aye aye, *mon capitaine.*" I said, Ninety is the longest interstate and one of only two to run sea to sea.

The *Nikawa,* eighty-seven miles above the dam, came abreast of Chamberlain, South Dakota, a good little main-drag town, and we made our way up American Creek to an anchored dock cut off from shore by the record high water of the impoundment. We tied in, hoisted pant legs, and, shoeless, waded ashore past a sandbagged café to where the Photographer waited for us.

That night at dinner, safely beyond the Great River Ears, Pilotis said, "Was it an easy day because we were lucky, or are we learning how to do it?" The apprentice Professor argued for education, but the cynical skipper, long in the wiles of the Big Mischievous, held for chance. Said his friend a bit mockingly, "I guess we don't have to get smart as long as we stay lucky."

Later, the Photographer and I walked down to the Black Hills Bar, a delightful place of embossed tin ceiling and a worn screen door, the kind kids used to bang shut as they ran out into their summer days, and there we took up a conversation with two surveyors working for the Bureau of Land Management. They told how some white farmers on the unfenced plains encroach on Indian land by taking in an extra row with their big plows each spring. Said one fellow, "Given the width of those rigs and the size of the fields here, we're talking several acres every year." The Photographer: "Will there ever come a time when whites stop finding ways to steal Indian land?" The surveyors, blonds from North Dakota, looked at him as if the question had been, "Will the Second Coming begin the day after next?"

A Conscientious Woman

THE PHOTOGRAPHER was an inventive fellow who could jury-rig a number of malfunctioning things with a length of coathanger, a chip of wood, or some oddment he'd found on the street, and, once, an old tennis shoe. To accomplish his simple wizardry, he functioned as an ambulant vacuum cleaner capable of picking up and packing away any loose thing weighing up to about sixty pounds. As a former Navy man, I insisted on maintaining *Nikawa* in near Bristol fashion, and as navigator I always watched our draft and concomitant fuel economy, permitting only necessities to be packed away in either the boat or her tow wagon, the latter already much burdened when *Nikawa* was on the trailer, with the mountains still before us. Almost daily I emptied our transport of residua, continually reminding my mates the boat required no ballast and the wagon no more stowage, and I threatened to court-martial any hand committing such slovenliness or acquisitiveness. Little changed. I would turn up materiel the Photographer had found and tried to squirrel away: a peculiar shard of broken glass, a large carriage bolt, a length of oily string, a rock shaped like a potato (any object resembling an object of another kind he was sure to pick up). Those were the small et ceteras. The big ones — driftwood for an end table, a boulder for a rock garden, a packing crate to hold the recrements — those I forbade whenever I saw him lugging them. For the last several years, after his wife turned up one of his caches hidden in their attic, he has tried to give me a large, broken metal-and-neon café sign that says EAT.

To my knowledge, the Photographer is the formulator of the Strap Rule: If a strap can catch on something, it will. That's a maxim I cannot gainsay, as I thrice proved that morning right after I discovered a piece of boiler and a lawnmower wheel hidden in the tow wagon: my belt, camera lanyard, and shoulder case attached themselves to a nail, doorknob, and boat cleat as if they were loath to leave port.

The Photographer came aboard, the Professor happy to have the shore time he was coming to prefer. We waded out to *Nikawa* and set off down the creek and onto Impoundment Francis Case, the morning again in flawless weather. Nobody said it, of course, but everything was right. That reservoir, like Lake Sharpe twenty miles upstream, is narrow, with submerged and exposed dead trees infesting its banks, places so stump-ridden a fisherman can hardly pull a lure through, so, although the way looked quite open, we proceeded up the lake by again trying to keep the old river beneath our hull. On the low hills we saw more decaying timber in the water than trees of any sort on shore, and on both sides of us, beyond the narrow U.S. government boundary surrounding the Missouri, Indian land stretched northward for some sixty miles.

A man who had watched us get ready to slog out to *Nikawa* that morning told us of a fellow passing through Chamberlain a year earlier. "He was running coast to coast like you, but he was taking seven years to do it. He did a stretch every summer, but he had a speedboat, so he was going to have to portage pretty much all through Montana and Idaho." With that qualifier I lost interest, but the Professor, wanting to spend more time where people were, said, "Seven years to cross sounds like a sane traveler." I agreed but told him that wasn't the plan for me who knew the towns and counties along our course; I wanted what I didn't know, the riverine route across America. One can drive over the Plains, to mention one instance, on highways nearest the Missouri and see its water only a half-dozen times, usually in places where everyone else is looking. No matter how marvelously open the land appears there, the Missouri and its bottom country are quite hidden away, and a traveler passing through the Dakotas could come to believe they are utterly dry. From a highway, perhaps one can get an idea of things like the Oregon and Santa Fe trails, but for a notion of what Lewis and Clark or Audubon or Father De Smet encountered on the river, *that* an automobile can't provide.

By noon we reached Big Bend Dam, a sinuous earthen and concrete wall athwart the Missouri, the spillway on the east and powerhouse on the west. The Professor waved the orange signal flag to direct us toward his voice over the radio and the waiting trailer, and we soon had *Nikawa* loaded and hauled up the slope and across the dam and back into the water. The weather remained neighborly, and the impoundment gave us nothing more than a washboard of wavelets. The Photographer said, "Why do I feel the Missouri is setting us up?" Pilotis: "That's its nature."

When we were again under way on Lake Sharpe, Mate stared back at the dam for some time, then nodded: "If we stopped up all the rivers, we'd be living underwater. They keep us dry. Without them, we'd have no bean patches or baseball diamonds. We'd be some kind of underwater species." The Photographer, who can tell you the plot of such movies as *They Saved Hitler's Brain,* said, "Maybe like the Creature from the Black Lagoon." Pilotis: "When we speak of land, we talk about our lives, but when we speak of rivers, we talk about life." I said, There's something in flowing water that can turn a bloke downright contemplative. Pilotis: "I think I know why I'm finding these impounded miles so slow — the river has no song in the reservoirs. It's quelled. I can't see the flowing, so sometimes it's like neither we nor the water is moving."

Seven miles above the dam, the Missouri strikes against a hard peninsula that forces it nearly ten miles north before it again reaches a more tractable terrain and turns to resume its southeasterly run to the sea. The Big Bend is, to my mind, more accurately a loop in the shape of a turkey's head, the long neck to the south, the beak to the west. From Lewis and Clark on into steamboat days, passengers sometimes went ashore at the narrow base to take a constitutional over the open but uneven ground to the other side, less than a mile distant today, but three times that before the dam. William Clark reported doing it and so did Prince Maximilian, both of them watching their boats labor around the bulgy spit, land now intensively plowed, a piece one would walk these days only to recapitulate a historical circumstance. While the river is wider today, its old braiding is yet apparent in the tricky shallows there, and I tried to match the chart with readings from the sounder as we hooked around the grand loop that slowly widens to nearly three miles on the upper end. At the base of the turkey neck, we passed our thousandth mile on the Missouri, almost three thousand water miles away from the Atlantic, but the erratics of the river gave us no moment to celebrate beyond high-fives.

The entire peninsula belongs to the Brulé Tetons, the tribe that came close to wiping out Lewis and Clark's Corps not far from Big Bend. The dramatic and angry face-off, a story often retold, is memorable because both sides checked their anger just enough to avoid blood, a détente that kept not only Jefferson's Expedition but much other Missouri River history from derailing early.

Each shore lay in reciprocations of treeless and anciently eroded slopes between leveled cropland, some of it with center-pivot irrigation insanely spraying water onto the entombed river. We turned north, went back west, and four miles farther reached another benchmark, the great hundredth meridian, the most popular definer of where the American West begins. Our day nearly done, we rolled along feeling in charge of our fate, but, a few miles below Pierre, South Dakota, the Photographer lapsed and said, "What an easy day," caught himself, and added, "Of course, it'll get worse." Damnit, I said, you know you can't trick a trickster.

Although thirteen thousand people live in the capital, we saw little indication from the water that there were even thirteen thereabouts; wooded islands and bankside trees once again screened us into the illusion we were isolated voyagers. In search of a dock, two miles below the mouth of the Bad River — called the Teton by Lewis and Clark, and the Little Missouri by the French-Canadian explorers, the Vérendryes — I took us up a shallow, dead-end chute along the east bank, a hazard area according to our chart. In the still water I tried to navigate with the depth finder, but the shoals sent the thing haywire, making it fluctuate wildly. When I noticed it register 196 feet, I cut power quickly but not before putting us onto an invisible mudbar. Surprised to be so solidly fixed, I looked back and saw a brown wake a quarter of a mile long. Wearily helping to pole *Nikawa* free, I said to my fine hearts, Part of standing watch is to look backward as well as forward, especially when I have to keep an eye on the goddamn sounder. One of them answered, "Billy Joe said we've got to learn to look ahead." Sure, I grumbled, and what direction was he facing when he said it?

I returned to the wheel and tried to fathom the way. Occluded water that doesn't move is like a face behind a mask — any horrible thing might be under it. Pilotis watched the transom for telltale silt as I eased us weavingly upstream toward several boys playing baseball in the shallows, upright sticks serving as bases. Behind second, in their outpool, several home run balls bobbed around. Over the radio, Pilotis hooted up the Professor who said he could hear *Nikawa* but couldn't see her, to which Pilotis replied, "We just rounded first and are going for second, but it looks like we'll have to slide headlong to beat the tag." That's when I realized the home run balls were actually little buoys, and I muddied us along them until the trees opened and there was the orange flag. After we pulled up, the Professor said, "That last transmission was really distorted. It sounded like you were gabbing about baseball."

Once *Nikawa* was on the trailer and we were wiping mud off her nose, someone crabbed, "That damn river's like a conscientious woman — she keeps you on your toes all the time."

Flux, Fixes,
and Flumdiddle

O NE FEBRUARY SUNDAY in 1913, a girl with her classmates was walking around by their schoolground on an arid bluff overlooking the Missouri and Bad rivers near the courthouse town of Fort Pierre, South Dakota, across from the capital; she noticed something strange protruding from the soil and pulled loose a metal rectangle about the size of her reader. So encrusted with hard dirt it was, the children could make out only a date, 1743, and they joked about its origin and threw it down, but one boy retrieved it and carried the heavy plaque to his father who called the state historical society. As the dirt came off, incised words began appearing, Latin on one side, French the other, and the historians grew highly animated; for some time they had been hunting the location of a lead-zinc tablet buried by the Vérendryes on their expedition in quest of a passage to the western sea. The French Canadians gave up in Montana and started home again, stopping for two weeks near the mouth of the Bad River. Wanting to accomplish something of note, they claimed much of the western country for Louis XV and left the plate as proof of possession.

Sixty-one years later, although a stone cairn still marked the site, Lewis and Clark unknowingly passed by the tablet that the Louisiana Purchase had just turned into nothing more than a rare and curious artifact, a relative of the lead tablets Pierre-Joseph de Céloron buried in 1749 along the riverbanks of the Allegheny and the Ohio. That three of the French tablets claiming about half of the forty-eight states would ever be found again is the stuff of a children's mystery book.

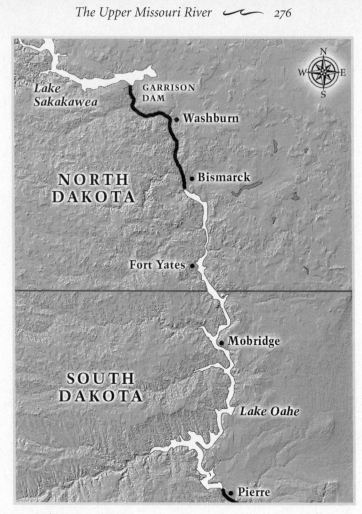

The Missouri, Pierre to Garrison Dam, 325 river miles

Hauling *Nikawa* through Fort Pierre, one of the oldest white settlements on the upper Missouri, to Oahe Dam north of town, we stopped at a filling station to gas her tanks and the five six-gallon reserve canisters we'd begun carrying since leaving Kansas City. A priss of a man watching us with his young daughter said, "See the men on the funny boat?" and she asked, "Daddy, are they going to die on the funny boat?" When we headed on, the Professor said, "Where in God's name did her question come from?" Pilotis: "Some parent whose fears take long steps through a short-legged life."

Behind Oahe Dam lies Lake Oahe, by several measures the biggest of the mainstem impoundments. Running for 230 miles, almost from Pierre to Bismarck, North Dakota — capital to capital — Oahe has more than two thousand miles of shoreline, and near the dam it is two hundred feet deep (Lake Erie has 871 miles of shore and is 210 feet at its deepest). Today the Missouri there is a river as Atlantis is an island.

We hoped to reach Mobridge, South Dakota, before sundown, eighty miles due north but 123 by water. From the dam all the way to the Montana line, the middle of the Missouri demarks, but for a notch here and there, the boundary of the Rocky Mountain time zone. The Professor commented, "If we fall an hour behind we can just meander over to the west bank." Although the Snow Imperative impelled us less fervently as we approached the mountains, another, if lesser, time constraint appeared. Each morning when we departed the tow wagon, we rarely saw it again until our arrival. Waiting for *Nikawa* to reach her daily destination could be nerve-racking to the trailerman who had to stand by helpless during a delay except to imagine the worst, trying to calculate the moment to go in search of a rescue team. Should we be clinging in cold water to a swamped *Nikawa,* minutes could make the difference in our survival.

The country we were about to set out for that June day was more isolated than any we'd yet entered, and there was but one practical place the tow wagon might spot *Nikawa,* the U.S. 212 highway bridge about halfway along our run. The marine radio could operate over no more than about a mile — far less if hills or trees lay between us — and a cellular phone, had we one, would have been useless in that vast noplace beautifully free of relay towers. Because I wanted as much independence from shore support as we could achieve, I disliked having to depend on a tow vehicle to get around the dams, and further, I enjoyed being cut off — it put an edge on the venture that too much safety, too much civilization would kill. On the Plains, that great pot that brews up much American weather, the element most likely to delay us was wind, but we, not dependent on sails, could afford to consider Aeolus a blackguard who surely must despise vessels no longer needing him. Our motors permitted me to love nautical doldrums.

Although the Missouri contorts to a fare-thee-well on Oahe, the bends are so big and the water so deep I could that morning lay down a sailing line and hold it for five or six miles before having to take a new heading; given that our vessel was something of a tortoise, running straight and steady was a joy no rabbit of a speedboat could understand. The wind puffed in irresolute wafts, and for a few miles we bounced over low waves, the effect something like riding a cart down the ties of a railway, but then even that mild roughness eased, and Oahe sang under our bow, and we were able to focus on a single concern — mistaking one of the huge arms or coves of the giant impoundment for the through river. On a map, Oahe looks like a skinny wiggle of harmlessness, but from its actual surface it is a small main waiting to confuse a pilot. If Galilee is a sea, then Oahe is an ocean.

Even prairie creeks like Okobojo can open to a debouchment four thousand feet wide and sprawl broadly upcountry for five miles, and the Cheyenne River, which I once waded bank to bank west of Oahe, opens to a mouth two miles across and runs into the hills like that for twenty-three miles before it returns to a Plains stream. In certain places, we could see beyond our bow fourteen miles of open water dead ahead.

Because I wanted to look at rivers and not instruments, I was happy the morning sun gave me an angle to steer against, a method I preferred to watching the compass. The device below our transom that might have measured mileage had not withstood the battering of Lake Erie and the drift fields of the Ohio, so to try to know our position, I roughly translated rpm's into miles per hour, and Pilotis attempted to match our chart with the far steep shores, things so distant they looked like coasts and made us feel we had somehow wandered out of the United States. I'd traveled every county in the Great Plains, but I'd never seen them look as they did there. It wasn't the treeless roll of the hills — that was familiar enough — rather, it must have been the littoral aspect that the grand spread of water gave under a big sky. Like the ocean, Oahe can be a near vacancy of everything except water and air. So we fluviomariners went coasting up along the vast shores of Dakota, where gulls, Franklin's and ring-billed, hung off our stern or rose before our bow as if *Nikawa* were at sea, and Pilotis sang a chantey that we happily endured, so apt it was.

Capable of carrying clipper ships and men-of-war, Oahe could be a portion of the Northwest Passage that Europeans long dreamed of and Lewis and Clark went looking for. That passage, however, leads not to the riches of Cathay but to the fertile abundance of the Plains, which were, of course, once an inland sea, and today, beneath them, lies the Ogallala aquifer, a reservoir of sand and porous rock holding as much water as Lake Huron. Considered truly for what they possess, the High Plains are as exotic as any oriental realm at the end of the Great Silk Road — their flora, fauna, and their native habitants whose ancestors learned to hunt and sing and chip flint points in Asia long before Great Walls, pagodas, or paddy fields. Those nomads out of Mongolia came in search of a Northeast Passage that led them into a new world where mammoths and mastodons died out and the horse and camel were born.

If Big Bend looks on a chart like a long-necked turkey, Little Bend resembles a skinny duck, wings ready to unfold, rising to fly. It too is a long peninsula, though narrower, thrusting northwesterly six miles into Oahe; a quarter mile across at the base and about four times wider near its headland, Little Bend is a river run of eighteen miles around. Treeless, half of it roadless, wild, and as isolated as about any place on the Plains today, its broken terrain drew me as plowed-over Big Bend did not. Everywhere, small embayments and snug bights serrate its margin, and Pilotis estimated it has more than a hundred miles of shore. On the back side, I turned into a sheltered cove, eased our bow onto a gravel beach, and we tied *Nikawa* stem and stern to the only bollards available, two shrubs, and then we broke out a cold lunch and left the boat. The Photographer experimented with our hand-held GPS to see if it might answer our frequent and sometimes crucial question about where we were. Pilotis wandered off, and I went up the slope, looked around, then sat down under the cordial sky and congenial sun, the wind amicable too. Low grasses and scrub dominated, but where they seemed unwilling to grow was nothing except friable, baked clay, the whole rise clearly a place that could be ungodly unforgiving in another season, a different weather.

I lay back on the warm soil, a pale broken crust, and watched the other end of creation pass above as cumuli dissipated their way eastward, air sailors that would not last long enough to see even the other end of South Dakota. I thought how far I was from where and when this journey began, how I was so distant from that fellow passing for me twenty months ago, the one so eager to learn the secrets of river passage. Could he — the me of that moment — and I sit down together, he would want to know what I knew and absorb what I had experienced, and he would regard me enviously, just as I do those men who have returned from the moon. But there would be forever a difference between him and me: I went and he did not. He set the voyage in motion, but he could not take it. Just as I, who lay on the Dakota hill, could not know whether *Nikawa* would reach the Pacific, he could never see the outcome of his preparations, unless somewhere, on some far other side, time permits us to meet our past selves, all those we have been. Our physical components change every seven years, so our brains are continuously passing along memories to a stranger; who we have been is only a ghostly fellow traveler. As for me, what might I learn from him who laid out the voyage or from all those others I once was? The eighteen-year-old who wanted to write, the thirty-year-old who wanted to teach, the waiter wanting a paycheck, the sailor boy wandering Port-au-Prince, the husband who didn't keep a marriage together, the son who heard his ailing father say one night toward the end, "I want to be like Black Elk and go into the mountains and die," the callow kid who nearly fainted the first time a girl really kissed him, the boy too old to be afraid of sleeping alone in the woods but who was.

What a report I might deliver to them about where they have sent me! And how they could remind me of first kisses and death, the Haitian mountains at sunset and the Ozark hills at night. They could redraw the faded lines on the long map of my journey here, point out clearly where it was I took a road other than the one they intended, and they could tell me whether they liked that divagation or not, whether they found it a good one or rankly stupid. Were human memory total and perfect, perhaps I'd be only one person from start to finish, but forgetfulness cuts me off from who I've been so that hourly I am reborn. To twist Santayana's words, I who cannot fully remember my past am condemned to proceed without it.

Close to my ear a voice: "How about a cool, refreshing phroso?" I opened my eyes and for an instant had no idea where I was. The Photographer said, "I've walked this GPS all over, and the readout changes with every step. It's incredibly sensitive, but we don't have a chart with degrees and minutes so the numbers are meaningless." He went off down the slope, and I thought, That's the way it is in life — you get a position *or* a map but not both at the same time.

So, where was I? I didn't really know other than to remember visually much of the way that brought me here. As a Navy recruit, I failed a course in celestial navigation, partly because of my innumeracy and partly because I thought the navigator's perpetual quest to fix his position created a bad precedent for piloting through one's life where the course must follow the eternal flux, a grand flowing that turns celestial fixes to flumdiddle. I've never been as interested in where I am as in what it was like to get there. On our venture I wanted to learn the rivers the way a pilot must in order to get a license, to see them all and draw them from memory mile for mile. Where I was at any particular moment wasn't usually that important because a fixed position lasts only a moment, but the times when I remembered a particular run of river and what it was like — remembered *her* and how *she* was — moments like those can reappear and last for hours, even until the end. The more miles I put under me, the more those recollections become the very vessels carrying me to the finish.

I went down to the boat where the Photographer held up an object as if it were of great price — a brass casing of a fifty-caliber machine-gun bullet, something probably ejected from a plane during World War Two when the military used this far beyond for aerial combat training. I had the feeling he would not long remember the GPS hike, but he'd never forget the thing that fell from the sky and lay waiting a half century for him to pick up and connect himself with a past.

I called out across the long peninsula, and soon Pilotis appeared from the far side, and we shoved off and headed upriver. To occupy miles, one looking much like the next, Pilotis read passages from Lewis and Clark, and I kept listening for the captains' response to traveling that vast openness which must have been even bigger then, given the way humankind has succeeded in wringing distance out of this planet — a process the Expedition furthered — for nothing is larger than an unknown. The Pacific was not as far away after Lewis and Clark found a route and returned with maps, with astronomical observations of precisely where they'd been, and, perhaps most of all, with stories of the new land. So I steered out the Oahe miles and listened for the captains to speak in their own terms of space and time, but along that section of the Missouri, Lewis (who was to become a suicide three years after he returned to civilization) kept to his astral fixes, his columns of mathematically expressed positions, and Clark stayed with practicabilities.

We swept around another bend so large it was almost impossible to perceive as a turn, and soon after we saw the U.S. 212 bridge. As we closed the distance, Pilotis through the binoculars made out the orange flag, and I called over the radio, and the Professor said, "Where the hell have you been? I thought you'd gone down!" No, I said, we just made a short landing in a long land.

Nikawa proceeded on, skimming the next miles like a clipper, and Pilotis read not to inform but merely to break what I have to admit was something close to monotony. There are times when the Missouri seems so long, you wonder how it ever manages to flow up and over the curvature of the earth. Then the river helped out by twisting again, regaining some shallows, raising its threats and lifting our grogginess. The Photographer said, "By the way, just what is a phroso?" One ounce ginger syrup, one ounce lemon syrup, dash of rum, dash of bitters, one egg, phosphate to taste; shake over cracked ice, strain, serve with nutmeg.

We ascended beyond the broad exit of the Moreau River and continued winding north for another twenty miles until, at last, we could make out a thin dark line across the water. "Please let that be it," the Photographer said, and it was, the span that gave the old ferry crossing a new name, Mobridge.

Off to port, from atop a windswept bluff, a stone face looked down on us. Beneath the rock eyes of the monument lie the remains of Sitting Bull, entombed by his descendants in twenty tons of concrete so that he, the child of nomads, might never again be removed from his land. We tied up in Smith Bay under another monument, this one to Jedediah Smith, whose history is the reverse of the great Lakota: a New Englander who left settled lands to roam the West, got caught, probably by Comanches, and killed. No one ever found his remains to bury them anywhere.

The Professor helped us fill gas canisters and stevedore them to *Nikawa* before we crossed the river into Mobridge to find supper in a big old place where, in another room, an Indian wedding rolled along. I recited a verse by Ed Miller:

> The bride
> is groomed,
> the groom
> is bridled.

I asked our waitress what tribe the people were. Her expression said, "Of what possible interest could that ever be?" but her words were "I don't know. They're Indians." We just looked at her, and, growing uncomfortable, she added, "Sioux, I guess," pausing, then, "I'll send some over to tell you."

Sitting Bull and the
Broom of Heaven

WHEN I LEANED OVER the side of *Nikawa* that Saturday morning to check the hull, a mural of a cumulus sky lay across the slick river, and from the clouds suddenly appeared a countenance smiling down on me, a bearded one. If I'd believed the Engine of Creation had a human face, I might have taken the visage for It, but It was only I, who soon dipped my hands into the river and shattered the firmament and myself, then held perfectly still to watch the fractured sky and a man's mug slowly return as if the river knew precisely where each piece belonged, and all was seemingly *just as it had been,* but it was an illusion of the reflection, another trick of the river, for in the minute the water took to return to a mirror I was that much older, the clouds had puffed noticeably into new shapes, world population increased by 162, the planet sailed another eleven hundred miles through the ether, the solar system traveled seventy-eight hundred miles closer to the Northern Cross, and the tectonic plate the Missouri flows across had crept microscopically closer to Siberia. A stilled river is an illusion of the human situation where stasis is only a concept, but a flowing river is a traditional metaphor for the way of all things. Mountains suggest fixity, but rivers give continuance.

Yet it was quiet water that showed humankind its face. Watching myself reassembling, I wondered about the first person to discover that the image on the water was his — or hers — and not the visage of a river demon, about the first someone capable of imagining the blind river might have made him — who was largely water — so that it could not just see itself — a toad could serve that end — but also perceive itself and imagine rivers as the legs and arms of the seminal seas sent onto land to learn to breathe, walk, smile, love, dream, and esteem its sources.

Pilotis caught me in my idling and asked, "What are you doing now?" I said, Just reflecting.

Beyond the sheltered nook where *Nikawa* lay, the river ran harsher, and we rattled along for some miles, our bellies solid for the moment with a breakfast of the Sitting Bull Special: eggs with chopped green peppers, salsa, hash browns. Just beyond the mouth of the great Hunkpapa chief's natal river, the Grand, the Professor put his hands to his stomach as we bounced hard and said, "I hope the old warrior doesn't decide to stand up." One more Red Man's Revenge, I said. The river grew smoother for a space, and I could throttle forward to bucket us along a fair course slowed only by my weavings past floaters, many of them dark and nasty low riders which Pilotis began calling dreadnoughts, a term more decorous than the maledictions we'd been heaping on them. As we rounded a bend, a crosswind picked up a piece of cold river and pitched it through the window into my face and helped settle my Special, but the roughness made the depth finder useless for guiding us above the channel, and the complexity of the braided Missouri under the reservoir rendered the chart nearly as bootless in revealing shallows of submerged trees.

Wind makes a river immensely complicated if not impossible to read, so as we went on, we tried to prepare for that sound from Hell, the props striking anything less yielding than water. We had a hit here and there, nothing terminal, but with each one the tense Professor expelled a loud sailor's blessing. After several of these I had to tell him that while I liked his sharing my concern for the boat, the sudden shouts were more unsettling than the strikes. Could he swear more serenely? I noticed he looked a bit peaked and asked how he was. He said, "Sitting Bull's crouching."

We crossed into North Dakota, happy about another mark behind us, and the water smoothed in the bends protected from the Plains wind. Where the broad river ran straight, it looked like a wide avenue reaching beyond the horizon into some huge openness that could be only a sea or, as it was, the fossil of an ancient one now raised high and dry. The Professor said, "The first time a river engineer visits an ocean, he's thinking, There's got to be one hell of a dam out there somewhere."

A dreadnought struck hard against the hull, a location I seldom worried about in spite of the loud vibration, but the others took it more seriously, their faces registering deep misgiving. I loved how my mates shared the burden of foreboding, and I was beginning to realize their anxiety served to raise my pluck, and I hoped it was neither inappropriate nor unmanly to feed off their edginess in that way. Their disquiet invariably made me want even more to see them safely through.

To distract us from the banging hull, I did what I sometimes tried during long miles — I asked a hypothetical question: Were Sitting Bull to rise again and see his homelands along the Missouri, what would he recognize? My companions considered. Certainly not the impounded river nor the overgrazed slopes nor vast acres of plowed flatlands nor hills barren of massed bison and antelope nor the miles of gravel roads. Pilotis said, "The question is, What have we successors changed the least? What has eluded our technical grasp?" And the Professor, "What's impervious to so-called civilization?" They were quiet too long, and I translated the inscription honoring architect Christopher Wren in St. Paul's Cathedral in London, "If thou seekest his monument, look around." Pilotis squinted down a long reach: "Water? No, no." Consider the face of the river, I said. The Professor: "Waves and more waves." Pilotis: "Wind! Sitting Bull would recognize the Plains wind." I said, The broom of heaven.

Near Fort Yates, an outpost named for a captain killed with Custer, the place Sitting Bull was a prisoner for some months and later buried for many years until his people came in the night and took him away, I spied a small wooden dock running into Oahe from a heavy willow thicket, a chance to tie up and get relief from the banging, although I wasn't sure precisely where we were and thought we might be about to trespass on the Standing Rock Reservation. The wind mastered me the first two tries to get us against the dock, then I slipped under a gust to get close enough for Pilotis to loop our bow line over a cleat and secure *Nikawa,* and we hopped onto the pier, the Professor saying, "How excellently firma is this terra." We broke out sandwiches, ate in silence, walked the shore, then packed up.

Two large, round men stepped from the willows. Eighteenth- and nineteenth-century novels and travelers' accounts contain many a passage about Indians seeming to materialize from a forest, a prairie, the night, as if they were resident souls of trees, stones, the dark wind. Those two men were not there, then they just simply *were* there. I thought an arrest was imminent until I saw they held beer cans. They approached, greeted us, gave us left-side handshakes in the gentle grip common among tribal peoples, and they asked about *Nikawa*, where we were going. Then a woman, also quite round, appeared, and behind her came two children, slender and pretty, and one of the men said they were his family. She carried a bottle of light beer, and her grin was an interspersal of incisors and cuspids between dark gaps that gave her the appearance of an awesome figure out of a shaman's vision.

One at a time, each person asked to go aboard *Nikawa*, to which I said yes, although I was uneasy because the beer had taken some measure of the adults. The children romped into the pilothouse and began tugging at the controls, the Professor's caution going unheeded. The father asked for a ride, but I declined for several reasons, the alcohol not the least; instead, I offered a couple of T-shirts imprinted with NIKAWA that I had made up for the crew and also strangers helping us. He was pleased, and said he would leave a Hunkpapa jacket at the Fort Rice trading post upriver. I said, You're Sitting Bull's people? And Chief Rain-in-the-Face? "Yes!" the children cried out, proud of the association. But the beer made good conversation difficult, and the parents knew little of the river ahead other than it was natural — that is, shallow and twisted.

They climbed back onto the dock, waved goodbyes, and the father pitched his beer can into the willows and the mother her bottle of light into the river, dispelling my illusion that our encounter — with its formal greetings, gifts, and queries about what was upstream — carried echoes of earlier travelers. I pulled into the current, the wind taking us again, and Pilotis said, "There's proof that respect for the land doesn't come with the blood." The Professor: "Education, education, education." I added, And a fair chance to escape poverty, to live hopefully.

I asked had they ever seen one of the old Savage Arms Company advertising posters with a portrait of Sitting Bull and the slogan "Savage Rifles Make Bad Indians Good." The famous Hunkpapa chief needed to be made "good" because he fought against the breaking of an 1868 treaty that guaranteed the Lakotas possession of much of their territory, and he had the temerity to resist gold miners swarming in to pillage the sacred Black Hills, the grubstakers soon supported by the U.S. Cavalry. Of all the enemy leaders the United States Army has taken on over the past couple of centuries, none has stood for a more honorable cause than Sitting Bull and Crazy Horse, a cause that any American — with our fierce allegiance to real property — should be able to comprehend. One may see the respect, commingled with bigotry, that soldiers and civilians once accorded Sitting Bull in their myth that he was a white man in disguise.

The Missouri gave us broad bends, each with an attendant warning on the chart of "Hazard Area," but we proceeded without hits or groundings past the shallows, some invisible but others perfectly outlined by willow copses standing in the high water. We ascended beyond the Cannonball River, known for round stony concretions washed out of its sandstone shores, and above it, Oahe began to diminish and become again the Missouri River. Near the site of old Fort Rice, we pulled up to a boat ramp where I'd arranged to meet the trailerman, and despite the wind and current made a nice landing and hauled *Nikawa* up to a farm. Pilotis received permission to leave her overnight while we reconnoitered the next miles of real river, ones we'd heard would be especially wicked.

How to Be a
Hell of a Riverman

ITH EACH MILE we set behind us, I felt some small achievement as if we'd really done something, and our creeping across America gave me a joy tempered only by the relentless lurking of the Grand Terminator, that unseen but probably not unforeseen error or malfunction or injury which could end the voyage for the year and perhaps forever. In so many ways we were defenseless because most of the threats were no more visible than a bunkered enemy, and our only shield was limited knowledge, our only sword insistence, and our lone ally luck, an ingredient no long venture can succeed without.

Even though I did not dwell on the dark possibilities, I never forgot that the last mile done might be the last mile we could do. One evening the Professor said to me, "Wouldn't it be easier on you to treat this voyage as a lark or a mere outing?" Yes, I said, if I can first teach myself to treat my life as a lark. Still, except in moments of real duress, I was not apprehensive, and I slept solidly even if I often did dream of the river, dreams that were never sweet. Above all else, what kept me from dwelling on the very real possibility of failure was my belief — with no rational basis — that *Nikawa* was destined to reach the Pacific if — *if* — I did not fail in resolve, for I could probably overcome my ignorance, but never could I surmount irresoluteness. So it was that bit of near irrationality that kept me atop a potentially crippling anxiety and let me love our river days even as they tried me and tired me, because, once we were on the water, past and future diminished into a long flowing and consuming present that reduced life to terms almost the simplest a human can know. Upon returning to *Nikawa* after the brief hiatus on the lower Missouri, Pilotis had reported an incapacity at home for dealing with the mundane requirements of contemporary life, an unwillingness to tolerate "pissants and nitwits," an enervating awareness that, without the invigoration of ever-present threats, life turns vapid and is beneath respect. For all the river took away from us, it returned the greatest of gifts — a clean and unassailable purpose to existence. We lived to go another mile, to try to encounter it fully so memory would register it deeply, and to stay around long enough for the next mile and a reward of repose at the end of the day.

We stopped at the Fort Rice gas station and trading post to ask what lay ahead, and we heard that the river was once again a natural waterway with the usual bugaboos, and a man told us, "Maybe you can make it up to Garrison Dam, I don't know, but you sure as hell picked the best year to have a run at it. In seventy-five years I never saw the water so high." Said murmuring Pilotis, "See, Captain's got this rainstick." The crew was delighted with the clerk's history even after I reminded them the dams existed for only about half those years, and further, a high river is not necessarily easier than a low one — it just changes the location of obstructions. What's more, the fellow probably knew nothing of the river five miles farther up, where, we'd heard earlier, the water was low because the dam was letting almost nothing through. The Photographer asked the man about the promised Hunkpapa jacket, but it wasn't there.

We retrieved *Nikawa* from the farm and put her in the Missouri exactly where she'd come out and set off for Washburn, North Dakota, under one more day of blue sky, a good weather about to become critical to our continuing. A mile above Fort Rice, the river turns northwest and enters a twisted section choked everywhere with bars and islands, false chutes, and stumps. I wound us through a broken forest of deadheads bleached like skeletons that eventually led to more open water but so generously braided we had to hunt the channel at every moment, and our progress was slow, then slower, then it stopped altogether when *Nikawa* grounded out.

We went fore and aft and poled off, not cussing, just working, because at last we understood that getting hung up was not like a flat tire — an unexpected and usually preventable annoyance — but rather part of the nature of ascent up the Missouri, just as lifting one's foot is part of walking. The Photographer, our fretter-in-residence, nonetheless said, "Are we pushing *Nikawa* too far here? Isn't it time for the canoe?" I said we couldn't know what was too far until we went too far, and we still had to play distance against time, against the June rise, and it was now June, and we were still about five hundred miles from the region of most questionable water.

On a narrow sandbar near the eastern bank, we saw for the first time white pelicans, veritable symbols of the high Missouri. I was telling about Lewis and Clark shooting a pelican to see how much water its big throaty beak would hold, but I didn't get to say five gallons before *Nikawa* crashed hard into something and rolled to starboard, halfway to her gunwales, charts flying across the pilothouse; it was as if she'd fallen into a hole. Then she righted herself.

I cut power, apprehensively raised the motors, and Pilotis went aft to face what sounded like the arrival of the Grand Terminator. As the props emerged from the dark water into the light, Mate called out, "No damage!" We checked the hull for leaks, but all was sound. Pilotis: "Chapter Forty-four of *One Goddamn Scare a Day*," and we took up another installment of the Canoe Debate, moot for the time being since the Grumman was on a highway somewhere ahead of us. We went on, relieved to have escaped once again, although I knew that those ringing hits accumulated on the crew, each blow less easy to shrug off, each one increasing our belief that the law of averages was gaining on us.

At a speed hardly better than what the canoe could do, we passed the location of an ancient riverside village now called the Huff Site that tractors, a highway, and the erosive river have not ground into oblivion. Raymond Wood, the archaeologist who excavated Huff, once told me that over the almost six hundred miles from the mouth of the Niobrara River to Garrison Dam, there was a prehistoric site along the Missouri about every mile, but the Missouri Valley farther west even to its headwaters is nearly free of them, and nobody knows why. We ascended beyond the mouth of the Heart River, once an important Mandan settlement. George Catlin spent time with those people when he came upriver in 1832 and wrote extensive and colorful accounts of them before disease all but eliminated the tribe. In one of his "letters" the painter wrote:

The Mandans are certainly a very interesting and pleasing people in their personal appearance and manners, differing in many respects, both in looks and customs from all other tribes which I have seen. . . . A stranger in the Mandan village is first struck with the different shades of complexion and various colours of hair which he sees in a crowd about him and is at once almost disposed to claim that "these are not Indians."

There are a great many of these people whose complexions appear as light as half breeds, and amongst the women particularly, there are many whose skins are almost white, with the most pleasing symmetry and proportion of features, with hazel, with grey, and with blue eyes, with mildness and sweetness of expression and excessive modesty of demeanour, which render them exceedingly pleasing and beautiful.

Why this diversity of complexion I cannot tell, nor can they themselves account for it. Their traditions, so far as I have yet learned them, afford us no information of their having had any knowledge of white men before the visit of Lewis and Clarke made to their village thirty-three years ago. Since that time there have been but very few visits from white men to this place, and surely not enough to have changed the complexions and the customs of a nation. And I recollect perfectly well that Governor Clarke told me before I started for this place that I would find the Mandans a strange people and half white.

The diversity in the colour of hair is also equally as great as that in the complexion, for in a numerous group of these people (and more particularly amongst the females who never take pains to change its natural colour as the men often do), there may be seen every shade and colour of hair that can be seen in our own country, with the exception of red or auburn which is not to be found.

And there is yet one more strange and unaccountable peculiarity, which can probably be seen nowhere else on earth, nor on any rational grounds accounted for, other than it is a freak or order of Nature for which she has not seen fit to assign a reason. There are very many of both sexes and of every age from infancy to manhood and old age with hair of bright silvery grey, and in some instances almost perfectly white.

This singular and eccentric appearance is much oftener seen among the women than it is with the men, for many of the latter who have it seem ashamed of it and artfully conceal it by filling their hair with glue and black and red earth. The women, on the other hand, seem proud of it and display it often in an almost incredible profusion which spreads over their shoulders and falls as low as the knee. . . . By passing this hair through my hands, as I often have, I have found it uniformly to be as coarse and harsh as a horse's mane, differing materially from the hair of

other colours, which amongst the Mandans is generally as fine and as
soft as silk.

We passed Fort Abraham Lincoln, the post the Seventh Cavalry rode
out from to their rendezvous at the Little Bighorn. Four miles farther,
we motored slowly through a scad of sandbars on the southwest side
of Bismarck, the river glomerated with Sunday speedboats and water
scooters, those aquatic motorcycles widely disliked except by the
sports roaring them in circles leading nowhere. A few days earlier
we'd heard a radio ad for the contraptions: "You'll own the water with
bold thrusts of power!" River-weathered *Nikawa* looked like the *Santa
María* arriving at a Caribbean beach party, but we looped around a
long bar and tied up at the dock of a rockabeatinboogie grill where we
hoped to find the Professor. Columbus's crew was hardly less baffled
than we as we stumbled into Sunday at the Beach, and the partying
made our long crossing seem something we'd only imagined, and I
said so, and Pilotis said, "It's the bikinis doing it to you." I realized our
isolation on the river during the day narrowed our lives to critical
focus and, in a way, made continuing easy since alternatives were so
few. But at that place, what choices, what allurements without the
"excessive modesty of demeanour" of the Mandans! Pilotis watched
me, and said to the others, "We've got to get him back on the river
quick." I said, Get me back on the river quick, otherwise I'm going to
call North Dakota the Pacific Ocean and drop our final anchor.

The Professor, exercising his talent for finding guidance, said two
fellows named Randy could tell us about the treacherous channel
ahead. Pilotis: "We're going to take advice from two beach boys named
Randy?" On the dock, we found them togged out in tank tops and
iridescent swim trunks, beers in hand, their radio thumping, and
Randall One said, "Where you're going, people lose their lower units
up there. It's bad and it gets worse." They so struggled to describe the
route through, Randall Two finally said, "Oh, what the hell, dudes, just
follow us. We'll get you started," and they roared off in their bright
speedboat of a design meant to restore self-esteem to men with small
penises and attract young women in search of a mobile tanning bed.
They left *Nikawa* behind, waited for us by opening more beer and
heavy-metaling along to "Symptom of the Universe." The Missouri
has listened to Teton war chants, cavalry bugles, Mandan courting

flutes, Arikara eagle-bone whistles, reels of Lewis and Clark's fiddler, Pierre Cruzatte, and now Megadeth. Perhaps that's what set Pilotis to muttering, and I said, A guide is a guide, so just consider the Randys Twain our Charbonneau and Sacagawea. "I'm considering going home."

We were soon beyond the beach parties and their roaring boxes, into a stretch where a thick cover of trees lined the quiet river and a high bluff rose from the east shore, dense bottoms to the west; the way was shallows split by channels of moderate width. Our Charbonneau ran aground once, then again, and it was apparent the Randallmen were trying to proceed by memory rather than by reading the river. Narrowly escaping another shoal, they wheeled about, waved, and headed back to the safety of beach-blanket bingo. Said Pilotis, "They must have gotten out of range of their radio station."

We pushed on cautiously, everyone on watch, I listening to the water against the hull for telltale changes in depth, and we slowly moved into more and more isolated country. After another ten miles, I noticed a spot of orange on a high bluff; it was, surprisingly, the Professor at one of the few places where a road, if for only a half mile, runs right alongside the upper Missouri. Over the radio he said, "About twenty miles more to Washburn and River Relief."

The pilothouse was still full of cheer and the expectation of ease when the Missouri reminded us how long its miles are. The water split into three broadly bending channels, one down each bank, one down the middle, all of equal size. I figured things couldn't be that easy, but for once we had a pilot in the sky, and I asked the Professor to assay our position from the blufftop. His was a long expounding ending with, "I'd recommend the middle channel, but I'm not sure. It's your boat." Those last three words I'd come to detest.

I considered and chose to follow the old piloting standard and take the chute on the outside of the curve where centrifugal force usually throws the most water. The current was fair and dark, the surface almost untroubled. Up we went, not fast. I asked over the radio, How do we look? "Okay, I guess." On we went. Farther. Each of us quiet, concentrating. Then: a loud cracking, shattering, horrific smashing that slammed us against the bulkheads, jammed forward my right arm, the one on the throttles, and the engines began racing to destruction, and my elbow bled over the levers. I jerked the power back, killed the roaring motors. For a minute, nobody could move or speak. We had met the Grand Terminator, and we were his. We knew it. Our lower units had to be on the bottom of the river. Already the Missouri was pulling us downstream.

One at a time, I raised the motors, my heart flattened, as Pilotis waited in the welldeck to see what was left. "Port stem there! Prop half gone!" I raised the other. "Starboard stem is there! Prop torn all to hell!" The Photographer: "At least it's just the propellers." We're done, I said, we can't run on unbalanced props or we'll ruin the engines. We stared at the river, then I went to the helm, fired the starboard motor, spun the prop just enough to turn the bow around, and radioed the Professor, We're dead in the water, and I have no goddamn idea whatsoever how we can get off this river. On down we drifted, helplessly. I remembered a fellow a day earlier asking me, "You know what 'Missouri' means in Indian?" I answered with a couple of popular interpretations, but he said, "You've got that wrong. It means river-that-eats-your-lunch."

The Photographer, in a consternation that may have surpassed mine, said, "Can we drift all the way back to Bismarck?" What the hell, I said, let's just drift all the goddamn way back home. I thought, This time we're in deep, deep trouble.

Every so often I spun the starboard propeller to keep little wounded *Nikawa* from being turned sideways by the brute river. Just as we were about to lose sight of the Professor and radio contact, I noticed a fisherman who had not been there twenty minutes earlier, and I called out to ask where there was a road down to the water. "There isn't!" he yelled. "Not around here!" Then an afterthought: "Unless you call that track over there a road." He pointed to a steep and curving dirt cut down a crumbling, treeless bluff. Pilotis looked at me in alarm. "There's no way the wagon can get down that dangerous sonofabitch, let alone haul a ton and a half up it. If that ground gives way, we'll lose more than just props — we'll be out a boat, trailer, *and* wagon. We're talking worse than destruction — we're talking death."

I said, Radio the Prof before we lose contact and tell him we're heading for it — tell him he's absolutely got to find it somehow. Pilotis: "Oh, jeezis." I brought *Nikawa* close to shore, but rocks kept her off, so the Photographer, an anchor of a man, took the bow line and waded to the bank to hold us. We waited. Pilotis was probably right: the track would be impossible. The Professor was probably right: the middle channel might have been better. The Photographer was probably right: this was canoe country. Believing in my experience, working from my insistence, I had put us out of commission. The fisherman came up after a while, looked at the props, and said, "You really done it." I did, I said. "If it makes you feel better," he added, "yours ain't the only blades out there. There's whole lower units and about two hundred of my lures."

"What did we hit?" the Photographer said. It had to be a rock, a big rock, a big invisible rock, a big invisible bastard rock. About then the tow wagon appeared, small atop the bluff, and warily started down the track, and I wondered whether I was about to turn a bad situation into the end of our voyage. Pilotis said, "Hold, earth, hold!" Down came the wagon, the Professor effecting a skillful descent, showing no fear of rolling over and over into the river. Slowly onward, lower, lower, and then he was down. He maneuvered here and there before we could find a boulder-free place for the wagon, shallow enough for the trailer, deep enough for the boat. I ran *Nikawa* up onto the cradle, and we tied her in. I stayed aboard in case we slipped back into the river, and Pilotis, relieving the Professor who wanted no responsibility should our rig go over the edge, got into the wagon, switched to four-wheel drive, shifted into gear, stepped on the accelerator, but the wheels turned and went nowhere on the slick, loose rocks. Now we had *all* our equipment imperiled.

I stood on the bow and shook my fist at the river, at the track. Then the Professor yelled, "It's Arlen!" I said, What the hell's an arlunn? "Arlen Simons. This is his ranch." Excellent, I said, now we've got trespass trouble. Simons crept down the track in a big, brand-new four-wheel-drive pickup. The Professor had just met the rancher as he was returning home, and now there he was to offer help.

We ran our chain from his truck to the tow wagon, and with eight wheels pulling, pulling, *Nikawa* slowly came out of the water onto the rocks. We undid the chain, I walked up the track and came down to take the steering wheel of our tow wagon, studied the track again, then started up with the boat immensely behind, everything under incredible strain. If the wheels began spinning, disaster was next. Backing that rig down would be a nightmare. The tow wagon had the biggest engine available, and it took all of its power to drag *Nikawa* up, slowly up, the wheels not spinning, not yet anyway, not yet, slowly up, up, up to the top, the ever-blessed top! I got out, looked at her a hundred feet up on the bluff, an improbable place for a boat, and I thought, This is a pre-departure fear, and any minute someone will nudge me and I'll be home, the voyage not even begun.

Laughing, disburdened Pilotis clapped me on the back, and I said, Let's do it again to prove it wasn't just another stroke of luck. Then I changed the props, Arlen helping, smiling, telling of his ranch where his people had been since 1882. We pulled *Nikawa,* again river-worthy, on across the bluff to leave it for the night next to his barn, thanked him profusely, and went down the road to the edge of Bismarck for dinner and River Relief.

Sitting in a grill with a good view of the Missouri, we cracked open peanuts and offered toasts, the abstemious Professor raising his mineral water, and Pilotis said to the crew, "You boys are new at this, but here's what just occurred: Ignoring the advice of each of us, Skipper makes two bad decisions, risks a third, and brings us to grief in an isolated stretch of river without a real access road for miles. Drifting helplessly downstream, he finds a fisherman who wasn't there a few minutes earlier, who points out the only possible escape around, which just happens to be exactly where we are. The tow wagon, which we almost never see during the day, happens to stop at that rarest of places, a good-visibility pull-off right against the river, but a spot high enough for the radio to work. Prof goes to find the most hidden track in North Dakota and just happens to catch the only resident in miles, who just happens to live near the track and who just happens to return home in the nick of time. The wagon somehow makes it down an eroded dirt trail a donkey would shy from, and the dangerous cut happens to be dry enough and solid enough not to give way. When loose stones make it impossible to move the boat, just then the curious rancher happens along in a new truck powerful enough to help pull our trapped contraption off the rocks. In an hour, *Nikawa* is safely high and dry and outfitted with new props. Now, here before you Skipper sits, mellowed out and watching the great Missouri as he sips a martini, and you're thinking he's a hell of a riverman, but he'll probably claim you don't have to be a hell of a riverman if you're lucky." No, I said, it was either clustered coincidences or destiny, the result being the same.

Yondering up
the Broomsticks

THAT EVENING so many months ago when Pilotis and I studied inch by inch the maps and charts of our entire route and nearly concluded we couldn't make the voyage in less than a couple of years because of several concerns, perhaps the greatest was whether a boat small enough to navigate the shallowest sections of the Missouri could ascend against its spring current, especially in a time of high water. On the fifth of June we prepared the canoe to learn the answer.

We returned the next morning to the place we'd come off the river, descended the narrow track again, unlashed the canoe, rigged it out, and struggled to get its four-horsepower motor, idle since the Allegheny, started. When I finally noticed we'd reversed the gas line from the six-gallon tank, we reconnected it. The Evinrude sputtered, caught, hummed its two dinky pistons, and off we went, Pilotis in the bow of the canoe, I at the stern, the others watching us head slowly out before they hauled *Nikawa* on to Washburn where we hoped to end the long day, although it was only twenty miles upstream. We carried a spare three-gallon gas tank because we had little notion how far nine gallons would take us against the current and twisting channels within a meandering river; because of his weight and the absence of checkpoints over that segment, I asked the Photographer to take his turn after we learned the range of the canoe. We tried to establish an arrival time, but all the unknowns made it conjecture, so we agreed that, should we not be able to make Washburn by dark, I would try to get off the Missouri to a ranch and leave a phone message on the Professor's home answering machine. To save weight, we carried the radio but no tent or sleeping bags and only enough food and water for two frugal meals.

The good weather of the past days, now that we were totally exposed in a seventeen-foot canoe, changed from overcast to massive clouds threatening a storm. *Rule of the River Road:* Take to an open boat — bring on bad weather. Even with its bouldery bottom, the Allegheny had been a delight in the Grumman, but now we faced something else; the difference between the two rivers was as descending a ladder is to climbing a sequoia. Still, to hunt out the elusive Missouri chutes, to go up them and discover slowly that the small engine (a woman had called it "a little pisspot of a motor") could move us forward, would give me pleasure and an increasing belief that the slender up-bound canoe could take on the big down-bound river.

We entered the channel that did in *Nikawa,* but we couldn't discover our enemy, so hidden it was. The water, carrying only a modicum of sediment, flowed lightly green with clarity varying from six inches to about three feet, a gift of mud-trapping dams, and its depth was thumb-deep to over our heads. The motor stem and prop bounced off rocks and snags concealed by glare or murky pools or mild turbulence, but after each hit I quickly pushed the engine back into place, so we scarcely lost headway.

Passing through a nearly recumbent country of modest elevations and declinations, treeless except along the river fringes, we crossed and recrossed the Missouri to follow what I deemed the best channel. Our weaving course was like that of blind worker ants returning to the colony: a zig, a zag, a zigzag, a triple zag, an oops, wrong way. If only we, like them, could have smelled the trail. Were it possible to follow the center of the river, Washburn was just twenty miles distant, but the frequent crossovers added almost half again that mileage. Pilotis: "We could make better time on foot," and I said, A hiker has to go up and down — at least our path is flat.

We guessed we might be doing four miles an hour, less the distance the current carried us backward, but our opposed directions gave the illusion we were moving faster, something I was happy to have since I thought the long hours in a canoe, seated in the same position and unsheltered from sun, wind, rain, heat, cold, insects — the usual appurtenances of such travel — might wear the crew into rethinking their commitment. The map was so inadequate I tried to measure our ascent by time elapsed, although I was careful to underestimate the mileage we'd done, because to arrive "early" is more an inducement to continue than to go on well past an expected arrival. These considerations — and more that will soon become apparent — explain why, of all the people I've heard about who traveled the Missouri in this century, I knew of only one other who claimed to have gone from mouth to headwaters against the current.

Pilotis dipped a paddle to check depth in places with invisible bottoms, and, spotting an obstruction ahead, would duck so I could see it. We called the practice yondering, as in "to see up yonder." Because the lower end of a chute can be quite unlike its head, and because often we couldn't see the whole thing, making it up one required equal measures of luck and experience, and for a while the luck held. Then I chose a small channel that turned into a slough, and we had to retreat and try another, not a difficult task, merely one that tripled time and distance. Miles of that piece of the Missouri were more riverbed than river, wet sand splattered with puddles and isolated pools, and it was obvious that little water was flowing through massive Garrison Dam fifty miles above us. The chutes into the shoals were sometimes only marginally wider than the canoe, and I could reach over the gunwales right or left and touch dry sand. On those segments, the longest river in America was also the coziest.

Pilotis at first resisted trying those skinny troughs and began calling them broomsticks. We made our way up one, drawing sand several times but scraping on, only to proceed till we grounded out. With no room to turn the canoe around, I raised the motor and let the chute wash us slowly back down. We got out, stretched our legs, studied the river, and decided that same trough was the only possibility. We started up again. Pilotis said, "A cow pisses a wider stream than this." I steered a more careful course, applied what I'd just learned about the channel, tried to avoid irritation, and, with hard assists from the paddles, we accomplished its length even though the difference from the first attempt was but a few inches here, a foot there. Then we reached a dark pool — darkness usually indicating deeper water — a stretch as quiet as a millpond that we ran so easily I could take my arm from its wrenched position on the tiller and steer us by slightly shifting my weight side to side. On came another slew of sandy strands, and the struggle to wrest a course from the river began again.

Pilotis advocated carrying the canoe over shallows with good footing, but I was determined to boat, not walk, across the country. Someday that might be another journey. Even a twenty-foot carry I considered a portage. So the ascent became a contest that I slowly drew my friend into, and the more sandbars and mud flats we managed to pass, the more Pilotis began to like the challenge, even when we had to use paddles as poles and push our way to the next pool. Because this travel was so different from our days aboard *Nikawa*, we enjoyed the laboring — and labor it was — but I knew too many miles of it might turn to empty drudgery ending in a desertion, and I wondered how long the crew could put up with such a traversal, such travail, especially if — *when* — the weather turned on us.

In the late afternoon big clouds of fouled darkness gathered at our backs like thugs ready to pursue a walker up a city alley. We were at last far enough west and close enough to mountain weather to encounter that daily summer phenomenon of a brief afternoon storm, so regular we could nearly tell the hour from it. We reached a good run of open water, the wind was at our backs, Washburn was surely not far ahead, and I opened the throttle all the way, and we fairly zipped along.

Canada geese had just finished nesting and were much about with their trains of little yellow and still flightless goslings; when we passed close to them there came a hubbub of complaint, accompanied by a mad paddling of webbed feet for the far side of whatever. Pilotis talked to all of them, explaining, lecturing, apologizing. On we went, our backs tiring, till finally we saw a feature to confirm our position, the Washburn Bridge, and we raced the weather to our waving orange flag and took the canoe off the river. Said Pilotis, "Anyone seeing that section of the Missouri from the air would think it a wet field. I mean, the rivers of the moon have more water."

We ducked out of the short storm and into a café with an announcement on the bulletin board:

SILENT AUCTION
TO BENEFIT THE SPEECH CLUB

When the weather eased, we went out, found a fisherman to advise us about the thirty miles up to Garrison Dam, an against-the-current distance I believed *Nikawa* should undertake. I laid out our Corps of Engineers chart, the aerial photographs of poor quality, and went over the route with the fellow, trying to annotate it as he talked. "When you come up this here, hang on this side over here. Now, that island there isn't there anymore, so you can go this way or on over here, but don't try that one over there. That island there isn't there anymore either, but if the wind isn't blowing, you can just about see the channel there. Over here's stumps, so hang over there, but don't get too close to here because there's trees there, and you can lose your props, you betchya. Okay, let's see, well, somewhere along here, no, this here is all changed from here to there. Is this the only map you got?" Asked the Photographer, "Would a canoe do better?" Our counselor: "Might."

When we were out of earshot, Pilotis said, "Haven't we heard those very directions once a day for the past week?" It seemed true, but the fellow had settled for one more day the Canoe Debate, that distance-versus-risk discussion. I doubted the Grumman could go thirty miles in a day against the current and winding chutes, but we were going to find out.

Chances of Aught
to Naught

THERE'S A LONG-STANDING journalist's maxim that it usually takes no more than three informants to direct a reporter to the right source; whoever devised the precept must have been a city-beat writer unfamiliar with breakfast in an American small-town café where a stranger has only to ask a waitress — no "servers" these women — to point out who in the place has answers to this or that. But for some reason it works only in the morning; unimpeachable sources apparently eat lunch and supper at home.

Our source that morning, according to the gospel of Glenda the waitress, sat with several large circular men at a large circular table, the difference between the two being the table wasn't wearing a ball cap. He worked for the North Dakota Game and Fish Department, and he said our chances of getting up to Garrison Dam, even in a boat like *Nikawa*, were "aught to naught." The Corps was releasing minimal water to avoid adding to the flood hundreds of miles downstream and, to our happy surprise, to keep from sweeping away the ground nests that piping plovers, an endangered species, build on sandbars. He wished he could trade some of the exploding populations of geese — Canadas and snows — for little plovers with their sweetly descriptive call, *peep-low, peep-low*. He said, "There was a time, if a hunter left four geese on the hood of his truck when he went in for a beer, they'd be gone when he came out. Today, if you leave four geese on the hood, when you come out there'll be eight."

The Photographer, a retired lawyer who had spent years protecting

Missouri rivers, told him of the fellow he'd met on his morning walk who was running for some state office and who agreed with not a single sentence from our man expressing concern for the environment. The Republican politician had concluded his preachment with, "Lookit, Nature's got to give if people won't." Pilotis said, "Well, let's just hustle on down to that old recalcitrant Missouri River and tell it to shape up and flow right." The Game-and-Fish man, who did not object to being called a wildlife agent, said, "While you're at it, tell the plovers to learn to nest in trees like sensible birds." And the Professor: "With more than eighty percent of Americans in favor of strong environmental protections, why do Republican politicians typically oppose them?" Said the agent, "The eighty percent isn't paying for their campaigns."

When we reached the water, fog lay over the Missouri in a dense layer fifteen feet thick, yet above was clear sky. A fine day for aviators. I nearly could have stood on the bow of the canoe to look over the top of the mist and direct us upstream, but with thirty miles ahead of us, we didn't wait for it to lift. I took the forward position to guide us through the ribbon of murk that turned black snags into specters, menacing shapes warning us to go back and claiming the alien morning as theirs alone. But we went on, happy for glassy water, a usual accompaniment to fog, the river so undisturbed it seemed vandalism for our prow to slice into it. With each mile the mist thinned, then was gone, and we moved under a Great Plains sky as blue as the mid-Pacific.

Now that Pilotis could run the shallows, I sat in the bow as navigator to keep the crew from feeling responsible for an error and, further, occupy them with the motor, deflect them from too many thoughts of home. Already the Professor was talking more each day about his garden, sometimes speaking of things I thought might undermine the others' endurance; his complaints, while mild, I could do nothing about except to commiserate and encourage river vigor. The bow position also freed me from the tiller so I could take notes and photographs without endangering us. I regretted only that the motor, though a little pisspot, was still noisy enough to make unshouted conversation impossible, but my mates understood that the concentration our canoe passage enforced would help perception and memory of the river, and they knew such focus was good since they had come to learn the Missouri and not simply get *Nikawa* to the Pacific.

Cottonwoods grew thick along the banks, and much of the surrounding country beyond the low bluffs was heavily cultivated, and with the fog and its eerie creations gone, we had to look closely — if not imaginatively — to keep ennui at bay. After all, this was North Dakota. The sun struck warmly into the cool air, and our moving through it provided a delightful mixture like an unstirred martini where one sip gives of vermouth, the next of gin; but as the day wore on, the air got more shaken than stirred by the Plains wind and became evened, dulled. I sat back trying to memorize the miles, occasionally pointing left or right to head us away from a snag or shoal or on toward a particular chute. From time to time, we had to paddle up a broomstick or push over a bar, but the exertion eased the confinement. When arms failed to relieve us, we'd stop at a sand bank and walk around, looking for curiosities or trying to identify some of the surprisingly abundant life that happens on places so apparently hostile.

In the long pools I could see three or four feet down and make out rocks and rampikes, a chaos of obstructions lurking only inches beneath us almost everywhere. To have come that far without such instruments of destruction sinking us seemed impossible, the result of sheer chance. It was splendid to skim above a wilderness of the inimical. I began to pick out creatures moving aside to escape our passage, some of them glittering an eye at us before flashing to invisibility, others lazy lumps of silt trusting in their ugsome camouflage. The bottom was a wavering garden of moss and slender plants, strands of algae, stones and gravel, sediments full of squirmings, slow currents of barbeled mouths, undersides slimed with egg casings, pools of turtle-clawed snags, and muddy humps that would suddenly show legs and scamper into a far murk. The inside of the river was slick with frog skins, sharp with fish fins, a dim realm still warming from the long Dakota winter and ready to be shot full of the spurt and squirt of milt, the bottom alive and everlastingly creeping about and wanting nothing more than food, safety, and a little sex, as if the creatures were the dullest of desk-bound scriveners with no urge to find the mountains, to cross them down to the sea — those undertakings they left to the world above them, to migratory birds from rain forests and jungles, to humans who could only dream of the ill-lit under-river world.

We had arranged to meet our mates downstream from the Knife River, but the nervous Photographer, whose well-intended concerns sometimes slowed our expedition, had left the Professor to wait for us while he retraced the road in hopes of finding a high place to spy the canoe. We pulled up and waited for him in what is probably the most deeply historied dozen miles of the upper Missouri. Just below was once Fort Mandan where the Corps of Discovery spent their first long winter and found their richest encounters with Indian life, ones not surpassed by the camp on the Pacific Coast the following winter. Soon after the Expedition departed, the Missouri washed away the site, but above it, safely on the high bluff, are outlines of a stockade and low circular swales marking an Indian village next to the remains of Fort Clark, a trading post established in 1830 and the scene twelve years later of a visit by the river traveler Peter Garrioch who described frankly topics other diarists usually ignored, perhaps the reason his fascinating journal has never been published. Here is a compressed version of one incident:

> Never shall I forget the awful and abominable scene I witnessed in the boat on the evening we landed. From about nine o'clock in the morning till dusk, the boat was literally crowded with men, women, and children of the Ree, Gros Ventry, and Mandan tribes. The great end which these poor, ignorant, and licentious wretches had in view in flocking so eagerly to the boat, appeared to me, not so much to cohabit with the whites for the pleasure of the thing, as the remuneration they expected after the rutting business was over. I cannot dignify the scene by any milder term — if I should, I could not but charge myself with detracting from common decency. Fathers and mothers led their daughters, and husbands their wives to the obscene and abominable shrine of Venus, as parents lead their children to the sacred Fount of Baptism or their daughters to the Divine Altar of Matrimony. Never perhaps since the days of Adam or since public markets were first instituted did any specie of animals or goods prove more marketable or meet with more general demand and ready sale than the hind-quarters of these ignoble and prostitute females. I am perfectly justified in making use of an epithet regarding these abandoned women which, I am aware, ought in justice to be applied to the brute creation alone, as they are totally divested of the very thing approaching decency — the very shadow of it even. Not the slightest regard was paid to virtuous appearance or personal qualities. If the object that was led to the shrine bore the semblance of a woman it was enough; the reality was taken on chance to be discovered in the secret chamber.

When the Photographer finally returned, revealing he'd hunted more for pictures than for us, Pilotis left the canoe so the Professor could have a turn upriver, and I went again to the motor so he might learn our methods of ascent over shoals and up chutes. He assumed watch in the bow and at first gave out loud alarms at anything larger than a toaster and at everything he saw no matter how far off our course it lay, but then he settled down and performed well.

Strange pockets of heat lay over the river, stifling cinctures alleviated by stretches of cooler air, but all of it unnaturally still, as if the Plains wind had paused before switching weathers. I began struggling to pay attention to the country we were passing through, and I tried to convince myself it was not really the same as what we'd been seeing most of the day; whenever I begin to believe that anything in nature looks identical, I'm usually losing the capacity to perceive. My dulled wits could find nothing to rouse them, and they retreated to dreaming fountain drinks and trying to recollect old recipes for — for what? a blood orange frappé? a claret punch? a buffalo eleven? a prairie oyster? (Draw a dash of soda in a glass, add one raw egg, a dram of vinegar, and season with pepper, salt, and lemon juice; serve with a glass of seltzer on the side.)

And thus we plugged on, almost eager for places forcing us to paddle. I practiced to improve my technique for flushing us over narrow shoals, and sometimes it worked and sometimes we had to pole on across, but the sand grating beneath the aluminum hull was like a cleanser to my brain, scratching it awake.

At about five in the afternoon we saw in the distance the silvery tops of the huge surge tanks of Garrison Dam. More than two miles long and 210 feet high, it is one of the largest earthen structures in the world, a thing so massive, from the river at least, it didn't look big, any more than, say, North Dakota looks big from a highway; it was just simply everywhere. By the time we reached the tailwaters where gulls gnawed on fish mortally bludgeoned by passage through the power-house turbines, and found the end of our day, we had made thirty-three miles against the Missouri, and at last I knew the canoe-and-pisspot would suffice, and one more possible impediment to our crossing vanished. When we lay down to sleep, we were only ninety miles from the geographical center of North America.

We Walk under
the Great River

THE WIND BEGAN RISING, inflating a hulking anvil cloud in the east, a nubilous sky up to no good. By morning a breeze had transformed into a norther and dropped the temperature thirty degrees and was buggy-whipping saplings and frothing Lake Sakakawea into a nastiness that would keep us off the Missouri until the air exhausted itself. Winds out of Canada can blow for half a week. Now, ever so close to the rivers requiring the snowmelt of the June rise, we were stopped cold like Antarctic explorers caught in a blizzard and perishing only a few yards from shelter. Because we knew the Plains winds should have struck us long before then, we didn't complain, but I did wonder whether we weren't now due days of blowing.

I tried to treat the halt as a welcome break from rivering, so we set up to wait it out in Pick City, nothing but a few wind-blasted buildings along a dusty state highway crossing Garrison Dam. In the American West, if a town appends "City" to its name, you can be sure it is anything but one (Salt Lake City the exception), and the traveler will do well to interpret "City" as "burg," with its colloquial meaning of Podunk. Perhaps the least meretricious name for these places would be one I've never seen anywhere: Businessburg.

In Pick City, with little of anything but space and wind, we were happy to find lodging across the road from the Sportsman Saloon Bar and Grill, a name Pilotis found tautological and said so to the bartender who replied, "No, you're wrong. We have very little trouble with drunks." The town, population 203 depending on whether Mister

So-and-so had yet joined the choir silent, would have been a faceless place devoid of anything redeeming — unless you consider utter openness redeeming — without the worn tavern and its antlers hanging like dusty cobwebs, its stuffed fish ready to leap through the ceiling, and its big schnapps cabinet stocked for winter. On our June day, the patrons drank thin, popular beers laced three-to-one with bloody mary mix which in that friendly bar made it easy to distinguish the locals by their ruby smiles.

To pass the time, we went to Garrison Dam, down inside the power-house, down deep until we came to a dismal and dank chamber filled with penstocks large enough to send an automobile through, steel tunnels carrying the Missouri toward the turbines. An aisle passed under the conduits, and we reached up to touch the cold metal shaking from the force of the river ripping down them, and as we stepped under the Missouri thundering inches above our heads, I thought how I was almost realizing one of my bottom-walker nightmares, this version hardly less chilling than those coming in my sleep. Farther on, we descended to another chamber where a vertical tunnel dropped the encased river into the turbines, and I laid my hand on a thick steel hatch: on the other side the river roared down with such colossal force we had to shout over the violence of its descent and the unnerving explosions of compressed oxygen bursting free.

When we came up again into the yellow light of the dusty day, it was as if we'd returned from the River Styx, and Pilotis said, "Not for one minute could I relax or breathe right down there. You can't comprehend the force in water until you obstruct it. Those tunnels give the river back its voice, and it sounded mad as hell to me." The Professor: "I had a sense the Missouri is just biding its time."

We repaired to our quarters, tossed a football for an hour, took a doze, called friends (the Professor learned his young daughter was playing the role of Cricket in her grammar school Wetlands Pageant), and went across to the saloon for supper. I talked to a retired teacher who came in to drink tea and absorb conversations. As we watched the wind blow through the dusk, I told her my concern that we might be trapped here even longer, and she said, "If there's enough blue in the sky to make a Scotchman's kilt, the day will be fine."

The next morning I awoke and listened. The only wind I could hear was exhalations from the sleeping crew. I looked outside. The saplings stood straight, leaves still, and above them was enough blue to weave kilts for all of Scotland. Later I saw the woman again and told her we were heading out onto Lake Sakakawea which was rising two inches a day and would likely surpass its record volume, and she said, "People around here watch that rise and think we have more water than we used to, but planet Earth has all the water it's ever going to get. If our lake's deeper, someplace else is shallower." I said, I hope it's not Montana. When we headed for *Nikawa*, I thought I heard her call what sounded like, "Beware the pillows!" Or maybe it was billows or willows.

Were Lake Sakakawea a sea, it would not be notably big, but as a river — or what used to be one — it's almost unnervingly big, by surface area the largest manmade lake in the United States, large enough to have navigational lights on a dozen headlands although it has no commercial traffic. Some years ago, North Dakota proclaimed the official state spelling and pronunciation of Lewis and Clark's Shoshone guide to be Sakakawea in spite of the popular Sacajawea or the version most historians prefer now, Sacagawea. The impoundment covers almost two hundred river miles running nearly to the Montana line, and happily for us it lies predominantly east and west. Less merrily, the eastern end has arms and bays so big we would have to work to differentiate them from the main river, and even less merrily, it's big enough to let the wind have a good long rip to maul little boats, so we set out onto Sakakawea with high respect for its several capacities to snuff our expedition.

Near the dam, *Nikawa* disturbed some western grebes huddled under a leeward shore, then we entered a few miles of rough water, then easy water, and rough again whenever we ran a reach open to the dying norther, but the buffetings were not enough to stop us. I feared the relative calm would pass at any moment, so, encountering only small floaters we called driftoids, I moved us as fast as the water permitted, fifteen to twenty miles an hour. The Corps of Engineers chartbook for that inland sea was again inexcusably deficient, nothing more than badly printed aerial photographs pasted into a composite that looked more like a high school craft project than a piloting aid. With not a single community along the shore between the dam and New Town, our destination ninety miles north, we all watched the lonely embayments and eroded headlands to try to match them to the

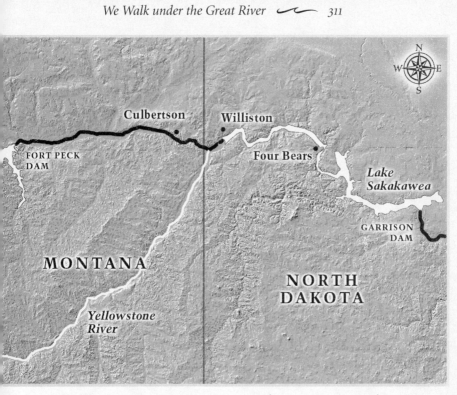

The Missouri, Garrison Dam to Fort Peck Dam, 347 river miles

chart, an easier procedure than picking out the small navigational day marks against the immense background of sky and bare hills. Despite our efforts, we thought ourselves lost until the Photographer noticed the distance scale on part of the chart was off by miles.

The inundated mouth of the Little Missouri is almost as broad as the main lake, and the huge bay called Van Hook Arm is more than twice as wide, and both of them, from water level, looked as if they might be the route we wanted. By neglecting that morning to set down compass headings, I increased the likelihood of following a faulty course, and, bucking the wind as we were, I could only approximately translate rpm's into miles per hour, so we once again guessed our way upriver until *Nikawa* entered the long, narrow reach above Van Hook that confirmed our position; from there the bays were smaller and easier to identify as cul-de-sacs. I gave the wheel to my mates to help them break the miles, and I photographed and sketched the striated

contours of the shoreline or just watched. Our relief at having escaped
the wind long enough to ascend almost half of Sakakawea was full
upon us, and we moved along so felicitously the Professor exclaimed
before we could stop him, "Couldn't ask for nicer water." Trying to
neutralize his words, I said how we all enjoyed his sarcasm, but I knew
I was too late, the Great Ears too large, and when we went around the
next wide bend *Nikawa* caught some miles of slammers. I took the
wheel again, and the Professor said, "Reason can't hold with that
listening-river stuff, but experience proves it does. A priorily, the Missouri does in fact have ears."

As we neared our destination across the water from New Town, we
passed another boat, the first we'd seen in days. When *Nikawa* was
secure for the night in Four Bears Bay, we went up the open hills to
the hotel and casino run by the Three Affiliated Tribes — Arikara,
Hidatsa, Mandan. About the latter William Clark wrote, "These are the
most friendly, well disposed Indians inhabiting the Missouri. They
are brave, humane, and hospitable." We took a big room overlooking
Sakakawea, then went for River Relief in the casino lounge where we
met a young man, Two Crows. The Professor asked him the significance of his name, and the fellow replied, "Haven't the slightest idea.
What's the significance of your name?" Said the Professor, "Right."

Another young man, an Anglo, came in and called to a comely
Hidatsa talking to Pilotis, "Maxine! Hey, what's happening? Where's
Tom?" She said, "On the road." And he: "Okay! Now there's room for
me!" In full nonchalance, she said, "Nothing comes between me and
my man. Nobody, nothing, not a blanket, not a sheet, and definitely
not you."

That evening I walked around the landscaped grounds above the
river refulgent in moonlight, the air vibrating with the clinking of
dishes, the electronic warbles of slot machines, voices whispering
Siouan, Caddoan, and English, sometimes in the same sentence, and I
thought how, for the last couple of centuries when these tribes lived in
villages not far downstream, they greeted almost every traveler who
ascended the river that far: trappers, traders, explorers, artists, soldiers,
steamboatmen, engineers, ethnologists. The location of their villages,
their friendliness, and a settled way of life made them the great hosts
of the Missouri, and many of their guests recorded their customs.
Lewis and Clark wrote rich accounts during the winter they spent with

the people, and so did Prince Maximilian and George Catlin, the last also painting them and their earth lodges and ceremonies, as did Karl Bodmer. Today the three tribes have an illustrated history of their ancestors unsurpassed by any other Plains Indians, perhaps by no others in America.

When I walked among them that evening, I looked at them closely, thinking how some of their great-grandparents had shared meat and corn with Meriwether and William, consorted with the crew, danced for the prince, posed for Karl and George, and I thought how the blood of some of those I saw surely carried the genes of two centuries of white and black travelers, all of us now linked by the old river under the hill, yet still separated by remnants of our history, like this one by Samuel Bowles in *Our New West*, his narrative of an 1868 journey from the Mississippi to the Pacific:

> We should stop making treaties with tribes, cease putting them on a par with ourselves. We know they are not our equals; we know that our right to the soil, as a race capable of its superior improvement, is above theirs; and let us act openly and directly our faith. "The earth is the Lord's; it is given by Him to the Saints for its improvement and development; and we are the Saints." This old Puritan premise and conclusion are the faith and practice of our people; let us hesitate no longer to avow it and act it to the Indian. Let us say to him, you are our ward, our child, the victim of our destiny, ours to displace, ours also to protect. We want your hunting-grounds to dig gold from, to raise grain on, and you must "move on." Here is a home for you, more limited than you have had; hither you must go, here you must stay; in place of your game we will give you horses, cattle, sheep, and grain; do what you can to multiply them and support yourselves; for the rest, it is our business to keep you from starving. You must not leave this home we have assigned you; the white man must not come hither; we will keep you in and him out; when the march of our empire demands this reservation of yours, we will assign you another; but so long as we choose, this is your home, your prison, your playground.

Why Odysseus
Didn't Discover America

E ARLY, WE WENT DOWN to the river and boarded *Nikawa* and took her out of the bay and upstream beyond the Four Bears Bridge, the span with nineteen names honoring as many Indian leaders, two of whom were Four Bears, the more famous called Mato Tope in Mandan, a chief Karl Bodmer painted luminously in 1833 and George Catlin rather less so soon after. Mato Tope repeatedly assisted whites coming up the river until 1837 when they again brought small-pox into the villages, a scourge that eventually left no more than 150 Mandans alive out of about sixteen hundred. As he was dying from the disease, the Chief reportedly said, in his own tongue, "Four Bears never let a white man go hungry. But now, how they have repaid us! I do not fear death — yet to die with my face rotten so that even wolves will shrink at seeing me and say to themselves, 'That is Four Bears, friend of the whites.'"

Just north of the bridge, on an immense but gentle treeless slope rising high above the river, is the largest geoglyph on the Missouri, and although not ancient, it's visible for a couple of miles: a medi-cine wheel with the Four Sacred Directions, precisely the shape of the one left in front of *Nikawa* at Omaha and now fixed to our forward bulkhead. To pass below the emblem is to share its native blessing and be reminded of the respect due creation, no matter how contrary it sets itself against small human purposes. Beyond it, Indian lands today cease, and the designs in the earth come from plowed furrows or circles of central-pivot irrigators that mine ground water as augers do coal.

We were headed for Williston. Because we'd heard the upper end of Lake Sakakawea was a complication of shallows, I changed our propellers that morning to older ones. The water was two miles wide with steep banks of eroding tan clay, sediments from the prehistoric ocean that the new reservoir has eaten into, removing as much as twenty-five feet of shoreline in just forty years, giving the banks again the look of a coast, something you might see in Cornwall. The lake lay quiet that morning, showing only a few driftoids, and we moved along at a pretty pace. Across the great openness our radio succeeded in picking up the Professor before we disappeared again into ever more isolated country. The impoundment progressively narrowed, not horizontally but vertically, its depth decreasing from sixty feet to a third of that, then a tenth, and the almost transparent bottle-green water became olive drab, then milky tan as the channel again began winding between big flats of snags, visible and otherwise, and at the river edge, the raw, striated banks became more weathered, turning into deeply rippled reclinations blown bare, and despite places of verdure, they said, Arid, arid, arid.

We talked of whatever came to mind. The Photographer asked about *Nikawa*, how I'd found her, and I said she was the last part of the voyage to fall into place. After more than a year of assembling what I thought we would need — charts, gear, knowledge — four months before we were to leave, I had everything except a boat. I had searched and searched and found nothing that could handle the tremendous variations of waters and conditions we'd face. One December evening I realized the whole undertaking was about to collapse. I went out into a light snow to the best newsstand in the county to look again at boating magazines. I'd been checking the racks for months, had been making calls, talking with rivermen, and still I was boatless and now nearly desperate. That night, time running out, I came across a skimpy, cheap rag, an unpromising one I'd never seen before. I turned through, slowly. Nothing, nothing. Three pages from the back I saw an advertisement with a small photograph of a boat having lines befitting a vessel for our purpose, a craft with the five requisite characteristics: flat hull, shallow draft, stern able to hold two moderate-sized motors, great range, small enough to be hauled around dams and over mountains. To use another parlance, I liked the cut of her jib.

A family company built only a few of them each year. At the last possible moment, in the middle of a winter night, holding a magazine

I'd never seen before or since, I thought I might have found *the* boat. The next morning I called the outfit and described our venture, and a few days later I flew to the West Coast. Within hours I was steering a demonstrator across Puget Sound as the builder told me of cruising alongside friends in speedboats that usually left him behind until they hit bad water — then his "little tortoise" would catch them. He said, "She's built to fish the Alaskan coast." The following morning I ordered a C-Dory, and only three weeks before our departure, a friend hauled *Nikawa* to my home, just in time for us to launch her into the rising Missouri and learn the ropes prior to pulling her on to New York Bay.

Said sardonic Pilotis to the Photographer: "You see, Skipper's the most luck-dependent man who ever came upriver, and this voyage may be the most coincidence-riddled trip ever undertaken. If Odysseus had experienced our good fortune, he'd have discovered America two thousand years before Columbus." I said, Will you please watch your expression around this river? Out the window I yelled, Belay that last — it's all jokes! But I knew I was too late.

The upper third of Sakakawea lies almost as due east-west as the lower section, and its bends are equally broad, but the shore is mostly free of bays that can confuse a pilot unfamiliar with the impoundment, so *Nikawa* skimmed along, and I began to hope Pilotis's loose talk had gone unheard.

I made sandwiches as we moved toward the end of the lake where it begins to dwindle into natural river again. "Amuse us," Pilotis said. I told of my aunt who wanted to become a professional dancer. In the late 1920s she saw an ad in a magazine for an instruction kit guaranteed to teach a young, flexible woman the bump-and-grind in five minutes. For two dollars she received in the mail a flimsy wide-brimmed hat, three lengths of red ribbon, two large buttons, a long feather, and directions to attach the buttons and feather to one end of each ribbon and the other ends to the brim of the hat, then put the hat on so the feather hung in front and a button to each side, the ribbons reaching to her hips. All she had to do was crank the Victrola, put her hands on the back of her neck, elbows outward, and rhythmically repeat this phrase while doing it: *Hit* the button, *hit* the button, *hit* the feather *twice!*

As Pilotis tried the method, something rose on the horizon, something we'd never seen before. I said, What the hell is that? We all leaned forward as if to get closer to identify it. Across the river, shore to shore, lay a faded brown line like a low fog. Pilotis: "What is that thing?" I said, It's either some trick of light off the water or it's trouble — if it doesn't shift, I think we're in for something. We each took a turn with the binoculars but could distinguish nothing more than a dun gossamer that appeared to be creeping toward us. "What is that damn thing?" The Photographer recited elements from two movies featuring deadly miasma. Whatever it was, it got bigger until it became a rampart, a streak of evil that was not fading away. I said, Bad news — that sonofabitch is no mirage. And Pilotis, "My heart's pounding again. How far's Williston?"

I slowed to a stop, picked up the field glasses, and looked a long time. Then I understood. Oh jeezis, I said, oh goddamn! "What is it? What the hell is it?" I shook my head and told them, Trees, a solid wall of trees. We moved forward slowly in water now only six feet deep. Across the entire widely braided river grew slender and almost leafless willows protruding five to seven feet above the surface. We'd found what the woman in Pick City told us to beware. As we approached, we could discern numerous small, twisted channels leading into the flooded underwood, each path looking like a dead end, each seeming more impassable than the others. "We may have to turn back," the Photographer said. I roved along the stockade, looking, looking, then gave up, took a chance, and just chose a channel. In a moment we could see neither upriver nor down, and in places even the low hills on the distant banks disappeared from us. The depth held at about six feet, so I went slowly on until *Nikawa* was engulfed. After a time, I stopped, climbed atop the pilothouse, but the elevation wasn't sufficient to let me see far enough over the thickets. The aerial photographs in our chartbook were only seven years old, yet they showed open water, not a willow anywhere, and miles of mostly barren surrounding land.

Pilotis said, "There's something eerie about this place. I mean, what kind of a place is a place that's not on the map?" I said, It's called Willowston. The Photographer again proposed turning back. Sure, I said, just point the way. The river suffered us to slog forward until the willows rasped the bow, sides, and stern all at the same time. I had only an approximate idea where we were, and I feared if we were as many as thirty miles from Williston, we'd play hell pushing through the tangles that far. Hoping the way would open, I proceeded according to the old Missouri River pilot's *Precept of Last Resort:* There's no other choice.

From time to time we found a channel with a good current and followed it, only to see it disappear, then we'd scrouge through the trees and eventually find another current that led us on before vanishing. At last I decided we weren't going to get out like that. I said, If we draw mud in here, we've had it — it's too woody to swim, too deep to walk, and too hidden for anybody to see us. What quicksand is to land, that boscage was to a river.

For the moment, we had three things in our favor: the water seemed to be holding a steady depth, the sky was clear, and the willows had not leafed fully enough to blind us further. When it seemed we were only becoming hopelessly enmeshed in that place which neither water nor earth had yet entirely claimed, I said, In a way, nobody can be truly lost on a stream because it always has two sides, and what we need now is a side. Pilotis: "Even if we get the boat to a bank, how do we get it off the river?" The Photographer: "Would you call this a river?" No, I said, I'd call it the Missouri.

I turned the wheel and set *Nikawa* on a course due northwest in hopes of holding it until we reached a shore we couldn't descry. If we were forced to keep shifting our route, we might not hit land for miles. Seeing little but sprigs, switches, and shoots, we went on. Six pelicans passed above, their easy, unhurried flaps and glides gibing us. On into that willowy wooden world we went, losing depth, but the trees still slipped aside or under us, a vast pliable wall whispering against *Nikawa* while Pilotis called soundings from the welldeck, the numbers ever declining.

Then it happened. No warning, it just happened: the nose of *Nikawa* popped through to a channel of fair size running along a steep clay bank about eighteen feet high, perhaps elevated enough to let us see an escape if we could get up the overhang. I held our course directly for shore, and as we neared, smack in front of us rose an improbable stair, a long wooden thing not unlike the one we'd found so long ago on the Allegheny. I beached *Nikawa*, and Pilotis and I jumped onto the soft ground and started up. "Do you hear that?" my friend said. "Is it some kind of weird motor?" Atop the broad first terrace was a man on a decrepit sputtering tractor plowing a garden.

Surprised to see people emerging from the willowed river, he came up to us and said, "It's a sonofabitch down there, ain't it? Them goddamn dirty bastard willas wasn't there a couple years ago." Between swear words, the most pleasing I ever heard, he described a route to open water, not a difficult path since we'd already stumbled onto a through channel. "The @!#@*! trees don't run all the @!@#*! way up to @!#@*! Williston, not @!#@*! yet anyway, but in another @!#@*! year, who the @!#@*! can say?" And so forth.

We went back to *Nikawa*, headed on upstream, and weaved along the twisted channel, and Pilotis said, "We just shoved through a wilderness of willows and came out right in front of a stairway — almost the only one we've seen in six days — leading to the only man around for ten miles, and I'm not even surprised. But I am concerned what happens when our luck runs out." I said, If I flip a coin ten times and each time it comes up heads, what are the odds on the eleventh flip? "Fifty-fifty. I know that, but how much would you bet that you could flip ten more consecutive heads? That's what you're trying to do." I said, I'm not trying to — I'm having to. The Photographer interjected, "I think we should worry about how many more willow flats might be ahead." Fine, I said, then we can worry whether lightning will strike on Monday or Tuesday.

After some miles we saw a road reaching into the river and stopped to go up it. We found ourselves on a picnic ground. A woman came toward us and said, "Are you the ones going long distance?" It sounded like a preface to bad news. "Your friend was here for a couple of hours, then he hurried away," she said. "He seemed real agitated, talking about who to call to get out a search-and-rescue unit." Her husband offered to drive toward town to hunt up the Professor and give him a message. Off we went again, happy in the assurance that there were no more @!#@*! willows between us and the Williston bridge. The braided river re-formed into a good channel of swift current bordered so closely and heavily by trees it looked like a bayou. Pilotis said, "What if the trip had begun on the Missouri instead of the happy Hudson and the easy Erie Canal? Would we have continued?" It was true: the eastern waters gave us the comforting notion that we could make it across the country.

Well before dusk we found the Professor, not glad but calmed and talking to a television crew that had apparently picked up his repeated and fruitless calls to us over the radio. As the Big Contrary would have things, it set against us a swift current and a vicious eddy that twice thumped and spun *Nikawa* before I could get her bow close enough to catch the winch line, the cameramen recording our struggle in water turned nasty by the Yellowstone River not far above. That night in a tavern, as we watched our difficulties on *The News at Ten,* I heard Howard, a man wearing a flowered bow tie, say to the bartender, "Pacific Ocean? Hell, Bert, those clowns won't make it to Fort Peck."

Because he might be right, I didn't tell him I was head bozo or that we jack-puddings passing for jack-tars had come 1,550 miles up the Missouri and 3,500 from the Atlantic, the distance from New York City to London. After all, we still had almost nine hundred miles of the Missouri to go. And then, *and only then,* the Pacific would be but a thousand miles farther. When I lay in bed that night, I wished I'd not heard his words and never done the numbers.

Pilotis Concocts an
Indian Name for God

O NLY SIXTY-FIVE MILES below Canada, we had reached the most northerly point of our voyage. For a river of such deviousness, the Missouri from the Williston Bottoms strikes a remarkably due-west course of more than four hundred miles until the short detour at Virgelle, Montana, then takes a long and winding southerly route paralleling the Continental Divide. As never before, we would now feel with each day that we were gaining on the Pacific. Ahead of us that Saturday morning was the first segment of waters fully dependent on the June rise to afford passage to any object larger than a washtub. From Williston onward — could we keep moving — the Rocky Mountain Snow Imperative would decline somewhat with every mile.

When we had pried from the natives as much river information as we could, we went down to the water, and I felt the draw of that state whose name is mountain. The current was swift, muddy, and full of stiff clots of brown foam formed from agricultural chemicals running off fields along the Yellowstone which we heard was charging down hard and high, a report that made the Professor uneasy. I tried to redirect his worry to the more real concern of finding a ramp or low shore solid enough to let us get *Nikawa* off the river should we need to. Through cultivated bottoms and anciently eroded uplands the meandering valley ran, four to five miles wide, the depth of the channel holding at about six feet; even against the spring rise and the perturbations put in by the Yellowstone — driftoids and low riders — we scudded along, yet still the Professor stood his watch in tension.

Not since the lower river had I been able to steer from boil to boil to keep depth and current under us; nevertheless, one strange upchurning struck *Nikawa* hard, a teeth rattler. Rhetorically, cussingly, I asked how we could possibly bang something in such a surge, and the unnaturally quiet Professor said, "That takes away the peace of mind boils gave us." Pilotis, concocting, said, "What's that Indian name for God which literally translates as the-one-who-now-and-then-but-not-often-understands-the-great-Missouri?"

The Professor remained edgy, no longer even speaking of his garden, and I feared we were slowly losing his continuance. Each thump from a boil or log seemed to hit him in the stomach, and I found myself trying to steer a course, erratic though it was, with the least chance of unnerving him. I asked if he were feeling the miles, but all he said was, "I'm with you."

As we approached the mouth of the Yellowstone, I began to anticipate that great defining river, another of the ever-westering nineteenth-century boundaries of the white domain, one of the final jumping-off spots before transcontinental railroads negated such places. The water became more embroiled, nothing *Nikawa* couldn't handle with ease, but the Professor's mandibular muscles flexed and flexed until I asked him to read aloud Meriwether Lewis's entry about reaching the confluence in 1805:

> After I had completed my observations in the evening I walked down and joined the party at their encampment on the point of land formed by the junction of the rivers; found them all in good health, and much pleased at having arrived at this long wished for spot, and in order to add in some measure to the general pleasure which seemed to pervade our little community, we ordered a dram to be issued to each person; this soon produced the fiddle, and they spent the evening with much hilarity, singing & dancing, and seemed as perfectly to forget their past toils, as they appeared regardless of those to come.

Below the Glass Bluffs on our Saturday, the famous confluence spread out like a lake, half muddy and half greenly and lightly occluded, the Yellowstone pushing brown billows of silt into the Missouri to form underwater clouds that rose and rolled in the river as a cumulus does in the sky. What the Big Muddy works on the Mississippi, the Yellowstone enacts upon the Missouri, so much so that some early rivermen argued it was tributary to the Yellowstone. After John Neihardt passed the joining of waters on his way downstream in a motorboat in 1908, he wrote in *The River and I:* "All unique characteristics by which the Missouri is known are given to it by the Yellowstone — its turbulence, its tawniness, its feline treachery, its giant caprices." On our crossing, we found some truth to his notion.

To say it simply, reaching the Yellowstone was splendid not for its flat shores or distant terrain but for its textured waters. I circled us twice that we might take it in, watch its try at overmatching the Missouri, and a good effort it made, not pretty but powerful. The Professor asked whether I'd considered the Yellowstone for our route west, and I said I had. While its smaller meanders make for a somewhat more direct route than that of the Missouri, the portage it requires over the mountains would be much longer than ours, but that's not all: after nine hundred miles of crossing the western plains, a traveler on the Yellowstone must still pass through days and days more of country only rattlesnakes and right-wing militiamen can love. Worst of all, highways and railroads bind in most of the river. I said, How could we have a sense of adventure with an interstate at our shoulders for two hundred fifty miles? Despite its wild grandeur in the mountains and the national park, the Yellowstone all too soon yields to civilization. While the Missouri suffers from big dams, something the Yellowstone is free of, the Missouri is the greatest and oldest highway of the Near Northwest, a river that flows through two latitudes and eight longitudes of remoteness, beauty, and unsurpassed history.

At the confluence, fishermen were snagging in the river for one of the most peculiar and ancient of its big creatures, the paddlefish, or spoonbill cat, a species that survived the rising of the Rocky Mountains, the drying and decomposing of Cretaceous forests of tree ferns now become coal beds, and the demise of dinosaurs. But paddlefish may not be able to withstand those new things called dams that block their spawning runs and drown the gravel bars their eggs require. Spoonbills continue today very much because of captive breeding in test tubes; although now it's rare to find one of such size, they can grow to six feet long and two hundred pounds, large enough to give credence to old tales of even greater ones jamming the paddles of steamboats. Since the fish are strictly slurpers of plankton and will not take bait or a lure, fishermen drag big treble hooks through the murky water the fish prefer in blind hope a spoonbill will get in the way; the catch there usually goes to a small caviar enterprise nearby that reportedly puts its profits back into local conservation projects. Pilotis said, "Call me retrograde, but I'm pulling for the paddlefish to mistake one of those guys for two-legged plankton and swallow him. 'Jonah and the Spoonbill.' Why should a New Yorker or Muscovite get to eat up the eggs of a species that watched the last diplodocus go down?"

Opposite the mouth of the Yellowstone once stood Fort Buford, now partially restored. During its construction in 1866, Sitting Bull made camp across the Missouri to observe and wait for completion, then he attacked and made off with a large circular saw he turned into a war drum. But the Buford soldiers got their revenge fifteen years later when the chief returned to hand over his rifle, his face covered by a blanket.

Not far beyond the old garrison, we came upon a man in a motorboat that had lost power and was being washed toward the swirling mouth, so we tossed out a line and towed him back to the Buford ramp and then headed again upstream. Four miles above the juncture of rivers is Fort Union, perhaps the greatest outpost along the once widely forted Missouri. The original stockade and buildings disappeared long ago, but recently archaeologists excavated the site before the National Park Service reconstructed most of the structures with stunning precision, so that in the midst of a vast, near barrenness, where perhaps the finest trade station on the river once cheered tired travelers with its high whitewashed plank palisades and gaudy red roofs fluttering flags and banners, it does so again. Upon reaching that location in 1833, Prince Maximilian wrote:

> Fort Union is built in the territory of the Assiniboins of whom a certain number generally live there. . . . Among the amusements and festivities are their eating feasts when the guests must eat everything set before them if they will not give offence. If one of the guests is not able to eat any more, he gives his neighbour a small wooden stick and the plate with food, the meaning of which is that he will make him a present of a horse on the next day if he will undertake to empty the plate; the young men do this in order to gain reputation.

Although we still had much of the afternoon left, to have missed ending the day at Fort Union would have been an affront to historical precedent, even if the place no longer took in rivering folk and set them down to full mugs and laden trenchers, and the only Indian involved in trade there was a park ranger in the bookshop.

Trickles, Dribbles,
and Gurglets

I N MY WRITING, when it comes to intuition versus advice, if the former is mine and the latter another's, I unfailingly choose intuition, but when the issue was the Missouri River on our last day in North Dakota, I did the opposite and followed the counsel of two government officials who said the high water should carry *Nikawa* well upstream. That ended the Canoe Debate for the morning and, nearly, the expedition. We started easily enough over those first miles above Fort Union, and took comfort in knowing the course of the Missouri for some distance was one of rather long reaches after we got past a trilogy of oxbows. The day was fair, the wind but a breeze.

We immediately crossed the Montana line and entered Mountain Time, congratulated ourselves, said how we had only one more zone to reach, and the crew spoke of the Rockies as if they expected them on the horizon at any moment. I reminded them that the only contiguous state wider than Montana was Texas with its eccentric borders; I said that even dawn took almost an hour to cross Big Sky country, and that our route to Idaho was anything but direct.

The old Great Northern railway bridge, one of the few in the nation where locomotives and automobiles share exactly the same roadbed (but not at the same time, we hoped), is a vertical lift span, its design evidence that steamboats really did ascend two thousand miles up the Missouri on their way to Fort Benton — a bit of the past otherwise hard to believe the farther we went. I thought, If a paddlewheeler can make the run, so can *Nikawa*. It is such insistent optimism that leads travelers into continuing up the Missouri against the evidence of the river itself which for two centuries has gone to great lengths to indicate its general unwillingness to be navigated by anything other than schools of the finned and gilled.

Even before we were beyond the oxbows, the lake-like river created by the joining of the Yellowstone and the Missouri disappeared, and the depth dropped from sixteen feet to six, and sandbars began breaking the channel into trickles and dribbles and gurglets, a piece of river so unmitigated I could use my century-old chart to steer through bends and even around some shallows. But the glare off the water at times made reading it most difficult, and I soon ran us onto a bar, a beaching that held *Nikawa* as if the shoal were adhesive; neither poling nor wallowing her by shifting our weight from side to side could free us. It was a grounding beyond any we'd yet had. As life must go, so it did in that moment of our struggle: a motley flotilla of young blades, their heads tied up in red bandanas as if ready for the bounty main, came canoeing around the bend to witness and comment on our predicament. Seeing they flew a jolly roger from their beer boat, Pilotis whispered, "Prepare to repel boarders." We heard a buccaneer sneer to his fellow picaroon, "Don't offer them help. They don't know how to read the river." To that Pilotis called out, "Try it *upriver* sometime, O jolly canoemen!"

When they had passed from view, my mates stripped down and went over the side to push and groan against the bow until they overcame the shoaly grip on the hull and I could steer *Nikawa* back into four feet of water. On we went, struggling against a river that rewrites mile by mile every law of hydraulics yet advanced by science. Where there should have been current, there was sand; where there should have been a deep, there was sand; where there should have been sand, there was sand. All the same, I thought I might be slowly catching on to the Missouri chop-logic for those particular bends and reaches, but not before we had to pole off twice more. The erratics drove the sounder mad, and I glanced at it only to remind myself that even an electronic intelligence couldn't quite fathom the Big Naughty. As I steered back and forth trying to keep to a good channel, trying to avoid an alluring and more direct route, Pilotis said, "It's hard to escape an asphalt mentality that makes a straight line look like the right way."

The worst part of a grounding was not the labor in escaping but the afterthought of wondering whether a strand of shallows was an anomaly or an indication the river was deteriorating into impassability and the June rise insufficient. On that day, the answer was six or seven miles of shoals followed by something worse, something that could not merely slow *Nikawa* but stop the voyage entirely — the archenemy upon whose nether church our venture could founder, Old Scratch-of-the-Rocks. By afternoon we were having to squeeze through narrow bankside channels where we clanked against stones, each time stopping for those dread moments of waiting to discover whether we still had props and motor stems. Even the halting was tricky, for if I proceeded too far after a hit, I might damage the engines, and if I didn't go far enough beyond a rock chapel, the current would carry us back over it. In all this I found a single favorable aspect in our edging, grudgingly granted progress, another feint a Missouri River traveler uses to keep from submitting: just such an ascent was the way boats passed up the great stream for two hundred years; since I was there not simply to learn American rivers but to learn the *rivers in their histories*, I tried to accept how that one was teaching us in spades.

Where rocks and bars played out, we passed through shallows of dark silt the props stirred up and the engines sucked in with the cooling water, but that too had historical precedent in the number of steamboats that came to explosive grief because of suspended sediment clogging boilers.

The consequence of our travailing that day was we could not make our destination, Poplar, Montana, where we'd heard there was a boat ramp good enough for the trailer to reach *Nikawa* and let us use the canoe. With the afternoon wearing on, we grew apprehensive with the realization we would likely have to get the dory out at Culbertson. As unruly, illogical, shifty, and willful as the Missouri is — here's one more river traveler's gambit — it nevertheless gives recompense, and in that country of long reaches and mild bends it returned to us some of the finest riverine landscapes we'd seen since leaving central Missouri. Plunging right into the shallows, the steep and high Bighorn Bluffs exposed banded banks of yellow and faded-ocher clays and soft rock eroded into cuts and washes and pinched coulees. We knew we were approaching the far edge of the Great Plains, and that on some afternoon, if we didn't founder, on the horizon a blue smear like an approaching storm would appear, but it would be the foothills of the Rockies.

From time to time we passed portable irrigation pumps sucking the river, and toward each of those I would mark out a heading because they indicated deeper water as a lighthouse does a shoal. On two occasions, beaver lodges built against the banks revealed where the river ran at a swimmable depth, and wherever we saw geese or ducks floating I made for them, knowing if there were enough water for goslings and ducklings to take their protective dives, *Nikawa* also had safety; but where we saw shoal-loving herons and pelicans, I took a different course. Still, since we were on the capricious Missouri, no method of piloting was without flaw.

By late afternoon, the Culbertson Bridge came into view, and Pilotis picked up the radio in hopes the Professor was there at the only checkpoint for miles, but we received no response. More calls. Nothing. Then a crackling that slowly modulated into a voice, and with the binoculars we could see him waving the signal flag. He radioed, "There's no good ramp here, just some muddy slopes that look bad for *Nikawa* and worse for the trailer. Which do you want, an earache or a toothache?" We searched the shore and finally settled on a place near the northern foot of the bridge that attaches to the Red Bluffs. It took some doing to get *Nikawa* over the rocks, and the Professor had trouble maneuvering the trailer around the worst of a quagmire. The boat struggled against things of earth, and the tow wagon against those of water. It was a match made in hell, a union the Missouri, no less than the Styx, makes a specialty of.

After I squirmed us into position and then partway up the cradle, the trailer wheels sank to the hubs, and I had to back off, beach the bow, and jump ashore to study the muddle we were in. All we could do was try to make the quaggy ground passable, so we went in search of stones, driftwood, branches, flotsam lumber, and then we began wading, digging, and laying down two narrow tracks. Pilotis paused to say, "On the Hudson, do you remember the line in old Ed's poem, 'Go soothingly on the grease-mud, as there lurk the skid demon'?"

When the trailer was again more or less in position, I went back onto *Nikawa* and brought her up, but now the trailer was too high. I asked the crew to come aboard and stand all the way aft to raise her bow. I gunned the engines for a second, the nose lifted, rode forward partway onto the cradle at an alarmingly steep angle, then could go no farther. She was so precipitously inclined, as if again on Lake Erie, I could see only sky ahead. I called toward the stern, Walk forward slowly, one at a time! The big Photographer came up last, and as he did the bow gently teeter-tottered down into position, but the props came out of the water and could push no more, so with much sweat we hand-winched her the rest of the way. Pilotis went to the tow wagon and put it in gear, but it couldn't overcome the poor traction and dead weight of *Nikawa* which moment by moment was forcing the trailer wheels through our cobbled-together ramp and into the mud. In another few minutes they would be locked in. With every inch they sank, so did our chances of getting out.

The Professor mentioned he'd seen a fisherman near a pickup truck just below the bridge, and Pilotis and I took off running. My friend's face seemed to say, "We've had it. This time Mister Lucky isn't going to escape." My mind, I'm afraid, was about to agree. "Will you help us?" Mate yelled down to the fisherman. "No time to lose!" The man walked all too deliberately to his truck and drove us back. As fast as the crew could work, we double-chained his pickup to the tow wagon. The trailer was now in nearly to its axle. Trying not to hurry and spin the tires and dig in deeper, we put the vehicles into gear, but nothing happened except strange sounds of steel under great stress, the engines pulling so hard I warned everyone away from the chain in case it parted. We took protection behind *Nikawa* and pushed on her stern while the trailer tried to break the suction of the muck; now the sounds were more sexual than mechanical as the wheels began to rise from their slimy pits, and suddenly our venture depended on the weakest link in our chain. "Push, you sissies!" Pilotis yelled. "Lean into it, you mama's boys!" And we did, and with a last slurping lurch the wheels came up and out and onto the upper end of our ramps, and our whole kit and caboodle rolled free and onto stable ground. Pilotis scowled at me: "Next time you disregard your instinct and take on the Skid Demon, I'm relieving you of command."

Our Montana samaritan said, "This bank is one nasty bastard, and it's like that because ranchers here keep opposing anybody who suggests putting in a good ramp. They do it everywhere because they don't want people using the river. They think the Missouri is theirs." As he started back to his fishing hole, he said, "Oh, by the way, welcome to

Montana, the place where they say, 'If it ain't yours, it's mine, so get the hell out.' It ought to be our new state motto."

We drove into Culbertson, three miles off the river, a bland little western plains place, once described this way: "Just when or how the town came into existence is not known, but the theory that there was a town gained currency between 1888 and 1892. In the latter year, however, a certain Lucy Isbel stepped off the train and spent some time looking for it." We found Culbertson readily enough and also a couple of rooms and a garden hose to flush mud from *Nikawa* and the trailer. After showers and a small ration of River Relief, Pilotis and I joined our mates in a railroad passenger car turned into a café — it wasn't a classic diner, just a railroad car turned into a café.

For the last couple of weeks we had made a standing bet about who first could divine the name of a waitress (waiters in rural America are as rare as passenger pigeons). The contest nearly got the Professor punched in South Dakota when he guessed Edna, a moniker from another time, for a woman just coming into her age-sensitive years. Pilotis, following some maverick interpretation of the odds, repeated the same name from café to café, but I tried to consider not only age but also locale, speech, and hairstyle. (I'll say here, without concern about jactitation or advancing the narrative too far, that I eventually won with Stephanie, a guess predicated on sentences of this order: "So like, are you guys like in a boat or what?") The wager usually amused our waitresses and got them talking about things beyond meat loaf. That evening Charmaine, toting a touchy load of cynicism not uncommon to the recently divorced, said, "Where you coming from to get way up here to Nowhereville?" Pilotis: "New York City." She: "What interstate does that?" The Photographer: "It's no interstate — it's rivers, lakes, a canal." She looked closely, evaluating us, then said, "Bullshit." Having just ascended thirty-eight miles of a wrung-out river, a route more damp than watered, I could see her point.

My Life Becomes
a Preposition

FROM CULBERTSON to Fort Peck Dam, the next place we could put *Nikawa* into the water, was just over 140 miles, a distance we'd traveled in her on our longest outing. If we averaged thirty miles a day in the canoe, we could make it to the reservoir in five days, a destination reachable by automobile in a little over an hour. These may be mere numbers to you, a reader seated comfortably somewhere, but on the river they are the essence of one's life. Sixty minutes in our canoe crossing the northern plains could seem something like the following "sentence," provided you read it slowly and are unafraid of losing your place and backtracking and you skip not a single word even after you get the idea (call this armchair participatory rivering):

River river river river river river river river river river river river river et cetera river river river river river river river river river river river river river and then some river river river river river hot river river river river river river river river river river river river river river mud river river river river pay attention to the river river river river goddamn rocks river river river river river river river river river river river river river oh boy river river river river enough river river river river river river river river nothing so endless as a river river river river except the universe itself river river river or time river river river river river even the sky has edges river river river river river on on up up river river river river river river river river oh jeezis river river river river river river river river river Möbius strip river river river river river always river river river river river more river river river river river river

river river river river river ever more river river river river river river river the river asks had enough river river river river river river river river river river river river against the river river long river river I'm ready to get stuck river river river more of you river river river river river river river river river river river river river river river river river sandbar river river river river river river river river river river river river river where are the river birds river river even they find this stretch too much river river river river river river river river river river river river O Missouri river river river river river river I know you're testing us river river river river river river river river butt hurts river river river river is that as fast as that peckerwood of a river motor can go river river river river river river river river the way's open river but are we proceeding river river river the Great River Boredom Test river river river river river river river river river river river river river me and my cockamamie ideas river river river river river river river river river river river no won-der Professor talks of leaving river river see what you did to him river river river river river naughty old river river river river river river river river I'm talking to you river river river river river river river river river river river river river river river where are those Ears when I want them river river river river river a brook can laugh say the poets river river river river but who ever heard of a river laughing river river river long long long long river river river river river river river river river river river river river oh mama river river river river river how many more days of this river river river river river river river river river river avoid river irritation river river river river river river all I know is river river river river river wet galactic equator of a river river river river river river the river is an eraser river river river river river river river river erasing my mind river river river river river long river makes traveler insane river river river river river river river river river river river river river and this is only one hour on the river river river river river river river river William Clark would understand this river sentence river river not a sentence river river river river no predicate here river river just all subject river river river river river no I'm subject river river you river are predicate river river you river are not a noun river river you're a verb river I'm rivered river river sing to me Billy! river river river river sing me a river song river river river river we got no fiddler Billy! river river river river river river river river river you big goddamn et cetera river river and you got no stop in you river river river river river you don't so much as pause river river river river river you don't got commas river river river

river river ceaseless river river river river river river river but please
river river what we want is a fuckin period

Now, good reader, you have the idea.

A ship's logbook, my pattern for this account of our try at a transcontinental voyage, will often take liberties with time and distance by
indulging freely in compression so that a reading of it gives information but hardly a sense of what the voyage felt like. To this point I have
given at least a chapter to each day on the water, but to do so for our
canoe ascent to Fort Peck Dam would try your attention beyond
endurance, just as the real miles did ours in the doing of them, even
though you, wearied, numbed, and perhaps cross, would come away
from those verbal Missouri miles with a keen sense of *how it was.*

Most of that long segment below Fort Peck presented the Great
Plains at their blandest, hours of low earthy banks just high enough,
like an English roadside hedge, to keep us from seeing beyond the river
so that even our vision couldn't escape to bring relief. The Missouri
became a kind of black hole, and our souls, like light, were unable to
escape. As if condemned prisoners, we frequently had only blind endurance to carry us on. One day, a person on death row may read that
sentence of a river sentence and surely will feel it as no speed reader
ever could.

What follows are edited excerpts from my logbook, concisions I
hope you, good lector, will fill in with what you already know and
perhaps expect: shoals, the incessant contesting the river, the perpetual
hunt for the most promising chute, the ceaseless crossing from bank to
bank, the hard thunks against the canoe, the occasional shocks that
rolled us gunwale to gunwale and made us wish we were on foot, sun
and heat, the aluminum canoe glaring almost as much as the endless
water, the continual unspoken realization we were never as far upriver
as we either thought or hoped. During it all, not once did the canoe
reach a certifying position before I estimated it would, and everything
was farther away than we ever believed. Such eternal self-deception
helped us continue and sometimes made me think the title of this
book should be *In Praise of Ignorance.*

MONDAY, DAY ONE

*Launch canoe at the perilous mudhole; crew happy to be in tow
wagon today. Morning clear, bright, breezy. Motor starts on first pull and*

P[ilotis] says, "That can't be a good sign." Indeed, an hour later, fuel line from gas tank gets plugged, and we go dead in water; repair and proceed. Standing Rock Reservation will be on our right all the way to Fort Peck. I tell P Continental Divide is now exactly halfway between us and Pacific. Not uplifted by report, P says: "I thought we were closer." Around Devil's Elbow and past site of old trading posts Fort Kipp and Fort Stewart. Beyond four-mile-wide floodplain lie rounded, eroded hills, but most of what we see are soft banks spending themselves into river to give the Missouri its essence of mud as filé does gumbo.

Mergansers, mallards, canvasbacks, shovelers — ducky world. Almost without exception, since above Harlem River we meet no other boats or people, and America seems land empty of residents; here, our fellow citizens are magpies, geese, gulls, terns, pelicans, the latter rising into echelons to wing past, their shadows sometimes falling over us and giving the only shade on sun-blasted river — if we could harness them into aerial umbrella! Above Hardscrabble Creek small rattlesnake swims toward us, so buoyant it appears airborne; when I reach out paddle, snake quickly coils, hoists tail like battle ensign, feints at blade; after we pass, it unspirals to weave on. Why would snake swim river? Can it conceive of another side to life? Do serpents have curiosity like bears that go over mountains? From cottonwood, two great-horned owls watch squintily, one yawning at the river; you said it, brother. Butterfly, with much exertion, comes alongside and overtakes us: new definition of our slow ascent.

Miles, miles, on, on, the river. The Great Ears hear tedium of my mind and correct it by stopping motor in swift channel, and we start drifting back, losing what we'd just gained; paddle to shore in midst of this grand privacy; pull off motor housing to find slipped throttle cable; reconnect and set off, now relieved for few moments to have boredom again.

Strange hump-and-pinnacle of soft rock weather-eaten into likeness of kneeling camel. Begin looking for tow crew as (we guess) we approach Brockton. Close to where Black Duck Indian village once was, see orange flag waving among trees; god, I love that flag. Make landing across from Mortarstone Bluffs. Because all towns along here are old Indian agencies next to railroad, they aren't on river but against tracks; no charm whatsoever; only things near the Missouri are sewage treatment pools.

In small tavern we meet Brendan Ryan, sixty-five-year-old Irishman from County Mayo, who left on bicycle from nearly same spot in New Jersey as we but five days later; even with rest periods he's caught us and will reach Pacific long before we can. Listening in, bartender says, "You guys' trip is a WPA gig just like construction up at Fort Peck Dam in the thirties." I explain to Ryan about Work Projects Administration but barkeep interrupts, "No, WPA stands for We Poke Along. Those boys building the dam got issued shovels with rope handles so they couldn't lean on them." Irishman sees this as sportive folklore.

TUESDAY, DAY TWO

Denver sandwich for breakfast. Up road to visit Lakota and Nakota Museum where poignant exhibit about Indians once incarcerated in old Hiawatha Insane Asylum (P: "A cruelly ironic allusion"); some inmates bore wonderful names: Mrs. Two-Teeth, Sits-in-It, Maud Magpie, Cecile Comes-at-Night, Drag-Toes, Robert Brings-Plenty, Yells-at-Night, James Black-Eye, Guy Crow-Neck, Poke-Ah-Dab-Ah. Photos of forlorn, lost faces.

As morning warms, put canoe in; terrain continues much as last few days; not unpleasing country, just too much of it between us and mountains. Water at first drably olive and murky except for reaches where certain angle of light makes them wobbly blue mirror reflecting sky. The beauty. Pass low riverbank with dead steer hanging on edge, dehydrated skin collapsed over rib cage like tattered and fallen tent, everything so dry even flies ignore it. River for hundreds of miles has been virtually free of litter other than occasional plastics: pop containers, fishermen's bleach-jug floats, broken-up Styrofoam coolers.

Through long pool of cottonwood-seed fluff lying atop like summer snow. We're reading chutes well now, backing down only one, although often successful ascent is but chance. Lunch on sandbar; too warm to enjoy. On again — Onagen, title of our voyage. Scoop up clot of foam from river: feels soapy but smells like mud, almost sensuous except for thought it's probably agrichemical runoff. Long stretch of sweet air that seems to be melding of sage and cottonwood; soothes day.

Out of west comes thunderstorming, but it slants away to leave us dry and hot. To pass time I try to concoct games; one this afternoon — think of four simple words I've never used in my books: hutch, razzmatazz, stapler, porkpie. Task takes up twenty minutes. Near bend where steamboat Big Horn *went down, we hit run of boils that thumps out tedium; ghost of* Big Horn *warning, "Vigilance, my jollies!" Passing time again:*

Words that will never appear in my books: scaphoid, epigynous, decalescence, monophthong.

Arrive at Poplar; not visible, of course; some young Assiniboins swimming; they stand up in shallows to watch, their wet hair shining like obsidian. We've made twenty-seven miles. Cool showers at old motor court, then hoof down to Buckhorn Bar for R Relief and supper and conversation with Richard Von Burton Courchene, massively shouldered and handsome mixed-blood Assiniboin (also Blackfoot, Chippewa, French). I say, Your name is almost Richard the Lion-Hearted. He: "I'm Oak Heart. I had one wife who thought my heart was wood." His grandmother played on the championship Fort Shaw Indian School basketball team at the 1904 World's Fair in St. Louis. Father was civil engineer, and Oak Heart grew up sharpening surveyor's stakes; he's now foreman for Montana highway department. P: "Are you a surveyor?" He: "More like a purveyor. I've had seven wives. One was barren. My first marriage was annulled when my wife's mother learned I was a halfbreed."

His speech has rhythm of Indians of Northwest; can recite Robert Service's "Cremation of Sam McGee" and his vocabulary is broad and slightly eccentric; character waiting for his novelist. He's read Koran and, "in three translations, the Bible." I ask would he like another beer. "I would — I want to cuss some more." And he does, an amusing billingsgate. P asks if Buckhorn takes credit cards. Oak Heart: "Only if you lay one out and turn your back." Later I grow alarmed at leaving my notebook on bar, and he says, "You think we can read?" Dinner is egg sandwiches. He's more curious about voyage than anyone we've met and wishes he could accompany us. Walks out to his truck and returns with large manila envelope and tells me, "Open this later. It's for guidance."

When we head back to our rooms, Prof announces he will leave ten days early, says, "I want to go home and see what's growing." Unable to dissuade him. Could his defection spread? Is weakness more contagious than will? Big trouble if it is. Later, on phone, [my brother] tells me [our eighty-five-year-old] mother each week seems to lose a little more of about everything. Should I come home? "No, no, keep going. There's nothing you can do here." Does she understand where I am, what I'm doing? "Not at all." Adding, "She's not near death — she's just dying more visibly than the rest of us." When I hang up I can hardly speak. Should I

have to return for funeral, I'll never come back — I know that. Founda-
tion of miles accomplished is crumbling. Before I sleep I open Oak Heart's
envelope; inside long tail feather of pheasant. "For guidance." Have to
love a man like that.

WEDNESDAY, DAY THREE

Rain in night, ending by dawn. Although thunderous sky still hangs in
northwest, clear directly above, wind fifteen to twenty mph. River looks
dangerously rough for canoe, so we pull on life vests and try water; little
pisspot shoves us along, then wind abruptly ceases. Thank you. After more
than an hour on a six-mile oxbow, we're only half mile west of where we
started, but above Spread Eagle Bar river straightens to fourteen-mile
reach with only one broad bend. I like those reaches.

Numerous boils shimmy canoe, and I caution P not to throttle down
but drive us hard across them. After one good rocking, P yells, "It's
like going through a rising cumulus in a small plane!" I've given names
to various river surfaces to help us recognize how to handle differ-
ences: teepee water 〰〰〰 *(vibrations, no peril); moun-*
tain water ⌒⌒〜 *(shakes, thumps, rolls, mild threat);*
shark surf 〰〰〰 *(avoid going broadside); chaos whites*
〜〜〜 *(time for lunch). And so we proceed.*

This morning woman in grocery told me when her grandson is thirsty
he opens can of sodapop; she asked him, "Whatever happened to going to
the faucet for a drink?" He said, "Pop's ninety-eight percent water." She:
"So I said, 'And how many resources did it take to quench your thirst?
Making the sugar and flavoring, carbonization, the aluminum container,
cooling it, plastic ring straps, delivery trucks? Then where did you throw
the can?'"

Pelicans frequently fly toward us, but geese and ducks go away —
response to hunters? Temperature rises to ninety; at one P.M. pass Assini-
boin sweat lodge; this canoe a sweat lodge; off with life vests. P speaks
about historical layout of transport lines all along here: typically, between
river and highway is a railroad track; "Turn the three ninety degrees and
you have a stratified archaeological site — steamboats on the bottom,
tractor-trailers on the top."

Long day ends at Wolf Point, again near sewage lagoons. Assiniboin
man fishing nearby has caught five species in an hour: goldeneye, white

*bass, sturgeon, buffalo, and a walleye, keeping only the last. Later, when I
rinse my face with cool water, in my mustache I can smell river like a
sweetly scented woman from night before.*

THURSDAY, DAY FOUR

*Morning conversation with Ken Ryan, big Assiniboin who P thinks
looks like me (mountain to molehill). Wm. Clark said tribe had "turbulent and faithless disposition." President Andrew Jackson invited one of
Ryan's great-grandfathers to Washington; upon return he told tribe, "We
must not fight the white people— there aren't enough of us to kill all of
them." Ryan's grandfather was Black Horse, name he refused to give to
soldiers, believing knowledge of it would allow Army to keep him. Ken
served in military (they got his name), has been tribal chairman, and
talks much about great usurpations of Indian lands and former forced
schooling of young Assiniboins: "The missionary idea was to save the
children by killing the Indian in them."*

*To my surprise I can understand Assiniboin name for the Missouri; it's
almost same as Osage use two thousand miles away. He says, "When our
people come upon the Missouri, we always say, 'Mini-sho-she, I'm glad to
see you.' When we leave it, we say, 'Mini-sho-she, ake wachishna ginkt' —
'Muddy River, I'll see you again.' Because we respect Mini-sho-she, it
hasn't drowned one Assiniboin. We teach our children about it. An uncle
taught me how to kick out of a whirlpool." I ask him to explain the
method, but he declines except to say we must not be afraid to ride funnel
all the way down. You first, I say. Years ago, he tells us, Wa Wonga, a
Missouri River creature, pushed relative out of whirlpool to save him.*

*When we head for river, Black Horse the younger says, "I wish I could
go on your journey with you," and I ask would he then tell us how to
escape whirlpools? He only smiles. "If you're strong and respectful, Wa
Wonga will follow you."*

*As we push canoe onto river, Indian children gather at shore to watch,
scene out of early-nineteenth-century traveler's account. I say loudly,
Mini-sho-she, we are glad to see you! and children laugh and repeat it.
None of them can speak Assiniboin. P: "Is it my imagination or do
Indians show more interest in joining us than whites?" Prof: "To Black
Horse the river is a living thing— to a lot of white Montanans it's a
sewage system."*

Prof has made extension for tiller to ease our otherwise wrenched arms;

crew doesn't like my hands-free method of steering by leaning from side to side. Pools sleeping under coverlets of cottonwood fluff; river as legs of tree. Proceed, proceed. I have to admit, at last, our ascent here drudgery; each morning, without thought otherwise, I automatically head to water—Wm. the lemming. Yesterday I was almost envious of Prof going home. I'm not angry, rather I long for freedom he'll soon have. Still, I disprize his weakness. When I feel like quitting, I reach for anything *to buoy me. Yesterday I trotted out line from some Christopher Columbus movie where CC, after his last voyage, says to adversary, "The difference between us is that I went and you did not." Message: remember how we must earn our differences. Look up that despair quotation from M. Lewis:*

> [The river for several days has been as wide as it is generally near its mouth, tho' it is much shallower or I should begin to dispair of ever reaching its source; it has been crouded today with many sandbars; the water also appears to become clearer; it has changed its complexin very considerably. I begin to feel extreemly anxious to get in view of the rocky mountains.]

Slowly, slowly, miles. Engage your mind! Find a topic! Soda fountain recipes aren't working anymore. Remember something. I once was smitten by auburn beauty called Cutches. Cease! No women stuff. Literary things are harmless. Words to use one day in book to annoy some reviewer from nitwit fringe: quadrate, xiphoid, epact, peplum. "The author, infatuated with arcane vocabulary, drags words from the underbrush of our language as a retriever does a dead duck." Miles not going away— I'm just getting older. Mini-sho-she! Give me topics! Then it does when we reach Prairie Elk Rapids, first we've encountered. We grab paddles, motor still pushing, and pull hard against water and rocks, straining enough for P to shatter one; picks up spare; hickory against river. Struggle, grit teeth, then reach good pool, and P says, "Back to boredom," words hardly spoken before western sky begins darkening fast, flashing, rumbling, blotting out hot sun; then the Missouri makes turn directly toward storm; obese, icy raindrops and small hail whacking us, rat-a-tat hard against canoe, and soon lightning on spiky legs comes walking down the river; head for shore, narrow mud ledge against steep twelve-foot-high bank that traps us; barely enough room to stand; pull canoe from beating water onto muck; we're drenched and shivering even before we can pull on rain gear, and we huddle soggy and sorry and trying to decide whether to get into the mud and under canoe to escape hail, but electric river reminds us to keep clear of aluminum. Waves break over legs as if we're pilings. Storm turns to near whiteout, air almost solid with water and ice, and in fact it is hard to breathe. Stand helpless and stupid like cattle and just get beat. P's lips blue, teeth achatter. Hypothermia here we come. After five hundred miles of cottonwoods blocking the view, there's not a goddamn one in sight. Plains hailstorms can produce ice the size of oranges, deadly missiles. P: "If this gets worse —" Electrocuted or stoned to death?

Hail stops, then wind, rain next, clouds move east, day slowly rebrightens and twenty degrees cooler. Find two eagle feathers stuck in bank — lightning rods someone left us. We set off again, behind one more thing that came and went so quickly we might have dreamed it. Our muddied clothes attest otherwise.

On gravel bars pelicans and cormorants raise big wings to dry; avocets, willets, Franklin gulls clean and groom as we wish we could; sandpipers worry themselves up and down rocks and cry, Wet-feet! Wet-feet! *Indeed.*

We finally find our crew at terrible place for landing, but we're tired so we clamber up muddy gulch, over putrefying steer, its stench fierce, shrubs crawling with ticks. Once ashore, I realize we're five miles short of destination; don't want to face either distance or putrescence tomorrow, and I announce I'm going back out; good P reluctantly accompanies. We go on, doing nothing more than proceeding in silence to about where steamboat Amelia Poe *went down some hundred years back, not far from Frazer, Montana. We call it a damn day. But these miles are like memory — can't be taken from us. Can they?*

FRIDAY, DAY FIVE

Most nights before I fall asleep, I read journals of Lewis and Clark or Maximilian, and strange thing has happened, strange because for years I've usually read before turning out lamp, yet never before — as much as I've wanted it to happen — have I carried a book on into a dream. This week it's occurred twice, once with Meriwether, now with William; the dream last night had Lewis peeping through brush to watch lubricious scene between Clark and "the Indian woman." I was present but apparently invisible. When I woke, encounter had somehow measurably strengthened my resolve to continue; once again I felt I had enough left to go on. I ascend in dreamboat.

Hard wind in night blows morning clear; mild temp. Beaver slaps tail at us soon after we set out. Hour later we reach Frazer Rapids, and for first time we must get out of canoe and cordelle it over rocks; fast current, slick stones, and invisible holes make progress touch-and-go; water ankle-deep to above the knees; foreheads sweating, feet almost going numb in coldness; but it's only for hundred yards; legs strung with long strands of algae we drag along as if tethered to river. As if?

Pools usually lie above rapids, and so they do here. With much curiosity we begin to await mouth of the Milk, sometimes vigorous watercourse Hidatsas called River-That-Scolds-at-All-Others. Along this segment of the Missouri, M. Lewis wrote of grizzlies, "I expect these gentlemen will give us some amusement shortly as they soon begin now to coppolate." Bears gone, no such entertainment for us.

Trying to slow erosion, farmer has bulldozed down cottonwoods for revetment along a bank — does he think dead ones hold better than living trees? On, on. I'm trying not to anticipate mountains; if Rockies continued due north-south orientation they have in New Mexico and Colorado, we'd now be at foot of Front Range; as it is, we have a couple of hundred miles to go before entering them. It's this northwesterly angling that permits the Missouri Valley to approach Continental Divide so far west; without Montana angle, this geologic shift, our portage would be quite long, as if we were to try boating across Colorado.

A few farmers abandon junked vehicles and machinery along edge of the Missouri in full knowledge river will sooner or later eat away sheer banks and topple junk into water.

> *Over the edge*
> *and out of view,*
> *I live upstream,*
> *my dear neighbor,*
> *so to hell with you.*

Then we pass south-side slope where rancher has dumped mess of dead and stinking cattle into river. P: "A rotten thing to do." Yes, but a kind of historical recreation — L & C complained about buffalo carcasses in the Missouri near here. Those bison, of course, were not vandalism.

Stop to stretch legs by old wooden ferry hauled onto shore but left too high for river to carry off. I fear we might have passed mouth of Milk River without seeing it, something that can happen when island inter-

venes, but soon the Missouri becomes two rivers side by side, blue-green one on south, muddy one to north. I steer exactly along division where I dip my right hand in and cannot discern ends of fingers, but on left I plunge in length of my paddle and can still see beyond its blade. In vertical cutaway how strange separation would look. Then we reach that curious debouchure, sometimes rich with creamy glacial silt. Cf. M. Lewis q.: ["The river we passed today we call Milk river from the peculiar whiteness of its water, which precisely resembles tea with a considerable mixture of milk."] *It's quarter smaller than the Missouri, and seems incapable of scolding it.*

Pass huge overflow spillway of Fort Peck Dam, about eight miles downstream from dam itself. Happy to have five-day canoe segment nearly behind us, and say so, forgetting Great Ears. Almost immediately enter one rock garden after another, striking stones again and again; cussing; where they cease, long strands of algae twist around prop; each pause to clear it causes us to lose much of hard yardage we've just made; cussing; effectively, we're ascending here nearly three times — up, back down a piece, up again. Heat waves off river make it tough to read; cussing; our eyes red and tired. Above Willow Point, current stiffens and threatens to overpower pisspot; cussing. Then we're into maze of islands and I lose track of our probable location, decide to keep turning left since dam lies south. Failing to avoid irritation. My life is down to one word, a preposition repeated repeatedly: on, on, on.

To P: If there's some possible way to miss largest earthen dam in America, I'd say we just managed to do it. "No time to get us lost, Skipper." But of course that's just when one does get lost. Rule of River Road.

At last I recognize roof of old lodge at Fort Peck and start taking what I think are shortcuts through the islands; if I'm wrong we'll be out here into night rather than sitting in cool dusk on great old verandah and sipping secret (not permitted) glass of iced gin. Finally, finally, finally, tops of tall surge tanks at powerhouse come into view, and soon we pass into shadow of dam that's so big it seems to be foothill; four miles long. Our fifty-seventh day on water: we've reached Fort Peck Reservoir. Learn Corps is holding back river because of flood conditions in Missouri 1500 miles away. Rockies now less than week distant? "O frabjous day! Callooh! Callay!"

Little Gods and
Small Catechisms

SOME FEW DAYS before I left home to take *Nikawa* east to launch her in New York Bay, I heard through a happenstance a piece of grave news. To control "traffic" between mid-May and mid-September of each year, the Bureau of Land Management does not permit boats with motors to go upstream on the 111-mile segment of the Missouri from Kipp Landing to Virgelle. When I learned of the prohibition, even though all other aspects of the voyage lay in order, I was troubled by such a long portage around the most famously scenic stretch of the river. A cartage where there was no alternative was one thing, but a portage where water — beautiful and historic water — existed to let a boat pass was something else. An agent with the BLM told me an exception was remotely possible, but a request would require weeks for a decision. He listened as I explained our proposed trip and my deep resistance to portaging. After some time, he volunteered to take us over those miles in a government patrol boat. We would have to travel faster than I wanted, but I had no other choice. With reluctance, I accepted.

At Fort Peck, I called the agent to tell him we were about two days out, but he needed more time, so we decided to spend the unexpected free day in the lodge rather than in a tent upriver. I had not had more than forty-eight hours off the water in two months and was visibly showing the wear, and I thought I saw a nearly commensurate fatigue in my mates. We didn't need sleep so much as change. After a nicely quiet Saturday breakfast alone, I went to the long front porch to sit and transfer notes into my logbook, study maps, and sometimes just lean back and listen to the robins and magpies. I liked that old porch because it was solidly still, not once rolling, yawing, or pitching. The Photographer, the most diligent of companions, spent the morning getting our motors adjusted and ready for the last quarter of the voyage. In the afternoon we all walked around to restore our legs, and I went to the Corps of Engineers office to ask about the reservoir and the river beyond. I knew our days in *Nikawa* were about finished until we could reach the far side of Idaho, but how much farther she could ascend I didn't know, nor could anyone tell me.

The Missouri comprised more than two fifths of our transcontinental miles, but emotionally it took up greater space than that, and once again an enforced layover repaid us even though the snowmelt question still loomed and would until we were far down the western slope of the Continental Divide.

That evening at our supper table in the lodge, while flitting critters bumped the window screens and night sounds and the scent of pine sap seeped in, our talk showed the effects of time off the river. Pilotis, who had been somber for several days, rose to the surface of the conversation like a hungry pike and pursued thoughts as if they were mayflies, but it was the Professor who started things when he asked if I'd gotten the idea for our voyage from John Cheever's short story "The Swimmer" where a man swims home by way of a string of sixteen neighbors' pools that form a kind of intermittent stream through his suburban neighborhood. I'd not thought of the influence although I had long considered Cheever's idea a clever one. I said something about liquid challenges, and the Photographer commented, "It takes time to see that a river is not just about water."

That's when Pilotis began talking. I couldn't get all of it down, but this is the gist of much of it: "I didn't know when I left home that I wanted something bigger than people and their little gods and small catechisms, their damned certainties and covered-over confusions. The Missouri *is* bigger. It's like a Roman deity — powerful, playful, cantankerous, lusty, profligate, changeable, dangerous, yet still interested in the humanity that approaches it. I'm not deifying it, just comparing it, but anyone who doesn't believe it's a living force — something far more actual than any divinity in any religion — is innocent."

About the time our pie reached the table, this: "That river isn't about people — it's too primeval. When I see an ocean, I don't see time, but on the Missouri I see time everywhere, along the eroded banks, down in the shallow bottoms in those worn and rounded stones, even in the current. Flow and erosion, flow and erosion. The valley is the face of a clock, and the hour hand's the moving river, always showing how our days are ebbing, getting washed downstream. Civilization will run out long before the sun burns up and turns rivers back into interplanetary gases."

And later: "Stand on the water's edge and see how easy it is to imagine a valley before you existed — then imagine it in a time when you're long gone. That river scours existence, pulls solidities loose and flushes them away. To it, our days are no more than cottonwood fluff. Our little selfish ploys and conceited aspirations are just so much sediment. People are about cleverness. A river's about continuance. We talk about dams and wing-dikes, but we don't need to fret about that Missouri. It's not endangered — *we are*. When I'm out on the water, I don't worry about it. I worry about me. I'm just too small for that river."

Eating Lightning

JUST ABOVE the big dam, we put *Nikawa* into the water the next morning and set off onto the Fort Peck impoundment, one of the most isolated big bodies of water in the lower forty-eight states, a lake reached, beyond the dam, by only about a half-dozen unpaved roads. As we launched, a fellow said, "Are you going out in *that?*" The antecedent to "that" was a darkening southwesterly sky coming on apace once we had committed to the deeps. Across the fifteen-mile-wide water the wind quickened and kicked up the lake and sent *Nikawa* into her crash-and-bang mode. Before an hour was done, lightning began slicing the growing blackness to spread it everywhere, and Pilotis's face flickered as if illumined from within, eyes candescent, things even more eerie than the ravening sky. The Photographer said, "It looks like we've been eating lightning."

I changed course and made for the nearest shore which just happened to be Grave Point. Against a black-violet overcast, the lake glowed greenly as the Caribbean can do on certain nights rich with phosphorescent plankton, and the day turned to an unearthly spectacle of bizarre firmament and waters that seemed a foreboding of doom, an assemblage of unnatural occurrences that can take small boats to the bottom. The treeless surround appeared to recede from us as *Nikawa* breasted the waves, the wind and the very darkness itself thick with the smell of ozone and voltage. When she at last did reach land, there was nothing to tie her to, so I set her nose up on a low bank of pulverized black shale that would hold us if the wind didn't come about. Our bow railing, ever the lightning rod, was the only metal anywhere around, but we remained in the pilothouse nevertheless and

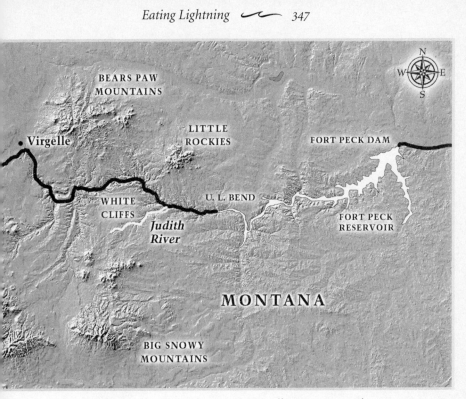

The Missouri, Fort Peck Dam to Virgelle, 262 river miles

watched the storm thrash the water and mess the sky, a blasting that had no good in it for anything of the earth.

Said Pilotis, perhaps to distract us, "How long would this lake last if the engineers cut off its feeder streams and let it empty at the rate it filled?" It took eleven years to fill it. "Then we have here eleven years of river in the bank."

Twenty minutes later the worst weather had rolled on to violate the east, and we set off again across short-spaced troughs and ridges about two feet high that slammed us hard, and the wind bore across us so steadily *Nikawa* proceeded with a decided list to starboard, an angle that made standing difficult and the motors drone in a disconcerting way. But such a nautical lean through the whitecaps, with the high headlands on the horizon, gave me a sense we were on a small and cozy sea rather than a large and blasted lake. In that manner, we moved along for some time.

Pilotis turned on the marine radio to the weather band to find predictions of "cold air funnels," things inimical in name, but what they were we could only guess. We proceeded on, trusting in the fickleness of the Missouri Valley skies. To be sure, the clouds soon began shredding, and in the rents a fine blue appeared, and the wind eased but not before tearing open the long horizon to let in shafts of sun that showed the way like searchlights. Our course shifted enough to permit *Nikawa* to go down along the wave troughs rather than across them, and the noisy banging gave way to a silent rolling that briefly wambled Pilotis's stomach, and again we were more mariners than lakers: port to starboard, starboard to port went our little bark.

Then, about forty miles out, near Hell Creek Bay where the impoundment narrows to less than two miles and runs due east-west, we came to a reach that let *Nikawa,* without any assistance from me, run the water like a bread-wagon horse that knows the route.

In early afternoon, under the broken and bare hills near Snow Creek, I pulled into one of the thousand coves of the lake. We tied off to a big sage and climbed a hill to eat sandwiches, walk our legs loose, and sit back happily knowing we were about to enter some of the most striking geological areas of the Missouri. The Photographer had brought along a big, magnificent book, *Karl Bodmer's America,* to help us identify locations the artist painted for Prince Maximilian, sites high enough to be unaffected by the impounding of the river a century later. There were few things we looked forward to more than discovering the painter's subjects and matching actuality with his peerless Montana watercolors.

The weather struck again soon after we were under way, an inky slanting rain but insufficient to obscure completely a horizon of blue ahead, a watery rainbow behind, and two other weathers to port and starboard; it was as if we were passing beneath a spigot, dryness everywhere but directly under it. We entered a realm of steep shores topped by low peaks and sharply angled buttes, spires, pinnacles, blunt pyramids, and squat trapezoids — a veritable catalog of solid geometries done in sandstone and shale and clay stratified into russets, buffs, grays, and white. To generations of travelers going west along this route, the Great Plains here begin to give themselves up in spectacular fashion as if all the delights of a thousand miles had been hoarded so they might be yielded in a final, grand bravura performance. Could they speak, the hills might say, "Ask in vain the mountains to show you these prospects." From there on, verticality would become increasingly a part of our days.

The long lake, its miles of shoreline equal to the coast of California, jogged northwest at Billy Creek, then opened to a six-mile reach due south to Seven Blackfoot Creek where we came upon one of the first Montana views unquestionably recognizable in a Bodmer painting. Maximilian wrote on July 25, 1833:

> A thunderstorm with high wind suddenly caused our vessel to be in great danger; but the same wind which had at first thrown us back, became all at once very favorable when we reached a turn in the river, and sailed for some time rapidly upwards. This brought us to a remarkable place, where we thought that we saw before us, two white mountain castles. On the mountain of the south bank, there was a thick, snow-white layer, a far-extended stratum of a white sandstone, which had been partly acted upon by the waters. At the end where it is exposed, being intersected by the valley, two high pieces in the shape of buildings had remained standing, and upon them lay remains of a more compact, yellowish-red, thinner stratum of sandstone, which formed the roofs of the united building. On the façade of the whole, there were small perpendicular slits, which appeared to be so many windows. These singular natural formations, when seen from a distance, so perfectly resembled buildings raised by art, that we were deceived by them, till we were assured of our error. We agreed with [Captain] Mitchell to give to these original works of nature the name of "The White Castles." Mr. Bodmer has made a very faithful representation of them.

We coasted to a halt, jubilant as if we had matched a lottery number rather than a painting to a geological formation. For some reason, the 160-year-old watercolor seemed more antique and exotic than the ten-million-year-old bluff, but being in the presence of those two renderings of the remnants of an ancient sea was like discovering a window in the long curtain-wall of time. We might have been standing on the keelboat *Flora* herself, with the prince's pen noisily scratching away, the artist laying down his washes, and somewhere beyond the hills roamed bison so thick it seemed that the plains themselves had gained legs, got up, and begun running, and from the high rocks red men watched the little thing-that-walks-on-the-water, part of the vanguard carrying in a new people who would inundate the old ways as the big impoundment one day would the river.

The clement weather held for the last thirty miles through the U. L. Bend Wilderness, a name that started the crew passing time by guessing its meaning: Upper Lake, Under Lake, Under Litigation, Utmost Length, United Limited, Utterly Ludicrous. We heard later it derives from a cattle brand. The vales coming down to the coves in that piece of the Mauvaises Terres were Killed Woman Gulch, Devil's Creek, Deadman Coulee, Lost Creek — a place of nefarious names that expressed some European-born fear of godforsakenness in a sublime landscape. Had the first nomenclature been put down by less narrow and acquisitively hell-bent newcomers (who wouldn't recognize God if It stood up in their bowls of slumgullion), the places in those Bonnes Terres could just as easily have been Sweet Angel Gulch, Transcendence Ridge, Playful Omnipotence Coulee, Surpasseth Understanding Creek.

We reached the long, slender peninsula creating the big bend at the mouth of the Musselshell River which we followed for a mile to a broken-down wooden dock at the foot of a steep slope of dark clay. Atop the hill was our tow wagon and the Professor, he much relieved to see us arrive at last at a place that must be high on any list of American remotenesses. I thought it possible, given the season, there might be no other humans within twenty miles.

As the crew set up a tent and I secured *Nikawa,* the weather snapped around again into a hard, cold downpour to turn the banks into the notorious Missouri Breaks gumbo, impassably slippery slopes that trapped me on the boat. At the next turn of the sky, Pilotis called down from the hilltop, "Do you need anything?" and I yelled back, How do you propose getting it to me? I ate as mice do, an ort here, a tidbit there, whatever flinders my scavenging uncovered in our larder, including a bottle of ale someone had overlooked. I went to the afterdeck and sat contentedly solitary in the great remove and watched a day of forty weathers close down to discharge the long western glimmering and give the night over to the scent of wet sage, the buzz of nighthawks, the far sorrow of coyotes, and then one of the strangest voices in all of wild America, a bittern in the reeds: gulping air, inflating throat, pumping out mellow, cavernous, liquid gurgles, wobbling notes seeming to rise from beneath the river itself, a voice made from the bittern world of slow marshy waters.

For all I knew, that lone bird, sometimes known as a thunderpumper, called down the lightning and wind which drove me into my bunk to lie in the easy rocking of the river, the Musselshell ticking the hull and putting a slow creak in the mooring lines. For a few minutes I knew all the reasons I was in that farness, why I'd come nineteen hundred miles up the Missouri. At such times, sleep is but a thief in the night who far too quickly steals what we've so justly earned in the day.

Imprecating the Wind

O N T H A T T E M P E R A T E Monday morning we knew we were going to run out of impounded water and enter natural river again, but we didn't know where it would happen, an ignorance that made us set out with two boats, the canoe tied across the afterdeck of *Nikawa* in an unwieldy and unsailorly manner. Off we went up the west side of U. L. Bend where the fifteen-foot-deep water was half what lay on the downstream side of the tongue of open land that is too narrow and straight to be properly either an oxbow or a horseshoe. The bottom rose steadily but remained flat enough to allow *Nikawa* to ascend due north for ten miles until the Missouri became a river once more and turned sharply to give us a westerly run. The broad and broken uplands, part of the Charles Russell National Wildlife Refuge, showed no evidence of ever having seen anything human and encouraged our expectations of finding birds and animals we'd not yet come upon.

Islands, chutes, and sandbars began reappearing to force us continually to change courses and speeds, and after an hour I had only a guess where we were or how far we'd gone. At what I thought was just short of twenty miles, we saw the dread thing again. I groaned out a god almighty, and Pilotis looked at me instead of upstream and said, "Are you sick?" Up there, I said, dead ahead. The Professor: "What the hell is that?" Pilotis stared, then, "That's what it is — hell."

Across the river lay a thin miasma of brown that turned into a line of saplings as we approached, and once again we were into the willows. I weaved *Nikawa* up channels that became progressively narrower, shallower, until she was doing no better than the canoe could, so we stopped, untied the Grumman and put it onto the river, fired up the motor, and putted away, slipping between gaps in the trees until Pilotis and I lost sight of our mates who were to return *Nikawa* to the camp at the mouth of the Musselshell and haul her on to the next place a highway crossed the Missouri, thirty-five long miles upstream.

The unadorned beauty of the arid Missouri Breaks helped us face the distance ahead, and even more to our relief, we soon passed out of the willows into open river, not deep but at least free of any bulwarks of shrubbery. A big Canada gosling, almost fledged, crossed our bow in a movement that was a combination of paddling, waddling, and flapping, a chaos of feathers that set up such a wake it rocked the canoe and set us to laughing and made us look forward to more wildlife in the refuge. The spring melt was reaching its peak, but the Missouri, although hardly a torrent, gave just enough depth to proceed without hunting out chutes, and often we could take a direct course and cut across bends; nevertheless, if that was high water, we didn't want to see it low. Coulees of many sizes interrupted the humpy hills, and here and about grew pockets of stunted junipers and little ponderosas, the whole scene beginning to look not so much like the plains but the farther American West.

Our progress was slow enough to allow mosquitoes to hover alongside and sorely beset us, particularly on our defenseless backs. We pulled on rain suits until the sun steamed us out of them, and we had to let the insects have at our posteriors, but on arms and legs we could kill three and four of the devils with every swat, a game that helped pass a few miles. When we stopped on a grassy flat for lunch, I took up my binoculars for a hike to spot some new species of anything, but as soon as we landed, the stench of cattle manure made us hurry our snack, and I found no pleasure in spending more time watching where I stepped than in scanning the bushes. The foul flat was barren of birds. We had landed in the Russell Wildlife Refuge, a narrow strip that boxes the river, a comparatively few square miles surrounded by thousands upon thousands of acres of grazing lands in every direction. In what way cattle, those Jaws That Ate the West, qualified as wildlife was beyond me, and I execrated the refuge managers for allowing such an abuse.

The place has come for me to say it: the antiquated Taylor Grazing Act of 1934 and two later modifications allow "ranchers" — many of them wealthy individuals living far from Montana and huge corporations like Anheuser-Busch and Hewlett-Packard — to run cattle almost anywhere on public land in the West, including wildlife refuges and nearly every mile of flowing water. Simply by paying an absurdly low $1.36 per animal per month (less than many fast-food burgers), these operators assault some of our most beautiful and diverse lands as well as American taxpayers who annually give a $500 million subsidy to corporate cattle operations. The very year we took to the rivers, the Republican-controlled Congress was considering changing the law even more to the liking of the industry. Considered against declining species — birds, plants, animals — the need for more meat in this nation is ludicrous; considered against the soil erosion and siltation that cattle create, the consumption of more beef is stupid; considered against the fecal pollution of our waters, the sale of more franchise burgers is criminal. For the past several years, big-spending cattle corporations have killed attempts in Congress to revise the grazing act to give a proper return to taxpayers and to control the degradation of our land and water. Yet what ordinary citizen would find it unfair to fence cattle and sheep away from our creeks and rivers just as we keep them off our roads? Windmills and pumps should water stock, not natural waterways. In the arid West, streamsides support three quarters of the wildlife, but Americans still unwittingly accept profligate and outdated laws that primarily benefit the wealthy while permitting them to poison the rest of us downstream.

Said Pilotis as we left that stinking shore, "How long do you think we'll let those rustlers of clean water, those corporate hamburglars, go unhanged?"

We proceeded through a refuge that, discounting mosquitoes, showed us no wildlife whatsoever, not even an English sparrow, a non-native bird that will live almost anywhere. The rest of the afternoon turned into something to be got through. Our backs tired, our legs twitched in the cramped space, our bums burned from the hot aluminum and the bites, our eyes went bloodshot from glare, our noses filled with the butt end of cattle.

The Missouri is great in part because, like the Grand Mysterious, it lets nothing go on forever. A wind, not a hard one, came along to blow the air fresh and cover the hot sky with dark clouds so that our last miles were tolerable. But when we came within view of our destination, Robinson Bridge, a fierce windflaw ripped down from a rocky bluff to shake the canoe and, as if it had hands, grab my hat and pull it off in spite of the chin strap which caught the safety cord on my sunglasses, then hurl the entire entanglement upward before flinging it down into the river.

I must confess, at that moment I'd had it. I went to my knees and thumped on the bow of the canoe, shook my fists at the gritty air, and yelled for Pilotis to wheel about toward my sinking hat and glasses, the only protective spectacles I carried. This was going to be a difficult loss.

Pilotis turned the canoe as quickly as the waves allowed and swept up alongside my cap just as the river was taking it to the bottom. I leaned over, grabbed out in desperation, snagged a strap, and pulled up. Still enmeshed in the cords were my sunglasses. Then I was laughing, thanking the river for keeping such a necessity afloat just long enough, and I turned toward the thieving wind to imprecate it as if it were the 104th Congress trying to steal away the beauty of American lands and waters.

Moments later we were ashore. That night the Photographer reminded me of a famous line from Aldo Leopold, author of the celebrated book *A Sand County Almanac:* "One of the penalties of an ecological education is that one lives alone in a world of wounds." But that was two generations ago, and now the world is not so lonely for those who act on behalf of our planet.

Into the Quincunx

SOON AFTER DAWN, the Professor left us to haul *Nikawa* to our destination at Virgelle before heading home to his wife and garden. As he packed his bag, I saw a pistol. You've had that the whole time? He nodded and spoke of his unease along the river while he waited for our boat to arrive. Although I said nothing, I then understood more: except for illness, nothing so burns out a traveler as fear.

When the rest of us assembled, I asked them, Are you still with this little ol excursion trip? Their mouths said yes and, I thought, so did their tired eyes. For that day, I reminded them, we would be in the government boat with someone else to shoulder the concerns. I said, Today we sit back in our ease — we're just tourists.

Chanler Biggs was nearly ready to retire from the Bureau of Land Management, whose badge and khaki uniform he wore that morning down by Robinson Bridge, and he brought to us much knowledge of the 150 miles of river up to Fort Benton. He was a sturdy block of a man with bristle-cut hair Marine-style, a broad mustache cowhand-style, and a stitched-up cheek where a solar cancer had recently been cut out to leave a scar pirate-style. He had high blood pressure but neglected to bring along his medication; as for his arthritic ankles, he treated them with little more than laughter and endurance. We took to him immediately and accepted him as our pilot.

He was, however, unhappy with the borrowed vessel we had to use, a beat-up johnboat powered by an engine that drew in water and forced it through a nozzle to create thrust; such so-called jet boats, being propellerless, can run fast in water only a few inches deep. I had chosen *Nikawa* over such craft because they are noisy, ferocious gas guzzlers prone to sucking up gravel or sediments and then malfunctioning. While we understood and respected the reason the government would not allow our four-horse pisspot to push the canoe up a portion of the Missouri designated a Wild and Scenic River, we still found it ironic that federal managers would permit a 150-horse jet boat capable of carrying us in six hours over a distance our canoe would require four days to accomplish. Of all the country we had passed through, the splendid and historic stretch of river lying just ahead was one we had hoped to cover in some leisure. A week or two earlier on the Plains, a jet boat would have been a godsend, but on that Tuesday it was an annoying requirement made somewhat tolerable because the Photographer and I had seen the White Cliffs from a canoe a few years before.

The heat of the previous day dissipated, and we put on jackets when we reached the river. Under a lifting overcast, we set out early, and Chanler said for the first of several times, "I wish I had my boat," words we all would soon be echoing. Another agent had fouled his motor with gravel, leaving us a hard-starting thing that nevertheless, once properly fired up, moved us nicely through the narrow valley where each mile onward took on the look of a foothills watercourse. The sedimentary bluffs showed layers of an ancient seabed in stratifications of tan sandstone intermixed with shales, the slopes more treeless than otherwise, and the enclosing shores varying between eroded badland breaks descending to the river and much higher hills farther from the water, gentle enough in their declivities to hold grass and even small conifers. From place to place between the coulees stood eccentrically worn spires, many of them topped with hard, flat rock that gave them the look of a procession of skinny graduates wearing mortarboards. Chanler stopped on occasion to comment. Once he said, "I've bagged seven bodies off this river. Every one of them the result of stupidity or not wearing a life jacket or both." The river, he added, was the highest in years, and Pilotis gave me a nod that meant, "There you have it, Mister Snowmelt Imperative."

Into the remoteness we rode easily as if we were steamboat passengers with nothing to do but prop back on the boiler deck and watch the territory ever so slowly begin to turn itself into mountains. It was a stretch of the arid upper Missouri country almost unchanged by humans, other than a few abandoned homesteader cabins, a defunct gold mine, and evidence of overgrazing. Where cattle could not get in, narrow flats of small cottonwoods that "woodhawks" years ago cleared out to sell for steamboat fuel had now returned to a river William Clark would recognize: "This countrey may with propriety I think be termed the Deserts of America, as I do not Conceive any part can ever be Settled, as it is deficent in water, Timber & too Steep to be tilled." And Lewis: "The country more broken and barren than yesterday if possible."

We stopped just below the mouth of a stream Clark named Judith, after the woman he would marry following his return to St. Louis. There, near a new highway bridge, the last we'd pass until Fort Benton, ninety miles upriver, our helmsman had arranged to pick up more gasoline, but nobody was present, nobody was apparently within miles, so we took out lunch and ate, walked around, waited, walked, waited. At last we decided the gas was not going to arrive, a detail that would have stopped us right there had Chanler not remembered ten gallons stashed in a nearby locked shed he happened to have a key to. Pilotis could not decide whether we were having good luck or bad. Chanler calculated mileage against gallonage, checked his figures, and concluded we should have *just enough* fuel to get us to Virgelle where a hot supper would be waiting. "If I had my boat," he said, "I'd know for certain whether we could make it." The man's command bearing gave us an unspoken assurance all would be well, and we proceeded on happily.

It was near here that William Clark climbed out of the river bottoms to the surrounding rim to see what progress the Corps of Discovery was making toward the Rockies:

From this point I beheld the Rocky Mountains for the first time with Certainty, I could only discover a fiew of the most elivated points above the horizon. the most remarkable of which by my pocket Compas I found bore S. 60 W. those points of the rocky Mountain were Covered with Snow and the Sun Shown on it in Such a manner as to give me a most plain and Satisfactory view. whilst I viewed those mountains I felt a Secret pleasure in finding myself So near the head of the heretofore Conceived boundless Missouri; but when I reflected on the difficulties which the Snowey barrier would most probably throw in my way to the Pacific Ocean, and the Sufferings and hardships of my Self and party in them, it in Some measure Counter ballanced the joy I had felt in the first moments in which I gazed on them; but as I have always held it little Short of Criminality to anticipate evils I will allow it to be a good Comfortable road untill I am Compelled to believe otherwise.

What Clark saw "with Certainty" was not the Rockies at all but portions of a topographical quincunx of clustered mountains at each corner with the mouth of the Judith River in the center; these clusters, rising distinctly from a somewhat level plain, are the Bears Paws, Big Snowys, Highwoods, and Little Rockies, all geologically distinct from the cordillera behind them. The Missouri passes among those stone outposts that seem to defend the great bulwark of the Front Range every traveler across the Plains longs so deeply to see. Clark, wearied by the "Deserts of America" and a consequent urge for destination, will not be the last to turn that longing into error.

We rode over Deadman's Rapids — once Drowned Man's Rapids — and ascended on toward the lower White Cliffs. There the most famous riverscapes along the Missouri begin modestly, almost faintly as if only a tracery of frost on a windowpane, in eroding sandstones topped by grassy contours steadily changing to ever more rock twisting into small pinnacles interspersed by crevices, pinched canyons, and sheer walls that might have once been fortresses were they not so fragile looking, their outliers elementally eaten into turrets, parapets, casements, barbicans, battlements, merlons; below them, broken boulders strew out like engines of war from some battle between the forces of earth and wind, rock and water, a scene of ancient antagonisms where the enmity of the elements had it out, where a piece of a continent, the old beachhead, lies moldering in perpetual dissolve.

Although the cliffs are not truly white, the glare of the afternoon sun on the bleached stone and the contrast with various dark volcanic intrusions made them seem nearly so. The eroded magma stands in large humps or low ledges and dikes fractured uniformly enough into blocks that a visitor innocent of geology could swear they had been cut and set by masons of the sort who laid up the great mortarless walls of Cuzco rather than by the aimless violence of sheer chthonic force.

To voyagers bound upriver, the White Cliffs are the last and grandest expression of the Plains, the prairie in climax, the flatlands in ecstasy; they are fulfillment, culmination, finale, and their power comes not solely from the harsh beauty or eccentric geology but also from a traveler's relief in knowing the Great Plains lie behind. To us they seemed like victory, our Battle of the Long Miles at last about to be won.

We watched the rocks rise minute by minute as the low sunlight burned them brightly and revealed aeries of golden eagles in whose yellow eyes we, far below, were a passing mote, a riffle in the river. Our voyage appeared to move with so gratifying a momentum I thought we could nearly glide the rest of the way to the Pacific; our miles had never been easier or lovelier. Such a blissful situation, of course, should have alerted me.

Sometime in the late afternoon, under the shadow of Last Chance Bench and across from Dark Butte, the albescent land began to change, and in effect the day started again, the alarm being the abrupt silence of the motors. Our guide nervously cranked the engine, cranked it, and it gave us nothing. The river captured our progress, once more pushing us back toward where we'd come from.

Said Chanler, "I guess this boat doesn't get three miles to the gallon." In the midst of sprawling beauty and little else, we were fuelless, tentless, foodless, nearly potable-waterless, and thirty miles from Virgelle. The hour was a few minutes after five, and Chanler's BLM office had just closed, yet he picked up his shortwave to try anyway. Why not? There was nothing else to do. I doubted the transmission would even get out of the canyon. No response, another try, nothing, once more, no. Then a rasp of static, a faint voice. His assistant had gone back to the office when she thought she heard the radio. A moment later and she would have been out of earshot and we, without sleeping bags, would be facing a cold night on the river. Pilotis said, "Stroke of luck number one hundred nineteen."

There would be no getting gasoline to us down the high north cliff, but on the south, almost where we were, there happened to be a coulee with a nearly forgotten track to the river. Said Pilotis, looking at the map: "Number one hundred twenty." Chanler described our position to a volunteer who, as luck would have it, just happened by the office and had a ready pickup and two jerry cans. Then we took up the long oars of the johnboat and began poling for the place Sheep Shed Coulee joins the Missouri, and after a mile we tied up and began our second wait. The river was now in shadow, the temperature dropping, but salvation was coming. Chanler said, "Hell of a way to run a navy." I picked up our copy of the Lewis and Clark journals and looked for White Cliffs entries and found the long descriptive passage from Lewis for May 31, 1805, the one containing the often noted last sentences, "The thin stratas of hard freestone intermixed with the soft sandstone seems to have aided the water in forming this curious scenery. As we passed on it seemed as if those seens of visionary inchantment would never have an end."

Chanler told us about the other Corps, the Engineers, and their wish in the 1960s to dam the Missouri a few miles away, an impoundment that would have turned the White Cliffs into a wave-lapped ledge and drowned most of the "seens of visionary inchantment." He talked about two sheep Lewis killed there and the extermination by the 1930s of those Audubon bighorn — a species now replaced by the smaller and less distinctive Rocky Mountain sheep — and told of the old homesteader who cut the tip off a long cow horn and shoved it in a gap in the logs of his cabin so, in the bitter winters, he could use it as a urinal.

To help our salvation reach us, I hiked over a broad sagebrush flat, hopped around a rattlesnake, and climbed the high south rim for a good look up the coulee, but I could discover no track or even the real possibility of one through the gullied bottom. I sat down and took up my dog watch.

As I had several times before, I wished we could make our crossing twice, once on the water and once along the surrounding shores and ridges that yield so different a perception of river country. At the very edge of the cliff was an exotic garden of small basins and concretions, stone toadstools reaching to my knees, a welter of rocks worn into oddities, grotesqueries, weirdities, nature gone whimsical if not deranged, a realm created by a fevered dreamer. In climbing to the top, I'd stepped over some bourn of the reasonable world to find a madscape hanging on the drop edge of a yonder, the kind of land I'd hoped — in vain — the first pictures from the moon or Mars might show us, a loony world we could recognize instantly as not ours, a place looking truly otherworldly rather than like west Texas. I felt I'd made an interplanetary climb above an alien river.

Far below slipped the slow downward sweep of the Missouri, propelled by the mountains toward the gathering of all waters, the river canyon illumined by low, supine sun shafts, thick and heavy as if light too were a topography, one I could walk out on to cross the river. The view was surpassingly splendid, one I'm not likely to encounter ever again. And then I came back to the practicalities of the coulee and its water-eaten bottom. There was no way our deliverer could pass through it. We were about to belong to the night.

I returned to the dead johnboat with my report, words hardly out of my mouth when the volunteer radioed to say he was cut off by a deep gully. We again went to the map. About six miles downstream was one last coulee with a track to the water; beyond that lay only hours of inaccessibility. We set out once more, poling the clumsy boat to keep it in the fastest current and away from shallows, the valley silent but for boils against the hull, the soft rattle of cottonwoods, the last whistles of the evening by this bird or that.

After an hour, in the gloaming, we came to an abandoned homestead, and Chanler took up the shortwave to radio we had arrived near the mouth of Flat Creek. We began our third wait. I asked him how, *should* our fuel reach us, we could make it upstream in the dark, something even many steamboat pilots wouldn't attempt. He said only, "I know the river." I asked, Those aren't famous last words, are they?

The hills were gone into the night when we picked out a pair of eyes gemming the dark, coming on slowly and erratically down toward us, disappearing, reappearing, vanishing again, and then the headlights of the pickup blinded us. I'd rarely seen our crew work so expeditiously, and in minutes we were refueled with what would either get us to Virgelle or leave us worse off than we were. Nobody ever raised the question of climbing into the truck and riding out for a return the next morning. We were too dauntless, or too distracted, or perhaps we thought our destination closer than it was. Soon afterward, I had an inkling that such an oversight might be the miscalculation of my life.

Our guide did not ease the boat upriver but rather let it rip along, damn the turns and impediments. Such conditions of speed, darkness, and an unpredictable and swift river left no room for one more error on a day of errors. Our pilot stood amidships to steer us over the black boils, Pilotis sat aft by the warm motor, the Photographer and I were in the bow as a human windshield where the frigid blast almost negated my two shirts, sweater, life vest, and slicker. Never had I been so thickly bundled yet still cold. Through the chilling darkness we went, Pilotis seeing the White Cliffs for the first time as few travelers ever have — bound upstream fast on a moonless night.

A river in the deep dark seems to give off radiance as if it had absorbed the day as a road does heat. The phenomenon was, of course, merely reflection from an origin I couldn't discern, and our pilot could just distinguish the gleam of the Missouri from its black shores and islands and, we hoped, hunks of drift. As for things beneath the looking-glass water, obstructions even only an inch below, those remained as unseen as a wall behind a mirror, and we proceeded upward, trusting in an image no deeper than a sheet of paper. At the speed we were moving over water infrigerated by snowmelt, to crash and go overboard in our heavy clothes would be to walk the dark bottom. The word for what we were doing is foolhardy, but something — perhaps the cold or my weariness or even my unfounded conviction we were destined to reach the Pacific — kept me from taking up my Lake Erie means of controlling fear: "We're doomed, so what use is fright?" But had the boat and decision been mine, we would have gone ashore, built a fire, and huddled around with stories and dozes until dawn opened the way. Despite my concern, I must admit to enjoying the thrill of the ride and the challenge of watching for rampikes and deadheads until about midnight when, flagging from the hour and effort, I began to think of death as a good sleep.

Tired and torpid, onward we went, trying to stay alert to be sure our helmsman did not nod, and we were almost reassured periodically when he would jerk the boat away from a sudden obstacle; it was like being saved from death two or three times an hour. For a while I let the scent-laden damp air keep me awake as we passed through pockets of sage, ponderosa, blossoming Russian olive, more sage, cattle stench, ponderosa again. The breaks became silhouettes, and the grand monuments merged with the tomb of night. Numbed by the chill and the drone of the motor, my senses seemed to fail as they must in death, and it was as if we'd passed down a nether corridor to an upper level of some Dantean infernality of cold, wind, darkness, and, worst of all, unendingness. Under such conditions, it is easy to abandon a luxury like hope and just give over to discomfort. So, through what to us were the Black Cliffs of the Missouri we went, neither awake nor asleep, neither alive nor dead. We were simply nullities. We were but darkly moving mindlessnesses like the river itself, and not until that moment had we and the river been so one.

On and on we went, time passing at the rate it does in a dental chair. Maybe we only presumed our progress; perhaps we actually sat still, our speed matching the current, while the only movement was the river passing beneath us, and if the tank did not again run dry, when dawn came we'd find ourselves where we began hours earlier — if there were such a thing as dawn in a place like that. On, on, on, the landscape increasingly indivisible, and then:

I thought I went deaf, the quiet became so abruptly complete. Or maybe I'd expired. Perhaps that was the way it happened: suddenly you go senseless while your mind spins for a few more moments like the wheels of an overturned wagon — slower, slower, then the revolutions cease, and that's it. R.I.P.

I heard a sonorous voice, a resonant one such as we expect God to have. Then It profaned the night. God can take Its own name in vain if It wants to. And the Voice said, "We've got a problem." I knew then I must still be alive, because surely, neither God nor the dead have problems — after all, problem is just another way of spelling life. "The motor won't turn over. There's got to be a short."

So, I was yet on Earth, in America, and this was life on the Missouri. The swift black river once again began carrying us down toward the wrong ocean, and our great adversary, gravity, was one more time overmatching our momentum, and all the while our helmsman fiddled with switches and circuits as we drifted back six miles to the hour until we understood the motor would indeed stay dead. At his command we rose stiffly, took up the cold oars, and began poling across our Acheron to the north shore, eventually reaching the mouth of Little Sandy Creek. As we tied up our dismal ferry, our Virgil lamented, "We were almost there. We were nearly done." I thought, We *are* nearly done. I managed not to say, even to Pilotis, For one day we're forced to put our expedition into other hands, and look what happens.

After clanking around in the metal boat, we climbed up a low terrace and came upon three tents spilling out groggy and partly clad women and one nominal man, all in high alarm and ready to confront the danger — us. Between our explanations and their objurgations, we shouldered our small packs full of materials more useful to a geographer or secretary than someone setting off on foot across Montana at half past midnight. I tried not to think of all that soft warmth soon to be again snugged into cozy tents, but wasn't this the time to break out a round of ardent spirits and regale the night with tales of our crossing? Even the Corps of Discovery had consort with natives of a certain gender. Of course, our piddling corps had not a drop of any social beverage.

We climbed the steep second terrace above the Little Sandy which in glacial times was the route the Missouri took around the White Cliffs as if it too found that a hard country. We came atop a vast black plain under a black sky, our moods the same hue. Chanler's flashlight soon failed, and the small one Pilotis lent him was suitable for scarcely more than finding a shoe in a pup tent. We could not see the ground, so each step was only a presumption of footing, a short and hopeful free-fall.

Our guide, to judge from the wobble of the penlight, was not having an easy time of it, his ankles arthritic and his blood pressure without medicine. Noting the gradual loss of his command bearing, Pilotis took up Chanler's pack and gave him most of our food, an apple. I asked for assurance that he knew the way to Virgelle and that it was close enough to make sense of tramping through the dark. "It's not that far. I just wish I had my medicine." Can you make it? "I'm all right." Off we went; the only thing greater than my doubt was my skepticism. I whispered to Pilotis, There have been a few miscalculations today, so if our little stroll starts to turn into another misreckoning, we may have a reordering of leadership. Said my friend, "Just remember, we're all here because of your grand transcontinental idea."

Thus set straight, I fixed the position of Polaris to keep us from circling, but that didn't mean we wouldn't end up far from where we intended; the difference between, say, a heading of fifteen degrees and sixteen after a few miles equals a whole lot of corrective footsteps and a possible mutiny. We were too fagged out and it was bootless to complain, so the Photographer, often given to bursts of optimism, named every positive element, which came to two negatives: no mosquitoes and no rain. And to myself I added, our Virgil is still alive. If he went down this far from help, the result could be dire.

For a while I was encouraged by a distant cluster of lights — probably the wide spot in the road called Big Sandy, fourteen miles north — not because it was anywhere close to our destination but because it reminded me there was yet life on earth. In my head was a map of where I thought we were, and I occasionally asked Chanler when we would turn west toward our goal of Virgelle (rhymes with "incur hell") which, by the way, was hardly more than a couple of buildings and a grain elevator hidden in the river valley. Every so often I closed my eyes for several steps at a time; since we could see almost nothing, it made little difference. When I opened them after one ambulatory nap, the lights of Big Sandy were inexplicably gone, and I thought it possible I had only wished such comfort into existence. The result was dispiriting: we were alone in a still land such as one can never find on moving water; anyone who thinks an ocean a lonely realm should try the plains of eastern Montana at night. I knew that to walk a straight course long enough in Chouteau County is eventually to cross a road, but the place is eighty miles wide, which, to pass some time, I calculated to equal about 150,000 steps, not considering the up-and-down of the terrain. That figure cheered me since footfalls, unlike miles, I could count off each moment.

We came upon twin parallel ruts that seemed to be a track, and our Virgil thought they were probably the right thing. Then, to my relief, we finally turned west and could begin to hope for a twinkle that would mean a warm bed. We walked on into the thickening dark by the thin blue light of stars which the ground absorbed but the sky gave back in just enough measure to create a horizon, and toward that we went single file, fettered to each other's silhouette. When I shut my eyes, I steered by the footsteps ahead until they were engulfed by the rumble of heavier steps, the hooves of phantom beasts we could only hear, like something from a dream of ghost bison. Remembering the manure we every so often stepped in, we assumed they were cattle, and we hooted into the dark in hopes of sending the stampede away from us. Said Pilotis, "Someone's going to explain to me tomorrow why cattle are inside the boundaries of a wild and scenic river, crapping up the place." I liked the sentence because it assumed we'd have a tomorrow.

After the second hour, I called to our pilot to ask whether we were still on a course he thought he knew, but he was too exhausted to respond other than perhaps by an invisible nod. Then the possibility came to me: Could we be on a death march led by a man gone loco? Was *I* loco? An insanity of exhaustion? A sane fellow would be back around the women's campfire. Or, failing that, wasn't the rational solution to lie down and sleep away what was left of darkness and then walk out by first light? As I was considering sanities, a pale green glow leaking a long milky tail suddenly appeared in the northwest and traced out a slow and flattened arc right under a dim Polaris. The thing didn't grow brighter as meteors do but simply sustained a leisurely glide across the sky, and then was gone. We all stopped in our tracks to watch it, make guesses what it was, before stumbling on in a darkness that seemed greater than before. Was the thing an omen?

Ha! Anything is an omen if you choose to see it that way! Yes! Those are words of real wisdom! So! I am not the one here gone loco! It's the others! Of course! The fatigue has done them in! They won't listen to reason! They've gone witless! I could test them! Ask them, let's see, yes! "Although the lion is a symbol of English royalty, are there lions in Britain?" Query them! Yes! They've quite lost their faculties! The Great Plains frazzled them! Oh, it's sad to see good minds falter! Poor, poor Pilotis, floundering along up there, couldn't tell a mouse from a moose! A dock from a duck! A butt from a butte! Quite mad, most apparent! But I'll say nothing until I can call the asylum! A couple of weeks in a small locked room! Perhaps a nurse in a crisp white uniform! Herbal teas to soothe jumbled wits! Yes! I'll bring cookies! Simple sugar cookies! The kind babies get! I'll look after my good hearts! Indeed! After all, their decline is my fault!

I stumbled into Pilotis who had stopped with the others to rest, which they chose to do like horses, standing on one leg then the other. They probably thought they *were* horses. But I was a man, so I lay down, not bothering to take off my pack, ignoring the dried cow pies, and in the two or three moments before I was sound asleep, I heard Virgil ask, "Is he okay?" Someone said, "He's got four thousand miles on him." Further proof of their lunacy: they took me for a used Buick.

When my mates called me to, I argued it was insane to proceed, only to arrive at dawn and go to bed. Continue! I intoned in a lordly manner, I shall follow along soon! As I started to slip off again, Pilotis said, "It's not a bad idea. What if we're off the mark and have to rewalk it the right way in daylight?" There you have it, I mumbled. Virgil concluded the discussion: "I need my medicine."

So they dragged me up, and we set off again into the botched night, our trudge as sorry as a body can do, one that could take days to recover from. I remembered our good Professor, by now home and curled in the warm arms of his wife, his pea patch waiting for the morning sun and his loving touch. But we? *We* went on across the invisible earth, the endless land, through the most complete night I've never seen.

Sometime thereafter — who any longer could care when it was? — I saw a gleaming, a sinuous glimmer. Glory! A psychic flourish of cornets! It was our friend the great Missouri! My piteously mad colleagues yoicked and yalped in exultation, and I joined them so as not to tip off my awareness of their grievous condition. Then we reached a gravel road leading down a ridge to the valley, and there before us shone the two lights of Virgelle, one of them in the old general mercantile that was our destination, the place where a bed waited upstairs, where a door opened and a lovely young woman in a white shirt said to a befogged writer, "You made it! You're actually here! I love your books!" And he said, "Books?"

Then, as a crescent moon rose, either to mock them or to celebrate their arrival, they learned they had walked nearly nine miles, double the distance by river. As the eastern sky lightened, the dewitted writer found not an herbal tea but a tall glass of fresh water and, upstairs, clean sheets, a warm blanket, and a small quiet room.

Planning for Anything Less than Everything

T HE MORNING BEGAN, I thought, as madly as the night had ended. Although the 1912 Virgelle mercantile had become a bed-and-breakfast a few years back and no longer sold hobbles, trousers, laxatives, stove lids, or a thousand other items, the cellar still held a deeply piled clutter of ancient and useless remnants once on shelves upstairs, a cross between a trove and a landfill. Pilotis told me our guide had phoned his mechanic who guessed the motor problem was indeed a blown fuse, and Chanler had gone down among the stacks to search for one. I shook my head at the absurdity of such a hunt — he would sooner find a fuse in our bed sheets or under the French toast.

About the time I finished breakfast, Chanler came from below, dusty and cobwebbed, his hand cupping an assortment of old automobile fuses. I was astonished he'd found anything even approximating one, but I knew the chances of a proper match were nil.

The Photographer drove him through the backcountry we'd just walked over to Chanler's broken-down boat in our tow wagon which the Professor had left for us. I set to work on my logbook, then poked down the road, happy to have the prospect of a day off the river and an afternoon sleep. About one o'clock, as I was ready to go upstairs, I heard a motor on the river and thought how good that it wasn't the johnboat. I'd no more than announced, Sack time! when in walked Chanler, who said, "It was a fuse all right." Do you mean, I asked, on all those shelves of old mercantile stuff you found one that worked?

"The third fuse I tried." Pilotis said, "I believe it. Of course I believe it. In fact, I believe now Skipper's luck isn't running out but somehow multiplying like mice in an attic."

We waited a long time for the Photographer to return and discovered when he did that he'd stopped to take pictures of old teepee rings — circles of stones that once helped hold Indian tents to the ground; he had been as sure as the rest of us we'd be going nowhere soon. The route we'd covered last night, he said, was aswarm with mosquitoes. Wearily Pilotis and I gathered up our kits and went to the boat, and my friend said, "It seems this river wants to get us up to the mountains." Either that, I said, or wear us down into quitting.

From Virgelle, the second most northerly point of the Missouri, the river runs southwest, then south to Three Forks, the so-called Headwaters, a distance of something more than two hundred miles. The sky was in gloom, the air cool, and the route at first was low earthen shores such as we'd passed between for days in the Dakotas. Soon after we set out, Chanler brought us alongside a bank the river had cut into a cross-section as neatly as if done by an archaeologist, and asked what we saw: in soil three feet below the surface lay a saucer-shaped orange stain surmounted by a bowl-like black discoloration. It was the remains of a campfire that burned before the people who made it were called Indians.

Over a winding route we passed the mouth of the Marias River which Lewis and Clark and their men debated over: Was it the true course of the Missouri? To take the wrong one and have to return could lose the Corps the season and, as Lewis said, "probably so dishearten the party that it might defeat the expedition altogether." The choice was critical enough the group spent six days exploring both routes for some miles and ended up with opposite conclusions: the men to the last one believed the north branch, which Lewis named Maria's River after a cousin he was enamored of, was the Missouri, while the captains held for the south fork. Had the leaders been wrong, their explorations might today be no better known in popular history than those of, say, Jacob Fowler or Howard Stansbury. On the day we passed the little Marias, we could not imagine anyone mistaking it for the Missouri, so strongly did the big river sweep along.

Farther, we stopped again to look at the site of Fort McKenzie, now a cultivated flat under a big center-pivot irrigator, but in 1833 it was

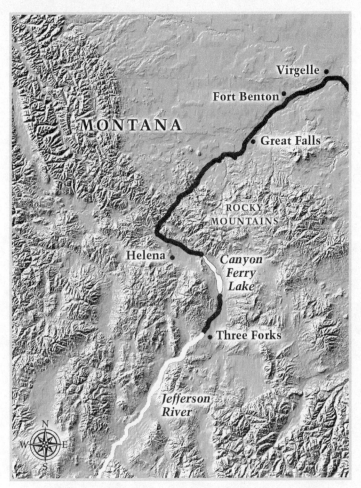

The Missouri, Virgelle to Three Forks, 289 river miles

here that Prince Maximilian and Karl Bodmer gave up their ascent of the Missouri because of Indian hostility on westward. The German ethnographer described their arrival in a place we saw only as an empty field:

> We approached the landing-place and at length set foot on shore amidst a [welcoming] cloud of smoke caused by the firing of the Indians and of the *engagés* of the fort, who were drawn up in a line on the bank. Here we were received by the whole population with the Indian chiefs at their head, with whom we all shook hands. The Chief of the Bears was quite

an original: his countenance, which was not very handsome, with a large crooked nose, was partly hid by his long hair. On his head he had a round felt hat with a brass rim, and a silver medal on his breast. We were led through a long double-line of the red men, the expression of whose countenances and their various dresses greatly amused us. When we arrived at the fort there was no end of the shaking of hands, after which we longed for repose, and distributed our baggage in the rooms. We had happily accomplished the voyage from Fort Union in thirty-four days and lost none of our people and subsisted during the whole time by the produce of the chase.

The riverbanks began to rise until they were considerable steeps of light-colored clays and shales utterly unrelieved by vegetation of any sort. On came rain and behind it a drying wind to wither the clouds enough for bolts of sun to reach us, and by the time we hove up in Fort Benton, we'd pulled off our wet gear. We tied to a small public dock just below the remains of the old fort itself and climbed the terrace to Front Street and an ice cream stand where we bought hotdogs and milkshakes, and once again river travel was easy, and *that,* we knew, was a bad sign.

About four thousand miles above the mouth of the Mississippi, Fort Benton was once the head of navigation on the Missouri and the most inland port in the nation, some say the world. On the river today between Hermann, Missouri, and Fort Benton, there are no longer any towns that really front the Big Muddy because those other places have moved to higher ground, or the river has moved, or up has gone a levee or floodwall, or a spread of industry has come in. Except in books, the historical link between the river and its towns has nearly vanished. But Fort Benton, a bit bedraggled yet genuine, still embraces the river, and one can walk out of a café or shop and take a few steps straight to the water. The landing is now a park, and at its south end, just a few feet from the Missouri, stands the fortress-like Union Hotel of 1882, closed but — as it has been for some years — reportedly under-going restoration. How fine it would be to take a third-floor room and lie abed and watch the river below! Northwest of town, behind the grid of streets, the big hills rise barrenly as they do in nineteenth-century photographs of the landing lined with paddlewheelers and stacked with cargo. Across the river, though, the scene is different: the broad flat is again full of trees as it was before the coming of the steamboats and their fireboxes. But the motto chiseled into the old grammar school is even now more hope than fulfillment: INDUSTRY IS USE-LESS WITHOUT CULTURE.

Recent rains were turning the Missouri into nasty currents and eddies, a downrush too powerful for our canoe to take on, and the rapids above Fort Benton precluded launching *Nikawa*. I asked our tired but true-hearted helmsman to take us another sixteen miles up to Carter Ferry, if he thought the motor would hold out. Someone said, "After Carter, then what? Why don't we stay here till we solve it?" But I had pledged long ago to accept even a single mile if that were all that was offered — in short, to proceed as the way opened. "But tomorrow, then what?" With almost four hundred miles of Montana yet before us, I had no idea. Months earlier, I made plans based on how the Missouri had run for the past decade, a period of low water; once again the Big Contrariness revealed the ineptitude of planning for anything less than everything.

The bluffs were even higher beyond Fort Benton, dark awesome things which only the afternoon sun kept from looking like promises of doom, the kind of terrain people die in. But farther on they became almost kindly, covered by hundreds upon hundreds of nests of swallows that unconcernedly glided over the awesome flush of water thumping our boat as if the waves were fists swung by someone in high conniption. Should the motor fail, we would have a quick ride back to Fort Benton either in the boat or in our life vests.

But the engine kept plugging. The unruly water had shut down the Carter ferry, although the TOOT FOR OPERATOR sign was still out. We pulled up on a gravel slope, fifty-six miles above Virgelle and only fifteen below the grand cascade section of the Missouri near Great Falls. How we would ascend those next miles of bad river to reach the base of the first of five dams built atop the big ledges, I didn't know. I could only hope for luck multiplying like mice in an attic.

Over the Ebullition

I N THE CAFÉ on Front Street in Fort Benton where we'd returned for the night, the sour waitress brought our breakfast eggs and hash browns with a side of caveats: "That river's more likely to kill you than an old grizzly bear. The water hasn't been this high in years. The ferry's shut down, so that ought to give you a clue. Just go on home and take a nice rest because ain't no damn canoe going to get through up there because when that river don't want nobody on it, nobody gets on it except people like you easterners — or some damn Californian."

Our boatman of the last two days had neither the time nor inclination to take us up to Morony Dam, the first of the five barriers built close to one another. The advice of everyone was to portage: after all, it would add only fifteen miles more to what we'd have to do around the dams anyway. I refused. Lewis and Clark made it to Belt Creek — they called it "Portage Creck" — before leaving the water, and although we were but a crew of three, we had a major compensation called the internal combustion engine. Somewhere we could find someone with a boat capable of ascending — surely, someplace there was somebody. We went looking and eventually met Jack Lepley, a retired high school teacher, a tall and friendly man who called the sheriff, persuaded him, and then told us the volunteer search-and-rescue team might take us those few miles in its small boat with a water-jet motor; perhaps we could make a contribution to the maintenance fund.

At six o'clock that evening we met Kurt Buskirk — a name we had to work at to get it right — a hefty young fellow glad to have the chance to log a few official hard-water miles. We hauled up to Carter Ferry and with some uneasiness set out in a drizzle that soon ceased. I didn't say it aloud, of course, but I whispered to Pilotis, Every time we look this river in the eye and call its bluff, it smiles on us. Pilotis: "Tell me that two hundred miles from now."

Sun shafts came and went, and when they appeared they deepened the green slopes against a blackly rolling eastern sky. The Missouri was wide — for Montana — and turned progressively rougher as we neared the area of rocks and rapids downstream from the five great ledges forming the series of cascades where, over just twelve miles, the river drops more than four hundred feet to create what was once one of the most stunning fluvial sights in America, a spectacle dams have nearly obliterated. Meriwether Lewis, awestruck by what he saw, set down a long entry in his logbook but then concluded with a wish for better expression unique in the journals:

> After wrighting this imperfect discription I again viewed the falls and was so much disgusted with the imperfect idea which it conveyed of the scene that I determined to draw my pen across it and begin agin, but then reflected that I could not perhaps succeed better than penning the first impression of the mind; I wished for the pencil of Salvator Rosa or the pen of [James] Thompson, that I might be enabled to give the enlightened world some just idea of this truly magnifficent and sublimely grand object, which has from the commencement of time been concealed from the view of civilized man; but this was fruitless and vain. I most sincerely regreted that I had not brought a [camera] obscura with me by the assistance of which even I could have hoped to have done better but alas this was also out of my reach; I therefore with the assistance of my pen only indeavoured to trace some of the stronger features of this seen by the assistance of which and my recollection aided by some able pencil I hope still to give to the world some faint idea of an object which at the moment fills me with such pleasure and astonishment, and which of its kind I will venture to ascert is second to but one in the known world.

The water changed from boils to riffles to rapids, and the metal boat began taking a beating. Pilotis said, "This Missouri is nothing but goddamn scary," a sentence I liked since it let me know I wasn't alone in wondering what would happen should we, should it, should whatever — et cetera. Mule deer stared at us from the scrub as if incredulous that anybody would be on the river, then in lovely arcs they bounced away, and I thought what good stuff ground is — for one thing, you can jump on it. We stirred an immense flock of pelicans into a low echelon that stretched ahead from shore to shore to form what seemed a fragile chain of gleaming white links, a heavenly lifeline. Could we overtake the big birds, I might reach up, catch hold of one, and let it carry me over, as Lewis has it, the "ebullition" and on beyond the dams.

At Belt Creek, the river turned the turbulence up a notch, and Kurt said, "It's sixty feet deep here with a current about twelve miles an hour. I'm not certified to go into water like this, but the dam's just around the bend. This is where Lewis and Clark took out." They had no motor, I said. "In these conditions, I really can't go that last mile." So we turned back for Carter Ferry.

By hitchhiking, we'd made it through what was likely the most tumultuous stretch of the Missouri we'd face. Relief swept over me, although I felt like the man who survived being hit by a steamroller and said, "Okay, boys, bring on the dump truck."

Ex Aqua Lux et Vis

T HE PHOTOGRAPHER woke on Friday to find a blood blister on the tip of his middle finger and spent some time trying to recall how he might have pinched it. When he put on his glasses to read the breakfast menu, he discovered the blister was in fact a well-attached tick. Another diner, a beautician who happened by and saw our examination, looked at it and called across the café, "We've got a tick on a funny-finger over here!" Then she said quietly to my friend, "Where have you been with that digit, sonny? Didn't Mama tell you about sheep?" For everyone to hear, she added, "This looks baaaaad. We're going to have to play doctor." She went to the kitchen for a dollop of shortening and returned to spread it thickly over the finger. Her treatment drew to us more diners who began defining their own sure-fire methods of tick removal while scoffing at others, the whole time our Photographer sitting silently, holding his greasy finger aloft. One man, who had spent perhaps too much time on the range, gave his technique: "Put a tablespoon of cayenne pepper in a glass of grain alcohol — whiskey will work too if you double the dose — drink it down except for the last swallow, then eat three jalapeños, then take the last sip and rinse it around in your mouth and get the tick between your teeth and pull real slow." I asked, What's the booze do? "It keeps you from caring you're biting a bug's ass."

Thirty minutes later the tick was still locked on, so, lacking jalapeños, I put a lighted match to the critter and out it came. Said the beautician, an inveigling woman, "That shortening loosened him up. I could write a book on what you can do with lard — and I'm not talking cooking." I said, Let us know if you need help with any of the, of the, uh, recipes. She leaned close and said, "Ohh, are we a naughty boy?" then smiled out the door. Her perfume fell over us like a veil, and I suddenly realized how far away I was from another life, how distant from cologne and evening gowns, shined shoes and Sunday matinees, easy chairs, a good book by the fireside. For a few moments I was close to believing I was ready to go home.

What the people told us about the next miles of river did not make continuance easier: the current would be too much for our canoe and motor. "Wait it out" was the consensus, a choice I couldn't risk because, although the Continental Divide was only days away, we would still need a week of good water on the western slope. I have not spoken of one final time constraint facing us: I intended to follow three mountain streams to the Salmon River in Idaho and take it through the deepest part of the western mountains to the Snake and hence to the head of navigable water. Because the Salmon is a popular wilderness run for rafters, the U.S. Forest Service controls the number of boats going down it in the summer to keep it from being overrun. Four hundred miles of white-water rapids, it requires in high water boats and skills we did not possess. To get us through, months earlier I engaged an outfitter and had to choose a departure date because regulations stipulated that hire-boats must leave on a preassigned day or wait until autumn. So our crossing from the beginning was compelled not simply by the opening of the Erie Canal and the spring rise but also by government edict, one I did not disagree with, but several days of waiting in Montana was not only bad for morale, it also set the calendar further against us.

That morning I telephoned a man we'd learned of, a car dealer in Great Falls, a generous fellow who might consent to take us up a few miles of the Missouri in his jet boat. I described our voyage, and after due consideration he said, "I can't go out this weekend. Not a chance." Our luck seemed at last to have snagged. He said, "I'm sorry to disappoint you. Too bad you can't go later today." But we can! "Okay," he said, "although I've got to tell you, I don't know how far we can go. Do you still want to give it a shot?" That's exactly our modus, I said.

We hauled our boats around the five dams near Great Falls, a portage of eighteen miles for Lewis and Clark that took them two weeks, where a welter of things from gnats to grizzlies pestered them. Wrote Clark, "To State the fatigues of this party would take up more of the journal than other notes which I find Scarcely time to Set down."

The chasm the Missouri has cut through the dark and renitent sandstone just above Belt Creek is mostly easy bends and continuous rapids between and below the five big cascades, all within only a dozen miles of each other, and lying like steps, ledges which for years have been either inundated or topped with hydroelectric dams. Small by Missouri River standards, the first was completed in 1890 and the last in 1958; it's hard to believe a power company could persuade the public today to allow, for the sake of a few megawatts, so massive an impairment of one of the most magnificent riverscapes in America. Indeed, some people are finally starting to talk about the eventual removal of the dams and arguing that the value of tourism to such a series of cataracts could overwhelm the income from selling electricity and, what's more, put money not in the already full pockets of a few electro-magnates but spread it more democratically across the area. (To megawattmen, the motto on the old electric company building in Helena has a special meaning: EX AQUA LUX ET VIS, From water, light and power.) Now, having complained, I'll admit the dams could be worse. Three of them sit several yards back from the ledges of the falls, so a visitor can yet see something of those cascades when the river is high enough to let a great volume of water top the spillways. Still, Meriwether Lewis's description of "this sublimely grand specticle [as] the grandest sight I ever beheld" points up what Americans have lost through an unregulated pursuit of wealth by a powerful few. There are many places and ways to generate electricity, but the Great Falls of the Missouri are unique, and they cannot be moved.

One of those early hydro-barons, so I heard, did decree that Rainbow Dam (1912) be built only to a height that would not flood another remarkable feature in the chasm, a fountainhead at the edge of the Missouri. The cold and tremendous outpouring of Giant Spring comes from the Little Belt Mountains about forty miles away, a journey lasting eons. I bought several bottles of it, the labels claiming that carbon dating proved the water fell as rain and snow three thousand years ago. Until the moment of my first swig from that source, the oldest beverage I'd ever drunk was fifteen-year-old bourbon, a notable spirit, but that ancient spring water was a sweet draft from an antediluvian world, a quencher from the time of Odysseus. (Incidentally, the streamlet flowing out of the spring into the Missouri runs only a couple hundred feet and, so says the *Guinness Book of Records,* is the shortest river in the world.)

About four that afternoon we met our new boatman at Broadwater

Bay in downtown Great Falls, not far upstream from Black Eagle Dam. Jim Pierce, about ready to enter middle age, was a rangy, slender fellow relieved to get away from the automobile dealership and happy to put into the river his new nineteen-foot boat driven by a motor with three times the power of the twin engines on *Nikawa* and three hundred times more than our pisspot. His craft was the kind that turns rivers into highways and — if it avoided sucking up sand — could cross the continent over our route in a couple of weeks. But such an effort would be like flying nonstop around the world: except to set a record, what's the point of it?

Although Pierce's machine was small compared to those insanities called "cigarette boats," I must admit I'm not fond of such tremendously powered vessels and had mixed feelings about taking to his even for one afternoon, but the alternatives were to wait for the current to subside and perhaps miss passable water farther on or to portage the next miles. Such choices made my decision easy. To get washed out now after more than four thousand miles was not tolerable. It helped also that Pierce was a man of consideration: "If trout fishermen are out in the little drift boats on up the river, I'll turn around. It wouldn't be fair to zip past them."

Meriwether Lewis, after the Corps had portaged around the falls and rapids and finally was able to see the country the farthest Missouri issues from, expected to encounter even more cataracts, as would anyone who looks into such a mountainous western sky; yet in truth there is nothing more than riffles, rapids, and islands, even though today many of those hindrances to ascent lie under three farther impoundments. Beyond Black Eagle Dam, the Missouri is a stretch of tight twists and narrow horseshoe bends running through a high meadow-like country, and the mileage to Holter Dam, the next barrier, is almost exactly twice the beeline distance. Pierce said, "With all this water, I don't know how far we can go even if the drift boats aren't out. We might not make it under that low bridge at Ulm."

Off we went, up past the mouth of the Sun, or Medicine, River; it was here that William Clark wrote:

> [We] have Concluded not to dispatch a Canoe with a part of our men to St. Louis as we have intended early in the Spring. we fear also that Such a measure might also discourage those who would in Such Case remain, and might possibly hazard the fate of the expedition. we have never

hinted to any one of the party that we had Such a Scheem in contempla-
tion, and all appear perfectly to have made up their minds to Succeed in
the expedition or perish in the attempt. we all believe that we are about
to enter on the most perilous and dificuelt part of our voyage, yet I see
no one repineing; all appear ready to meet those dificuelties which await
us with resolution and becomeing fortitude.

Some miles on we reached the mouth of the Smith, a canoeist's river
with a sign at the juncture prohibiting motorboats. Paralleling, but
mostly out of view except when crossing the Missouri, was Interstate
15 where vehicles gave another perspective on our speed of forty miles
an hour. The surrounding country was at first gentle contours brightly
green from the rains and late sun, and glowing yellow fields of canola,
and the river long glassy pools interspersed with swifter water of boils
and a few shallows we skimmed easily; nowhere did we have to con-
tend with broomstick chutes, a good thing since at our pace even big
channels were tricky to interpret. We stopped to look at a nest of
golden eagles, the unfledged young staring down, the parents in another tree doing the same, and from yet another cottonwood a bald
eagle watched all of us.

We went around a sharp bend and saw ahead the Ulm Bridge, the
lowest immovable span on the Missouri, and we slowed to a near halt
as we approached. With the water so high and boat canopy so lofty,
clearance would be by inches if at all. Pilotis watched intently and
intoned, "Please. Oh, please!" I said, If we miss by a whisker, we'll
get ten fat men to step aboard. Pierce concentrated and visually calculated. Passage looked unpromising, and I said, Everybody to the side —
lean over and take a big drink. On we went, holding still so we
wouldn't bounce the boat, and then we started under. Graffitoed on a
pier was DONT LITTER BUTTFACE. We sneaked forward and, by a
handspan, passed cleanly beneath. Said a relieved Pilotis, "It's like the
dentist saying, 'Okay, I'm finished.'"

Near Cascade, we entered a country of old volcanic interruptions
and perpendicular upthrusts and thousand-foot buttes, distinctively
shaped things, and beyond them, for the first time from the river itself, we could make out what we'd waited so long to see — a deep and
jagged blue shadow across the horizon. We stared in silence for a
moment before Pilotis said, "Somebody assure me what we're looking
at isn't clouds or an atmospheric illusion." And our boatman: "You're

going to know soon that's no illusion, but in a week you may wish it was." We were at the foot of the Rocky Mountains.

Beyond Hardy, the Missouri has a clarity downstream residents could believe impossible, a transparence that makes the segment through the Big Belt Mountains a fine trout stream, and on that day of deep sky, the river was astonishingly blue. The terrain before us, while not so eccentric and unexpected as the White Cliffs, we thought the most postcard-scenic along the entire Missouri. Among brown volcanic walls were lighter sedimentary erosions, vertical humps too round to be pinnacles and too slender to be hills, risings like the apparently impossible formations common in Chinese brush paintings of the riverine landscapes around Guilin. Even a stretch of dumpy little vacation houses smack along the water did not totally dispel the excellence of topography.

Pierce gave me the wheel and cautioned to keep the speed up to maintain our plane so we would pass over the riffles. As I spun us through the sharp bends, I thought again how a boat like this would have served us better along the slow miles in the Dakotas. I had no time to correct a navigational error and nothing but a moment to choose the channel with the best water. At that speed, which mocked the fast current as it for so long had mocked us, I simply looked and reacted then hoped in a kind of thrilling and treacherous piloting my friend called "a glance and a prayer." Pierce said, "There are places up here usually so shallow you have to drag a canoe through. You're lucky to catch the water like this." Pilotis muttered, "This is probably the one time it's not a question of luck."

As we entered the section troutmen love, we saw no drift boats, the current presumably too strong for good fishing, so I happily requested to attempt the last miles on to the dam. Pierce said he'd never been able to make it this far upriver before, and he was invigorated by the easy run and began to envy our crossing. To that Pilotis said, "Think twice." Soon after, the hydroelectric dam came into view, an ugly concrete door to the splendent region Meriwether Lewis called Gates of the Rocky Mountains; just below it we pulled the boat out for the haul back to Great Falls.

At supper that evening in a Chinese café, I tried to revive the crew with a toast to our good fortune in finding Jim Pierce and a reading from Lewis and Clark detailing their serious hardships which I hoped would give perspective to ours. I concluded with this satisfaction Meri-wether wrote not far from where we sat: "My fare is really sumptuous this evening; buffaloe's humps, tongues and marrowbones, fine trout, parched meal, pepper and salt, and a good appetite; the last is not considered the least of the luxuries."

Our own fare did not seem to lift my comrade who said, "Even after we run the string of lakes tomorrow in *Nikawa*, we still have way more than two hundred miles of cold water charging down at us before we reach the Divide. We know now we don't have a proper boat for mountain rivers, so what do we do? Are you counting on Old Friend Luck?" I don't have the answer, I said, except to tell you our canoe could have made it up to Holter Dam, but I listened to locals even though I know they're full of misinformation and negative opinion.

What I didn't say was that our easy ascent in the powerful boat had saved us a couple of trying days in the canoe at a time when I was beginning to see the toll our voyage was taking on us. I was increasingly aware of the possibility of suddenly losing my mates, and I knew, as devoted as they were, this journey could never be to them what it was to me. I realized that, at least until we reached the Great Divide, I had to make our passage up the slope of the continent as easy and jolly as feasible, and I believed that, without a jet boat here or there, just then I might be sitting alone, eating lemon chicken and opening up a fortune cookie with no one around to share it. On the little slip, which I pasted in my logbook that night, was this:

> NOW IT IS BEST TO TAKE THINGS
> JUST ONE STEP AT A TIME

I passed it to Pilotis who read it once, then again, and said darkly, "Don't ever try to write a novel. Lucky coincidence after coincidence kills good fiction. And that's the way you're proceeding." I thought, Do they really believe it's just luck and coincidence that got us here, or is this only repining?

Weaknesses in
Mountains and Men

WE HEARD THAT the snowpack was nearly half again higher
than its average, and that was good news since such excess
would make the spring melt-off last longer if temperature
and rainfall didn't wildly increase. From then on though, it was apparent, each morning we would have to play the height of the water on
that particular day against the expected decreases of days ahead, and
we might have to take on a torrent now and then to avoid a river
turned to rocks farther along. If we avoided too much today, we could
have too little tomorrow. Or, in the cynical words of a certain cohort,
"Drown today to avoid dragging tomorrow."

Because we'd gained time in the jet boat, and because of the threat
in our incipient mental fatigue, I took a chance and suggested we get
off the river for a day, so on Saturday we slept in to different hours and
spent the morning on our own, each of us enjoying a brief solitude.
When we gathered again for dinner, some vigor had returned, and I
saw no repining. On Sunday, considerably recovered, we took *Nikawa*
to Holter Dam to launch her in fine weather. I very much wanted blue
sky to embolden our little company.

Just below Holter, the Missouri takes an unfortunate southeasterly
turn for westering travelers, and although I didn't mention it, during
the entire day we'd be moving away from the Pacific through a string
of three impoundments, the first two quite narrow and linked by short
sections of nearly natural river. Canyon-bound Holter and Hauser
lakes, only marginally wider than the Missouri, are like distensions in

an artery, yet those two smallest reservoirs on the river are arguably the loveliest, and the best section in them is a severely constricted defile today called the Gates of the Mountains. I don't like to confess this, but it may be that the lake created by Holter Dam actually enhances the naturally stunning gateway. Before reaching it, we went around a pinched horseshoe, then a broader one, then beyond scarred Mann Gulch, the scene of the horrific 1949 forest conflagration Norman Maclean describes in his book *Young Men and Fire.*

Had we been without a chart on our approach, we might have thought the Gates a cul-de-sac, but the truth is, the Missouri only hides itself like a prankster behind an open door to a curving hallway. Because the stone walls so narrow the river, we knew for the first time we were moving precisely in the wake of Lewis and Clark, albeit a good many feet above the surface they saw; there are few other places on the Missouri where a voyager can say with such certainty, *Exactly here they passed.* That the river could breach those high rocks seems to attest more to its power than to any inherent weakness in the enduring stone, although that is scarcely true. Here as everywhere, whether mountains or men, a river finds faults, weaknesses, rifts, and exploits them, and that's why rivers outlast rocks. And men.

The cliffs rise straight above Holter Lake about a thousand feet and continue upward for another three thousand as they recede from the Missouri. Due west, the Continental Divide lay only thirty-five miles off, but we would have to parallel it south for more than two hundred miles before we could turn to cross via a comparatively short portage — short *if only* we could overcome the increasing torrents.

When we reached the upper end of the canyon, we stopped to meet the Photographer pulling the trailer toward Townsend, our intended destination that evening, and took him aboard and returned through the magnificent cleft that he might see it too. Then we set him ashore and proceeded on to a widening of the river called Upper Holter Lake and passed one forested gulch after another as the Missouri constringed to a stream before finally becoming too shallow for *Nikawa* to advance. There, below Hauser Dam, we hauled around the barrier and set off again. Each time we landed, we asked about the water ahead and how far *Nikawa* might go. After the third or fourth query, Pilotis said, "I notice you consider anyone with bad news to be ill informed, but those who babble 'Nothing to it' you believe." If I did otherwise,

I said, we'd still be looking at maps on my kitchen table and wondering whether *Nikawa* could get under the last bridge on the Harlem River.

Much as a merely good-looking man or woman standing next to a beautiful one suffers from proximity of comparison, so Hauser suffers next to Holter, or it once did before it began to turn into a suburb of Helena. This second-smallest Missouri impoundment would be a logical purlieu for a couple of grand lodges rather than a sprawl of ranch houses and more pretentious nouveau dwellings, but of course to advocate that certain great American places are better shared than owned can cause some citizens to reach for the dynamite.

Our charts had gone off in the tow wagon, and the river was so chopped up by water scooters and Sunday folk in inner tubes towed by speedboats, I failed to read its direction and took us a mile up the wide mouth of Prickly Pear Creek before I realized we were heading for Last Chance Gulch in downtown Helena. The Missouri narrowed again into steeper country, the houses fell behind, and we had a good run up to the face of Canyon Ferry Dam before turning back to a ramp on the east shore where we took *Nikawa* out for her final portage around a dam. As we were tying her in for the short haul to the other side, a man of no authority came along and upbraided me for going so close to the spillway. I pointed out there were no off-limit markers and the water release was negligible, then I described the nature of our trip and my insistence on keeping water under us. "Don't carry it too far," he said, and Pilotis nodded. Only as far as the Pacific, I promised.

A more useful warning came from a fellow who told us about the south end of Canyon Ferry Lake — by much, the largest of the three upper impoundments — twenty-five miles away. "It gets real stumpy down there. It's almost a bog because this reservoir goes from over a hundred feet deep behind the dam to a few inches around Indian Road. That boat of yours can get hung up in that place — no doubt about it." Pilotis, believing that I was increasingly failing to respect the power in water, watched me closely. I said, I'm listening, I'm listening. "And discounting."

We arranged for a checkpoint with the tow wagon about halfway along at Goose Bay, and off we went, the water blown into some roughness but the sky still kind. The mountains begin edging back from the river at Canyon Ferry as the Missouri enters a long valley reaching, but for a couple of mild incursions of hills, all the way to the so-called Headwaters below Three Forks. We ran down past the mouths of gulches with names from prospectors' nightmares: Hellgate, Avalanche, Bilk, Snag, Beer Can. The upper two thirds of the dogleg lake is a couple of miles wide and the lower section is twice that before it peters out in a tangle of shallows, a stretch that before the impounding was a navigational fright of labyrinthine channels. By comparing our century-old chart to a modern one, we could see that, in another time, a pilot might have spent hours finding a way through a mile of the shifting Missouri maze now, for the most part, lying many feet beneath us.

We clipped along as the wind dropped with the setting sun and the water slicked down to polished steel, but I still maintained a compass heading to keep from weaving. Trying to point up our progress and bring cheer, I said, *Nikawa* is in her last couple of miles on the Atlantic side of things! The comment backfired. Pilotis: "That's what I was thinking. Now it's the canoe for two hundred miles before we even reach the road up to the Divide." Would you please cease arithmeticking, I said, numbers only make it harder. Then, as a diversion: If you want to calculate, tell me the fewest number of states a traveler can pass through going coast to coast in America.

That one worked, and before we knew it we were into the boglands near Indian Road Camp, just upstream from Townsend. "Don't risk it in here," Pilotis said. "We can pick up this stretch in the canoe tomorrow." I wheeled us around, and we went back a few miles to a small pull-out called The Silos and put *Nikawa* onto the trailer. When her hull touched river the next time, we hoped it would be at Clarkston, Washington, where nothing but deep water would lie between us and the Pacific. Near the ramp was a sign, one I wished we might have seen on some other evening, a sign of arithmetic noting the drowning of twenty-one people in the area. It said: DON'T BE NUMBER 22.

A Nightmare Alley

THAT MONDAY in Townsend, population 1,600, an elderly fellow wearing a cap imprinted WHO? ME? asked where I was from — the standard opening gambit in rural cafés — and I told him, and he said, "I got a dog from back in Missouri." He wondered how I came to be out in Montana country, and I explained, and he said, "So you're out to see the watery part of America?" His daughter, her gray hair tied so severely back she couldn't move her eyebrows, grumbled something into her coffee mug as if she knew what was coming; I had a feeling she'd spent a lifetime grumbling into coffee cups.

He said, "I saw me enough water when I was seven and my preacher daddy baptized me in Clear Creek back in Tennessee. He was an old-time brimstoner who would pray over God for creating Satan, chiggers, and the Republican Party. He prayed over me so long I nearly drowned in my baptizing, but he kept me down for enough to see the face of Jesus. It swum right up to me in the form of a big old terrapin and opened its beak to say something, but that's when I got jerked back up into the air. All these years later I've wondered ever since what it was going to tell me. Maybe the secret to life. I don't mean that 'Trust Jesus' junk of those teevee phonies, I mean something about the real way creation works, the secret you got to die to learn. I guess it didn't come to me, because I didn't quite die. But it sure would've been something if that terrapin let the secret slip out and I could've made it back up with it. I bet I'd be wearing silk shirts today, and maybe my girl here might take to smiling once in a while."

She turned to me. "Don't get him going." I said it was part of my job to get people going. Her father, I think to provoke her, asked, "What did the cowboy say in the Chinese opium den?" And the woman, again into her coffee mug: "To hell with you both." And he: "Many men smoke, but Fu Manchu."

I went outside to find my mates, not a hard thing to do in Townsend, but I first ran into a river outfitter we'd met the night before, and I asked him what the Missouri was going to do in the next few days. "The fields are wet, so nobody's taking water out for irrigation. Whatever's coming down the river is going to keep on going." When I gathered the crew, we bought a gasket for the motor, then took the canoe down to Indian Road and slipped it into the water, and Pilotis and I struck out onto the braidings, then turned toward a wider section where the Missouri flowed swiftly over riffle after riffle. The current ran so hard we could cross from bank to bank in order to follow the best chutes only by ferrying — that is, running a diagonal course to set the downstream thrust of the river against the angle of the hull to push it forward, something like tacking upwind in a sailboat. The chutes took us right against the shoreline, but the rush of water let us make barely a couple of miles an hour, and we literally had time to smell the wild roses overhanging the low banks.

It was a cool morning of hovering ospreys dropping to trawl their claws across the river, of magpies descending from the sage hills, mergansers taking off in their distinct tippy-toe, killdeer running along the few dry shoals and refusing flight until they had no more rocks beneath them, sandpipers seeming to vibrate their wings rather than flap them, and also cormorants, blackbirds, doves, great blue herons. It was a birdy morning, not with the abundance apparent in nineteenth-century travelers' accounts, but nevertheless one we treasured because of our disappointment in the amount of wildlife we'd seen since the beginning, a paucity that gave us concern about the health of the countryside. The river widened yet again, deepened, and we bounced over boils but had less current to fight. To measure our speed, I held up an empty produce bag, a flimsy plastic one, as a kind of windsock, but we moved so imperceptibly it simply hung limp. Slower than a walker, slower than ever, we ascended the valley, the distant mountains still in snow, that lovely stuff that was making it possible for us to ascend at all.

At a place where the Missouri rubs almost against the shoulder of U.S. 287, we unexpectedly came upon the Photographer smiling down on us. We stopped to consider our position, and I told him all the river asked for that day was patience, then off we went again. Between the riffles lay pools providing some ease, but just below Long Ripple the weather began its afternoon performance with a sky blown to darkness and crackling with lightning, and I realized too late I'd defined what the river asked for well within the range of its Great Ears. At sorry little Toston, population even less than you might guess unless you guess fifty, we pulled ashore below the old highway bridge, the first or last functioning one on the Missouri and went up to a roadhouse making the same claim, both of them referring to location, not history. Over something passing for lunch, we fell into a competitive reminiscing about the worst meals we'd ever found. Pilotis won with "The Wet Patty Melt — the Sandwich You Eat with a Spoon."

We spread out charts on the pool table and figured our last miles on the Missouri, and to no one's pleasure I determined we needed to reach Toston Dam before nightfall. "What about the weather?" the Photographer said. I offered that it seemed to be easing, even if not by much.

Above the Toston bridge, the gradient of the Missouri increases as it nears its apex, and it poured down fast enough to make us consider responses should we overturn. Although only five miles from the dam, we knew the route would no longer test just our patience but now also our persistence, a word Pilotis claimed I used instead of recklessness. Our "run" would be a slow ascent made slower by apprehension, but the only way of knowing what we were getting into was, as always, to get into it — that's the nature of river travel, especially in remote places, and you either like or hate it for that. Pilotis shouted, "This rascal is really cooking!" Indeed, it looked like the impossible — some great pot of icy water in a fierce parboil.

After the first mile, we came among boulders the size of casks and puncheons that put voice into the river and made it speak threats. The motor stem and hull clanked against smaller stones, some of them rocking us in every sense of the word. We did our best to stay in the chutes, but they were running as fast as log flumes, and each successive one seemed more likely to stall the canoe. If we went dead in the water, the current would have us, turn us sideways, send us sprawling. Between the chutes was a more accommodating water of only rolling waves where Pilotis would call out, "What do you think?" Trying to mask my uneasiness, I would signal forward to the next pounding. I was both concerned and glad there were few places to get the canoe off the river, so we *had* to continue, and fear offered one less alternative. Then we arrived in a nightmare alley.

Partway up a strikingly vigorous chute, the canoe began to shudder, seemingly unable to advance. We bent over to lessen wind resistance and lower our center of gravity, but the little motor had finally met its match; thrust and resistance equal, it could not push us forward. In such circumstances you don't turn around — you wait to get turned over. Both of us on other trips had been dumped, but neither of us in water like that, the kind where authorities pull out corpses wearing good life vests. The motor screamed and still the river checked us. Pilotis yelled, "Get ready to abandon ship!" Keep her cranking! I shouted, and leaned out slowly to a pendant branch, grasped it, pulled steadily, pulled hard, and we inched forward, creeping, creeping on to the top of the chute. Pilotis called, "And what if that willow hadn't been there?" But there was no time to answer before we entered another sluice, this one shallow enough I could get my paddle against the bottom to pole a few difficult yards. As we reached calmer water I turned to discover Pilotis in almost a Hell Gate Grin. I guessed tension had taken its toll. I yelled, I don't know about this! My friend pointed ahead to a long line of seething turbulence across the entire river, a wall of white chaos.

I started then I realized it was Toston Dam, an old diversion structure and by far the smallest one on the Missouri, yet roaring enough to drown out the sound of our engine. We were almost there! We went on toward the spillways, made invisible by the cataract pouring over them, until the ferociously churning tailwaters threatened to roll the canoe, and we looked for a friendly eddy to turn us quietly back downstream, and there we pulled out at a path through the overgrown west bank. With a struggle we got the boat up the slippery slope so the Photographer could reach us. Pilotis, exaggerating, told him, "This man's not happy unless we bang the bow into the spillway," yet the words were full of vigor and victory at having survived one more day.

At last, one more day on the Missouri was all it could set before us, but we weren't up to talking about it until supper when Pilotis mentioned our reaching the place where the current and our power were going to be equal much of the time and said, "I still think you fail to respect the power in water, but I know, no matter how you hide it because you like to look lucky, you're always calculating the odds. But tomorrow the odds are lousy." Don't ask me to wait two weeks or to portage around the last miles of the Missouri, I said. "Okay, but unless somewhere in this emptiness we can find a properly powered boat, that leaves just one other choice — downstream." We sat in a long silence, then I said, If we do it, it'll be the only time we do it.

No Huzzahs in the Heart

I ASSUME THAT a certain peculiar and knotted conjoining of three mountain streams flowing north from the Yellowstone Park country looked different in 1805 because Meriwether Lewis, almost three thousand miles up the old unengineered Missouri, decided it should have a change of name. What we saw as two tributaries flowing closely together into a main stream, the Corps of Discovery deemed three almost equal rivers; thinking politically, they named them the Gallatin, Madison, and Jefferson. For the last one, we thought a more accurate name would be, if not the Missouri, then at least the Jefferson Fork of the Missouri, and we considered that juncture of streams no more a headwaters than, say, the mingling of the three rivers just north of St. Louis is the fount of the Mississippi. The true Missouri riverhead, its farthest source, its vertex, lies ninety-eight miles — more than two hundred by water — due south of the mouths of those three mountain streams.

I had been to the so-called Headwaters, near Three Forks, Montana, several times before, and following the footsteps of Lewis, I'd climbed the limestone bluff to discover the view of the famous complexus of tributaries. Once, during low water, as I was trying to wade across at the place the captains incorrectly deemed the top of the Missouri, I nearly ended up being swept toward Toston Dam, sans boat, life vest, or even swim trunks. Partly because the area was not new to me, I acceded to Pilotis's wish to play it safe and descend the last twenty-one miles of the Missouri, a decision I was soon to question.

The morning was gray, chill, and windy, not the kind I'd hoped to have for our farewell float on the great river. Before setting out, I put down two small stones I'd taken from that shoreline a year earlier and kept on my desk as I planned the voyage: one in thanks for a safe return, the other to honor my late father who taught me to read not rivers but books and maps. Near the ghost town of Gallatin City, we launched at the mouth of the Madison and let the high water pull us into the Missouri where the swift downrush immediately began to shove the stern ahead of the bow, and we had to paddle hard to steer. Going with the current is not always easier than going against it, especially when it's kicking as it was that day, and Pilotis seemed unusually tense.

Ten minutes out, we got pulled in dangerously close to a deadhead, and my friend, despite considerable canoeing experience, overreacted and thrashed the paddle wildly, throwing cold water over me. On a hot day such a flub is a relief, but on a sunless morning with a wind-chill of forty degrees, I failed to avoid irritation and barked out something about tension making danger worse, so please relax. There were a few moments of injured feelings before the river turned us into a nasty angle of wind that nullified the shove of the current as air and water fought for control of the canoe. Over the next half hour we worked the paddles hard. Stroking, thinking of the 4,220 miles behind us, I finally said, What the deuce — this is no weekend float. I started the motor for a more fitting farewell-and-hallelujah downstream cruise. I called out, How are you doing? Thumbs up.

Immediately below the nominal Headwaters is Trident, not a village but a mine, and the first we'd seen along the river; the operations had destroyed much of a big spread of bluffs near Headwaters Park. Pilotis, considerably disturbed, yelled, "Of all places to tear into the mountains! Doesn't the importance of the geography or what happened here mean anything to these people?" Some hundred miles northeast of Trident, I'd seen the North Moccasin Mountains with an eastern side blasted away by a mining company searching for gold ore of such low grade it has to be extracted by a cyanide leaching process that adds poison to the colossal defacement. The 1872 law that governs mining in this country may have made a degree of sense six generations ago, but today it's so obsolete it actually requires taxpayers to underwrite the pillaging of some of the finest lands in America. As with the out-of-date grazing law, Congress, stumbling along under its usual opiate of venality, still listens to mining moguls rather than the citizenry, perhaps because too many people are yet ill informed about the robbery of our tax till and natural inheritance.

About eight miles below the mouth of the Madison, hills reach right down into the Missouri, and the intertwining of chutes and islands simplifies into a single broad channel deep enough to flush up big boils, but the pisspot pushed us smoothly through the swirls. We paused at a forgotten log cabin of a homesteader or long-gone cowhand, a pitiful little thing overgrown and turning green with decay, then set off again. Paralleling the water is an abandoned railroad grade that, given the beauty and the historic and geographic significance of those first official miles of the longest American river, should be converted into a trail, a path for walkers to enter the headstream country. Americans need and would use that slender strip of our history far more than a couple of dozen hamburgers-on-the-hoof defecating it into foulness.

We passed a pother of cormorants in a cluster of dead trees, their dark shapes doing nothing to alleviate the gloom but instead only adding a foreboding to it that came to fruition about two hours out as we approached an enormous outcrop of gray rock slanting into the river, a remarkable exposure of geology unlike anything we'd seen. We reached for cameras. As the water drew us toward the slab, Pilotis, keeping watch in the bow, suddenly yelled out, "Gun it!" Blindly, without questioning, I answered the alarm and twisted the throttle all the way, and we lurched forward, then dropped as if over a low ledge, the canoe rocking gunwale to gunwale, yawing, shipping in water, a chaos preliminary to capsizing. The Missouri finally had us. Trying to stay loose and move with the canoe, a serious challenge when one is not expecting such violence, I knew we'd escaped an upset far too long. The time had come. All the way up the Missouri, we'd heard people talk of whirlpools, a word more common than the actualities of boils and eddies, yet we had not seen a single one wider than a few inches. But that vortex, a havoc created by the river deflecting off the face of the huge slanted rock, was fifteen feet across and turning fast.

We had no time to pick up paddles. The canoe tossed, shook horribly, then stabilized just enough to ride forward and bounce up over the far edge, taking on more water. I started to call out something, I don't remember what, when Pilotis yelled again just before we dropped into another whirlpool, smaller but nastier. The motor kept driving forcefully enough to give us headway, and we banged up and out. When we were safely beyond, I throttled back. Pilotis turned slowly and said, "Well played. Now, how many more of those little gifts do you think there are?" I said, Only Mini-sho-she knows. "Do you remember the Assiniboin who refused to tell us how to escape a whirlpool?" I nodded. "Do you think if he'd known of our encounter, he would've given us the secret?"

We proceeded on. My fear subsided, but for some days it did not leave me completely, and Pilotis never again mentioned my alleged lack of respect for moving water. I said, We should have known the Missouri would say goodbye in a way we'd never forget. Pilotis: "I would've been disappointed had it done otherwise," pausing, then, "Well, maybe not *that* disappointed."

Not far into Red Rock Canyon, we stopped at an old mine with small, collapsing smelters and ovens — or so we took them to be — of well-laid native stone, one of the most picturesque ruins we'd seen along the river. Said Pilotis, "To corrupt a cliché, in country like this, the only beautiful mine is a dead mine," and off we went again.

The Missouri, naturally, had one more surprise: as we rounded the horseshoe bend above Toston Dam, we came under a clearing sky of a deep blue the river reflected splendidly, and we saw ahead three dozen pelicans, brilliant in the sun like seraphim, take wing to lead us right down our final Missouri mile. We had climbed its back, all 2,290 miles by my measure, and it had lifted us 3,400 feet — about three stacked-up Empire State Buildings — above its mouth. I can hardly believe it, I said, and my friend finished the sentence, "but we did it."

Out of the river came the canoe and onto the top of our vehicle, then we headed toward Three Forks for the night. Beyond, to the southwest, we could see far into the higher Rockies still topped in snow, a forbidding horizon, and Pilotis said, "That's where we're going to cross?" Yes, I said, after we tend to the little business of getting up the Jefferson and Beaverhead. "You mean the streams Lewis and Clark dragged up?" Those are the ones, I said.

That nippy evening, as I sat in a rocking chair alone on the big porch of the Sacajawea Inn, a place carefully restored, I thought how the Missouri at last — *at last* — was behind us. Of course, it did give one final unforeseen turn: something about our ascent was missing in me. I had a sweet sense of relief, but where was the jubilance of doing what so few people have ever done — go *against* the Missouri all the way? There was no hallelujah in my heart, not even a huzzah. Then I knew why. We hadn't quite gone against it all the way. We had turned downstream for those last several miles. By agreeing to descend for just a few hours, the final hours, I had fouled my sense of arriving at the traditional top of the long river. When we should have been toasting a dram in Headwaters State Park, we were instead standing numbly twenty miles away at Toston Dam. Toston! Goddamn!

Was it right to give caution precedence over an unwritten rule of the voyage? We were, after all, still alive to continue tomorrow. But as I sat rocking on the porch in what should have been a golden hour, in hand a tired glass of spirits meant for celebration, I thought, whatever else, I'd made an emotional miscalculation, and I vowed I'd not again turn away from westering.

IX

THE MOUNTAIN
STREAMS

JUST WEST OF THREE FORKS, MONTANA

ICONOGRAM IX

August 4th, Sunday, 1805

Proceeded on verry early and Brackfast at the Camp Capt Lewis left yesterday morning; at this Camp he left a note informing that he discovered no fresh Sign of Indians &c. The river continued to be crouded with Islands, Sholey rapid & clear; I could not walk on Shore to day as my ankle was Sore from a tumer on that part. The method we are compelled to take to get on is fatigueing & laborious in the extreen, haul the Canoes over the rapids, which Succeed each other every two or three hundred yards and between the water rapid oblige [us] to towe & walke on stones the whole day except when we have poleing; men wet all day, Sore feet, &c., &c.

William Clark

Monday August 5th 1805

The river today [Capt. Clark] found streighter and more rapid even than yesterday, and the labour and difficulty of the navigation was proportionably increased; they therefore proceeded but slowly and with great pain as the men had become very languid from working in the water and many of their feet swolen and so painfull that they could scarcely walk. At 4 P.M. they arrived at the confluence of the two rivers where I had left [another] note. This note had unfortunately been placed on a green pole which the beaver had cut and carried off together with the note; the possibility of such an occurrence never onc occurred to me when I placed it on the green pole. This accedent deprived Capt. Clark of any information with ripect to the country, and supposing that the rapid fork was most in the direction which it was proper we should pursue, or West, he took that [wrong] stream and asscended it with much difficulty about a mile and encamped on an island that had been lately overflown and was yet damp; they were therefore compelled to make beds of brush to keep themselves out of the mud. In ascending this stream for about a quarter of a mile, it scattered in such a manner that they were obliged to cut a passage through the willow brush which leant over the little channels and united their tops.

Meriwether Lewis
The Journals of the Lewis & Clark Expedition

We Meet Mister Eleven

I F, ON FOOLSCAP, you drew an elongated S the length of the paper, then let a three-year-old scribble over it for a minute, you'd have a map of the Jefferson River that would serve a navigator almost as well as any you could otherwise come by. Above its junction with the Madison, the Jefferson wanders, staggers, and crankles, flushing half its water askew, the other awry, and throughout its upper and lower miles manifests little urge to go anywhere other than sideways; when it's not hunting a new route or sending one channel off in search of two others, it will flow properly just long enough to fool a boatman. In short, it is the little Jefferson that puts the mischief into the big Missouri, and, like its descendant, it seems always to ask "Where am I?" although it stays not for an answer.

For sixteen months my concern had been with finding our way up that torture of lost waters, but once we reached it, the question was moot, and instead we went looking only for somebody knowledgeable enough to suggest we had even a slim chance of ascending what had become for a couple of weeks a most unambiguous route of hard-flowing water. The worry now was not getting *lost* on the river, it was simply getting *on* the river. We found no one to say anything other than "It's impossible," although one man added, "And if it isn't, you should wish it was." Outfitters, fishermen, and a government agent each trotted out the hazards we already knew: diversion dams (small barriers for irrigation), barbed-wire fences (illegal), bridges with clearances low enough to decapitate (if the fences didn't do it), logjams (perhaps the deadliest of all), and overhanging trees called sweepers. I pointed out that those perils posed less danger to an upward-bound

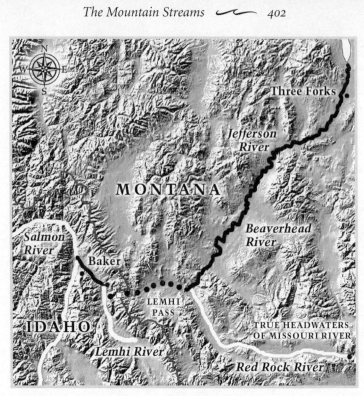

The Jefferson, Beaverhead, and Lemhi,
Three Forks to Baker, 241 river miles (112 air miles)

boat because the current would not ram us into them. "Sure," said an outfitter, "but how're you going to make headway against that uproar? There's a ten-horse legal limit for motors on both the Jefferson and Beaverhead, and that river's coming down in places more than twelve miles an hour. Maybe you don't know, but current increases geometrically, not arithmetically. A twelve-mile-an-hour current is much more than twice as powerful as one at six. You get it?" He looked to see whether I comprehended. "If you go on that river, I can just about guarantee I'll be along tomorrow afternoon cutting you out of the trees." Then, "But hell, last year you could have poled up the Jeff." As I stared disconsolately, Pilotis said, "What we need is a little stream boat."

Here was one more thing I'd evaluated the wrong way like a simpleton who reads a comic book back to front and wonders why he's confused. The issue for us in the Snow Imperative was no longer missing it and finding a river too low but rather catching it and finding a river too high. Could I have foreseen a big snowpack breaking a decade of diminished precipitation, I might have made plans for an additional craft of some sort. I complained so much about my short-sightedness in not having a bad-water contingency boat standing near, Pilotis said, "Enough, enough! Just remember your history: Meriwether Lewis walked all the way from here to the Divide and on over it, while Clark and the others dragged the pirogues for a hundred miles. To go up the Jefferson and the Beaverhead in a boat is unhistoric."

Such a remark is further evidence why one should never undertake a venture such as ours without companions, intelligent companions who can restore common sense and open the way to any skipper blinded by insistence. I thumped my hand on the table. That's it — we'll do it on foot! Pilotis: "Oh, no. What have I said?"

I pulled out our best topographic maps and a magnifying glass. By sweet chance I found what appeared to be a railroad grade running along the south bank of the Jefferson, a route through the most scenic terrain the river passes, a confined way where Lewis himself likely walked. But Pilotis wanted wheels: "You and your historical precedents — me and my mouth." What lovely precedents they are, I said, and sometimes your ideas too. "It was no damn idea."

We spent the afternoon looking into that passage and phoning for permission to hike the abandoned grade, and by nightfall we ended up in Willow Creek, a village just off the Jefferson. At the venerable Blue Willow Inn we took supper, finishing with peanut butter pie, then went into the adjoining taproom where we discovered a worn player piano and a cabinet with rolls of music. I looked inside, came across "Cruising down the River," put it into the antiquated instrument, and began treadling the thing into creaking motion and wobbly music. As the notes rolled across the room, fair-voiced Pilotis sang along with words slightly altered for the moment:

> Walking up the river
> on a Thursday afternoon,
> the clouds above
> no one we love —
> waiting for Heat-Moon —
> an old piano playing
> a mountain-river tune.

The next morning we began fulfilling the lyrics. A couple of days earlier, the Photographer had hauled *Nikawa* over the Divide to a farmhouse of acquaintances and tucked her under some big poplars near the Lemhi River. Thus unencumbered by boats, we agreed that the only point in walking, other than historical precedent, was to *see* the Jefferson, so we decided to hike just the portion that would allow us next to the water, a segment almost a quarter its length. From Three Forks (a town where in season you can witness ice fishermen engaged in racing their bait, that is, maggots) we went west to near the Sappington bridge and set out on foot up the abandoned grade of the Chicago, Milwaukee, St. Paul & Pacific Railroad, a name only a little shorter than its route. Stripped of tracks a couple of decades earlier, the way at first was fairly smooth but became progressively rougher, yet never enough to hinder a good pace. I liked hearing my footfalls and thinking each one took me a twentieth of an inch higher up the slope toward the Divide and a yard closer to the Pacific. Although the portage across would have to be longer than I'd wanted, I made my peace with it: from the Missouri Headwaters — as flies the mountain raven — the next certain river was 112 miles away. Given the imposing barrier of the Great Divide, that distance was negligible.

It isn't happenstance that the old railbed and a functioning one across the stream rub shoulders with the Jefferson through those singular miles because the high, hard walls of the London Hills admit passage only via a canyon the river has taken three million years to cut. The sixteen-hundred-foot cliffs drop to the water and leave scarce space for works of humankind, and for fifteen miles the deep defile is hardly wider than the river itself — about forty yards across — and shackles it into a single, powerful channel. Beyond the cliffs of whitish limestone rise easy hills, mostly treeless, a strange aridity to encounter so near all that pounding water, a place opposite in every way from the low bushy meadows above and below the canyon.

The day was fair but warm and so breezeless that mosquitoes attacked whenever we came near a copse of willows. We had hopes travel by foot would turn up more and different wildlife than we'd seen — I repeat, our numbers and varieties did not match even remotely the accounts of early travelers — but the ramble yielded only a couple of towhees, a nesting osprey, and three magpies pulling their long tails like pennants across the canyon. Down in the hard flush, beyond the banksides of wild roses, swam brown and rainbow trout, some of the largest in the West, so we'd heard. Near our halfway mark and not far from Lewis and Clark Caverns high up the cliff — caves they didn't know existed — we saw a mule deer at the edge of the river. Paying attention only to the cold swirlings, it watched the flow for a few moments, then leaped in and began a strong but unconcerned swim for the north shore. By the time the beast reached the other side, it was more than a hundred yards downstream at a bank of easy ascent. Said the Photographer, "I think he aimed for it." In dry weather the Jefferson can get nearly "dewatered," and we wondered whether the deer had learned to cross during those easier times, for hard current like we saw, on the Missouri anyway, once swept migrating bison to their doom.

The walk was long and hot but otherwise a vacation from the confinement of our boats, and several times I bolted ahead of my mates only to wait at some choice observation post, but by the time we reached the South Boulder River at the far end of the arid canyon, our drinking water was gone, and we were tiring and parched. Mosquitoes swarmed in as we came to the bosklands near Jefferson Island, and, thirst and weariness be damned, we scurried toward cover across the Cardwell bridge and went on to La Hood Park. There we found a 1930s tavern near a long-closed filling station with a large wooden canopy still covering the broken pumps, its underside painted with an illustrated map of one of the formerly great transcontinental routes, U.S. 20 running from Boston Harbor to Yaquina Bay in Oregon, from scrod to oysters. Although it lies ninety-five miles south of La Hood Park, the fame of 20 was such that it effectively obliterated the lore of Highway 10, which the station once sat alongside. Today the numbers have changed, and the way west in that place is Interstate 90, only a mile north of us. When I mentioned we were seeing the last of that four-lane we'd first crossed under on the Hudson River, Pilotis looked up surprised. "New York seems as remote as New Guinea." By river passage, emotionally, it almost was.

At that point, our miles from the Atlantic and our elevation in feet above it happened, by my figures, to match: 4,250. To celebrate the coincidence, after a mathematical discussion of whether or not mileage and elevation at some place *had to* coincide, we went to evening prayers in the old tavern (the word is related to "tabernacle") at the mouth of the canyon. Inside stood a noble altar of a back bar, with a large mirror framed with a hundred signed dollar-bill offerings above an assortment of bottles gleaming like candles, upon each label in bold numbers the price of a shot, and at our backs a bookcase neatly full of prayerbooks like *The Blonde That Rode Texas.*

Before ordering up spirits, I drank two glasses of ice water and asked for a third, whereupon the bartender, Baron ("a name, not a title") Stewart, said to me, "Come around and I'll show you how the drink hose works. I'm here to serve — booze. Now, when you're quenched, what will you *drink?*"

My mates ordered lager, but that seemed insufficiently celebratory for the happy coincidence of our travel numbers, so I said, How about a martini? "What?" Stewart said. "If that's your call, come back here and make it yourself." I took the white towel, stepped behind the polished wood, mixed my potion, and tended our little company and the friends they were making — a demanding lot, I must say — while our host disappeared into the kitchen before returning some time later with plates of burritos and a stack of hot tortillas.

Soon filled to comfort and ripe for meditation, Pilotis engaged a fellow, a science teacher, in a tedious fifteen-minute discussion about the length of an "instant," a ramble that made me redefine the duration of a quarter of an hour. During most of that debate, I fell into an interior commemoration of our mileage, and for the first time I thought not how distant we were from the Pacific but rather how far from the Atlantic.

Stewart told me, "I'm just here on hiatus — is that Greek or Latin? I'm a helping hiatus. You all have been talking a lot of numbers, but standing before you is a living number — meet Mister Eleven." He was a short man, balding, round billows of white hair at his temples, possessed of a jolliness confirming he was not a bartender except by hiatus, the sort of fellow who might step from a crofter's cottage in the Scottish Highlands to invite you in to a bowl of cock-a-leekie, but in fact he was from Florida, Weekiwachee Springs, "that place where mermaids swim in glass tanks and eat bananas underwater — but never a fish." He had just learned to tap-dance and proved up our new friendship by not insisting on a demonstration. "That's me, Mister Eleven," he said again, so I obliged: Why are you a number? "I play eleven musical instruments, I've totaled eleven cars, I've been bitten by eleven snakes. Now I'm afraid I'm opening up a new category — falls. I fell down the stairs, I fell off a bridge forty-one feet onto a highway and broke both arms." He held them up to show the large calcium knots on the ulnas where the bones had knitted less than perfectly. "Not long ago," he said, "a neon sign fell out of the sky and hit me on the head. So now I wish I was just Mister Three."

As a reporter, I'm pledged to try to ascertain the veracity of tavern talk, so I challenged him to name his eleven serpents, and without hesitation he said, "Black snake, green snake, blue racer, bull snake, chicken snake, garter snake, ring-neck, water snake, tree snake, copperhead, and water moccasin. That cottonmouth bit me in the navel when I was twelve. I grabbed it and pulled it loose. Threw it a mile."

Just then there was an explosion from the deck behind the tavern, and we ran to the door. We should have known. I mean, this was Montana: outside, nothing more than two men shooting potatoes. Not shooting *at* potatoes but shooting them out of a homemade contraption called a spud gun. From the porch above a deep field reaching down to the Jefferson, a man named Parker and his assistant launched the potatoes to see who could get the farthest trajectory. The spud gun was about four feet long and made from four pieces of PVC plumbing pipe: the assistant rammed a raw Idaho potato down the barrel to the firing chamber into which he then injected a spritz of hairspray; Parker aimed the gun as his friend put a match to the igniter hole, and with a loud *!whump!* a spud went sailing some hundred yards toward the river.

Parker handed the gun to me. "Try it." I said, I don't have time right now to get a new face. "There's no danger. Not much." Don't you have something smaller — say, a parsnip pistol or a radish revolver? "I've thought about that," he said.

The temptation was too much, so I loaded in a nice, firm Idaho and fired the thing into kingdom come. "Hey, you're a natural." I said, Not quite, although I nearly finished seventh at the Missouri Turnip Toss back in 'sixty-three. "These things were invented in California," Parker said, "but I hear they're illegal there now." Pilotis: "That's right. The Association of Los Angeles Grocers got them outlawed when a masked man held up a produce stand with a large russet."

In the dusk we retrieved our tow wagon and went down along the Tobacco Root Mountains, through the valley of the Jefferson, a pleasant flatlands where, except in fast-water years, the gadabout river lingers as if in love with the bottoms. At Twin Bridges, under Old Baldy Mountain, near the junctures of the Big Hole and Beaverhead rivers, we found a cabin for the night, a place from the forties but clean and spacious. After we turned in, I heard across the dark room, "If Meriwether Lewis amazed the Indians with his air rifle, think what he could have accomplished with a spud gun." A long quiet, then through the blackness, "If only he could've gotten the boys to haul from St. Louis those two hundred cases of Aqua Net."

Eating the Force
that Drives Your Life

FROM THE BEGINNING of the voyage, I had little hope of ever
ascending the Beaverhead River. The Corps of Discovery accomplished it only by making the men wade the treacherous bottom,
ropes over their shoulders to drag the loaded pirogues, a task that
perhaps more than any other could have precipitated a mutiny. Clark,
overseeing the effort, wrote almost the same sentence at the end of
each day of the long haul: "Men complain verry much of the emence
labour they are obliged to undergo & wish much to leave the river. I
passify them." And Lewis: "Capt. Clark found the river shoally, rapid,
shallow, and extreemly difficult. The men in the water almost all day.
They are geting weak, soar, and much fortiegued; they complained of
the fortiegue to which the navigation subjected them and wished to go
by land." But without the Indian horses Lewis had gone ahead on foot
in search of, lining the pirogues up the river was the only practical way
to move their heavy stores.

While we considered the Jefferson the same river as the Missouri,
the captains thought the Beaverhead to be but more miles of the
Jefferson. By whatever name, those waters below and beyond the
Tobacco Root Mountains are a hell of a tangling. Like an indigent, that
river will take any bed it can find and the next morning go looking for
another. One of our small maps warned:

> The Beaverhead is a maze of braided channels, sloughs, and irrigation
> ditches that are numberless for all practical purposes. Also, there are
> more bridges than have been indicated here. Showing all details at this

half-inch-to-the-mile scale would simply make the map unreadable. Don't even count the bends, because from season to season they may be in different places. To have shown the islands would only have added another element of chance, for they come and they go. For example, the one that Lewis and Clark named "3000-mile island" — that far from St. Louis, they calculated — washed downriver many years ago.

We had other maps, the best available, including nine adjoining charts that when laid out were ten feet long and seven wide, all for a river only forty-six beeline miles, head to mouth, and about seventy-two by water. I say "about" because it's impossible to be accurate with something as uncommitted to going anywhere as the Beaverhead usually is.

The difficulties are more than simply meanders or the narrow channels Lewis called bayous or the dead-end sloughs and old irrigation ditches, for the Beaverhead, possessed of all the impediments of the Jefferson, adds roots extending from the shore, undercut banks, irrigation pipes, sudden water releases from Clark Canyon Reservoir, and a controlling agency called the Bureau of Reclamation. As a result, people don't go *up* the Beaverhead — they wait for the water to reach a certain level then go *down a portion* of it, sometimes carrying wire cutters for illegal fences. The Corps of Discovery required almost three weeks to ascend the 150 miles from the mouth of the Jefferson to the start of the Beaverhead, a trip they accomplished on their downstream return in less than three days.

All of those obstacles, of course, do not include seriously high water. Confronting us on the morning we hoped to ascend was a river, like a teenager, determined to get nowhere in particular as long as it did it fast. Once again, we could not find an experienced boatman willing to face such currents, especially to buck them. *Rule of the River Road: When veteran pilots blink, head for dry ground.* But walking along the brush-encumbered banks was also out of the question, an age-old circumstance that explains the several well-worn Indian "roads" Lewis and Clark came across in the Beaverhead country. So, without other recourse, we also took to a road and drove up the valley past a ridgeline that pushes against the river to form what many historians believe is Beaverhead Rock, the landmark Sacagawea recognized as proof she had arrived again in her home territory. Another outcrop some miles on south has always looked far more like a beaver to me, and some residents say *it* is the true landmark, explaining the lower ridge as a swimming beaver, the upper a walking one. Other people shuffle off the debate by noting there are formations all over the area that look like beavers walking, swimming, copulating.

We followed the valley. To the west lay the heavily mined Ironrod Hills and on the east the Ruby Range, dug up for garnets and talc. The road, rarely more than a mile from the river, led us into Dillon, a small college town of four thousand, then onto Interstate 15 and a twelve-mile run through the canyon of the upper Beaverhead, a place of umber-colored rock walls and an aridness even the swift water couldn't relieve. On we went toward Clark Canyon Reservoir, an impoundment that buried the campground Meriwether Lewis named Fortunate at the union of the Red Rock River and Horse Prairie Creek, the latter leading westward to Lemhi Pass where we intended to cross the Continental Divide.

Our failure to move by water had suddenly gained us time. Since the date set for our start down the Salmon was still some days away, I proposed we take a few hours to visit the true headwaters of the Missouri, its farthest source, the one the Corps of Discovery missed. We were singularly unprepared for such an off-the-elbow expedition, even to the point of not knowing with certainty where that head-stream was; I had read only that it rose someplace in the mountains beyond Upper Red Rock Lake. Our maps were insufficient, and we could not come up with proper ones on such short notice, but we headed off anyway for the road that parallels the Red Rock River, stopping along the way to ask questions in hopes of finding an oral map, but the veritable source of the Missouri was there terra incognita. Everyone kept trying to direct us back to Three Forks or toward a spring at Lemhi Pass which Lewis considered the farthest water, and a half-dozen times we heard variations on, "What? You think the Missouri actually begins where? Who says so? When did you hear that? Why do you want to go there?" Who, what, when, where, why.

We proceeded on, following the Red Rock around its turn eastward into the long, wide, wet meadow of Centennial Valley, a prehistoric lake bottom still spongy enough to hold a rather new reservoir and two ancient pools, today heavily silted up by just 120 years of Euro-American activity. Once about twenty-five feet deep, neither Upper nor Lower Red Rock Lake will now cover a short man's head, and they are well on the way toward eutrophication and the attendant demise of the last indigenous population of grayling in the forty-eight states, as well as a colony of trumpeter swans. Although much of it is a national wildlife refuge, the valley still holds many cattle, and we had to look hard to see any creature not intended for an abattoir: a few antelope, a mule deer, a curlew, three Swainson's hawks, a pair of swans. At the Red Rocks, federal regulations still effectively permit the extirpation of uncommon wildlife in order to protect grazing rights; that is to say, 120 years of humans cancel the prerogatives of any other life, no matter that those other rights of tenancy are twenty thousand years older. Coincidentally, in the lonely valley (so we heard) is a vacation home of the richest man in America, and with good cause: the place is markedly beautiful.

From the road, we followed the flow of the Red Rock River through the two marshy lakes and its turn to the south again at the point it becomes Hell Roaring Creek, an accurate name on that day, and passes under a gravel road and disappears into a narrow and forested canyon. We were in the shadow of Nemesis Mountain, a name confirming that we were on the right track of the Missouri. Unable to follow the creek, we tried to flank it by taking the road on up to Red Rock Pass where we stopped to make a short climb into the aspens and conifers to get to some patches of winter snow. I reached down and packed a handful into a ball, tossed it to Pilotis, and said, Have a little Rocky Mountain Imperative. My friend: "So this is what has compelled and impelled you since Elizabeth, New Jersey." But not propelled, I said and bent to palm up more, brushed away the top inch, and put the rest into my mouth. It isn't often you can eat the force that drives your life. Pilotis watched and said, "There's one scoop of precipitation that won't make it to the Atlantic." Rethink that, I said. Pilotis considered, then, "Yes, I guess it still will — unless we cross the Divide tonight."

As we sipped what the Photographer called "Imperative Stout," a young hiker happened along and told of his trek down the Divide from Missoula to Loveland Pass in Colorado. Although he had not yet reached the portion above the farthest source of the Missouri, he had read that to get there we would do best to go around the Centennial Mountains and try to approach from the south. At an elevation of nine thousand feet, the alleged trail was still snowbound, a tramp three river travelers were improperly equipped for, but I knew then I would return someday to see the true source of the longest river in America.

An Ark from God or
a Miracle of Shoshones

WE TOOK A DAY of respite at the Red Rock Inn, the nicely
refurbished old railroad hotel in Dell, a one-street settlement with a population often less than what's passing by on
the four-lane just to the west. We went out into the territory again,
wandering, looking, and returned to the inn for supper and then a
nightcap in front of the fireplace. Our companions were a couple of
cowhands working for a wealthy Boston physician who held several
grazing permits. Said one of the fellows, a former paramedic, "Doc
doesn't know much about ranching — he's in it for the investment and
tax breaks — but he's better than what my friend's got up north. His
boss is Japanese or Taiwanese or some kind of Ese. That's the Great
American Ranch Legend for you today."

The next morning we set out for that place we'd so long anticipated,
the Great Divide, and our first look into the far western mountains
lying between us and the Pacific. From the high waters of Clark Canyon Reservoir, we drove through rising grasslands drained by Horse
Prairie Creek and up the foothills of the Beaverhead Mountains in the
Bitterroot Range. The country, not so beautiful as Centennial Valley,
was pleasing enough with stands of conifers, splots of sage, volcanic
outcrops, and history: we were more or less on the Indian trail
Meriwether Lewis followed to reach Lemhi Pass. The way changed
from asphalt to gravel to a dirt track with a sign: ROAD CLOSED. A far
better crossing lay about fifteen direct miles south, the route the Photographer took when he hauled *Nikawa* over the Divide, but I was bent

on staying with history, so we continued on to see for ourselves whether the way was open. The deeply rutted track did its best to keep close to Trail Creek, a narrow downrush of clear water marked all across the open foothills by a bordering serpentine of small willows. Hanging on in the lurching tow wagon, we could ascend at only a walking pace, and we hoped we wouldn't come around a tight bend and find our passage blocked, because above us somewhere was the tiny spring Lewis believed to be the farthest water of the Missouri.

Then, beyond the last hairpin turn, we saw a long and lightly forested ridge sloping down to a saddle, the gentle dip that was the crest of Lemhi Pass. We followed on to just below it and another track leading south a few hundred yards; we stopped and began walking, past a small campground, through a stand of firs and pines, on to a hilly meadow of sage and blossoming lupines, bluebells, strawberries. We stood, I sniffed the air, listened. When the sough in the trees, a sound like gurgles from a brook, paused, I heard real water. We started again until we came to a rillet only ten inches across, its margins thick with watercress, and we pursued it up the slope a short way to a bubbling circle of clarity no larger than a platter for a Christmas turkey, no deeper than my immersed hand, and cold enough to make knuckles ache in a few seconds.

We had read the famous passage Lewis wrote about that spring, knew it by heart and felt it the same way. Among the thousands of significant moments in American history, we have few records of what a participant thought at the time: as Lincoln stood reading at Gettysburg, what did he feel? or Dorothea Dix the first time she stepped inside an asylum? or George Washington Carver when that sweetpotato glue actually stuck a postage stamp to an envelope? At the springlet below Lemhi Pass, Lewis, after nearly a year and a half of struggling to reach that spot, gave account of his response:

> The road took us to the most distant fountain of the waters of the mighty Missouri in surch of which we have spent so many toilsome days and wristless nights. Thus far I had accomplished one of those great objects on which my mind has been unalterably fixed for many years; judge then of the pleasure I felt in allying my thirst with this pure and ice cold water. . . . McNeal exultingly stood with a foot on each side of this little rivulet and thanked his god that he had lived to bestride the mighty & heretofore deemed endless Missouri.

I kneeled to drink. The Photographer, ever the man of concerns, said, "Do you think it's safe?" As a long-time sampler of American waters, sometimes only tasting where drinking would be harebrained, I said, I know that water pollution is widespread in this country, but I'm going to trust it's not so bad it's reached a spring a hundred yards below the Divide — I mean, how much closer to the top of a stream can you get? The only water above here is rain. Leaning to the spring, I said to myself, Even if I'm wrong, this, of all places, is worth the risk.

The taste was like melted snow. Then I took a few steps down the rivulet, and I too straddled it and watched the rush between my legs and realized it would reach my home country before I would. I looked up, thinking I should say something appropriate, but nature did it for me: from a high dead branch came down a rasping *khraaaa*, a Clark's nutcracker, one of the fifty-some birds the Corps of Discovery first brought into American ornithology and the only one named for the captain, and I answered, Indeed, William.

We went on up to the pass and stopped again to walk across the line between Montana and Idaho, to step over the very ridgepole of America and into the world of Pacific gravity. From the Atlantic at the Verrazano-Narrows we had come 4,432 miles, and we were almost a mile and a half above it. Now, stretching out before us through range after range of gray mountains — mountains set athwart our course — was the deepest horizon I've ever beheld, and somewhere among it all lay waiting eight hundred more miles of river. Looking at the ten-thousand-foot-high ridges of deep and successive forest, a view unchanged since Lewis took it in, Pilotis said, "Only a madman could believe he could reach the Pacific through those things." Or a guy with a good map, I said. "One of us qualifies on both counts, and I don't have the maps."

Of the several Divide passes Lewis and Clark used in their explorations, the Lemhi is the only one both crossed, and for them it marked the boundary of the Louisiana Territory and the end of the United States. I went down the western side to look for the spring that Lewis, assuming it was the source of the Columbia River, also drank from; although he missed the true headstream of the Missouri by only ninety miles, the farthest water of the Columbia actually lies north almost four hundred miles. The forest was heavier on the Pacific slope, the valley more pinched and steep, and I wandered some time before I gave up on finding that other spring and climbed back to join my mates, and we started down the old stagecoach road, a narrow and much twisted track scarcely improved in six generations. We followed Agency Creek through a declivitous terrain of weird volcanic formations that on a foggy night could surely change into phantasms and chimeras, a haunting if not haunted place. Sky darkening, the wind poured down from the continental summit, rattled the trees hard, and pushed us along as gravity pulled us. Pilotis said, "From here on, if we have a mechanical malfunction, at least we'll get washed along in the right direction." And the Photographer: "Going downstream only means different problems, not fewer ones." Pilotis: "That's a difference I can live with."

At the foot of the Beaverheads we came into the valley of the Lemhi where it passes in front of the Tendoy store, a general merchandise sandbagged against the rising river. Pilotis looked at the bags and said to me, "Well, Mister Flood, here we go again. You really overdid it last winter with that damn rainstick." We stopped to walk to the edge of the narrow torrent smashing against rocks and rolling over a small irrigation dam and shaking the hell out of overhanging trees. Above the noisy Lemhi, Pilotis said loudly, "Won't be any canoes going down this little ripsnorter!" We've got only twenty miles of it! "Twenty miles of near-death experiences!"

In the glooming evening we headed on north alongside the river toward rooms we'd arranged for at the place where *Nikawa* waited. It was in the Lemhi Valley that Lewis stepped into one of the remarkable and almost incredible events of the Expedition, one so stunning it blurs the line between coincidence and miracle. Having seen virtually no Indians since leaving their winter camp at Fort Mandan four months earlier, the captain was desperate to trade for horses, an immediate and absolute necessity to carry their stores over the mountains to the next navigable water. Going down into the valley, he caught sight of three terrified women whom he managed to approach and calm by rolling up his sleeve to reveal his white arm and show he was not an enemy from the Plains. The women belonged to a small band of Northern Shoshones, Sacagawea's very people, and their chief was no other than her brother. As for horses, they had many.

The valley takes its name from Limhi, who (so purports Joseph

Smith in *The Book of Mormon*) was a son of Noah, the old master of flood. The way I figured things that gloomy night, to get down the little roaring river we would need an ark from God or a miracle from the Shoshones. Pilotis said, "Along here, you've got a better chance of coming across Limhi himself than you have either of the others."

A Shameless Festal Board

O F THE problems we would have in trying to get down the little Lemhi, one of them would not be Mary Turner, once rejected in love and thereafter at war with the world — especially where it was male — her disappointment enough to name her ranch the Broken Heart and proclaim it with a painted wooden sign at the gate. A woman of the valley, she especially had it in for those on the river, snatching fishing rods and snapping them over her knee or shooting holes in boats. What sort of weapon she used I don't know, but I hope it wasn't the Thompson submachine gun in the county historical museum, her "Chicago typewriter" engraved with names of gangsters she claimed to have known Back East: John Dillinger, Ma Barker, Baby Face Nelson, and, at the muzzle, hers too. Other than taking neighbors' apples or trying to bullwhip a woman who gave some offense, I didn't hear of any other crimes attributed to Mary, known to valley people as Old Blister.

Three winters previous, a few days before Christmas, the eighty-two-year-old fell on the ice near her isolated house, the one with secret compartments, and froze to death, a demise some residents found fitting for a woman who had long considered the outside world a cold and heartless place, even believing the power company daily shut off the electricity to chill her. Linemen, ironically, were the ones to find Mary a few days later. When the sheriff arrived and went inside, he discovered a house heated to eighty-four degrees, three starving Dobermans, a room full of insane chickens, a cocked bear trap, and in a drawer a plastic snake on a coil ready to spring. All the "secret" compartments were empty, but in her purse, next to the food stamps, was forty thousand dollars. People now speculate that Mary, always contemptuous of governmental programs, did not consider relief stamps a violation of her efforts, as she said, "to live free in an unfree world," since she more or less returned the money through a hundred-thousand-dollar bequest to the University of Idaho.

Her Lemhi was the smallest river, in breadth and length, we would face, of such size Missourians would call it a creek, but the heavy and fast-melting winter snowpack was driving it into such confounding impetuosity, no one in the county would entertain even a notion of setting out on it until it dropped considerably. To the dangers of the Jefferson and Beaverhead, it added a treacherous narrowness and dozens of blind bends that can bring a boat suddenly upon a decapitating bridge or barbed-wire fence or, lying bank to bank, a downed tree as deadly as any cheval-de-frise. Because the Lemhi is the major source of irrigation for the otherwise arid yet fertile valley, ranchers did what they could to discourage people from putting on the river, even using as evidence one of their own who drowned fixing a fence just before our arrival. The law provides for open access to such waterways, and all we wanted was to descend a mere twenty miles without harassment, but once again a swollen river made our passage moot because it was the Lemhi itself that was keeping us off.

While waiting for a drop in the water before our federally assigned departure day down the Salmon, we laid over in Baker, Idaho, at a red farmhouse that, so we learned, had also been a stage stop, a railroad "depot," and a bordello frequented by Al Capone. Other than our quarters, Baker was a couple of small dwellings, a closed-up general mercantile, and two highway signs, one on each end, the distance between them seventy-two yards; I could walk across town in three quarters of a minute.

Our hosts were kindly people, Sharon and Roger Solaas, who came into the valley in the early seventies to raise a family and had spent much time refurbishing the house and its yard, putting in a garden, pruning the ninety-year-old poplars. Mrs. Solaas, a woman of smiles and teasings, kept rabbits and chickens, and to one tree she had nailed a sign, COUNTRY FRESH EGGS; she also offered travelers several bedrooms decorated with antiques and curiosities, each chamber opening to a view of the Beaverhead Mountains eastward or the Lemhis westward. During our several-day wait, we sat on the front porch and read or wrote or listened to the narrow irrigation ditch that was in effect a brooklet, or we just looked across the Divide Valley and wondered what it was like when young Sacagawea lived here or exactly where along the Lemhi River William Clark set up camp. Mrs. Solaas's breakfasts were big spreads of eggs fresh from the cacklers, or French toast, or pancakes, potatoes and muffins, meals that negated lunch and necessitated long walks. Sharon and Roger, she adept in the culinary arts and he in the chase, told many stories, hers occasionally concluding with, "Now don't write that down," and his ending with a bang — that is, with a bullet. Across the country, we had met no better people than they.

On our first afternoon there, I sat quietly, happily thinking how we'd at last shed the constraints of the calendar, and once I paused in my reading only to doze off for three hours. Every night thereafter, with the sweet summer air from the Bitterroots coming through my second-floor window, I knew the sleep of a seventeen-year cicada, and indeed, when I awoke, I too felt changed. Sometimes in the evening we went up the road to a café with both a good salad bar and view of the Lemhi, where I watched the tumult pour past and imagined the flow lessening; afterward we would go into Salmon, twelve miles north of Baker, to hunt out a conversation that might lead us to a boat capable of descending the river, but we turned up nothing except refusals. Most of the town soon learned of our mission, in part because of our continual queries and partly because in front of the farmhouse *Nikawa* sat in full view of the highway. A woman, cocking her head like a hen hunting up a morsel, asked me the second day, "Where you trying to get to in that little boat *Nirvana?*"

I went to the public library in Salmon to read about the valley and happened across a nineteenth-century book containing a lexicon of Shoshone; I copied into my log the translations of certain phrases because they amused me and seemed a hidden history of red and white relations here before the Indians moved north and the townspeople named the high school teams the Savages. (Someone said, "You're surprised? Man, you're in Republican country. The University of Idaho is the Vandals.") When I looked at the phrases I'd copied down, a found poem materialized:

> Are you good looking?
> Stop rambling about.

> Both of you kiss.
> Your face does not look good.
> Got no nose.
> You are a great liar.
> You think you talk smart.
> Let me loose.
> Break his toe.
> Do your best!

I tried to learn the lines in Shoshone, but the pronunciations surpassed my capacities, so I settled on the last line, rendered as *too-nuts,* then went up the street for a snack of spud fudge made from Idaho potatoes. It managed to taste like both, losing the best of both.

Every morning I checked our company's resolve not to test the river by using our small kayak and canoe, each time finding their will unshaken, and secretly I was glad because the Lemhi was still ripping at full pelt. One afternoon on the porch during a chess game (the scrounged-up pieces were two sets of salt-and-pepper shakers for royalty, .270-caliber bullets as bishops, shotgun shells for castles, quarters as knights, and pennies for pawns), a fellow rode past on a bicycle, saw *Nikawa,* and turned back toward us. He said, "I knew we'd cross trails. I've been hearing you were out here somewhere."

A native of Long Island, New York, Rob Pike, a forty-two-year-old lawyer, seven years earlier had begun crossing the United States by boat and bicycle, using wheels where his V-hull would not go. Each summer vacation he put in several hundred miles. Except for Fort Peck Reservoir, the solid fellow had pedaled over Montana, and to that Pilotis said, "You're smarter than some people who insist on struggling along completely by water." I asked if he were biking through the Idaho mountains, he nodded, and my copilot said, "Worlds smarter." Pike was bound for the head of navigation on the Snake River at Lewiston-Clarkston. "So are we," said Pilotis looking dimly at me. I said I admired his soloness, but his concept was different — his was a boat-and-bike. Pilotis: "Ours is a hope-and-hike." More like a goad-and-gripe, I said.

I asked the lawyer what led him into such an undertaking, and he said, "I watched the wife of a friend struggle through a car crash and its aftermath. I saw her broken body go from an ICU to a hospital bed to a wheelchair to a walker to crutches and onto her feet again. It all made me take a hard look at myself coming into midlife and the way I was spending my time. One of the results is this trip, my American Passage." He liked our company and the porch and decided to stay for a few days of rest before taking on Idaho. He said, "I'll tell you, heaven is an ignition switch."

Because we would travel down the Salmon River with a local outfitter, a man I considered a master raftsman with proper boats for white water, I needed more than our company of three to make the long descent worth his time, so I had lined up several friends to join us on the River of No Return. Toward the end of our layover, they began arriving. To celebrate the start of our run to the Pacific, I asked our hosts to prepare a special and historically appropriate dinner, an idea that came to me when I was reading Meriwether Lewis's account of a lunch break with the Lemhi Valley Shoshones, one of the most graphic descriptions in the journals:

> When [the Indians] arrived where the deer was which was in view of me they dismounted and ran in, tumbling over each other like a parcel of famished dogs each seizing and tearing away a part of the intestens which had been previously thrown out by Drewyer who killed it; the seen was such when I arrived that had I not have had a pretty keen appetite myself I am confident I should not have taisted any part of the venison shortly. Each one had a peice of some discription and all eating most ravenously. Some were eating the kidnies, the melt, and liver, and the blood runing from the corner of their mouths, others were in a similar situation with the paunch and guts but the exuding substance in this case from their lips was of a different discription. One of the last who attracted my attention particularly had been fortunate in his allotment or reather active in the division; he had provided himself with about nine feet of the small guts, one end of which he was chewing on while with his hands he was squezzing the contents out at the other. I really did not untill now think that human nature ever presented itself in a shape so nearly allyed to the brute creation. I viewed these poor starved divils with pity and compassion. I directed McNeal to skin the deer and reserved a quarter, the ballance I gave the Chief to be divided among his people; they devoured the whole of it nearly without cooking.

Mrs. Solaas could dress out farmyard creatures or a grouse or deer or anything else that made an unfortunate wander onto the highway, and Roger kept the family table additionally supplied with game from the field and fish from the rivers, as well as filling their large vestibule with taxidermied salmon and heads of mammals (a mule deer, antelope, caribou, black bear, cougar, several sets of antlers, and a bison skull he found). Even though no one in our outfit hunted any longer and some of us gave fair allegiance to vegetable diets (I asked one member to go easy on calling the foyer "The Hall of Death"), I proposed we sit down to a farewell meal the Corps of Discovery might have eaten.

On their twenty-seven months away from St. Louis, the men shot and devoured at least:

Deer	1,001
Elk	375
Large fowl	252 (probably more)
Bison	227
Beaver	113
Antelope	62
Wolves/Coyotes	48 (ate only one)
Grizzlies	43
Black bears	23
Otter	16
Fish	countless

They also ate 190 Indian dogs and a dozen horses, the latter keeping them alive north of the Lemhi Valley. Although they occasionally cooked up smaller creatures, the near absence of rabbits, squirrels, and prairie dogs suggests such game wasn't worth expending the limited supply of shot and powder. Clark said the company could consume in a day four deer or one bison. There were also meals of various grains and legumes, wild berries, wappato, and enough camas root to give the Corps gastrointestinal upsets.

One morning I read the list to Mrs. Solaas who said her freezer held nearly everything except a bear, wolf, and otter; instead she had cougar, mountain goat, and thought she could get a raccoon and maybe some moose. No coyote? I said. She looked shocked. "I raised a pup from before its eyes opened. It was darling. Our children taught it to howl in the living room." We'll forget the coyote, I said. Just then the Solaases' Labrador, Duke, ambled past, and I commented that although Lewis was inordinately fond of loin of puppy, the only animal the often-hungry Corps refused to eat was the captain's Newfoundland, Seaman. Mrs. Solaas said to the dog something on the order of, "We won't let the bad man put you in the oven."

I proposed the menu to Pilotis who has been alleged to weep when passing a meat counter. "So now our participatory history is turning into gustatory history?" Pausing, then, "Okay, but no puppy and no horse." And I: Explain to me the ethical difference between a fish and a pony. While I drew up a menu, Pilotis, watching over my shoulder, said for both of us, "Mea culpa!" A few days later, early in the morning, Mrs. Solaas began preparing the feast, a shameless festal board. To recapitulate history, she used only the simplest means of cooking, few seasonings, and made no attempt to remove any "wild" tastes. On our last night together, she set out a spread such as I'd never before seen or ever again could condone for myself. Over two tables were platters, bowls, pots, tureens, pans, broilers, and trays, and in them:

Mule Deer Roast
Bighorn Meatloaf
Chicken-fried Cougar
Roasted Mountain Goat au Jus
Haunch of Bison Stew
Grouse in Cream Sauce
Skillet-fried Elk
Roasted Flank of Antelope in Gravy
Baked Leg of Raccoon
Steelhead Trout in Cream
Roasted Beavertail
Boiled Beavertail

*

Salmon River Wild Cherry Pie

I affirm here that what might seem a menu of the forbidden was all taken legally and that we ate it respectfully but with due relish. I proposed the toast: May these critters before us forgive us, and may none among us even once utter the words "Tastes like chicken" — and now my boon friends, *too-nuts!*

Our preferences varied. I found the mountain lion the most delicious, the only feline I've ever eaten, except perhaps one time in China when the smiling host once too often reassured us, "No, no, American guests, house cat not in soup bowl." The bighorn was a close second, but I was alone in tolerating raccoon for more than a bite. We were unanimous regarding only one dish — no matter how prepared or how favored by Captain Lewis — our distaste for beavertail, a glutinous mess. About cooking it, even our chef, her face pinched as if she'd sniffed offal, said, "Never again." In all my days, including China, I've never eaten a meal more singular.

Thus full of American history, we moved to the cool porch to look off into the mountains that had abundantly provided most of our supper; toward the north lay the range that nearly starved to death the Corps of Discovery. The Photographer said, "It's sad that the great river of these valleys, the one we've got coming up, can't any longer provide the fish it's named for." That comment about sockeye salmon depressed conversation until I asked whether anyone had noticed in town the shop selling T-shirts imprinted:

THE RIVER OF NO RETURN
WHERE NO ONE HEARS YOUR SCREAM

X

THE SALMON RIVER

NEAR GOSPEL HUMP WILDERNESS, IDAHO

ICONOGRAM X

The Salmon River is one of the upper branches of the Oregon or Columbia and takes its rise from various sources among a group of mountains to the northwest of the Wind River chain. It owes its name to the immense shoals of salmon which ascend it in the months of September and October. The salmon on the west side of the Rocky Mountains are, like the buffalo on the eastern plains, vast migratory supplies for the wants of man, that come and go with the seasons. As the buffalo in countless throngs find their certain way in the transient pasturage on the prairies, along the fresh banks of the rivers, and up every alley and green defile of the mountains, so the salmon at their allotted seasons, regulated by a sublime and all-seeing Providence, swarm in myriads up the great river and find their way up their main branches, and into the minutest tributary streams so as to pervade the great arid plains and to penetrate even among barren mountains. Thus wandering tribes are fed in the desert places of the wilderness, where there is no herbage for the animals of the chase, and where, but for these periodical supplies, it would be impossible for man to subsist.

The rapid currents of the rivers which run into the Pacific render the ascent of them very exhausting to the salmon. When the fish first run up the rivers, they are fat and in fine order. The struggle against impetuous streams and frequent rapids gradually renders them thin and weak, and great numbers are seen floating down the river on their backs. As the season advances and the water becomes chilled, they are flung in myriads on the shores, where the wolves and bears assemble to banquet on them. Often they rot in such quantities along the river banks as to taint the atmosphere. They are commonly from two to three feet long.

Washington Irving
The Adventures of Captain Bonneville, U.S.A.,
in the Rocky Mountains and the Far West, 1843

Bungholes and
Bodacious Bounces

O F AMERICAN RIVERS outside Alaska, the undammed Salmon, the River of No Return, is one of the longest entirely within a single state, and probably the most unabused big one, chiefly because its lower two thirds passes through the least accessible large tract in the contiguous forty-eight, a fiercely mountainous region where roads cease and humans thin to almost nothing along a chasm deeper than the Grand Canyon and second only to Hell's Canyon not far distant; for 180 miles the Salmon gorge is more than a mile down. It is the only river Lewis and Clark turned away from. Meriwether wrote of Sacagawea's brother explaining the terrain:

I now prevailed on the Chief to instruct me with rispect to the geography of his country. This he undertook very cheerfully by delienating the rivers on the ground. But I soon found that his information fell far short of my expectation or wishes. . . . He placed a number of heeps of sand on each side which he informed me represented the vast mountains of rock eternally covered with snow through which the river passed. That the perpendicular and even juting rocks so closely hemned in the river that there was no possibilyte of passing along the shore; that the bed of the river was obstructed by sharp pointed rocks and the rapidity of the stream such that the whole surface of the river was beat into perfect foam as far as the eye could reach. That the mountains were also inaccesible to man or horse. He said that this being the state of the country in that direction that himself nor none of his nation had ever been further down the river than these mountains.

Not fully trusting Indian geography, Clark followed a "wolf path" over the high and broken north bank for fourteen miles only to reach a vista running to a horizon of ridge after ridge of rough metamorphic rock uplifted into a chaos of ten-thousand-foot mountains. He said:

> This river is about 100 yards wide and can be forded but in a few places. Below my guide and maney other Indians tell me that the Mountains Close and is a perpendicular Clift on each Side, and Continues for great distance and that the water runs with great violence from one rock to the other on each Side foaming & roreing thro rocks in every direction So as to render the passage of any thing impossible.

Clark, who not once recorded a disparaging word about his friend, named this most difficult of rivers, the impossible one, the Lewis, and the Expedition bypassed it to go north into mountains that nearly killed them before they reached easier descent on the Clearwater. A century later, a settler said the Salmon gorge looked like "Creation chopped it out with a hatchet."

We planned to put in immediately above the mouth of the Lemhi, at the island under the Main Street Bridge in the county-seat town of Salmon, and follow the morning shadow of the Continental Divide twenty-two miles to North Fork where the river turns west to assume broad bends and a generally direct course toward the Pacific. The rock-riven river drops more than three thousand feet from our start-ing place to the mouth, a distance of only 130 air miles. Pilotis said, "This isn't a river — it's a wet elevator." If we could stay off boulders and get through sixty-some rapids, the least of them greater than anything we'd yet encountered, the hard current would give us a swift float. On the international rating scale, rapids on the Salmon range up to 4 ("difficult"), with the exception of the one nearly at its mouth, a mean constriction with the seemingly playful name of the Slide which in high water can become a class 6, "a substantial hazard to life." I asked a fellow, What's it like? "Roughern a stucco bathtub." Because of our assigned departure date, we could not wait for the water to subside even though we knew the final rapid was at that moment impassable by boat or on foot. If the Salmon didn't drop sufficiently before we reached the Slide, we'd be trapped there until it did.

The ominous nickname River of No Return refers not to self-destruction but to the inability of early-day boats to ascend against

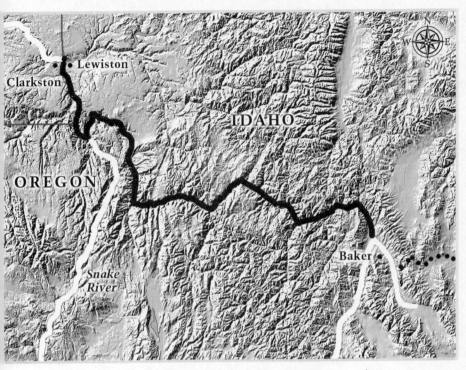

The Salmon, Baker to Snake Confluence, 260 river miles

current and rocks; a scowman might dare his way down, but he couldn't fight his way back up. Other than my wish to follow westering American history, it was the Salmon that made me decide months earlier not to cross America west to east and thereby gain twenty-five hundred miles of down-bound Missouri River. From the late nineteenth century to the Second World War, big wooden scows carrying cargo (and an occasional tourist) to gold mines and a few homesteads all ended up as tunnel shoring, barroom floors, brothel walls, outhouse seats. With the advent fifty years ago of powerful, lightweight vessels, especially the jet boat, the Salmon became a River of Grudging Return because what it lacks in depth and width and open channels it makes up for in velocity and turbulence, and its comparative narrowness is a poor measure of its power, its beauty a subterfuge for potential havoc. Our chart book warned, "The Salmon is not a place for the novice boater. Accidents can occur in seconds, but rescue can take many hours. The cost in both lives and dollars can be enormous." Of the rivers we'd used or would yet use, the Salmon had by far the fewest travelers but, I suspected, the highest fatality rate.

On a Tuesday morning in early July, we assembled beneath the bridge to meet our outfitter, don life vests, and get in his twenty-two-foot Hypalon raft, a flexible boat stiffened by a steel frame. Under fair skies we set out on a kind of shakedown cruise before all of our contingent joined us at the entrance to the so-called primitive area where stone vies with water for mastery of the gorge. Our helmsman was Bill Bernt, a former Nebraskan by way of Missouri, now a two-decade resident of the Salmon country, a forty-seven-year-old who knew the river and its lore — a craftsman of cataracts. For a few days I was de-skippered and could sit back to take in the territory and enjoy the first leg of our coast to the coast. Again, because of a frequent certain sameness hour to hour, I will push along the narrative with my logbook:

TUESDAY, DAY ONE

B[ill] B[ernt] lanky, boy's face still showing beneath weathering; thinning hair almost always under hat to keep pate from western sun; in college studied "something that had to do with angiosperms and gymnosperms, and I've forgotten much of even that." Speaks slowly, calmly, precisely, western drawl; calls his outfitting company Aggipah, shortened version of Shoshone name for the Salmon, Tom-agit-pah, "Big-fish-water." He guesses current at seven mph. Almost immediately we pass through several standing waves that raft tries to bend itself to fit, water we begin calling jolly rollers or, where accompanied by a "pit," holey rollers. BB sits amidships to work long oars, not for propulsion but only to keep us pointed downstream. Morning full of Lewis's woodpeckers, another species Corps of Discovery brought into American ornithology; in all my travels, never saw this bird before — now a couple every mile. Eastward high cliffs of sedimentary rock; on west sky-shredding metamorphic rises; stones close to river covered with yellow lichens like mirrors reflecting sun. Motorless, we can talk where rapids don't drown us out, hear birdsong and rattle of cottonwoods. Too easy to be real travel. BB: "Count on it to change." Indeed: soon after, blue sky dies and turns black as if decaying, wind cracks down hard, brings sheet rain, and we scramble ashore for half shelter of tall outlier called Tower Rock. Half hour later proceed on; to starboard is U.S. 93, one of the loneliest federal highways in America, but not here with houses and more going up; goodbye old valley; at last, relief of hay meadows; along banks magpies flit and natter in serviceberries. Average annual rainfall about eight inches, virtual desert we're floating through. Pass big cottonwoods holding heronry of 150 nests, gawky birds gawking as do we; one lets fly squirt of excreta that could sink canoe. Nature's opinion of us. Valley narrows to limit human works; on hills beyond grow shrubby and twisted mountain mahogany, wood so heavy it won't float. P[ilotis]: "Widely used in the early days for Salmon River submarines — if only the water had been more than six feet deep." Arrive North Fork late afternoon; will enter Wild and Scenic section tomorrow. Compared to past ones, day so uneventful feel I've been on Sunday outing, not transcontinentaling. P: "Why do you think our passage must be continual travail? You've got to adjust to going downhill. Quit uprivering. Just follow the drainage down."

WEDNESDAY, DAY TWO

Adage here: "The river peaks when the roses bloom." Someone tell it: Petals are dropping. I ask BB how far unsteered raft might go in this water: "One got loose a few weeks ago and traveled fourteen miles before it got hung up. An untended boat can do embarrassingly well." Especially if not loaded down. At ten A.M. we make big turn west; each mile now deeper into wilderness. Pacific, here we come. Gravel road along bankside stops on below after forty-six miles; I wished it ended sooner; P: "Sure of that?" Escaped European plants, common tansy and knotweed, creeping into canyon, making problems for natives; another metaphor. Tansy, strange tansy: its oils can promote menstruation, but tea from steeped leaves can help prevent miscarriage (Make sure Doc gets it straight). Beautiful spread of virgin's bower draping over banks, and actually forming bower; also called traveler's joy, don't know why; Indians chewed peppery stems to ease sore throats and crushed roots to place in nostrils of horses to invigorate them. Long pool named Deadwater requires oaring through; slow passage makes P groggy — needs a snootful of traveler's joy. Photog[rapher] apprehensive about big rapids ahead. Relax, I say, a river can smell fear. Dump Creek Rapids mild, tune-up for what's coming. BB points out logjam in sidewater where canoeist drowned last week. Cliffs slowly closing in and forested where not purely rock or too steep; creeks entering every couple of miles. Only beauty keeps canyon from being forbidding. Try lunch stop but mosquitoes drive us on; eat in raft: home-made antelope and elk jerky and fresh grapes — excellent. See occasional derelict gold diggings, but most signs of humanity are CCC projects from thirties: pack bridges, narrow road, campsites. Pass below high vantage where Wm. Clark looked westward and knew the Salmon was not North-west Passage, but for us this dark jagged, ragged, snaggled, scraggled, cragged, and haggard gorge is a NW Passage. What were Clark's words? ["Those rapids which I had Seen (the Indian guide) said was Small & trifleing in comparrison to the rocks & rapids below at no great distance & The Hills or mountains were not like those I had Seen but like the Side of a tree Streight up."]

Above us grave of H. C. Merritt who drowned in 1884 while passenger in supply scow. Stop to walk at Shoup, once gold-rush village, now only couple of buildings remain; place heavily salvaged in 1941 for armament metal; gold to guns. BB says last hand-crank phone system in U.S. here until recently. On again, deeper into narrows, on beyond Clipper Bullion Mine, richest around: sixty-five million tons of mountain torn out for thirteen pounds of gold, about enough to decorate neck of NFL wide receiver. Ever darker, more serrated cliffs of metamorphic gneiss, their age spectacular billion and half years although canyon only (!) about forty million years.

Line of white across river is Pine Creek Rapids echoing up gorge; I think nothing of it till BB quits talking, his silence more disturbing than roar of river. Then he says only, "Get hold of something." I've looped line around steel frame and will try to ride through on bucking stern bronco-buster style; want to feel river, feel the surge and rip, get rid of passive passage. BB pulls hard to set up for drop, water louder, boulders now visible, and jumbled river looks like tops of thunderheads, rising, changing color, water trying to become air, rock trying to resist becoming water. Current grabs claws into raft, point of no return; bow drops about four feet, seems to pause atop standing wave then stern drives it forward into hole, our heads snapping back — crack-the-whip. Second pause, then everything repeats, and third one; pounds hell out of me till rowdydow lies at our backs and raft quits crumpling, straightens atop tailwaters, and on we go. We do as novices do after first good banger, laugh with joy and relief. Real transcontinental passage! P: "So that's what it's like to go down the

Rockies by water." BB: *"A little bit."* Six bighorns make impossible walk down nearly vertical rock face to drink from river — amazing feat/feet. Ahead Dutch Oven Rapids, double set looking worse than last but prove only commensurate. A mile beyond, canyon now shadowy in late afternoon, we pull ashore near Panther Creek. Made twenty-seven miles — seems like ten. P: *"I like this downhill stuff."*

In evening, conversation about sign we saw a few days ago: HUNGRY? EAT AN ENVIRONMENTALIST. Such antagonism, often manufactured by big self-serving corporations or Farm Bureaus, makes solutions ever more difficult. The Salmon received Wild and Scenic designation through compromise, including controlled use of jet boats. Photog: *"I agree with looking for common ground, but in this place it just seems that people should have to earn their way in. Jets are too easy."* When I fall asleep, I'm imagining difficulty — the Slide.

THURSDAY, DAY THREE

I fear, above anything else on this river, losing my logbook; better I should go under than this most important object in my life. Entries in waterproof ink and journal bagged in plastic and boxed in aluminum where it stays while on river as I rely on pencil and pocket notebook; if I saw logbook go down I'd dive for it — stupid but necessary resolve. Morning of gentle rapids; stop at old homestead now cherry orchard where owner lets us climb and pick; one *"wild"* tree gives sweetest fruit. P: *"The wild is always sweetest to you whether it's —"* Cease! Along riverbank large serviceberry; blueberryish, seedy but pleasing, exotic taste like something out of Asia. Indians desiccated fruits and mixed them with dried bison meat to make pemmican. Spot first dipper of voyage, little loonies that walk underwater to feed. P thinks river may have dropped slightly from yesterday. Realize running out of water is no longer concern! Lake Creek Rapids give such mild bounce, I ask to start going through the heart of drops, and so we do next one, Proctor Creek Rapids. Oarsman lines us up to *"thread the needle."* Keep her dead-on now! He does. Thump into standing waves, fall into big hole, unexpected pit, and I go flying forward, crashing into P, then bouncing up toward side. P reaches desperate arm out to grab me and yank me back into raft; saves me! Then second drop trounces us until we're a tangle in bottom of boat; river quiets; both P and I hurting, begin to unsort ourselves: This is my leg. That's your arm. No, *that's mine. Whose knee is this? I don't care, take it. Too skinny for me. All right, maybe it is mine. What about this hand? The one with the bleeding finger or the bent thumb?*

Half mile farther, rapids with name I didn't catch. Set myself more securely. Rollers, too goddamn big to be jolly, carry us up, give that horrible pause; all I see ahead is yawning black hole, a grave if I ever saw one. Nerve fails and I dive to bottom of raft where P and I again bounce like beans in a hopper, all of us drenched. Raft bounds into easy afterward, and P says, "Wet your pants, cowboy?" How would I know?

Seated again, determined not to dive anymore, I ask, Can a poor helmsman turn a class 3 rapid into a 4? Perhaps. Photog, working to enjoy white water, says, "What if we miss the slot at the Slide?" Chance for one of my favorite quotations: "Only the curious, if they live, have a tale worth telling." Somebody else: "Live little, change little." P: "Live lots, change your lot with the dead." Somebody: "What is this, a competition of homilies?"

Just past beautiful canyon of Middle Fork of the Salmon, otter watches, plunges to cover. Fountain Creek pours long and lovely white tail/trail of water down high cliff. P: "Want to shoot that little drop, buckaroo?" Reach Corn Creek where road ends and serious rapids begin, but that's tomorrow. Take rooms at lodge across river. By early evening, rest of contingent arrives for next five days of descent; we're now a baker's dozen ready for grand inaccessibility.

FRIDAY, DAY FOUR

Near cabin is Butts Creek (never mind name — one of prettiest rills I've ever seen); follow it up slope; in mountain mahogany, watch thrifty little orb weaver take her web down, roll it into tidy ball, tuck it under small branch. We now have two more helmsmen for two more inflatable rafts: fifteen-foot "paddleboat" (requires us to use paddles) and twenty-two-foot sweepboat (steered by long, rudder-like oars fore and aft, modification of nineteenth-century Ohio River flatboats). Sweeps used here on scows years ago; although our version mainly for supplies, P and I will take it today to get sense of how such things rudder through big rapids. Like its predecessors, it's unwieldy and at risk between rock slots and tough to coax out of slack water (so we hear).

Under way into the big Seldom Seen, and soon into rapids — Killum (too mild today to deserve name) and Gun Barrel *(shoot through)*. Near Legend Creek take break under cliff and climb a ways to see wall of orange-red pictographs of two mounted men and several dots and arrows. P says haltingly, "Let's see, yes, yes, aha! 'Two horsemen four days away — on warpath.' Oh, excuse me, we're not supposed to know how to read these things yet." First people in canyon about eight thousand years ago, although figures here, as horses prove, no more than c. three hundred years old, yet, finger marks in iron-oxide paint clear as if drawn last week. What did scribe think of the gorge? What is this red message? A river song?

Roll on until reach rivulet pouring hard and clear into the Salmon; no beaver dams higher up, so send man to fill jugs; assume it's giardia-free; better be — we're not purifying water, and this no place for illness. Deep canyon only about hundred yards wide now, river less than half that; hotter, drier north slopes *(facing south)* have ponderosa; cooler, moister south side with firs; area never seriously logged, no clearcuts visible. Along steep cliffs mountain goats move as if aerial creatures; wonder they haven't evolved wings. Move through two slackwaters so slowly tiger swallowtails alight on shoulders, heads — burly Photog looks to be wearing yellow bow. In faster water, dragonflies whip up and stop cold atop us for little ride; makes me feel welcome. River wordless but not silent like infant who hasn't learned to speak. P: "Is there anything else in inanimate nature so companionable as a river?" Ask that when we head into the Slide.

Now on our starboard is Pacific time zone although we won't really enter it for another five or six days. Sit back in easy water and feel pull of ocean, one of finest sensations I've known on voyage. On the Missouri we moved always with sense "this could be our final mile," but not here, not with certainty of gravity at our backs and promise of at least four more months of open water once we leave the Salmon. Now we measure days not by miles but by next big rapid or degree of shadow in deep gorge; dusk and dawn here seem to last for hours and midday but a moment. Life in a narrow realm.

Stop at pleasant beach of white quartz sand by mouth of Little Squaw Creek. Set up tents, bull snake crawls from under logs, examine it, release it; pour out half cup of Old Mister Easy Life; supper, no mosquitoes; sit listening to newcomers tell what's been happening in cities; lie back on warm sand to watch starlight slip down the deep night, count meteors.

*Overhear passionate P in discussion: "Of course William Carlos Wil-
liams could have written 'The mind can never be satisfied,' but there's no
poetry in that. The poetry is in what you call 'wordy': 'It can never be
satisfied, the mind, never.' Don't you hear the difference? I'll bet you're a
Republican." Steady, I say. Photog quiets things by announcing his favorite song is "Celery Stalks at Midnight." Then he says, "Did anybody ever
hear the Toad Suck Symphony play? They're very good." Last thing I
remember is meteor number five and the way long river trips quite knock
one off one's chump.*

SATURDAY, DAY FIVE

During summer, six thousand people go down "Main" Salmon, but
we've seen only dozen or so. Permit system works well and so do regulations that make campsites seem almost pristine: except for useless notions,
we carry out everything we bring in, from ashes to dejecta; we do not
bathe with soap in river; even drag a branch over footprints when we
leave. Gorge nearly free of floating detritus, including elsewhere-omni-
present Styrofoam; also cattleless. BB says wherever number of cattle
goes up, big game goes down — guaranteed. Photog, inventing: "I hereby
found upon this spot HABITAT — Hunters Against Bovines in the American Timberlands." We are in area where USFWS reintroduced gray
wolves a few months ago; much grumbling in Lemhi Valley about it and
praise for rancher who illegally plugged a wolf; mantra there is "Shoot,
shovel, shut up." Yet we saw time and again certain favored painting of
wolf approaching its quarry and entitled Woe the Prey! Mythic fascination with what they otherwise kill and hide.

Onto river under continued excellent skies — how long can such perfec-
tion hold for us in open rafts? I move to paddleboat, snap on required
helmet; each person slowly matching expectations to vessel proper to fulfill
them; moving over to big sweepboat are those who put too high a price on
exhilaration. Under way, mild water. Stop at hot spring once used by
scowmen; climb rocks to semi-natural cauldron and, six at a time, get in.
Water, although cooled by second spring, at first so hot it's uncomfortable;
men make interesting faces when they feel their ballocks about to be
cooked, surely some atavism to preserve generations. Soak out Atlantic
anxietudes. Photog: "This is the first time you've gotten us into hot water
that I've liked."

Return to cold rapids, standing waves we can paddle through, wetted but not thrown; then Bailey Rapids where sweepboat cannot set up in time and gets pulled through sideways. Little oarsman pitched down, struggles to feet only to catch wildly swinging rudder across jaw that puts him down again; rises slowly, gamely, automatically, and grabs control as boat emerges; terribly close call. Worst part of watching friends go through bad rapids is being helpless to prevent accident. Soon after, we pull up at narrow sand ledge for night, supper of grilled chicken, rice, salad, stories. Cap Harry Guleke, a century ago one of first to descend river and perhaps greatest of Salmon scowmen — his motto, "Until a man is afraid, he'll be all right" — went downstream to assist injured person and returned some weeks later. Asked how things went, he said, "Done what I could for him." What was that? "Buried him." We're a hundred miles down the No Return.

SUNDAY, DAY SIX

Before breakfast seven of us hike toward rumor of fine waterfall. Route goes up edge of forested canyon, trail only eight inches wide; no place for misstep; one fellow turns back, but seventy-eight-year-old V— [of the Doctor Robert] continues but can't keep pace. Bringing up rear, I find him standing dazed, stung by hornets when he stumbled against ground nest; lumps on forehead, neck; says he'll pause and maybe return to camp; I go on; way gets worse in boulder field with rocks size of haycocks. Hear yell from behind; go back to find V— has taken tumble; bleeding but determined to see alleged waterfall; wait with him then on we go, up big rocks, using hands to climb; rumor turns to splendid cataract of three drops into pools. Our other hikers there. In 4,500 miles we've had no accidents until we became thirteen people; feel I'd overstep myself were I to set down guidelines, but what if I don't? I say only to stay together on return. They don't.

Stop to watch moose; hear birdsong somewhere above, telltale notes. Can it be at last? The one I want to see most? Scan ponderosa with binocs — yes! Most brilliantly colored western songbird — western tanager! M. Lewis first to describe it, coincidentally, one he saw not far north of here. More participatory history.

Return to camp, breakfast of eggs and asparagus that horrifies Photog whose culinary acme is mashed potatoes. Set out into day promising to be continual rapids, including Big Mallard, second only to the Slide in threat. High water turns lesser ones into jolly rollers that merely drench; "coxswain" calls to paddlers "Right!" or "Left!" to align raft for drops. Above Big Mallard, pull ashore to dispatch Photog and J[ohn]B for photos of our passage. Give them time to climb high bank, then we push off. Hear roaring around bend; noise with unseen cause more alarming than when source evident; finally see rapids ahead. Oh no, view is worse: two great rocks to shoot between, wall of water, river gone vertical, battling stone for dominance; we're innocents wanting only passage. Uneasy chattering, then we fall dead silent, adjust helmets, boatman tries to align with slot, paddlers ready for commands, current locks on, tension of commitment, into standing wave, up, pause, ahead black hole, worst I've seen, all around water confounded, down the bejeezis we go into thundering pit, spines slammed, necks whipped back, center of maelstrom, raft twisting, contorting, waiting for kick-out, only sound of roaring water, then up, charging forward again into daylight. Saved! Oh god! Into another vortex that holds water higher than sides of boat. Raft more vertical than I thought possible, down again, ditto, ditto, ditto, then onto tailwaters, emergence, sunshine, alive. Eventually, P: "That, friends, is one reason the Northwest Passage is a fiction." Pause to watch sweep come through — logbook aboard — down, up, and out, once more safely; away from rapids they look like kiddie play. Ashore to pick up Photog and JB, but they don't appear. Impatient member grumbles about waiting: "Let the oarboat take them." Thinking of my indecision of morning and injuries, I say we're not moving until they turn up. Muttering. Finally I get out and start up bank of jeopardous boulders treacherous as rapids in front of them; could snap leg clean off in here. Men nowhere to be seen. Return to boat — not there either. Waiting. "We're wasting time!" P speaks for me: "So would you waste a life?" Back over rocky shore. See glint off helmet, go toward it. JB sitting blankly, not speaking, ashen. Photog says JB fell headfirst down bouldered bank. Ask: Can you wiggle your fingers? Does so. Raise your arm? Does. Stand? No answer. What's your name? What year is it? Who's President? Slow answers. Down to cold river to soak my shirt and wrap around his head and neck; begins to revive, talks sentences, lifts legs. Stay here. Return to raft and two of us cordelle it upstream, terrible task over rocks, current against us; put JB aboard; he's considerably unnerved. On downriver to shady lunch stop; he revives further and goes into talking jag; calms slowly. Who would have thought walking around Big Mallard would be more dangerous than rafting through it? What if he hadn't been wearing helmet? Dead probably. Someone: "How long would it take to get a guy out of here?" Another: "In this place, he who dies slowest has the best chance." P: "Enough!"

Again to river: onward, downward, seaward. Elkhorn Rapids almost equal to Big Mallard; on farther, high water turns Growler into purring rollers. At Ruff Creek pull up for night on another fine, if narrow, sand strip where we swim until 65-degree water too much; strike out against current to see what it's like — I manage only to stay in place. After much paddlework today, P says, "I feel my hands turning to fins." Supper is trout we carried in; two anglers have caught only three squawfish and one old tire, probably from abandoned mining camp. As stars appear, I tell an intimate story to my friend who worries about his memory, then say, Forget it now. He: "Easily done." Made only nine miles today.

MONDAY, DAY SEVEN

Years ago old cargoman took big wooden scow down the Salmon. One rapids after another tore it up, forcing him to cannibalize it for repairs; by time he reached Riggins he was in boat "without hardly room for his butt." Day uneventful although we stop often, once at gold mine abandoned sixty years ago but recently bought by jerk who hauled bulldozer to his pocket of private land within Wild & Scenic segment and began tearing things up, threatening to subdivide acres, all with idea he could scare government into buying him out; feds ignored him, and now dozer sits rusting, trapped by River of No Return. Reach Mackay Bar and old ranch, now lodge served by pocket airstrip; a few of us rent house there; showers, beverages on porch where P says, "That last rapids we'll face, it keeps turning up in odd corners of my mind. A while ago the part of my brain that helps me dress found the Slide under a clean shirt." Yes, I confess too, I got a glimpse of it behind the bathroom mirror. "What's happening to us?"

TUESDAY, DAY EIGHT

Morning. Someone calls into room, "Did you know Nikawa spelled backwards is Awakin?" Throw boot. River full of long backeddies we enter to wait until sweepboat comes along; currents gently haul us up-

stream right next to the hard charge down of main river; weird sensation, seems impossible. Metamorphosed canyon walls cooked brown by ancient subterranean fires; a few stands of Pacific yew (Taxol), more ponderosa. Along north bank is Gospel Hump Wilderness. P: "What's a gospel hump?" Somebody: "Ask one of those de-churched evangelists." Rapids mild, helmsman lets me steer paddleboat through. Pleasure of white water lies in its navigation; otherwise it's theme-park ride — almost. Dried Meat Rapids our oarsman calls Dead Meat because five people drowned here thirty years ago, including helmsman named Lucky; but for us Wet Meat is more accurate. Hot day produces water fight. After twenty quiet miles, we make camp on triple terrace beach at Johnson Creek; take nippy swim. Around evening campfire — our fire in large metal pan so we don't mark sand — our baker's dozen, on last night together, bestow on me Trogdon Memorial Peckerwood Award (unspecified whether for conduct or frequent use of term); trophy is driftwood remarkably like Lewis's woodpecker (jokes about that and Clark's nutcracker); all sign it; lucky they didn't find one shaped like posterior of horse. Night so lovely we sleep outside tents, under rotation of stars, beneath clock of heavens; all around small conversations dying out slowly like embers until only river speaks, and I remember old riddle-song:

> You passers-by
> who share my journey,
> you move and change,
> I move and am the same;
> you move and are gone,
> I move and remain.

WEDNESDAY, DAY NINE

Pack for departures; quickly under way and soon out of Wild & Scenic portion. Only five miles to our point of separation but way is hearty rapids, fitting farewells to those leaving; soak all peckerwoods down. Arrive Carey Creek at head of west-end road; reorganize gear and four of us move to another oarboat, this one fitted with small outboard motor for run from here to Clarkston. Goodbyes.

Four of us, plus BB at helm, continue on; pass accurately named Fall Creek — drops five thousand feet in five miles — now that's a wet elevator. An hour out, the Salmon deepens and slows enough to use ten-horse motor for first time, and we putt through warm afternoon, country much more open, vast treeless hills, no longer gorge but valley, gravel road again alongside, a few dwellings, great wilderness behind. We all feel a letdown, especially when we pass island some screw-you-world guy keeps sheep on in winter; when spring rise comes, it flushes manure — E. coli and giardia — right on downstream; such poisoning still permitted. Past Music Bar, name having nothing to do with harmonics; rather, years ago German miner Fritz Music lived near; so fearful of serpents he walked the seven miles to town with metal stovepipes clanking around his legs. Explain to P how snake is ancient Indian symbol for river.

Water makes sweeping curve toward little Riggins atop steep and high bank; find rooms, showers, and supper where BB says, "We had one old raft we'd pump up in the morning to get it going, pump it again at lunch to keep it going, pump it at bedtime to keep it from sinking." P: "There's my life in a sentence."

THURSDAY, DAY TEN

From Riggins, the Salmon runs about fifty miles north before making broad loop topped by six-mile horseshoe, then continues due south to confluence with Snake River. Photog asks will we meet the Slide today, and BB: "Don't rush it. Give it time to drop." Every hour should help. Photog: "I just want it over with." If we rush it, that's exactly what could happen. Below Riggins, pass under "Time Zone Bridge" and enter Pacific clock; small cheer goes up. Water easy although many jolly rollers; to starboard for about thirty miles runs U.S. 95; people wave from car; reminds me of I-90 along Erie Canal — seems I've lived many lives since then. On the Salmon I descend like Cleopatra in her barge; sit royally atop baggage which I fashion into soft throne; or, in slack water, sometimes stretch out on locker box; take notes, pictures, speak little, just delight in such happy pace down miles toward ocean. From shore, oyster plants releasing parachute seeds, and in places on hills hackberry and mountain mahogany, but also invasive yellow-star thistle, exotic taking over whole slopes through root inhibitor lethal to other plants; nasty spines prevent even cattle from eating it.

Snack at Hammer Creek; 92 degrees; on again; river sloshes us cool at right intervals as if it knows our need. Rollercoaster Rapids leave us laughing. Into Green Canyon, first of four splendid gorges — Cougar,

Snow Hole, Blue — each one successively more austere and magnificent,
fuliginous stone having tinges of color; grand gifts of gravity-driven water.
Into Demon's Drop, curling waves and good pounding, then series of
rapids with names better than their challenge, at least in high water:
Lorna's Lulu, Lower Bunghole (where else?), Bodacious Bounce (espe-
cially if you don't hit it right), Half-and-Half (half the time you make it),
Gobbler (eats your lunch). But Snow Hole is different, partly because
motor quits twice on approach and BB has to grab oars at last second;
sharp drop, huge boulders, deep pit. Holey rollers help interrupt miles —
could have used a few on the Missouri. Stop at long sandbar to unkink
legs; near here, Chief Joseph and Nez Perce in 1877 crossed as cavalry
chased them north, conflict that eventually led him to utter perhaps most
famous of Indian sentences: "I will fight no more forever." Sudden smash-
ing wind rips down narrow defile like cannonball in gun barrel, blasts us
with blinding sand, then gone as swiftly; a shock of wind. P: "Was that
Chief Joseph or the cavalry?"

Make camp near Skeleton Creek, a name we trust not prognostic; last
night we hope; tomorrow the Slide, only six miles below, perhaps final
block between us and Pacific. Having shed baker's dozen contingent, our
reduced company made seventy-three miles. For future transcontinental
crossers, DoggeRule *of River Road:*

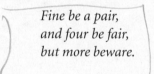

> *Fine be a pair,*
> *and four be fair,*
> *but more beware.*

How
True?

FRIDAY, DAY ELEVEN

Sleep under stars again and rise dewed over; to river to check rock
placed at water line as I've done last few nights; the Salmon dropped a
few more inches; no better morning message. Decamp and enter multiple
but easy moils that get us ready for big one. Blue Canyon is steep black
walls free of vegetation; stretches out cold and lonely, lovely like beautiful
corpse. Listening for the Slide to announce itself.

BB unusually quiet except to say twenty thousand cubic feet per second
of water passing through will send us back upriver to wait it out; do we
have enough food? Sheer walls prevent portaging or lining raft down.
Nobody shoots hard rapids flawlessly every time, yet we trust in our

craftsman-raftsman. Slide lies only three miles from very end of the Salmon — theatrical suspense; drama increases as we hear it, hidden around bend, echo up canyon; hear it even better when motor abruptly quits again just above thundering. BB rushes forward to oars, nearly sending me overboard, his pell-mell revealing what his wordless calm covers. He strokes hard to pull into backwater. Tie up so he can clamber over boulders to scout passage. As he loops line around rock, I ask, Did you kill that motor to make good drama? No. He gives smile that, were it any grimmer, would be a scowl. What if motor quits when we enter? "That would be drama." *Can't believe timing — the luck, she is still running good?*

The Slide a result of collapsing canyon wall forty years ago constricting river to about half its width — now a fire hose trying to shoot through keyhole. Does good job of standing river on end. Unnoticed, P and I climb high above to see rapids and observe BB who studies a long time, turns away only to come back; studies more; starts toward raft, stops, returns again. I say, It's that third look that bothers me. P: "More drama?" *Don't think so, I'm sorry to say.*

At boat we wait for bad news. BB: "In low water you can run plumb through, but this is the highest I've ever known it, about seventeen thousand cfs." *A couple hundred cfs in this channel would float canoe. And?* "Just low enough to give it a try." *A try? I think, A try is something where alternative to failure isn't death. Photog to BB:* "Are you sure about this?" *I answer for him: Let's go.*

Motor still dead — bad word. Oar into center of river, negotiate for position, get set as current locks on; decision made like parachutist's first step out of plane; rapids of no return; lying behind us now only our deeds done, and ahead maybe nothing more than Judgment Day. To myself: Too-nuts! Raft begins to shimmy, standing waves hump it, violate it; coming on fast white dread of water bashing hell out of boulders, working to grind them down and unconstrict passage; rivers eat mountains, not vice versa. Sucked forward fast, barely miss nasty flipper wave, bump and bounce; pitch, yaw, and roll at same time, then skim easily onto tailwaters; we're barely dampened. BB's cautiously masterful steering is perfect except for negating ten days of expectations and chance for dramatics. Feel like one who just died in sleep and wakes on other side: "That was it? That's what I dwelt on for a lifetime?" *P oxymoronically:* "That's the happiest letdown I ever had."

BB sends me to oars while he tinkers with motor. On to Sluicebox, Checkerboard, and Eye of Needle; I head smack into centers, drenching us, "wahooing it," as BB says; just trying to bid proper farewell to River of No Return. He glances up, says casually, "That green ridge ahead is Oregon." Sentence overwhelms me. Oregon? I remember shouting to workman at Third Avenue Bridge on Harlem River, We're bound for Oregon! Now it's there, it's there, we are goddamn-the-hell there! Between us and Pacific only two more rivers, fully navigable; no Snow Imperatives. We're alive and we're down-bound.

XI

THE SNAKE RIVER

NEAR RIGGINS, IDAHO

ICONOGRAM XI

[On the Snake River] Ice Harbor Dam was finished in 1962, Lower Monumental in 1970, Little Goose in 1970, and Lower Granite in 1975. Hydroelectric generators produce 1,305 average megawatts — enough for Seattle. Though navigation was the impetus for the project with power being incidental, hydroelectricity provides ninety-six percent of the benefits, navigation two percent. Construction of Lower Granite alone cost $370 million; annual operations require $14 million. No one has analyzed actual benefits and costs since the projects were built. "We don't sit around and worry about that anymore," says "Dug" Dugger, public affairs director for the Army Corps of Engineers in Walla Walla.

Even though laws mandate mitigation for lost habitat, little has been done to replace the 140 miles of river, 14,400 acres, and forty-eight islands. . . . What would real mitigation entail? Private riparian lands that would otherwise be developed could be bought. Overgrazed riparian acreage could be acquired for wildlife. Obsolete dams could be removed. Flood-prone development could be cleared instead of using disaster relief funds to rebuild on the floodplain. Wetlands could be acquired and levees removed. Water rights could be bought for instream flows. The Army Corps of Engineers is barred by law from doing most of these things. Much *could* be done, but almost nothing *is* being done, not because biologists lack the will or competence but because riparian values are not recognized in the political system.

Tim Palmer

The Snake River: Window to the West, 1991

My Hermaphroditic Quest

BECAUSE OF the river canyon, we could not discern from below that we were leaving the Rockies, nor could we see how the Blue Mountains to westward descend toward the Snake as an outwash slope opening to the great Columbia Plateau — an open and arid country of cindery hills and basalt exposures cooked up in volcanic kettles and pitched across the miles only to be heated again by the sun day in and day out in the shadeless land. The mountains still ahead of us, the Cascades and the Coast Range, lie sundered by the Columbia River and its engineers and their dammed and locked pools, a route we expected *Nikawa* to run easily after our arrival in Clarkston, Washington.

From the mouth of the Salmon, the Snake River rattles over a few rapids hardly more than riffles until it broadens and deepens enough to lure weekend boats of high gloss and power. Their slickly swimsuited occupants stared at our beat-up raft and the motley and disheveled band within as if we were poorlings wandering into a debutante cotillion. On both sides of the river above its rocky shorelines, treeless hills rose from layers of ancient magma stratified into terraces, and where there was sufficient soil, grasses, yellowed by July, topped out the slopes. The green realms east of the Rockies were gone, and we descended through a country of golden midsummer. Idaho was still on our starboard, but now, to the west for a dozen miles, lay Oregon, succeeded by Washington; two hundred miles farther we would loop back to the Beaver State.

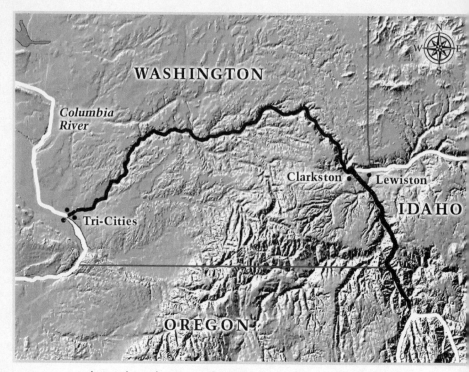

The Snake, Salmon Confluence to Tri-Cities, 190 river miles

Along the east bank, under low hills hunched as if ready to shrug, were a number of vacation homes, nearly all new places that our isolation in the wilds made appear inimical encroachments on a cleanly open land. We felt like Indians of another century as they watched log cabins go up beside their paths, in their old campgrounds, next to their springs, and we went down the river in silence, resigned toward features we could view only as temporary inevitabilities; such is one result of living, even for a few days, in an unsullied billion-and-a-half-year-old canyon. I found it difficult to see myself as other than floating ephemera, and I believed the images and words I was gathering were headed for the same place as the red pictographs of Legend Creek — eventual erasure. Yet, of the times in my life I must count as wasted, squandered, spent aimlessly, I knew our river days would never be among them because, ephemeral as they too were, the river had done what it could to make them memorable enough to carry forward to the end. I floated along contentedly. Brevity does not make life meaningless, but forgetting does. Of the gifts of the rivers, none was greater than their making our time upon them indelible, or nearly as indelible as the old pictographs.

On the fringe of settlement by Heller Bar — a sand spit, not a tavern — we pulled ashore for lunch at a riverview café. The table of food we ordered up reminded us that civilization and its discontents were also not without their contentments, and of some of those we partook roundly. There we came upon four middle-aged men swimming 450 miles from Redfish Lake in central Idaho to Lower Granite Dam, to dramatize what sockeye and chinook smolts face as they try to descend from their hatching in the mountains to the Pacific, a nine-hundred-mile journey that federal hydroelectric dams have turned into a virtual suicide run. Each of the eight massive dams on the lower Salmon and Columbia rivers kills about ten percent of the fingerlings. The year before, only a single adult male sockeye, called Lonely Larry, returned to the lake, even though its route was once so full of redfish and chinooks that riders had to scare back the plunging salmon to get horses to ford a stream. Our raftsman said the last good spawning run he saw was in 1973: "It just isn't pleasant to be a witness to a disappearance like that." Some time later, I came across an 1882 issue of *Harper's Magazine:* "[The salmon] is indeed a noble fish, and if means are taken to prevent the diminution of the run, will prove a source of wealth for many years to come."

One of the swimmers, whom the media called "the Sal-men," said, "We're doing a crazy thing to get the word out that there are some insane things going on with the Corps of Engineers and their dams. We want to save our river, and we want to save its fish. Without question, there are problems with ranching, logging, and mining, but that's not what's killing most of the fish. The salmon were thick all through here until the dams started closing. We want those dams operated to assist the seasonal migration of fish, and we want people to know that the aluminum industry and power authorities are influencing Idaho politicians to say that saving salmon will cost jobs. It's untrue. Salmon bring money with them."

Each swimmer had managed the rapids by wearing a wet suit over a dry suit, neoprene boots, gloves, neck cowl, helmet, goggles, shin guards, hip pads, shoulder pads, and flippers as he clung to a kickboard. Even with such protection, their descent of the "Big-fish-water" made a voyage by raft seem cheating, and I said so. Pilotis: "Call me a sissy, but I'm not swimming from here to the sea — *that* you do alone." We watched as one of the Sal-men took up his relay in the down-bound river; although he left only fifteen minutes ahead of us, it was almost an hour before our motored raft overtook him. When we passed, I stood and gave my old naval salute.

I regained some perspective on the varieties of river passage when we crossed the wake of a jet-boat bus, coiffed and cleanly dressed tourists seated next to a banner, RIVER ADVENTURES! As we neared the twin towns, we floated into a swarm of ripping water scooters and bikinied speedboats that gave further perspective. In the late afternoon heat we pulled up on the Washington shore at Clarkston (formerly Jawbone Flats), deflated the raft, rolled it up, and packed it onto a trailer, then went off to find a couple of rooms overlooking the Snake. We showered and crossed the bridge to Lewiston (formerly Ragtown), a historic center of brick and stone more pleasing than the one on the other side, and took dinner in a place of some elegance, the food less so. I started off at the bar so I could make entries in my logbook undisturbed, but I drew the attention of two psychologists, a couple who referred to my scribbling as "writing behavior." Her eyelashes, genuine ones, nearly dipped into her cocktail when she put it to her lips, and he had a black mustache that could have, were it attached to a handle, swept a floor. The wife was working to calm herself after visiting her father recovering from a stroke. Said the husband when she went to the women's room: "Papa's taking it hard. He was a soft-drink distributor for years, in good health except for the cigarettes. He told us today he was just an old, broken-down pop machine and we should hang a sign on him like they do: OUT OF ORDER, SORRY."

The wife returned, and the husband said, "You okay?" She: "Sort of. Sort of not." He to me: "Clinical lingo." Then, as he put his arm around her: "We have a wonderful permeability — we seep into each other — tears, hopes, lives." I nodded, and he asked about me, and I said the Snake River and I were doing a little co-permeating just now, and gave a précis of the voyage. Glancing again at my logbook, she said, "Are you illegible?" I said my boatmates read me about as well as they did my handwriting. "No, no," she said, enunciating. "Are you il-eligible?" For what? "Oh, good god! Are you married?" Sort of not,

I said. In full certainty she said, "When a man takes to the road, even if it's a river, he's running away, but when a woman takes off, she's looking for something." I said I was running away from looking for something. She considered, then leaned over to tap my logbook and whisper, "Here's a title for your journaling: *Crossing Waters: A Hermaphroditic Quest.*" Does that mean, I said, you don't like *That Dang River?*

Kissing a Triding Keepsake

THE PHOTOGRAPHER, in fine yeomanly manner, returned on the truck hauling the deflated raft back to the Lemhi Valley where he hitched our tow wagon to *Nikawa* and trailered her up along the Bitterroots, across Lolo Pass, and down the narrow defiles of the Lochsa and Clearwater rivers to the Snake, his route similar to the one Lewis and Clark used to avoid the Salmon gorge. During his absence, I prepared for our last two waters by gathering what materials I could, trying to learn whether the way was truly as open as it appeared. Twice Pilotis and I walked to Wasem's drugstore in Clarkston, drawn not by the addled slogan stuck to a window (SOVEREIGNTY FOREVER — U.N. RULE NEVER) but to the soda fountain that let me answer a desperate lack of ice cream sodas with an excellent pair while Pilotis ate a slice of huckleberry cheesecake pie and one of peach cream, the latter tasting like 1949, not in freshness but in that distinctive way gustatory memory can summon up the past.

On the third afternoon in Clarkston, once we'd prepared the engines, idle since middle Montana, we stopped at a filling station to fuel *Nikawa* and then went to the river to launch. I'd not been behind her wheel in four weeks, and taking the helm again felt strange and good, like kissing a long-absent lover. She responded immediately, her motors humming out eagerness, and we set off under a warm but cloudless sky, and the Photographer drove off westward. The Snake below Lewiston is not so much a river as a tail end of the long impoundment behind Lower Granite Dam, so we ran smartly, and I tried to control a growing notion that we had nothing ahead but easiness. The main mechanism checking such overconfidence was a little burr of a thought resident in phrases like "And we almost made it" or "Well, we came close." As a marathon runner knows, it's one thing for a long race to fail in its early miles, but quite another to fall just shy of the finish. I realized that still before us there were likely even more potential coups de grâce than the Photographer could dream up. Yet, that day *Nikawa* and I hummed along in a heretofore unexperienced ataraxia that even certain reaches where the wind got a hard run at the water could not dispel.

The Snake is one of only five rivers of more than a thousand miles entirely within the contiguous states, but we would see just a fifth of it as we descended to its union with the Columbia. Of those five rivers, the Snake is unique in that once it leaves its natal territory in the Yellowstone basin, only sixty miles from the true headwaters of the Missouri, it traverses desert. Any water flowing through such extensive aridity is going to get dammed, and the Snake suffers from twenty of them. The lower four are huge things with locks, although as far as we could testify, commercial navigation on the upper Snake right then was as scarce as on the lower Missouri. Despite other pretexts, those dams exist largely to employ the Corps of Engineers and make big corporate money selling power to citizens as far away as California who simply must have their cans of beef stew opened electrically, their roofs outlined with Christmas lights, and their socks dried by turning a dial to number seven. A bumper sticker I once saw in Oregon: HATE THE DAMS? SQUEEZE YOUR ORANGES BY HAND.

Below the mouth of the Clearwater at Lewiston, we again picked up the wake of the Corps of Discovery, not because we sought it out but because it is the most complete water route to the Pacific. The section of river we skimmed that day was, before impoundment, white water that gave the Expedition fits by smashing canoes, throwing men, sinking the stores. Clark, in this passage representative of several, wrote:

> Examined the rapids which we found more dificuelt to pass than we expected from the Indians information. A Suckcession of Sholes appears to reach from bank to bank for 3 miles which was also intersepted with large rocks Sticking up in every direction, and the chanel through which we must pass crooked and narrow. We only made 20 miles today, owing to the detention in passing rapids &c.

From Clarkston, the Snake westers through generally broad bends along a gentle arc to the Columbia, no longer slowed by rapids but only by four stair-step impoundments, each about thirty miles long.

Unlike the great pools behind the Missouri dams, the less silty Snake has not yet so visibly begun to return to a natural river in its tailwaters. So before us lay merely long, deep "flatwater" troughs that would present not riverine but lacustrine problems, most likely wind, for the blowing season in that vastly open place was fully at hand. Indeed, once we were well under way, the Snake considerably thumped *Nikawa* and forced us to slow and bucket along through water so sun-struck it was like sailing a small sea of fractured mirrors.

The shores rose steeply a few hundred feet into bastions of basalt broken by fallen ramparts of volcanic crust and long ledges weathered into delicate traceries like petticoat hems or coarsely eaten into lacunas and strange shafts, the canyon virtually devoid of anything human but an empty rail line and impounded water. Grasses grew where they could among the dead magma, the stems toasted golden, the stones burned dark like meat held too long to the fire, and for hours we saw, other than water and sky, only grass and rock, the latter here and there stacked on end in long skinny columns as if so many igneous noodles and in other places tumbled into the river like massive granules of brown sugar. It was as culinary a landscape as I ever saw, one that — unless it was my hunger — got me rambling about food and how I longed for an old-fashioned plate of chow mein. Such happens during long hours of water passage. Pilotis extended the empty-fortune-cookie metaphor I'd heard on the Missouri: the year before, my friend finished a meal in a Chinese restaurant with the usual slender slip of prognostication; not long afterward, at a different place, the cookie that night contained precisely the same fortune; a few weeks later, at yet another restaurant, arrived a third cookie, it too containing the exact words. It's great, I said, to get your kismet triply promised — was it on the order of, "You will travel far with a great master of waters"? "Not at all," said Pilotis. "Each time it was 'Someone is kissing your triding keepsake.'"

Thirty-five miles out we reached Lower Granite Dam where we happened upon Rob Pike, the boater-bicyclist, in his swift runabout, waiting to lock through. We wished he were *returning* from the Pacific so that he might give us word about conditions downriver but settled for asking him as he went oceanward to tie warning messages to trees, as Lewis did for Clark. There were in that country, of course, no trees anywhere visible.

The descent in the locks of the Snake-Columbia system is far greater than anything we'd yet faced on the Ohio or the Erie Canal, as much as ten times greater, three of the drops about a hundred feet. More than ever before, *Nikawa* was but an oyster cracker bobbing in the dark soup being drawn down into the valves. Enclosed in the deep concrete casements, her smallness made our venture too seem picayune, a game played by idle kids, for unlike those first captains to come this way, we were after neither empire nor science; we were there simply to experience the empire, learn the science, and report it to those who might not ever make the journey. As Pilotis said on another occasion, perhaps presumptuously, "Our voyage is a kind of fulfillment of their voyage." If so, maybe that was enough to justify for an hour the massive manipulation of river it took to get us down. Once we were free of the lock, Pike jackrabbited away, and I knew he wanted, whatever else, to reach the ocean before us, as well he should — after all, he'd been at it seven years.

We proceeded on through the canyon-torn shores, a river edge that could not decide whether to rise vertically or stretch out horizontally, so it did a little of both beautifully. The wind dropped with the sun and temperature — hence also the waves — and our river horse moved at a merry canter. But I reined her in, why I'm not sure. Perhaps I could feel the voyage coming to an end.

Messing About in Boats

ENTRAL FERRY, WASHINGTON, should be today — were history to catch up with contemporary fact — Central Bridge. The highway span, the first we'd passed under since leaving Clarkston, served as a piloting mark to direct us into a hidden little sidewater harbor on the north bank and a dock for the night. The ranger who oversaw the place asked where we were headed, a common question but one with an answer no longer interesting; now a better query was where we were coming from. We answered both, but he, a wide-shouldered, slender-hipped man who cast a triangular shadow, cared only about destination, as if bored by multitudes of voyagers from New York Harbor stopping over. He gave such a disquisition on the perils of trying to cross the bar at the mouth of the Columbia River that the Photographer again grew uneasy. I listened, perhaps too nonchalantly, although I was only practicing my belief that fearlessness is contagious, or, perhaps more accurately in this instance, semi-fearlessness is semi-contagious.

I knew the mouth of the Columbia is, by wide consensus, the third most dangerous confluence of river and ocean in the world, a place mariners call the Graveyard of the Pacific. I reminded the hands that we no longer had a calendar working against us, and we could afford to wait for good weather and boatable water when our approach into the ocean arrived, but I carelessly said, Too much caution can stop us dead. The retort: "And so can too little."

The ranger talked about something else that concerned me far more — wind. Two days earlier a bad blow had come through with gusts he estimated at 125 miles an hour. I discounted that figure by a third, yet it still would have been enough to lay low a small craft like *Nikawa,* particularly when blasts get channeled up the gorge against the river current to become two flailing fists smacking into each other. Other than losing my logbook to the water, I most feared wind. When not itself a direct threat, it lay behind almost all the nasty moments we'd encountered, and now we'd come into one of the blowiest places in America during a season of winds.

The next morning we moved out in yet more fine conditions, good water and sky, but by afternoon it had become, in William Clark's inventive orthography, "a verry worm day." Other than brief squalls, we'd been spared nasty weather since South Dakota. That streak surely couldn't continue, but somehow I believed it would. Pessimism and negativism are cankers in the soul of long-distance voyagers, and continuance of journeys owes about as much to blind faith as realistic assessment — at least that is my interpretation, drawn from reading many travelers' accounts, including those of Columbus.

Shortly after noon we reached Little Goose Dam, named for an island now inundated. The Snake today is poor in islands as if it were a forest without streams, a prairie without ponds. The lock, we got told over the radio, would not open for nearly three hours, and I was unable to interest the voice in our crossing, so we found a safe landing and went ashore to look at the long fish ladder that allows adult salmon (and other species) returning from the sea to reach spawning grounds but is almost useless to down-bound smolts, partly because the little ones head for the ocean tail-first.

We talked to a Corps of Engineers employee who asked the question the way we now liked to answer it, and we told her where we'd started from. Deciding we weren't lying, she tried to guess a possible route, became more interested, then said, "Maybe we can help you," and went to a phone and called someone who called someone who called someone, and finally she said, "Get your itsy-bitsy boat in position. You're going through." The lockman, the one who had cut me off on the radio, grudged himself toward the control house to fill the chamber. In excellence, he manifested the swiftness of a mollusk, the leanness of a possum, and the smile of a badger. To him, *Nikawa* expressed everything that was wrong with his job, and were it possible to suck her down the giant drains of the lock and flush her seaward like a turd, he would have done so. Said Pilotis, "Our little cruiser just doesn't have much command bearing." True, I said, unless you know her history.

On we went, past occasional orchards in the broadening valley bottom, past the mouth of the Palouse River and its marvelous cataract a few miles north, past Skookum Canyon. We were twenty-five miles from any place one might call a town, and we saw no other small boats and only one tow. By holding to a steady speed, we had a chance of reaching Lower Monumental Dam for the next scheduled opening; while we understood the efficiency in assigning times for locking through, an open-on-request system gave more freedom. Even though the big federal dams of the lower Snake fascinated me and the challenge of their locks enlivened our passage, I can't say I believe them either necessary or ultimately beneficial because their two major purposes, commercial transport and generation of electricity, other means can readily provide. It is not cheaper to move wheat or timber by barge rather than rail when you figure in the costs of extinction of species and the decimation of salmon fishing, nor is it expedient to haul bauxite from South America to the hydropower-rich Columbia Basin to be turned into pop cans if that means the destruction of native cultures dependent on a naturally abundant river. The damming of rivers today is primitive engineering, like paving highways with flagstones or moving ocean vessels with paddlewheels, and our time has seen that gothic management reach its zenith. Despite the dams of the lower Snake being only twenty to thirty years old, I thought of them as cabooses, things at the end of their era. To someone who might counter, "But they let you get down the Snake River," I would say, They let us get down the Snake faster and easier, but it was not speed or ease we were after. We wanted the crossing *itself*, however we found it at the time of our passage. I've never believed speed and ease are conducive to living fully, becoming aware, or deepening memory, a tripod of urges to stabilize and lend meaning to any life.

We passed under the big, isolated upthrust of basalt that gives its name to Lower Monumental Dam, and as we neared the lock Pilotis radioed our standard message: "Lower Monumental, this is *Nikawa*, the boat crossing America, requesting passage through." No answer. Repeat. No answer. Repeat. Keeping a small vessel in position above a lock, especially in high water, is tricky and trying (as the *Doctor Robert* discovered when she lost power on the Ohio and had to be rescued from being swept over Montgomery Dam), so we were always happy to receive quick instructions. Working to check the current by turning *Nikawa* in a tight circle, I said, Norman Numbwit's either asleep up there or thwarting us. We couldn't go to shore and wait because the hour of operation was at hand and no lockman will start the machinery until he sees a boat in position, but after thirty minutes I headed for the nearest landing. Immediately the radio crackled alive, and the tender ordered us to get ready and alleged we had not been receiving his transmissions. Pilotis: "I think that last lockman had a little chat with him."

When open, the gates of Lower Monumental hang above like massive guillotines and on a hot day drip cool relief on any line-handling sailor on a bow. Pilotis liked the dousing. The gate closed, locking *Nikawa* in to lock her down, and we dropped ten stories in fifteen minutes, then headed again for open river.

At last, the engineered barriers between us and the ocean were no more than digits on a hand; we celebrated the number five with a tuck of something from a small, labelless tin that we could identify only as deviled something, but the other food we could recognize: dried cherries and chocolate bars. We were near a place called Windust, not for its weather, accurate though it can be, but for an old ferryman long ago become his name. In that spare and demanding part of southeast Washington, beyond the bending river, a road can run for thirty miles with no more deviance from straightness than you find along the immaculate edge of an engineer's rule, yet because of the broadbacked hills, travelers may not realize they are on a perfect course. Pilotis, never before in the fertile if arid Palouse, watched the smooth, sensuous slopes, fondled them visually, and said, "How would it be to take a tractor into a fallow wheat field and plow in a short poem, a haiku, something writ short but large?" Geograms? Tractoglyphs? "Sky poetry."

The long, enclosed river began opening into something too broad to be a canyon and too steep-sided to be a valley, but it remained treeless, an arboreal vacancy that made it seem yet vaster than it already was, and the afternoon lay across the big pool in such stillness that even the slow and punctilious step of great blue herons seemed quick and careless. We went along, moving the water more than it moved us, a golden glide in full leisure, and for the first time in weeks I sat back to steer with my stockinged feet. Pilotis said, "In *The Wind in the Willows*, Water Rat says to Mole, 'There's nothing — absolutely nothing — half so much worth doing as simply messing about in boats.'" Then, moments later, "Does the ease of downstreaming make you second-guess yourself about refusing to take a jet boat up the River of No Return so you could have cooperated with the flow of the Missouri for halfway across the continent?" No, I said, because those two rivers that so defined our voyage forced us to earn passage — I think it's like rock climbing where the point is to go a difficult way, otherwise ascent is almost meaningless — the object isn't just to get to the top but to get there in such a way you learn the nature of the mountain — I'll bet somebody, if all went flawlessly, could jet boat our route across the country in a quarter of our time, maybe less, but it would be a stunt, or like stock-car racing, going nowhere fast. "Four-lane highways are for passing, not passage."

We waited about an hour in the warm afternoon to be admitted into the relief of the mossy coolness in the lock at Ice Harbor Dam. When we left it behind, evening was upon us, and we slid down the final ten miles of the Snake and into the Columbia, our last river, and turned upstream a couple of leagues to Kennewick and a quiet berth behind Clover Island, a place dredged up from the river bottom, where we helped tow a disabled cruiser to the dock. Nearby we found both quarters and supper overlooking the Great River of the West, the one that more than any other has borne Americans to the Pacific. As I sat with a small and satisfying shot of budge, then ate my meal, and later lay abed, I watched the Columbia roll darkly down carrying fish and flotsam, sand and silt, and soon a small boat come from the Atlantic 4,892 miles away. But for a rising wind, all was exceeding well, a bad portent on a river if I ever saw one.

XII

THE COLUMBIA RIVER

NORTHWEST OF ASTORIA, OREGON

ICONOGRAM XII

The Columbia is our twentieth-century river. Its dams represent the optimistic faith in technology of the century's beginning, and the restless misgivings about large-scale engineering at the century's end. It is the river of the turbine, dynamo, the reactor, and airplane. It is the river of Tom Swift, Franklin D. Roosevelt, *Popular Mechanics,* and Nagasaki. In the first three decades after World War II, major dams were completed in the Columbia Basin at a pace faster than one per year. It is a river so transformed as seemingly invented. If you want to see how America dreamed at the height of the American Century, come to the Columbia.

William Dietrich
Northwest Passage, 1995

The Far Side of
the River Cocytus

HAD WE NOT BEEN so lucky as to have a Coast Guard station next to our dock at Clover Island, we might have been spared what lay ahead, the kind of encounter that teaches one the nature of a river as climbing a rockface does a mountain — so my words would come back to me. While I filled the fuel tanks on *Nikawa*, I asked the Photographer to step next door and get a reliable weather forecast from the Guard. The wind of the night before persisted into the grum and unpleasant morning, and I thought it a good time to lay over, take a nap, try to find an interesting dinner, read something other than charts; after all, we were only a little more than three hundred miles from the ocean, a run we surely could make on the navigable Columbia in three or four days. Those numbers got me thinking of destination rather than of daily navigation and caused me to neglect other figures. The Photographer had been many days absent from his wife, and I should have considered his urge to get the tow wagon and trailer to Astoria, Oregon, where I planned to put *Nikawa* aboard it for the haul back to Missouri once the voyage was over; the quicker we finished, the sooner he could see her; perhaps that colored his report. Men who keep bachelor's table forget such things and can believe everybody else lives in independence.

So, when the Photographer returned with an inexplicably rosy forecast — winds about fifteen miles an hour, waves to three feet — I thought, What the hell, *Nikawa* can handle those numbers, and found myself happy to trade repose for a batch of river miles. When we set

The Columbia, Tri-Cities to Hood River, 155 river miles

out under a gray sky, I checked the time and discovered it was more than an hour later than I thought; because wind tends to increase as day progresses, we had lost what little morning calm there was. The first four miles gave us only chop, but once we passed below the mouth of the Snake where the Columbia widens to two miles across in an impoundment called Lake Wallula, "many waters," the river began showing one of its natures.

Pilotis was unwell that morning, quite off the mark and fearful of a recurring "fouled gyroscope in the inner ear"; such an onset of vertigo could turn my friend into a lump of flesh incapable of even standing properly. Failing to match that condition with those on the river was my third error of the morning. When we turned south and shifted the wind from athwart our course to one head-on, we saw the currents in a like way directly counter the blowing as the gusts tried to pull the river upright, make it run toward the sky instead of the sea, working to stop it dead as if an Aeolian dam. It was a blast to blow the lights out of heaven.

But the Columbia, driven forward by nearly a thousand miles of itself and an equal length of the Snake, simply got vicious and smashed forward, its passage not to be denied, and let the air batter it open. I'd heard that water spouts occur on Wallula. *Nikawa* began rearing and plunging like a horse confronting an old terror, and she threw wobbly Pilotis. A saddle has a pommel for a terrified rider to grab, but the pilothouse of *Nikawa* had not so much as a nubble. Then she bucked the navigation table into the air and sent dividers, straightedge, pencils, and a smashed cup flying. Suddenly the cabin was full of daggers and razors. As on Lake Erie, the swells were too close together for us to rollercoast, and *Nikawa* could only drive forward, rising, hanging, crashing thunderously into the troughs, poor Pilotis trying to stand and keep eyes fixed on the stable horizon, fighting fear of vertigo while being pitched against the bulkheads. We were dice in a gambler's cup, shaken, rattled, thrown, and the wager was our lives. Trying to brace in the opening of the cuddy, Pilotis was gasping. Breathe slowly! I shouted in the mayhem. Slowly! Mate's ashen face locked on to a beyond that must have looked more like the edge of some hereafter than a horizon. Yelling, Can you secure the table? No answer. It's dangerous like that! No response. Shouting, If I have to give up the helm, I've got to cut power and we're going to get turned broadside! It's going to be hell! A nod. Okay! Here we go! You're not going to like this!

Freed from my grip, the wheel spun wildly, and the river took naked *Nikawa* and wrenched her around to molest her and set her rolling so that to starboard all I saw was trenched river and to port only menacing sky. If the welldeck shipped enough water, we'd founder; if the motors drowned out, we'd be less than a broken-winged duck. I got pitched down, my arms now bleeding like Pilotis's, and from my knees I worked to secure the table and grab up loose objects and stow them, all the while getting clanged from side to side like a bell clapper. When I tried to get to my feet, I saw what a brutal broadside thrashing our helpless steed was taking, and I had no problem imagining the black bottom waiting for us below. I struggled up and made a lunge at the insanely jerking wheel, trying to grab it without breaking my fingers, and then working to wrest control of it from the river. My whole body went into cranking us back to meet the swells head-on, and when I did, Pilotis went down a second time. *Nikawa* climbed, hung, fell, then again, and again. So much water was coming across the windows, I could see little of the shore even when we crested. Those waves were hoodlums bent on kicking in the ribs of a flattened victim, and each shattering impact was a shout of worse to come.

I yelled, We've got to get off this bastard river! Pilotis stood unresponsive. You've got to read the chart! Nothing. To hell with the vertigo, pick up the goddamn chart! Nothing. You've got a goddamn choice — dizziness or drowning! Move! You can do it! Slowly bending, thrown down, seizing the chart, clawing back up only to find it impossible to read the thing. Hold the wheel! Give me the chart! But it was hopeless — I might as well have tried to look up a number in a phone book from the back of a Brahma bull. All I could make out was map colors, yellow and white — land and river. In the pounding I'd lost track of where we were, so the chart was useless anyway. I threw it down, wiped at the forward window, tried to make out the shoreline, but it was unbroken, without an inlet anywhere, and I wondered whether I should just head toward the bank and hope to wash up on a shoal. We were making only the slowest headway against wind and waves, so on we plunged, how long I don't know, but I'd guess twenty minutes short of forever.

Finally I yelled, What the hell is that off to starboard, about two o'clock? Pilotis turned slowly to follow the horizon around but said nothing. I yelled, We're down to hope and luck! I crashed out a course toward what seemed an opening. As we closed the distance I could see that it indeed was a small inlet, the kind of place that eats motor stems, but I was willing to trade them for our lives. It would be better for us to say tomorrow, "We almost made it," than for some undertaker to announce it a week later. We got hammered into the cove, a long crescent of quieting water, and made for the far shore.

Then I said, without having to shout, We're the hell okay. Pilotis nodded. That's when I saw a line of dancing water. In the seconds it took for me to remember such motion means trouble, my pull on the throttles was too late, and *Nikawa* coasted onto a rocky shoal, props dragging, hull scraping, noises only slightly better than the splintering crashes of moments earlier. For a minute I was even relieved to draw gravel — from that we at least could walk away.

Pilotis spoke: "Those stones make the sweetest music I ever heard." Indeed, I said, and now we can fiddle our way off them. But there was no prizing free from that reef; neither trying to rock an immobile *Nikawa* nor pushing hard with the poles would loosen her. If you've ever attempted to get a terrified horse to face its terror again, you can imagine how securely she held to that shoal. "Why can't we just wait here till the wind lets up?" When the big dams on the Columbia release water, I said, the impoundments drop so fast you can almost see it — I don't want to be sitting here next week, and that means we've got to go over the side and try to shove her off.

Pilotis didn't move. A debilitating vertigo last happened right after my friend got heaved off a dock into the Atlantic to celebrate a softball game; cold water seemed to cause the problem as readily as violent motion. I couldn't help except to remind Pilotis there was no dizziness yet. I said, If the Corps has opened the gates at McNary, we've got no time to discuss things.

Off came our jeans and over the side we went, deep chill in the feet and belly, hard heaves and shoves, but *Nikawa* would have none of it. I waded atop the narrow reef to size it up and saw it was apparently a relict railroad grade running the length of the inlet, and worse, the rocks seemed to be rising from the water by the minute. I cursed back to the bow; one moment there was too much goddamn river and the next not enough. I guessed we had about fifteen minutes to set *Nikawa* free. We pushed, shoved, groaned, swore, slipped down, and went nowhere.

Then the wind, the coy wind, shifted a little and sent wavelets toward us, under the transom, enough to rock the boat a bit. We watched for a good ripple, let it ride beneath, then shoved mightily, and *Nikawa* edged sternward a few inches. We watched for another wave, pushed, and she moved again, then one more and she slid into float-water, and we scrambled aboard and I fired the engines to keep us from being washed back. Pilotis went to the pulpit rail to watch for obstructions as we headed toward the only possible shore, one that at the moment let the wind hold *Nikawa* against the black-sand beach. The slope was so gradual we had to wade to dry ground, and the trees were only scrubby Russian olives, all of them too far away to be of use as bollards, but Pilotis stumbled across a promising post, and with our longest line we tethered *Nikawa*. We dropped onto the sand as the overcast started to break up, and Hell-Gate-Grinning Pilotis said, "All of that beating didn't stir up any vertigo. If that thrashing didn't cause it, and neither did the cold plunge, then I'm free to do things I used to avoid." One of the gifts of the river, I said, is liberation. "If you survive to use it."

We lay on the beach, and I tried to see the wind against the sky, but it was as invisible as the mind of God. I quoted, "There's nothing — absolutely nothing — half so much worth doing as simply messing about in boats," especially if those boats are on the toy waterways of England. I got up, walked down to the point at the entrance to the cove, and watched the manifestly infelicitous river, still wrecked by the imperium of wind. I couldn't identify any pilot mark to help me figure our position other than we apparently were somewhere on the far side of the River Cocytus.

As I came back around the crescent beach, a darkly pretty thing, I saw a Jeep drive up at the west end and an elderly couple get out. They made no move in our direction. I hiked over, spoke to them, asked where I was. They seemed leery, but he gave an uneasy smile. "This is Hover, or it used to be before McNary Dam flooded it out." He pronounced the name to rhyme with "Dover." "It was just a whistle stop on the old Great Northern. That's the railroad grade you reefed on. Nothing else left except some foundations out there under the water and that pole you're tied to. If there's such a thing as an underwater ghost town, that's where you are."

The couple lived a mile up the long slope, part of the Horse Heaven Hills, an appropriate place for *Nikawa* to find shelter. His shirt, unbuttoned all the way, revealed a long vertical incision running down his bare chest, and he pointed to the fresh sutures. "Triple bypass. Just got home yesterday. I was sitting on the porch, you know, recuperating, eating a sandwich, looking at the river when I saw you come into view. You were really getting beat." She said, "He called me out to watch, and I was so afraid for you, I said, 'God, don't let that little boat sink.'" He nodded. "Then we saw you turn into Hover, and I thought you'd made an even bigger mistake." He looked at me closely. "Did you get a weather report this morning? They were calling for winds of fifteen miles an hour, gusting to forty-five, and swells of three feet building to six." I said, We got half a weather report — the front half. "You got away with a bad move then. Is this your first day on the river?" I said, I think it's our ninety-sixth. "Where in the world could you be coming from that takes ninety-six days? Or are you just lost?"

I explained, and they may have believed me. I asked how long the wind might keep at it. "It can go on like this for a couple of days, but this time of year and coming from that direction, I think it'll play out by sundown." He pointed to the trackless railroad grade, now high and dry. "You can tell they're letting water out down at McNary. Don't get yourself stranded in here, son."

When I returned to the boat, I said to Pilotis, We're caught between a grounding and a drowning in a ghost town called Hover under the Horse Heaven Hills. Pilotis: "Isn't there a poem or at least a good metaphor in there somewhere?" We waded out to push *Nikawa* farther into the dropping cove, and I wondered whether the inlet would run out of water before the day ran out of wind. I said how odd it seemed that, in the midst of our peril, two people sat watching us from on high, the woman praying from Horse Heaven, the man recovering from having just shown the world his heart.

We went back to the sand to warm up, and I said, All we can do now is hover in Hover where we've hove up — take cover in Hover. "No doggerel." So I sang a corrupted version of the World War Two song:

> There'll be blue skies over
> The black beach of Hover
> Tomorrow, just you wait and see.
> There'll be joy and laughter
> And love ever after,
> Tomorrow when *Nikawa*'s free.

Pretending to ignore me, Pilotis said: "If the Columbia is this violent three hundred miles from the third most dangerous river mouth in the world, then what's it going to be like crossing the Bar?"

I didn't say it, but I knew pilots in the so-called Graveyard of the Pacific considered twelve-foot swells calm water. Until that day, I had interpreted the Columbia according to what I'd learned from the deck of a small ship in a gentler season two years earlier, and for several months I'd foreseen our final river as a Sunday cruise. What a happy and beneficial fiction to believe that our last days, could we hold on long enough to reach them, would become easy. My ignorance and miscalculations drove us forward every bit as much as knowledge and planning, for no sane person would work hard only to end up with a fearsome and possibly fatal final drubbing.

We had to move *Nikawa* again, and this time the mooring line reached its bitter end; the next shift would mean anchoring and staying aboard. The day wore on and seemed to wear out the wind, and before sundown we waded in, shoved off, clambered aboard, Pilotis on the bow until we cleared the concrete and steel bones of the ghost town, and we went again onto the river. The water, turned clinquant by the sunset, lay rather than stood. We ran down four miles to cross the Columbia above the Walla Walla River just below the huge, peculiar twin basalt towers called Two Sisters, or Two Captains (I suppose for Lewis and Clark), to a weather-beaten little dock in the shelter of a hump of shore, and tied up near Port Kelly for the night. As we squared away the pilothouse, I noticed red splotches all across the bulkheads. It was dried blood. Pilotis started to wipe it clean. No, I said, leave it.

We were but a dozen miles below the mouth of the Snake. At that rate, we'd cross the Bar in a month. When people are exposed to repeated threats, they either become inured to them or finally find their nerve eroded. A craven inkling came to me that I'd entered the latter category when I heard a weather report predicting more wind for the next day. Before I fell into weary sleep, I guessed I didn't have a week of risks left in me, and I lay in a blackness of soul that exceeded what the sorry night was passing off as darkness.

Place of the Dead

A S IF IT HAD BEEN following me cross-country — upstream and down, over the plains, into mountains — my life off the river caught up that morning. By spending most of the day before trapped in the Hover cove, I'd given that other existence time to find me and bring with it much I'd recently failed to do well or even adequately — marriage preeminently — so that when I fully woke, even before I thought I heard the wind, I wanted nothing to do with anything, and I lay wishing I could evaporate like a creek when feeder streams dwindle in summer heat until one day the water is gone, leaving behind only an imprint in its bed.

With destination so near, how could such a deflation of heart happen? I tried the proven nostrum of simply getting up; if that didn't work, at least I'd confirm the miserable conditions on the river. What I found was a bright Thursday fresh from the Horse Heaven Hills, and before I could stop myself, I fell into the routine of rivering, perhaps half believing that going through the motions might call up real purpose and squelch thoughts of an empty house waiting for me at home. I roused Pilotis, and in the full bloom of morning we set out with nothing more than a narrow hope of gaining a few miles before the wind would drive us to cover.

The night had much dulcified the air and river, and our passage through the great Wallula Water Gap, where I was expecting to catch a zephyrean fist in the face, was nothing but a mild flowing between beautiful shores of brown basalt cliffs. At the point Oregon comes up to share the Columbia with Washington, the river was like an oiled tabletop, flat and slick, and *Nikawa* marked across it a long, trailing V.

The banks, about a mile apart, ran nicely parallel as if the engineers had been at them too, and we saw not another boat anywhere under the ideal July sky.

At the Gap, the Columbia ceases its southerly run out of the Canadian Rockies and makes a grand western turn, a bend that allows the river to become a truncated Northwest Passage. Were it not for this shift — that is, were the Columbia to keep running longitudinally as do most of the other big rivers west of the Rocky Mountains — the old Oregon country might today be in Canada because that three-hundred-mile westerly flow to the ocean was just long enough for nineteenth-century Americans to use it to gain the territory. Once more, and for the penultimate time, *Nikawa* was heading directly for the Pacific. With only a single short northern deviation ahead of us, we could look down the broadly sweeping bends and believe that soon the west wind would carry across her bow the smell of the sea.

McNary Dam gave us a prolonged wait while an upriver tow locked through, so we went to see fish ascend the ladder past a counting window. Although the trough at that point is high above the lower river, we stood watching fish and lampreys wriggle against the current as if we were in a diving bell on the bottom of the Columbia. In the subdued light, the viewing station was a weird, clammy, netherly place where we were interlopers, voyeurs into a life otherwise hidden, and Pilotis said, "The best human beings can do is borrow a river. We can live in a forest, in the mountains, in the earth, in the grasslands, but not in a river. That's strange for creatures two-thirds water." When *Nikawa* descended the deep lock, dropping through what only minutes before had been seventy-five feet of dark river, we could smell the heart of the Columbia as if it had just exhaled. Before us lay almost eighty miles of open water.

Umatilla, Oregon, is a dusty town on the stark Columbia Plateau, a victim of careless agriculture which sometimes turns the wind brown, a treeless vacuity of sage and other plants that can live a year on the amount of water a human drinks in a day, a land of dead magma and wuthered heights, wind-haunted canyons and gulches, a country seemingly able to suck even a big river dry, an ostensible barrens requiring an artist in summer to carry a palette of nothing more than yellow ocher, burnt umber, and Vandyke brown to paint everything below the horizon — even the tail of a lizard, the eye of a rattler. You

can find white men's early estimation of this terrain in three names —
Golgotha Butte, Dead Canyon, Freezeout Ridge — or six words — ord-
nance depot, bombing range, Indian reservations. Yet, like any landscape, the scablands are not ugly except where the hands of people
have made them so.

Beyond the dam, the ridges don't rise quite sufficiently to be foothills, and the river widens and becomes shoaly as if it too were leveling;
that place once full of low islands is now, after the dammings, a spread
of mud flats and shallows requiring a pilot to consult the chart, something we failed to do when I took a severely direct route down a wide
stretch and *Nikawa* got dragged to a halt. I tilted up the motors to find
a thick green wreath around each prop and twin hawsers of stringy
weeds tying her to the swampy bottom. After we unwrapped and cut
free, I turned perpendicular to our former course and, within the
length of the boat, the depth went from three feet to five fathoms as we
floated off the edge of a drowned island, perhaps one Indians used to
call a *memaloose,* "place of the dead." In the midst of the river they
built wooden charnel houses, structures Lewis and Clark, violating
their usual code of not disturbing native possessions, twice disassem-
bled in the timber-poor canyon to fuel their fires.

Before impoundment, the Blalock Islands were a couple of estimable if low rises about six miles long but are now only a scramble of flats
and islets presenting a temptation of shortcuts down sloughs and
weedy channels. Yet for a few miles they give the Columbia the aspect
of a real river again instead of deep pools of human artifice controlled
by keyboards and silicon chips. Near the Blalocks, Interstate 84 leaves
the Oregon tableland and descends almost to river level to run beside
the Columbia right next to the Union Pacific Railroad — across the
water is the Northern Pacific — all the way to Portland. In narrow
strips of river terrace were small irrigated orchards and higher up the
steep slopes occasional vineyards and wineries, but those things did
little to deny that this place is forever a locale where human habitance
is marginal with its continuance depending more on technology than
on the land itself. If you've ever walked a vast and isolated piece of
nature and not thought it lonely until you unexpectedly discovered
someone else's bootprint, then you know the feeling of that scarceness
which only the river keeps from desolation.

The Columbia narrowed to about a mile across and deepened to holes of more than a hundred feet, but in spite of the sediment traps dams are, the water was a murky jade, we guessed from agricultural runoff. Near Arlington, little more than a grain elevator atop a dredged-up jetty, the Columbia Plateau begins loosening its grip and gives up trying to wring the river dry. We could see to the north forested foothills of the Cascades, and the desert of scant green, the land of rain-shadow we'd been in since the Bitterroots, fell behind.

We came upon a fisherman, about thirty years old, whose boat motor had quit, and he worked in vain to propel himself to shore with a water ski. Pilotis called, "Very inventive, but don't you believe in spare paddles?" and threw him a line, and we towed him to shelter in the mouth of Rock Creek. I asked what he would have done had wind come up. He considered, then said, "Drowned comes to mind." When we went on, I told Pilotis one of the constants I'd seen among water folk was their notion that a river is just wet land, and I thought they no more feared dying in one than a farmer does of dying in his field.

I've always found it peculiar that Oregonians named two rivers, one valley, one town, one geologic stratum, one rich fossil bed, a lock and dam, and I don't know how many transmission shops and laundromats after John Day, since the trapper's fame rests on losing his britches to Indians in 1811 and his mind to the desert soon after, thereby becoming the first recorded white man to walk the Northwest naked and unhinged. Perhaps, had he a more singular name to match his history, say Eliphalet Nott or Belazeel Wells, the nomenclature might make sense. While I'm at it: I try never to pass up a chance to complain about the undistinctive name for a most imposing volcano just fifty miles away, Mount Adams. In fact, in the grand string of volcanoes of the Northwest, several have names sadly deficient in color and vigor: Baker, Hood, St. Helens, Jefferson. I told Pilotis I wanted our great and deadly mountains to have names I couldn't find in the White Pages. Where are the American equivalents to Popocatépetl, Krakatoa, Stromboli? Said my friend, "Did Canadians do the naming?"

A couple of miles below Mr. Day's river, the version in eastern Oregon, we entered his lock, one of the deepest drops in America, and descended to the accompaniment of an ungreased mooring bitt tracking down its slot and trumpeting uncannily like an elephant. As we left the chamber I said to Pilotis, I consider that flourish proper for the reach of river ahead. "What makes it special?" Our five thousandth mile, I said.

On a high, sloping terrace on the north shore is rail magnate Sam Hill's full-scale replica of Stonehenge in ferroconcrete, a monument that happened to mark another significant moment, the halfway point on a journey I'd made seventeen years earlier, a long loop around America over what have since come to be called blue highways. Equally by chance, across the river is the place where travelers on the Oregon Trail got their first glimpse of the river that, had it truly been part of a Northwest Passage, would have made the famous American trail unnecessary. Some settlers did use the river to finish their western journey, but most found the rapids too risky and paid a toll to follow a track around the base of Mount Hood. Pilotis: "You couldn't have orchestrated a better conjunction of national and personal history," and I said, If you travel long enough, space and time and self will coalesce here and there.

The Great River of the West went into some short bends and twisted past the mouth of the Deschutes, and we entered what was once the big bottleneck of the Columbia, a ten-mile run of rapids and cascades that stymied whites but provided a way of life for at least four thousand years of Indians. From Celilo (rhymes with "Ohio") to The Dalles (rhymes with "fowls"), the river once was a constriction of white water visited by natives during the salmon run, a place so important that tribes agreed to share it as their paramount bartering and social rendezvous. Today, even after the damming, atop certain rocky overhangs Indians still build flimsy wooden platforms that allow them to reach down with eighteen-foot dip nets to snare fish, a means only they may use.

White people found the rapids not a faucet of nourishment but a nuisance, and they blasted out a boat channel, and below the cascades they erected huge fish wheels, one of them in 1913 scooping up in a single day thirty-five tons of fish. Not for Anglo-Americans any of that inefficient catching coho or chinook one at a time. A few years later the devilish wheels were outlawed to keep from exterminating the salmon, a job the dams quite legally now threaten to complete. In 1957, when engineers closed the gates of The Dalles Dam for the first time, the river took only five hours to cover the rocks and the ancient way of life they fostered — an event analogous to the virtual eradication of the bison and the consequent cultural decline of the Plains Indians.

Three miles above the powerhouse, at the edge of the pooled river, is a basalt boulder, forged in the hot heart of earth and shaped by the cold river and hammered by human hands into an unequaled petroglyph, a large beast-like face with great encircled eyes, a visage called She-Who-Watches. For centuries, that stone gaze has looked onto the river, onto people coming and going, descending and ascending — Indians spearing and drying fish, deceased chieftains borne to a *memaloose,* captains of discovery and those of mere haulage, settlers, idle travelers, engineers with blueprints, laborers with dynamite and concrete, programmers with computers. There is a chance she will still be watching when dams, like Roman aqueducts, are relics of an empire that prized technology over vision and natural harmony, creations of a mechanically clever people who in only a couple of hundred years, give or take a day or two, worked consciously to turn a zoggledyteen-million-year-old river valley into a great *memaloose.*

While we waited to enter The Dalles lock, we watched three young osprey beat their fledging wings on the rim of a nest in a steel tower that was part of the dam. Across the country, ospreys have found the great American power grid of transmission poles a boon to their survival. Now, if only salmon could learn to fly like some of their ocean cousins, or, only somewhat more realistically, if only *Homo sapiens* could practice the long vision of She-Who-Watches.

When the massive guillotine gate rose to let us out of the deep tomb, the low sun flooded into the chamber that moments earlier had been the inside of a river, and we passed over the tailwater turbulence. Straight ahead on the horizon loomed the snowy cone of Mount Hood in splendid symmetry as if drawn up by engineers to be another artifice like a river regular and rockless. Two miles down we pulled into the Port of The Dalles docks, tied up, and climbed the stacked streets of the narrow hillside town to find a room for the night. We had gone ten times farther than we had the day before, and I thought it a good thing I hadn't evaporated.

Theater of
the Graveyard

BEFORE I EVER set out on the voyage, I had thought mere duration, our heaped-up days, would be the element likely to best
me, do me in, and put an end to passage. Because the potential
for respites from the river would be few, I believed the sheer volume of
miles, whether I accomplished them easily or otherwise, would be the
enemy. But that isn't what happened, perhaps because there's something timeless about river travel, especially through lands nearly hu-
manless, where flowing water somehow dissolves days down to a resi-
due you could pour into a thimble. Never had I experienced such a
quickly gone sixteen weeks. The Brooklyn Bridge, our Hudson lunch
of smoked shad, the Flight of Locks up the Erie Canal, all seemed quite
distant in space yet as fresh in memory as the cove at Hover.

Nikawa moved in country I'd much traveled before, even up and
down the Columbia itself, and from time to time I was animated more
by exploration of memory than of topography. Details bobbed up like
so much flotsam (but certainly not jetsam, for I try never to cast
overboard from the small barkentine of my life any incident, whatever
its color), details that didn't so much define a place as a moment in it.
At times Pilotis must have thought me like a person revisiting the old
neighborhood to search the wall for that penny hidden years ago, the
kind of journey back we sometimes follow through our tumble of days
gone to emerge with a refreshed memory that, almost by itself, can
awaken one's life.

I told of a dinner one chilly night a couple of years earlier in The

Dalles. The bartender was a Japanese-American woman, a Nisei, about forty, sprightly, flirtatious. She said to me, "I'm from Maui. I wish I was there now. It's sunny, eighty degrees, and I'd be with my cats and Daddy." She stepped away to take an order, and an eavesdropping man next to me said in my direction, "At her age, cats and Daddy! I'd call that a goddamned sad cry for help." A woman with him said, "And you're just the man to help out?" And he: "No, Sally. If you'll remember, I firebombed the Japanese." The bartender heard the last several words, and even before she could grow angry, tears ran down her face, the man said nothing to her, and I realized he'd used my presence to speak out the aftermath of *his* war. I ignored him, but it was too late. When I left, I put down a large tip as apology for just being witness, and she pushed it onto the floor.

At The Dalles, the Columbia flows from under the rain-shadow cast by the Cascade Mountains and enters its great gorge, one of the loveliest river canyons in America and one easily accessible by auto, train, or excursion boat. The deep defile is fifty miles of hard evidence, if any were needed, that water is the master mason of mountains, seemingly able to cut them where it chooses. Yet, in the long and massive Sierra Nevada–Cascade cordillera, the gorge is the only place reaved by a big river, and to pass through such a cleft is to be dumb-founded that anything so inconstant, unfixed, vagrant, and undisci-plined as water could achieve such an opening, even if the obdurate rocks resist and force the lower Columbia into its narrowest miles, a dark constriction of fierce gusts and water 150 feet deep.

We got under way slowly, giving the wind time to rise, then we thumped on west, down the shadowed canyon, past where the little Klickitat puts in. I wanted only twenty miles out of the day, just enough to reach Hood River, Oregon, a pleasant town and the home of a brew house, Full Sail, that offered a taproom with a high overlook of the Columbia and an exceptional glass of cask-conditioned India pale ale to lubricate lucubrations of time and the river. The run was bouncy but soon done, and we walked up into town.

For the last several days, as we neared the western terminus of the Great American Real Beer Desert, I'd been talking about the ales of the little brewery and leaving so many verbal clues across the dry miles even a bumbling Doctor Watson unaided could have found Pilotis and me there. Indeed, in walked a relaxed and smiling Photographer and his wife, then came the Reporter and his cameraman to follow us to our destination, and soon after even Cap'n Pike, our fellow voyager, whom I insincerely promised to overtake and beat across the Bar. Although the time had not yet come to celebrate, we were ready to try to remember how one expresses carefree joy and expectation of unburdened days, and the only thing that kept me from dancing atop tables was our last care, those dozen miles lying in wait at the very end. So we merely practiced at celebration.

But that night I read Pilotis a passage: "Where the Columbia meets ocean tides at journey's end can be a fearsome place. Here, where waves often leap a hundred feet into the air to cascade down in torrents of sand and silt and sea life, have occurred some of the most violent adventures and tragic dramas in the history of the marine world."

My friend said, "The Bar hangs over us like one of those three-hundred-fifty-ton guillotine gates." Then, later, having thought about the situation: "The real reason you chose not to cross the country west to east is that you wanted the theater of the Pacific Graveyard as finale." No, I said, I just needed five thousand miles to work up my nerve. Pilotis said nothing for some moments, then, "Most people have a cross to bear, but we, we've just got a bar to cross."

A Badger Called Plan A

WHETHER IT'S TRUE that Dan'l Boone when living along the lower Missouri River actually said something on the order of "A durn badger at yore feet is worser than a big ol bar off yonder," I don't know, but based on our experience soon after leaving Hood River, I can testify to the validity of the proposition, something I ended up proving through my casualness in getting under way. When we set out, the wind was up, gusts to forty miles an hour, maybe higher when chucking through the gorge which provides such strong, steady blowing it has become a premier location for windsurfers. Because I knew the air was usually calmer beyond the narrows, we entered the river anyway and made a jolting course among weekend boaters and darting sailboards ("barge bait") and went down a reach too removed for the "boardheads," but we were soon on water free of everything but funneled wind. Measured from the summits there, the forested mountains rise three to four thousand feet above the Columbia, and we beat along past places like Wind Mountain and Viento Creek, and a fine little cove now closed off by a railroad embankment and turned into misleadingly and maybe mischievously named Lake Drano, as in pioneer William Drano.

About five miles beyond it, the gorge opens to allow the river to spread out to a mile or so until it reaches another narrows just below old Cascade Lock, an artifact today but once the means of circumventing the severe rapids Bonneville Dam and its pool now cover. Nearby local toponymy goes from the waggish unflattery of Drano to, at first glance, the reckless grandiosity of Bridge of the Gods, a name surely not befitting a truss bridge, handsome as it is; but its moniker is true to

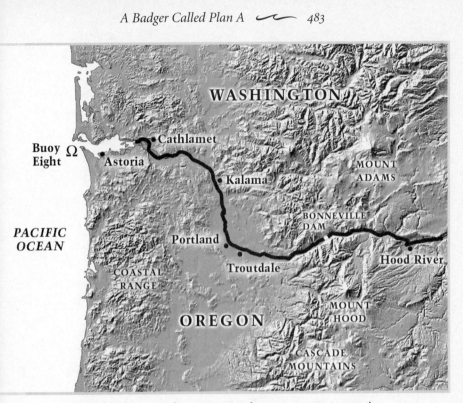

The Columbia, Hood River to Pacific Ocean, 178 river miles

Indian legend which holds that a great span of stone once ran from shore to shore, the only foot-crossing on the Columbia until the arrival of technicians. Given the landslides that occur here, some geologists believe such a bridge may have existed. Just beyond the splendid trusses, a traveler comes upon the Eyesore of the Gods, Bonneville Dam, which crosses the river in three sections separated and anchored by two islands. Recently designated a national scenic area, the gorge gets a good mocking from the heap of concrete and steel of the old spillway that appears to have been simply dragged in and stacked up like a beaver dam.

Nevertheless, we were happy to see the infernal thing because it was the remaining engineered barrier between us and the Pacific. In our five thousand and some miles of crossing, we had locked through or portaged around eighty-nine major dams (and one fallen bridge), and now only a single final plug stood in our way. At last,

Nikawa was about to enter a river running freely to the sea. We were a jovial lot.

I radioed our request for passage, the lockman answered we would have to wait for an upriver tow, so we went to the shore of Bradford Island and rafted beside a docked speedboat a third longer than *Nikawa* and capable of producing power on the order of Bonneville itself; hook up that boat engine to a transformer and you could light Portland. Still, such wasn't enough for its skipper, a fellow not yet into his third decade, who told Pilotis that next year he would buy a bigger one. He and his two pals had broken the windshield the day before by ramming the boat through swells at a speed truckers would find almost satisfactory for a trooper-free four-lane, and he boasted of the damage as if it were a hit from a kamikaze. Said he, wearing a T-shirt imprinted UP YOURS, "I'm going to get a boat that'll eat this river." He hated the dams because the runs between them were not long enough, to which I said, Without these dams your boat wouldn't be here. He shook his head: "They oughta take them down and dredge this river all the way into Canada."

After an hour the upstream gate opened, and out came a string of barges pushed by the *Maverick,* a name unlike any I'd ever seen on the towboats of the Mississippi or the Ohio where the nomenclature runs along the lines of *Emily P.* or *Miss June Watson.* As a long-time believer that names tend to become self-fulfilling, I was about to encounter further evidence. When the last barge was nearly out of the lock and the chamber almost cleared for our final descent, we heard a terrific crash and a tortured screaming of steel against steel. The tow came to a halt between the gates, and a distinct odor of putrescent garbage wafted up to us.

After some time I radioed the lockman who snapped, "We're out of commission here!" I said to my mates, The single accident in a lock occurs at the last one, just when the salt spray of the Pacific is practically off our bow. The Reporter chided: "If only we'd been here a couple of hours earlier." From the radio, although not addressed to us, we overheard, "Go to Plan A." Any procedure requiring a letter designation sounded grave indeed, and we settled in for a tiresome wait, the lockman refusing to tell us any more. We sat long enough for the party boat to run out of beer; the three boys shifted to gin and, in the blast of heavy metal, began dancing on their bow and stern as they held up docking lines and strummed them like electric guitars, making lyrics of the situation:

> We're tied down, we're tied up,
> Locked out of Heaven and nowhere to go
> 'Cause we ain't got the Power,
> The Power of the Gate!
> Yeah, yeah, yeah!
> Only the Man's got the Power,
> The Power of the Gate!

Our condition thus expressed by a trinity of drunken whelps who would dredge the whole Columbia, we sat, we waited, we grumbled, and wondered whether to yield and head back upriver until tomorrow, or until the day after, or until the unthinkable. Practically truckling to the lockman, I finally pried out that the *Maverick,* now happily on its way, had smashed loose a piece of steel that seemed to prevent the upriver gate from closing properly. I did what all pilot manuals instruct the prudent mariner to do under those circumstances: mutter and cuss. Pilotis looked, in a needlessly obvious manner, at the aft plaque: AVOID IRRITATION. It isn't irritation, I said, it's frustration, and *that* the Code of Cross-Country Pilots allows. A mere 145 miles from the ocean, we suddenly were blocked off by a blunderhead who couldn't steer a garbage scow straight.

At the end of the third hour I started the motors to head back upstream. The Reporter, making note of my action, gave me an idea. Over the radio I said, We have aboard a staff writer from the *Kansas City Star* who's doing a story on the river and locks. A pause. Then, from the tender, "Stand by," and in the background we heard someone say, "We've got two pleasure boats going down. They'll be a good test." The lockman told us to form up, and the Reporter said, "You're actually going to go through on a test?" There's a rule of thumb about plans designated by letters: the farther you go into the alphabet, the more desperate they become.

We set up in front of the gates, a safe distance from the well-ginned party boat, then we answered the signal to heaven or hell and entered the lock. A day earlier, I'd spent time thinking of a bear called the Bar instead of a badger called Plan A, and now we were about to find out how much of a miscalculation such foresight was. We took our usual positions, Pilotis on the bow to handle the line to the bitt, I in the welldeck to use the boat hook against the lock ladder. The gates closed ever so slowly, and we began a prolonged descent, the sluggishness indicating the questionable conditions. I watched the wall for signs of our nearly imperceptible creep downward, worried not about the tons of water building behind us nor about some disastrous malfunction that could sweep us to destruction, but rather only that we might stop and be floated back up. Again and again I chanted to the swirling water, Go, go, go! Drain, drain, Drano! The Sirens of the North Pacific sang full in my head, and I thought how far we'd come to hear the melody of the Hesperian surf now playing not far beyond the steel gates, thought of weeks of travail to reach the country of the Golden Apples and other sweet fruits of destination.

Bonneville Lock has the shortest drop on the Columbia, sixty-four feet, but our descent was taking twice the time of one nearly two times deeper. From the bow: "This rate isn't reassuring." About then I realized I'd been staring at the same lump of algae on the wall for several minutes. "We've stopped." Nothing happened. "What if they can't open the gate and can't get us back to the top?" A climb up the slimily treacherous ladder was not so fearful as the notion of *Nikawa* having to stay in that tomb for a day, a week, for a who-knows. We sat trapped behind the speedboat in a ringing hell of Judas Priest's "Breaking the Law" and Quiet Riot's "Cum On Feel the Noize" — we doing the latter, they, with the gin, the former.

Should I have portaged around? Had my insistence on keeping water beneath the hull finally vanquished us? Had I traded a couple of hundred yards of river passage for the chance to complete the voyage? Was the way open or wasn't it? "Be glad this happened on the last lock instead of the first — then you would have had eighty-nine new worries." No fervent Christian ever waited for the gates of heaven to open more intently than did we those dripping and tenebrous doors.

Nikawa sat on the stilling water near the bottom in the dismal dank, and we did nothing but watch the front of the chamber. "Let there be light!" But there wasn't. "They're up there figuring on how the bejeezis to get us out of here." Then: a rumbling, a deep and sonorous opening, clanking and grating, chains of the entombed, valves groaning a cold, dead misery. A long white crevice no thicker than a ray of hope slid down the gates, and at the speed glaciers move to the sea, the slit opened to the width of my wrist, then my shoulders, and the bright western horizon unrolled before us. Between *Nikawa* and the sea, between our pulpit rail and the Pacific, ran nothing but open water. I went to the helm, started the engines, and at the signal we proceeded on. I had not felt so free, so unencumbered since the morning I walked across the brow of the USS *Lake Champlain,* saluted the flag for the last time, and followed the ladder down to the shore of civilian life.

Beyond the lock we entered into the tidal Columbia, the sea-level river where it exchanges depth for width and forces a navigator to use a chart. On a waterway of grand pilot marks, the finest lay just ahead, Beacon Rock, a distinctive black monolith some eight hundred feet high and shaped like a bishop's miter; it is a hardened clog caught in the throat of a volcano long ago washed away. I've read, although I don't believe it, that Beacon is, after Gibraltar, the biggest rock in the world. I do believe it's the finest coign of vantage on a river full of them, a view achieved by a steep trail that in places clings to the sheer sides by means of steel catwalks. Lewis and Clark named Beacon Rock, and that it still exists is the work of a descendant of the first editor of their journals. To prevent a company from blasting the huge thing into road gravel, Henry Biddle bought it in 1915 and built the cliffhanger of a trail to the summit; his heirs later gave the monolith to the state, a gift Washington initially declined but then accepted when Oregon said it would be happy to include the marvel in its park system.

A river traveler cannot see all the seventy high and slender falls that drop off the deeply green and precipitous edge of the Cascades on the Oregon side, but the several that are visible, delicate white tails and veils, caused Pilotis to say, "In six miles we've gone from whoa! to ahh! From woes to Oz." The cascades are stunning enough to cast doubt on their authenticity, as did a child I once overheard, whose vision of natural America perhaps owed too much to Disney falsity, ask, "They're not real, are they?" And her mother, "I *think* so, sugar."

We went on, on past Phoca Rock stranded in the middle of the wide river like a pedestrian caught between streams of five o'clock traffic, and then to port another upthrust of once hot magma, a tall phallic rise today called Rooster Rock, but to the early rivermen it was Cock Rock. The later name, while making no topographical sense, may have come about not because of any urge for decency but rather by a mere preference for alliteration over rhyme — simply a matter of poetics, wasn't it?

On the precipice above the Top of the Cock is the celebrated view from Crown Point, the cliffs there a kind of portal between the mouth of the Columbia Gorge and the broad Willamette Valley to the west. Soon we gained the outreaches of Portland. At the bend where the Sandy empties into the big river and has built up a delta, I tried to steer a straight course and ran *Nikawa* onto a gritty reef that we had to pole off of. It was here, wrote William Clark, that he "arrived at the enterance of a river which appeared to Scatter over a Sand bar, the bottom of which I could See quite across and did not appear to be 4 Inches deep in any part; I attempted to wade this Stream and to my astonishment found the bottom a quick Sand, and impassable."

Free of another encounter with history, we went on to a good dock and stepped ashore to greet the Photographer waiting for us. Away we went to nearby Troutdale on the Sandy River and into the Edgefield Inn, perhaps the most merrily eccentric in America, a hostelry once the county poor farm but now well refurbished, its walls painted by artists with phantasmagoria from nature, history, and dreamlands of the drugged — doors done as windows, pipes as trees, six-foot pigeons beating against skylights, angels in wheelchairs riding the Milky Way and plucking stars as if they were daisies. I hoped such jolly lodgings would lift a tiring crew for our run to the sea. Like smolts, we were wearing down.

Robot of the River

THAT NEXT MORNING was my hundredth day of the voyage, eighty of them on the water, and when I woke I decided to leave the river for a Sunday on the old poorhouse porch so I could work on my logbook and sit rocking in a chair like a pilot retired from boats who spends his days just watching the water; down the long slope from the verandah I could see the Columbia making its way oceanward free of us. When I announced a holiday to the crew at breakfast, to my astonishment there were hats in the air, and it came to me that our recent difficulty in getting out of bed had more to do with exhaustion than apprehension of the Bar or anything else. But, as the day would reveal, I was only half right. Things unacknowledged were about to claw into the light like moles desperate in a flooding field.

A young friend, a writer for the *Los Angeles Times,* joined us for the push to the Pacific; having such a wordsmithing crew about, I offered to take them in the afternoon to downtown Portland and that Beulahland of bibliolatry called Powell's City of Books. Despite my forewarnings, my sailors lost their bearings in the place and did not again heave into view until four hours later, whereupon I led them a couple of blocks away to a century-old seafood house, Jake's Famous Crawfish, with an excellent menu and a bar that is one of the historical sights of the city. We took a table by a window blessedly free of any views of water, but I soon went to the brass rail to stand against such good bibulous history and mull over a voyage nearly done. Next to me was a couple, he reading *The New Yorker* and she a worn copy of *Fear of Flying.* Readers are to Portland as musicians to New Orleans — everywhere. The woman was winsome but wore a mute sorrow that seemed to admit no hope, an expression painted by Modigliani. She turned to me and without prologue or preamble began speaking openly about her life as if I'd been present on all but a few days of it. I grew uneasy and finally said, Your friend here may be missing your attention. He, who had not turned a page since she began talking, was deep into a Pisa-like lean toward the conversation, a tilt ready to topple him onto the floor. He said emphatically, "I'm not with her." She: "Don't you two guys talk over me. I'm too much of a bitch for that." Her conversation, devoid of humor and wholly and relentlessly about her life, nevertheless compelled me as honest words usually do. She suggested we go someplace quieter, and I pointed to the crew and mentioned our long tour. "A hundred days?" she said. "I think they'll understand." I must admit I suddenly felt the deprivations of river travel as I hadn't before and considered the invitation. After all, none of my jolly jack-tars, even Pilotis, had gone the entire five thousand miles; they had found respite, escaped the river, seen family, bussed a spouse, so maybe they really would understand.

I turned back to say something to her, I don't remember what, and she threw her arms around my neck and pulled herself close and gave me a smashing, open-mouthed kiss. I had to pull hard to extract my agape face. She stepped back, stared angrily, and said for all to hear, "You're a robot! A robot!" In that instant I was indeed an automaton incapable of speech, my machinery fully engaged in putting every ounce of internal propellant into a blush that even a hundred days of wind and sun couldn't hide. Then it got worse. "You need a cure!" Now we had the attention of management. It was a moment to decide fast whether to treat this as conscious comedy or to dive for cover, so of course I did neither. "Get yourself a cure!" Can we drop the word "cure"? I whispered. The crew, figuring I'd provoked things, watched impassively. Before she could lash out again, I ordered her a drink, excused myself, and fumbled back to our table. I said, Let's not any of us ever throw a frigging life ring to a drowning friend.

When we returned to the quondam poor farm, I found a quiet rocker in a dark corner of the porch, but there was no escape any longer from a certain unacknowledgment. The bar incident had nudged me, not for what happened but for what it shook free in me, something kept in restraints for the last months. The woman was unwittingly correct: I *had* become a robot, a robot of the river. What it commanded, I did to the exclusion of almost everything else. Seventeen years earlier, I'd passed through Portland on a long trip I'd set out on largely because my marriage had failed; here I was again, this time on a long trip that flattened another marriage. On that hundredth night I understood that I had gone and had entered a place, and I knew where I'd gone, but where I'd entered I had no idea. When our voyage was only memory, where would I wash up? Just where is the great delta of old river travelers? When the journey is done, *quo vadis?* That's a question adventurers leave out of their accounts, and if you read of their later days you can be glad, because often their after-life seems to be aftermath. From the poor-farm porch, I couldn't see the Columbia rolling on in the night, but I could feel it — and all the other waters — as if they ran in my veins. Why not? The backs of human hands are nothing if not pulsing river maps. It then came to me to read the writing on my own bulkhead: Proceed as the way opens.

The next morning we set out under fair skies over a course free of Sunday boaters. We followed the big bend past industrial tailings and then on north beyond the mouth of the Willamette, above which, ten miles up, lies downtown Portland. The city *on* the Columbia is Vancouver, a smaller town but older, the descendant of the Hudson's Bay Company trading station and a later military post, a place in its earliest days once described as the New York of the Pacific. As we rolled northward up the forty-mile deviation the Columbia makes from its westering, the last we'd do, we could see four of the big Northwest volcanoes, an astounding view: behind us Mount Hood, and to starboard at various bearings Adams, Rainier, and St. Helens, the last still charry, its symmetry blown away fifteen years earlier, the result of things kept too long under restraint.

We passed docks with marine cranes swinging their cables and hooks through the August morning, passed broken pilings of dilapidated and dead industries, and we overtook freighters both under way and moored, the empty ships with Plimsoll lines far above our pilothouse, but *Nikawa,* a fingerling among leviathans, held her own in the deep-water lane and showed them a sassy stern. Against the Oregon shore lay the biggest island in the Columbia, Sauvie, fifteen miles long. Beyond, we entered into reaches of smaller islands, bosky and full of ponds and sloughs, each a lure to exploration. The Coast Range trailed down wooded hills and approached the river on one shore only to fall away on the other, then reverse itself to give an equality of ridgeland to both states, and along the riverbank here and about lay narrow beaches — one of them, Hewlett Point, the place where picnickers in 1980 turned up a decaying boodle of twenty-dollar bills, some of the two hundred thousand dollars stolen nine years before by the soi-disant D. B. Cooper who had parachuted from a hijacked airliner into the night only, according to one theory, to be swallowed by the black cold of the Columbia and flushed out to the Bar. On we went in a rising wind, on under the courthouse cupola of St. Helens, Oregon, high on a bluff, on past stick nests of herons, our approach sometimes stirring a bird from the shallows into a slow flap upstream; behind us, gulls dipped to inspect our wake for whatever gnawables it might thrum up.

By afternoon the wind and water conspired to pound *Nikawa*, so after a spell of nasty bouncing, I made for protection in the small-boat harbor at Kalama, and we left the Columbia. The town was gritty, drab, and overwhelmed by the roar of Interstate 5, a place only blasted river could drive us into. When we found quarters for the night in a motel Elvis Presley once used — photographic proof of the miracle everywhere like crutches affixed to walls of the grotto at Lourdes — I spent some time apart from the crew.

The winter before I had heard, "Are you going to trade a boat trip for our marriage?" an impossible question for me since to walk away from the river, once the idea of crossing took hold of me, was to walk away from a long dream, a deep aspiration. The voyage was not more significant than the marriage because it had become one pillar of it — or, at least, one pillar of my life. Either way, I believed the long rivering necessary to my continuance as a man. To the question I said, If I fail even to try the trip I won't be worth being married to. And I heard, "Then you've made your life contingent on rivers." To that I could say nothing.

When I found the crew for dinner, one so poor it got us to laughing in the way desperate people laugh, the Reporter said, "If the wind keeps us here tomorrow, you'll find me hanging by my neck from the shower rod," to which someone said, "One more Kalamaty."

A Taproom Fit
for Raggedy Ann

JUST AFTER SUNRISE — an occurrence I knew from the clock rather than the dark sky that was neither fog nor mist but the heart of a deep cloud — I went down to the river to see how it ran. The surface was like cobblestones, nothing more, so I hurried back to wake the mariners with coffee and pastries, and they turned out readily but for Pilotis. I called out, The wind's on its way! Nothing. The men are here to launch your mattress! Groaning, no movement. How about a swell little cruise on Lake Wallula? That's what's going to happen! Grousing, rising at the rate tectonic plates make their subterranean way along, sulking to the shower.

Before seven we were under way and beyond the gloom of the stilled Trojan nuclear power plant, on beyond the mouth of the Cowlitz River which fifteen years earlier poured into the Columbia tons of heated ashen mud from the Mount St. Helens eruption and for two weeks dammed in ships upstream. The Cowlitz, so I heard, flowed with enough warmth to make salmon try to jump out of it. When it comes to a great river coursing through a land of fire, the Columbia is almost a Phlegethon, and for eons it has treated magma as other rivers do silt. No matter how the earthen plates shove, shift, slip, and melt the earth beneath and send it back up in massive violences even humankind has yet to match, the Columbia, like a patient lover, crawls over and feels out the hot country, finds its crevices and gaps, and then thrusts its wet way in, penetrating the rock to shoot it full of life.

We couldn't see Longview despite its name, a double-entendre from lumber baron R. A. Long of Kansas City, Missouri, who, inspired by Pierre L'Enfant's elegant (if sometimes incomprehensible from the ground) hub-and-spoke plan for the federal capital, had his milltown similarly laid out in the 1920s. What we did see — and smell — was riverside timber industries and freighters being loaded with pulp and logs cut for a pittance in national forests and now ready to become Japanese newspapers and hot tubs. The nickname of Washington is the Evergreen State, but a few days earlier, in front of one large clear-cut, we saw a hand-lettered protest: WELCOME TO THE WAS-GREEN STATE. Nevertheless, west of the marine facilities the way was green indeed, with conifers and a ground cover of ferns and salal, and the river was full of marshy islands that are its beauty as crags and cliffs are farther upstream.

In my dawn hurry to check the water, I had banged into a bulkhead and put a lump on my forehead, a defect the native people here a couple of centuries earlier would have found nearly hideous before they gave up the head flattening that could turn a human profile into a perfect forty-five-degree slope from the tip of the nose to the hairline. They achieved the effect by a several-month compression of a new-born infant's skull between a cradleboard and another strip of wood, cushioned by moss, pressing down across the brow. Meriwether Lewis made several sketches of their peculiar profiles, and the naturalist-explorer John Kirk Townsend in 1834 wrote:

> I saw today a young child from whose head the board had just been removed. It was without exception the most frightful and disgusting looking object that I ever beheld. The whole front of the head was completely flattened, and the mass of brain being forced back caused an enormous projection there. The poor little creature's eyes protruded to the distance of half an inch and looked inflamed and discolored, as did all the surrounding parts. Although I felt a kind of chill creep over me from the contemplation of such dire deformity, yet there was something so stark-staring and absolutely queer in the physiognomy that I could not repress a smile; and when the mother amused the little object and made it laugh, it looked so irresistibly, so *terribly* ludicrous that I and those who were with me burst into a simultaneous roar which frightened it and made it cry, in which predicament it looked much less horrible than before.

We passed around the rock-stacked bend known as Cape Horn, a label repeated at least twice on the river and a place that compares to the real Cape as an Iowa snow field to the Antarctic. Perhaps, given the likes of names just north of here — Queets, Oyhut, Humptulips, Duckabush, Dosewallips, or a wilderness called Colonel Bob — early residents just wore themselves out with naming and found emptily derivative toponyms a refreshing change.

The Columbia was now two miles wide, but it let islands large and small nearly fill it and thereby hide its size and character so we had no sense we were moving atop an American river that discharges into the sea more water than all but the Mississippi. I once knew a woman, a dancer with erect carriage, who managed always to keep her shoulder blades pointed forward so that her full breasts could disappear in the drapings of blouses; as the Columbia approaches the sea, it too does its best to disguise the truth of itself. I, an appreciator of small bosoms and gentle waters, had no special urge to encounter either the woman or the river in such a potential reality, so we took the islands leeward and fairly skimmed along up to Cathlamet, the tiny seat of Wahkiakum County, smallest in Washington, the village encompassed by the woody rumples of the north end of the Coast Range, a darkly and deeply forested area of only three highways, two of them dead ends, but with more logging roads than Seattle has streets.

Cathlamet carries an aura of being hidden away, the kind of place one might abscond to with the company payroll or the neighbor's spouse instead of, say, Bolivia or Tasmania. We went up tree-lined Elochoman Slough (no shortage of good names here) and put out our docking lines in a quiet and secluded harborette surrounded by damp evergreens and gray weather, the air full of the scent of each, a combining that made the place a veritable image of the Pacific Northwest: blindfold me, spin me around four times, throw me willy-nilly across the country, then ask me where I am. Were I to land here, I could tell you.

It was just nine in the morning, and my mates urged me to press on to Astoria, but they had never before seen the Columbia estuary, the one that made William Clark think he had reached the Pacific when he was still three leagues away. My plan for our last fifty miles was to find a route "behind" the string of islands and through shallow but protected sloughs and channels, and thereby turn the flat hull of *Nikawa* to advantage rather than otherwise. Soon enough we would reach unforgiving water where we'd have no choice but to set out on it and take our chances against not mere river winds but the greater ones off the ocean. I said to Pilotis, Consider it — the estuary of the Columbia by itself could hold half a dozen Lake Wallulas.

We climbed the slope above the sailboats to find the harbormaster, a jovial man appropriately surnamed Mast. We could indeed, he said, run a course through the backwaters, using the islands as shields, but even with our hull, to minimize shoals and deadheads we should do it on a flood tide. For that day we had missed it. "Tomorrow at seven-fifteen," he said, "you'll have water and light." "And no wind?" said Pilotis. "I guarantee tides and sunrises — air I don't do."

We walked into the village, essentially two streets, Main and the other one, population 500, and only three or four fewer espresso bars than in all of Pittsburgh and St. Louis together. No Mormon town this. We found breakfast, then went to the old hotel, about halfway through renovation, including installation of an espresso bar in the lobby, and took second-floor rooms connected in pairs to a central bath. I turned on my Northwest-coast air conditioner, that is, I opened the window, propped it up with a Gideons Bible, and thought how holy writ was now wafting along Main and maybe working on those dismal, caffeine-blighted souls below. I was happy to see across the street the Cathlamet weather channel — a large flag on the courthouse lawn; already it was lifting into the wind, and I knew the next morning that banner would tell me whether or not we would sail into our last day.

If you like good coffee, exploring Cathlamet can take longer than you might expect, but even then, not so long as to preclude an afternoon snoozing or, given the espresso, an afternoon tossing. An hour before sunset we walked down to a rickety tavern, the River Rat Tap, sitting on tired and uncertain pilings at the edge of the water, reputedly the oldest bar — after *the* Bar — on all the Columbia. We looked around the place for any remaining ninety-degree angles, but tides had so long danced with pilings as to bend and soften walls, floor, and ceiling into flexibility if not limpness, a sagging Raggedy Ann room. Even the pool table was chocked and propped to give its slate top an approximation of levelness, although before we picked up cues, an old fellow with a bit of sag in himself advised us to play for a strong lie toward the north rail on the incoming tide and toward the south on the ebb. He said, "Check your watch before you shoot." Having spent so many recent weeks atop water, the creak and sway of the place seemed steady enough to me, and I reckoned table angles like a navigator, my sextant of an eye giving me the best stick of my life, which still failed to beat anyone.

For most of the last light of day, I sat mellow against the weary wall and watched through the west window as if, across the river and through the forest, I might see our final mile and the Bar and even beyond to the whither-thou-goest my life was about to become. Pilotis put down a cue and asked where I was, and I said, In this area the Indians buried — if that's the word — their dead in canoes placed in cottonwood trees, prows pointed west, ready for the flood tide to the next life. My friend seemed to turn the image mentally, then spoke Tennyson:

> For tho' from out our bourne of Time and Place
>> The flood may bear me far,
> I hope to see my Pilot face to face
>> When I have crost the bar.

I said, Tomorrow, whatever else we see, I hope it's not any Great Pilot's face — your visage will be quite sufficient.

Salt to Salt, Tide to Tide

I WOKE AT DAWN with equal measures of expectation and apprehension, and rose to look out at the courthouse flag. While it didn't
lie against the pole, it was far from garnering enough air to reveal all
fifty stars, and we could move into a morning that might lead us to
destination. The rush of water in the shower brought the others to
their feet and soon down onto Main for the walk to the dock. The
weather was good for that place — that is, depending on direction,
skies of gray, grayer, and ominous, but all rainless. As the flood tide
rose to its peak, I started the engines, synchronized them, Pilotis pulled
in our lines, and we set off down the slough of black water and dark
trees in a boat bright with hope of entering the Graveyard of the
Pacific. It was August the second.

Pilotis took up a snag watch, the Reporter tried to interpret the
chart we'd heard was unreliable, the *Los Angeles Times* writer made
notations for me, and we entered Clifton Channel to find a Columbia
of moderate waves, the shores wooded and quiet. *Nikawa* pottered
past an occasional settlement, some of them once wooden fishing
outposts, one a ruined salmon cannery, and the route became a maze
of crooked channels, inlets, shoals, and marshes — a strange realm at
the end of a big river rather than what you might expect to lie so near
the largest ocean on earth. As the sky lightened, the wind picked up
just enough to throw wrinkles over the places where backwaters
opened to the main river, rucks that disguised the shallows so that
gulls seemed to walk the surface. Said someone, "Jesus birds."

There were snags aplenty, but *Nikawa* avoided them as if she'd been
there before. Over almost twenty miles we wended through the dark-

water narrows, a riverland so quietly lovely it seemed enchanted, and all the way we hid from the wind like a field mouse from the fox. Then at last the islands thinned and fell away, and we came into a bight, and from there on we could hide no longer. But the river was only harder and not a bludgeoning. After four miles we reached the bluff at Tongue Point, the name reminding me to taste the Columbia to discover whether we'd yet reached the salt line. Not yet.

Then we rounded the point, and for the first time since the Atlantic, straight ahead through the parted headlands lay nothing but a perfectly level horizon of water, a flat gray line uninterrupted by shore. I spoke the sentence William Clark jotted in his notebook at about that same place: "Ocian in view! O! the joy." We too felt joy, a deep one, though we knew a *prospect* of arrival is hardly the same as arrival, and for us arrival meant the far side of the Graveyard.

Harbor seals rose to break the water and peer at *Nikawa,* and we passed a big freighter taking aboard a Bar pilot, one of only a few people licensed to direct ships through the collision of river and ocean ahead. We would have no pilot other than me, although I had asked the Photographer, who had gone before us, to check on conditions at the mouth and try to find a fully reliable chart. Of the several concerns I had, not least was being tricked by the size of the lower estuary into believing we'd reached the Pacific when we hadn't. Pilotis: "That would be like hitting a Series-winning grand slam and being called out for missing home plate."

On the Oregon shore, Astoria occupies a peninsula where the Columbia bends ten miles northwest before curving back to run due west into the sea through an opening four miles wide. The town lies against the hills of the Clatsop State Forest, and when sunlight falls over the Victorian homes and waterside buildings, Astoria has a fine look to it from the river, but otherwise it can be a place of hard coastal weathers, as Lewis and Clark found out on their arrival in the stormy November of 1805. Across the estuary, toward the Olympic Mountains, the annual rainfall is a hundred inches and the Yellow Pages runs a heading for "Moss Rid." Our luck that day was better. The dark sky began lifting, even though still without sun, and we thought Astoria a good haven to pause in before striking out for the ocean.

We passed under the three-and-a-half-mile-long bridge over the Columbia, and for us it seemed a gateway to our destination, a balance to the Verrazano-Narrows Bridge at the virtual mouth of the Hudson River. Pilotis said, "To go from Gravesend Bay through the Graveyard of the Great Lakes and on to the Graveyard of the Pacific, that's, well, a grave undertaking."

Just beyond the southern pier of the bridge we pulled into the West End docks where we'd agreed to meet the Photographer. When we stepped off *Nikawa*, I hooted and did a little jig because at last I could smell the western ocean and had no words to match my feelings. Watching my joy, Pilotis said, "You know, it would make sense to call this journey's end." Not a chance, I said, our voyage is sea to sea, salt to salt, tide to tide.

The Photographer found us and gave his report: "I talked to the Coast Guard Auxiliary, told them what you're doing. They said if we'll wait an hour they'll accompany us out to the Bar." I asked for the weather forecast, and he paused. "This is the calmest day in some weeks." Another pause, longer. "But the swells are still eleven to twelve feet." That was almost twice what hit us on Lake Erie. The words were a dirk in the heart. The Photographer: "They said if you're going to try it, today's the day to do it." Twelve feet? Twelve goddamn feet? "They said *Nikawa* could probably make it." I remembered the Photographer's weather report before we went out onto Lake Wallula, and I said, Twelve feet building to what? "Eleven to twelve feet is all I heard."

I paced around on the dock. Three other people would be out there with me, three friends trusting in me. Should I go alone? Should I go at all? I said, Let's get some breakfast. While we ate, I mulled figures for the Graveyard: two thousand vessels sunk, seven hundred people drowned. And that damnable story about Captain Jonathan Thorn of the *Tonquin* in 1810, ordering seaman John Fox into a longboat with four inexperienced crewmen to seek out a channel across the thundering Bar. When the sailor protested, Thorn rebuked him, "Mister Fox, if you're afraid of water you should have remained in Boston." As the boat was being lowered, Fox told a fur clerk, Alexander Ross, that an uncle had drowned there not many years before and said, "Now I'm going to lay my bones with his." The longboat went into the breakers, and only a hundred yards away it disappeared, never to be seen again.

At ten o'clock we went back to the dock to meet the Auxiliary, three retired men in a vessel about the size of ours. The leader, Ralph Gilbert, looked at *Nikawa* and said, "Even a ship can get into trouble out there, but your C-Dory looks like she can take it, at least on a good day like this." I said, Good is a twelve-foot sea? "It is, but I wouldn't wait any longer. Things are supposed to get worse." Rob Pike, whose boat coincidentally lay tied up nearby, happened along. He had made the run the day before. That was all I needed to hear. I turned to Gilbert and said, Just make sure you get us into the Pacific — I don't want to fall even one inch short.

At half past ten we set out, the Photographer and his wife and two friends aboard the Auxiliary boat leading the way, with Pike and the Shooter nearby. Astoria fell behind, and the great mouth of the Columbia turned from heavy chop-water to banging swells as we passed old Fort Stevens, shelled by a Japanese submarine one night during World War Two, and we moved on beyond a shoal called Desdemona Sands near the Oregon side. Northward rose the rocky headland British Captain John Meares named Cape Disappointment because the Bar so obscured the mouth of the river rumored to be the fabled Northwest Passage, he didn't believe the Columbia was actually there. That foggiest place on the West Coast began to give us broken shafts of sun as the clouds furled, and when I looked aft, I saw a wing of seven gulls following us. Pilotis said, "The mariner's number — seven seas, seven continents."

The angle the river makes kept us from seeing anything except the shoreline of the estuary until we rounded Clatsop Spit, a bulbous sandy hook that is the most northwest corner of Oregon. Then everything opened and before us lay the ocean, the swelling ocean, and we rode up the backs of the broad waves and down, *Nikawa* disappearing from view of the other boats when she reached the bottom of a trough, then pushing high again to the top of the wide crests. Those were not the short-spaced bangers of Lake Erie that so trounced us but Pacific giants that let us ascend and descend as if we were crossing a great rolling meadow, and the only noise was that of our own engines. Up and down, up and down, and once again my expectation proved wrong: the ocean didn't beat the tar out of us — it gave us only a merry ride, merry enough to throw the Reporter's wallet to the deck when he stood to put the binoculars on a sport-fishing boat that had lost power. I said, If we get there, our arrival — arrival! — will be about as close as I'll ever get to a Columbian experience — Columbian as in Christopher.

At every crest the view ahead was ocean, ocean, ocean, and I said, Should we hold this course for the same distance we've come from New York Bay, we'd just about bump against the Great Wall of China. No response. I turned to look at my true hearts: three blanched faces, eyes closed or locked on the horizon. Believe me, I said, these broad swells are a piece of cake — I mean, this is the place where the Coast Guard tests its rescue boats, the ones that can be corked up like a jug so they can take the violence — some of them get completely turned over — the crew sits strapped in. No response until Pilotis pointed north. A second fishing boat lay dead in the water, rolling in the merciless swells, and our radio picked up their distress call to the Coast Guard: "We don't have any power." A long break, then a frightened, "We're not feeling real comfortable out here." The Guard was on its way. Pilotis said, "Did you hear how he said 'out here'?"

We proceeded on, slowly getting used to a scarp of sea rising above our pilothouse, until we seemed to be far beyond the jetties supposed to protect the dredged channel through the Bar, but the Auxiliary boat kept pressing westward. At Buoy Eight, the sky opened wider into a benison of light that spangled the blue water into an undulous American union jack, and when we rode up again, the radio crackled and cleared its throat and said, "*Nikawa*, this is the Pacific."

A finer sentence I'd never heard, but my own words failed me utterly. All I knew was that we were 5,288 watery miles from the Atlantic and had gained six degrees of latitude and forty-eight of longitude and that the moment had arrived to do what I'd so long dreamed of: I passed the wheel to Pilotis and went aft to the rearing welldeck with the pint of Atlantic Ocean. Holding a rail securely with one hand, I raised the bottle high, sunlight striking through the glass, salt waves rising to it as if thirsty, and I said, We bring this gift from your sister sea — our voyage is done. Then I poured the stream into the Pacific and went back to the wheel of our river horse, and I turned her toward home.

THE PACIFIC OCEAN

POURING OUT
THE ATLANTIC WATERS

An Afterword of Appreciation

I can't imagine this book without the generous and often crucial help of Stephen Archer, Molly Barile, Jean-Ellen Jantzen, Edward Richardson, Jack LaZebnik, Eamon Dolan, Larry Cooper, Gail Cohen, Peter Davison, and Lois Wallace.

Along the way, these people assisted the voyage, the research, or the writing: William Abney, Lucinda Baker, Jody Baltessen, David Barton, Richard Blake, M. K. Blakely, Jim Bracken, John Bradley, JoAnn Brown, William Bullock, David Burwell, Scott Chisholm, Elaine Clark, George Clark, Sr., Charles Clifford, Suzanne Cole, Ramona Combs-Stauffer, William Comfort, Harold Cramer, George Cummings, Steve Cunat, Ted Curtis, John Cutten, Rita and Wayne Daniels, Harry Ditty, Ray Eakin, Darl Eck, Connie Fitch, Ellen Fladger, Rod Frick, William Gardner, Kelly Grant, Thomas Grasso, Frank Grizzard, Rod Guthrie, Douglas Helmers, Janet Henderson, Strode Hinds, Jackie Hinshaw, Nancy Horan, Rebecca Howard, David Howes, David Ivey, John Jermano, Dana Jones, Linda Keown, Alan Kesselheim, David Kibbey, Daryl Kleyer, Karl Kruse, Roger Langendorfer, Christopher Layer, Robert LaZebnik, Linny and Larry Livingston, Pauline and Tom Longnecker, Michael Mansur, James Mast, Robert McCaughan, Shirley and Paul McLaughlin, Tom McManus, John Metcalf, Stephen Morehouse, Gary Moulton, Chris Mullen, Matthew Nelson, Bruce Padgett, Patrick Parenteau, Chuck Parrish, Paul Pence, Thomas Prindle, David Pulliam, Larry Purcell, Mary Reynolds, Kelly Riforgiat, Barbara Rollin, Forrest Rose, Alissa Rosenberg, Ruth Rosenberg-

Naparsteck, James Ruddy, Cathy and Kit Salter, Roger Saucier, Debra Shampine, Tricia Shaw, Wanda Shields, Diane and Robert Shott, Rhonda Stansberry, Ken Steele, Thomas Stevenson, Terry Strasser, Norm Stucky, Linda Swatfager, Ralph Swift, Wayne Taylor, Vivienne Tellier, William Tilton, Peaco Todd, Mark Toland, Randy Vance, James Voorhees, Chris Walker, James Wallace, Joseph Warner, Kim Weeks, Mark Wellenstein, Jack Wicker, Craig Williams, Andy Wilner, Clyde Wilson, David Wink, Andrew Wolfe, Raymond Wood, Stephen Wunder, Beffa Wyldemoon, Brett Ziercher.

I also thank Apelco, Bass Pro Shops, Boat/U.S., Cabela's, C-Dory, Garmin, OMC (Grumman), Recreational Equipment International, and Perception (Keowee kayak).

I am indebted to the Minnesota Historical Society for permission to quote from the typescript of *The Garrioch Diary* and to the University of Nebraska Press for *The Journals of the Lewis & Clark Expedition,* Gary E. Moulton, editor.

If You Want to Help

There are many organizations working to improve or correct certain environmental problems (including historic preservation) that appear in this book. If these issues concern you and you want to act, here are a half-dozen groups (described in their own words) out of many others that have proven their worth over the years.

AMERICAN RIVERS

American Rivers is dedicated to securing a future of healthy rivers supporting diverse species of wildlife, fish, and plants, as well as working to make our rivers safe for human consumption and recreation and able to contribute to sustainable local economies. This nonprofit organization has protected more than 22,000 miles of rivers and 5.5 million acres of riverside lands.

> 1025 Vermont Avenue NW, Suite 720
> Washington, D.C. 20005
> 877-347-7550
> www.americanrivers.org

THE NATIONAL TRUST FOR HISTORIC PRESERVATION

The National Trust for Historic Preservation is a private, nonprofit organization dedicated to protecting the irreplaceable. With more than 270,000 members nationwide, it provides leadership, education, and advocacy to save diverse historic environments and to preserve and revitalize communities across America. It has six regional offices, owns twenty historic sites, and works with thousands of local community groups in all states.

1785 Massachusetts Avenue NW
Washington, D.C. 20036
202-588-6166
www.nationaltrust.org

THE NATIONAL WILDLIFE FEDERATION

The nation's largest nonprofit conservation advocacy and education group, the National Wildlife Federation unites people from all walks of life to protect nature, wildlife, and the world we share. The commonsense approach to environmental protection brings individuals, organizations, and governments together to ensure a brighter future for people and wildlife.

8925 Leesburg Pike
Vienna, Virginia 22184
703-790-4000
www.nwf.org

THE NATURE CONSERVANCY

The Nature Conservancy is an international nonprofit conservation organization with a mission to preserve plants, animals, and natural communities representing the diversity of life on earth by protecting the lands and waters they need to survive. It has protected more than 10 million acres in the United States and Canada and helped partner organizations protect millions more in Latin America, the Caribbean, and the Pacific.

4245 North Fairfax Drive
Arlington, Virginia 22203
800-628-6860
www.tnc.org

RAILS-TO-TRAILS CONSERVANCY

Rails-to-Trails Conservancy is a nonprofit organization dedicated to enriching America's communities and countryside by creating a nationwide network of public trails from former rail lines and connecting corridors.

1100 17th Street NW, 10th Floor
Washington, D.C. 20036
202-331-9696
www.railtrails.org

SCENIC AMERICA

Scenic America is the only organization solely dedicated to protecting the natural beauty and distinctive community character of America. The nonprofit group works in Washington, D.C., and through state affiliates and associated organizations to reduce billboard blight, preserve scenic roads and places, conserve and promote the planting of trees, and offer alternatives to sprawl development.

801 Pennsylvania Avenue SE, Suite 300
Washington, D.C. 20003
202-543-6200
www.scenic.org

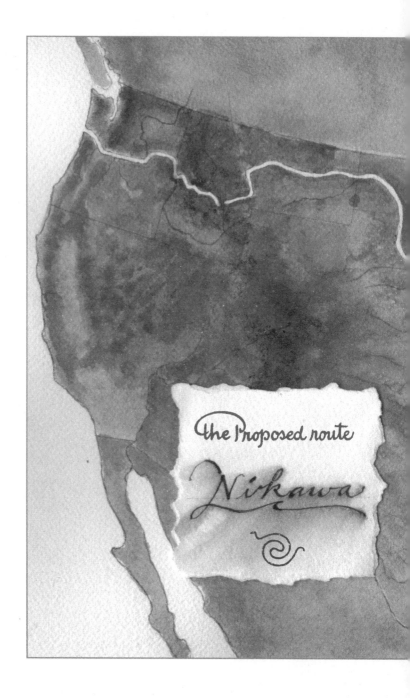

the Proposed route

Nikawa